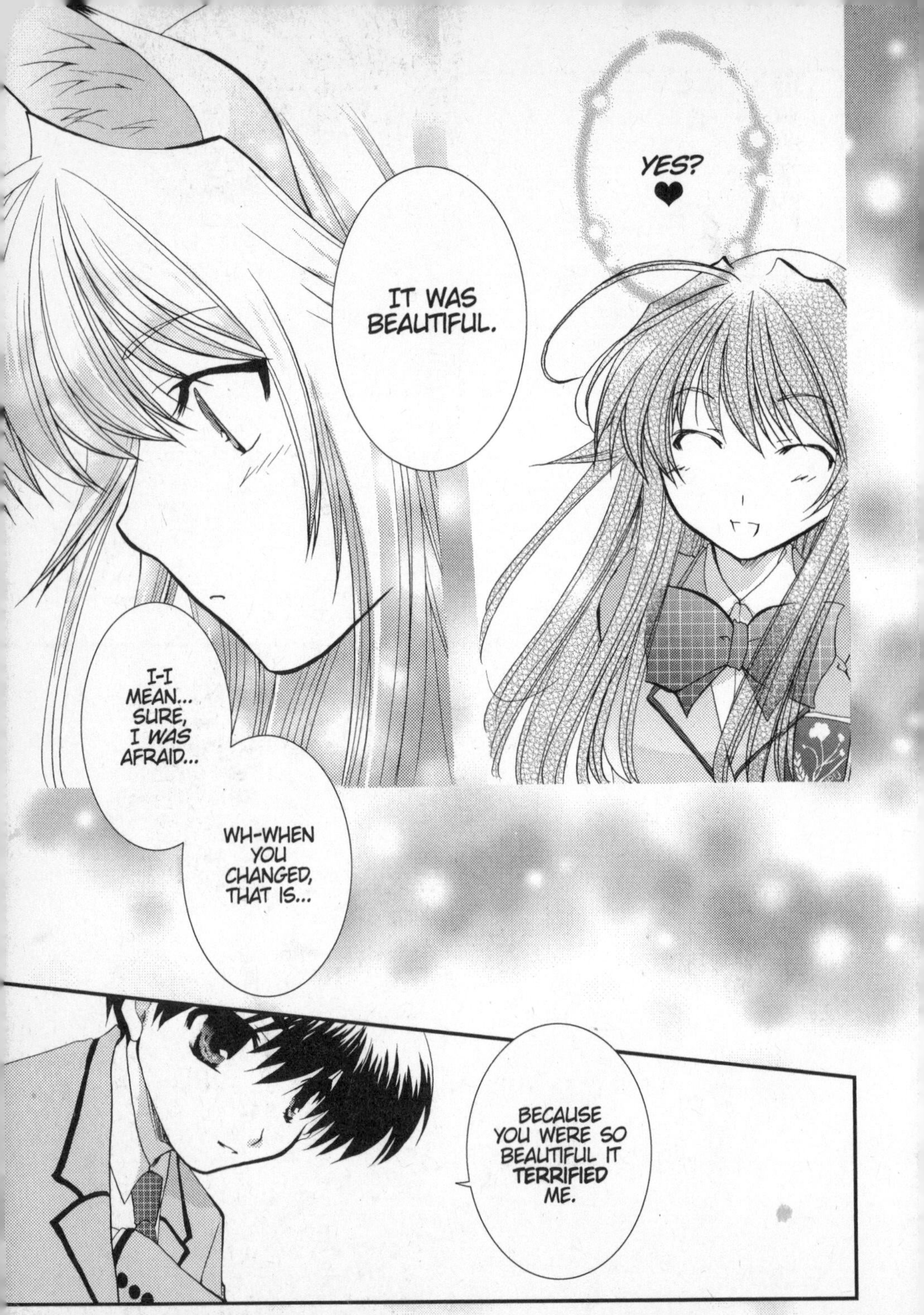
YES? ♥
IT WAS BEAUTIFUL.
I-I MEAN... SURE, I *WAS* AFRAID...
WH-WHEN YOU CHANGED, THAT IS...
BECAUSE YOU WERE SO BEAUTIFUL IT TERRIFIED ME.

Continued in...
Kanokon Omnibus 1-2!

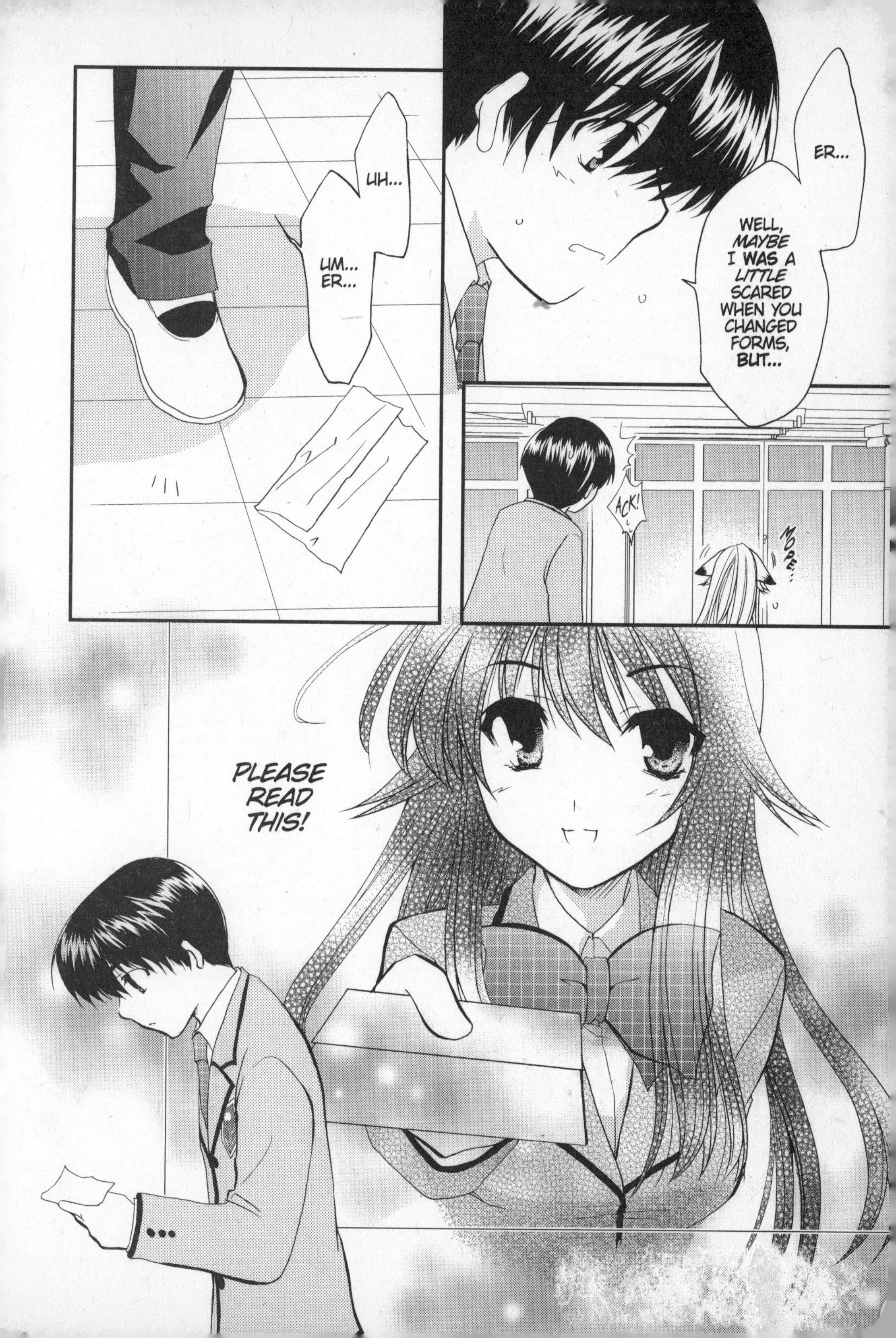
ER...
WELL, MAYBE I WAS A LITTLE SCARED WHEN YOU CHANGED FORMS, BUT...
ACK!
MOPE...
UH...
UM... ER...
PLEASE READ THIS!

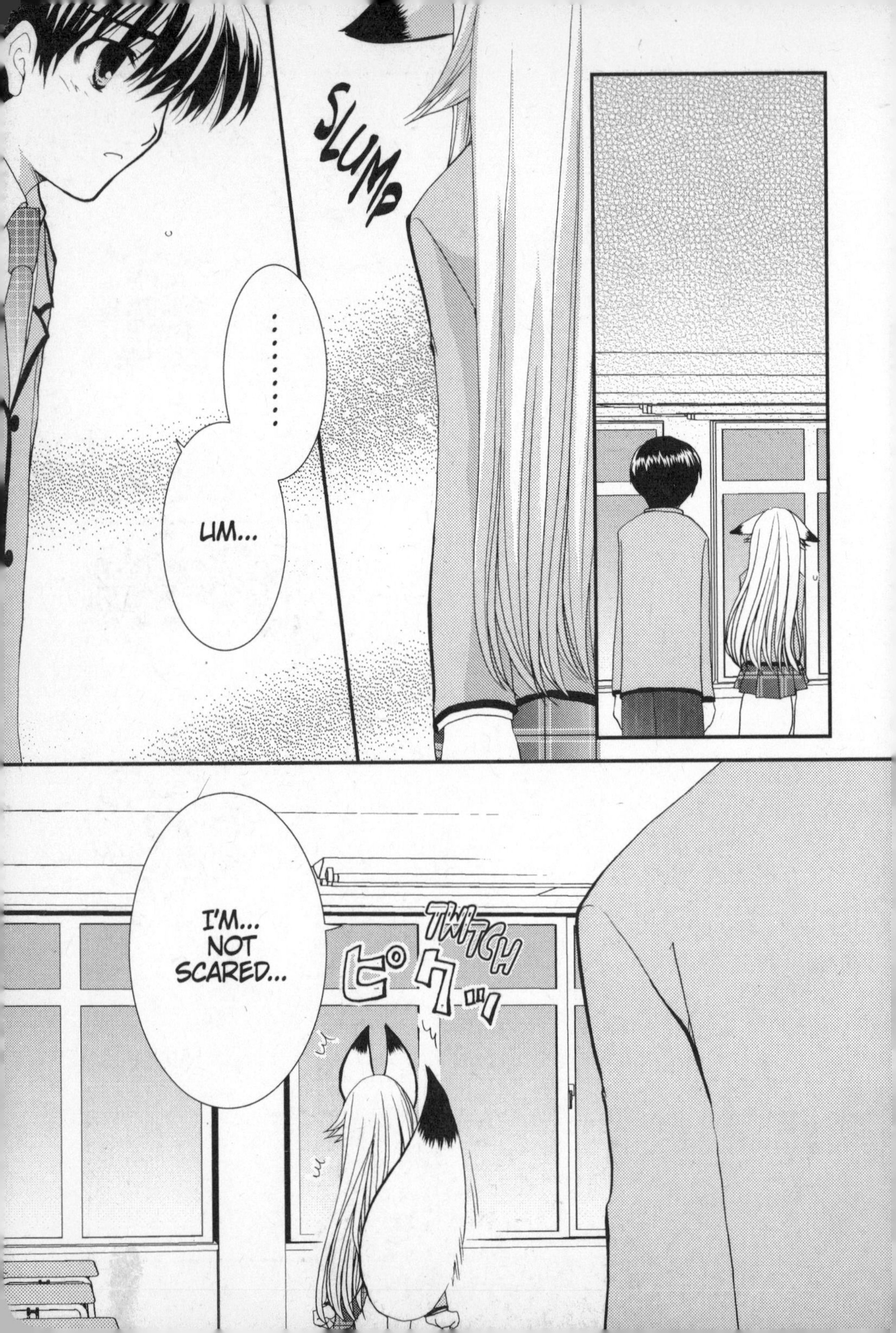
SLUMP
......
UM...
I'M... NOT SCARED...
TWITCH
ピクッ

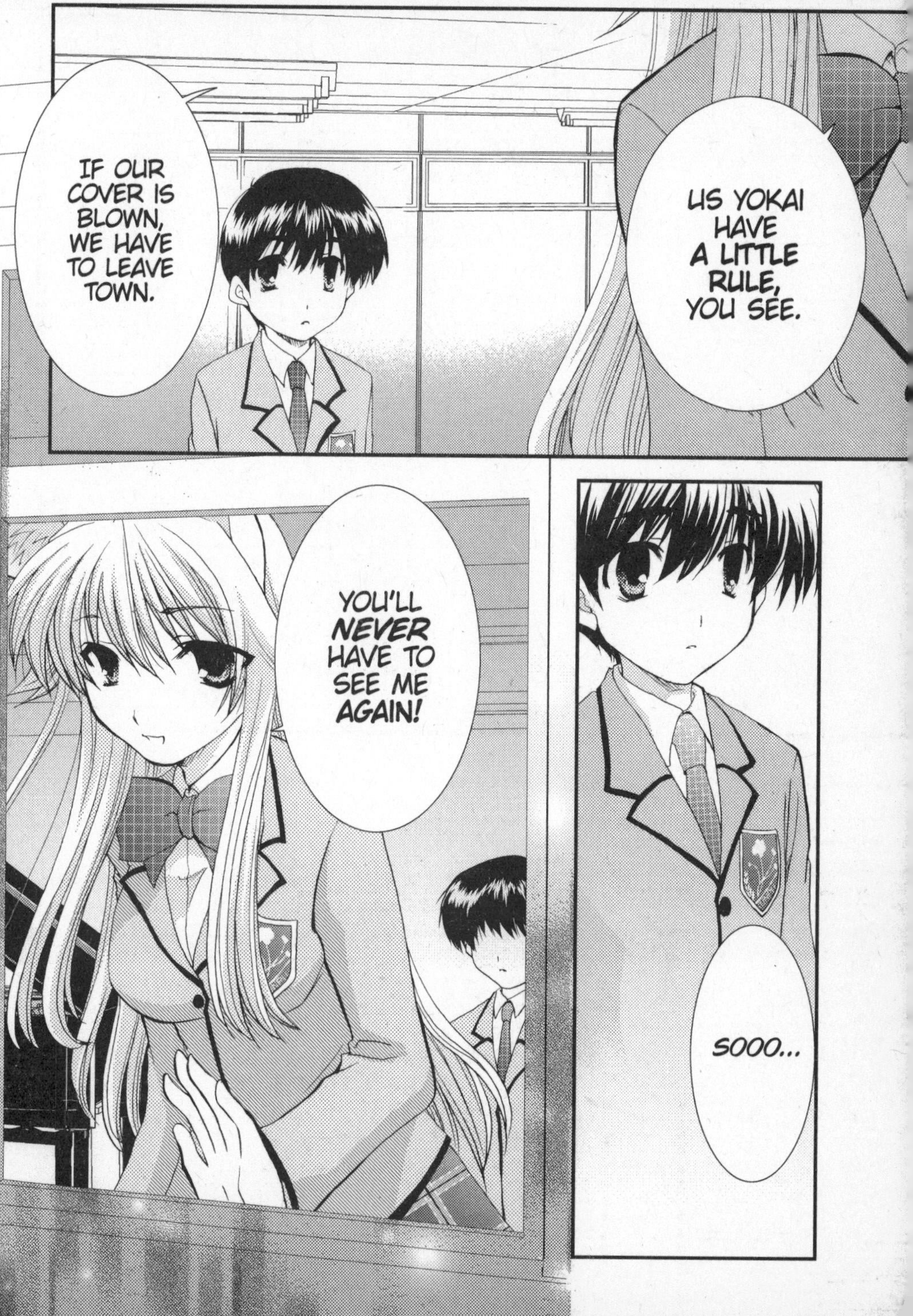
US YOKAI HAVE A LITTLE RULE, YOU SEE.
IF OUR COVER IS BLOWN, WE HAVE TO LEAVE TOWN.
SOOO...
YOU'LL NEVER HAVE TO SEE ME AGAIN!

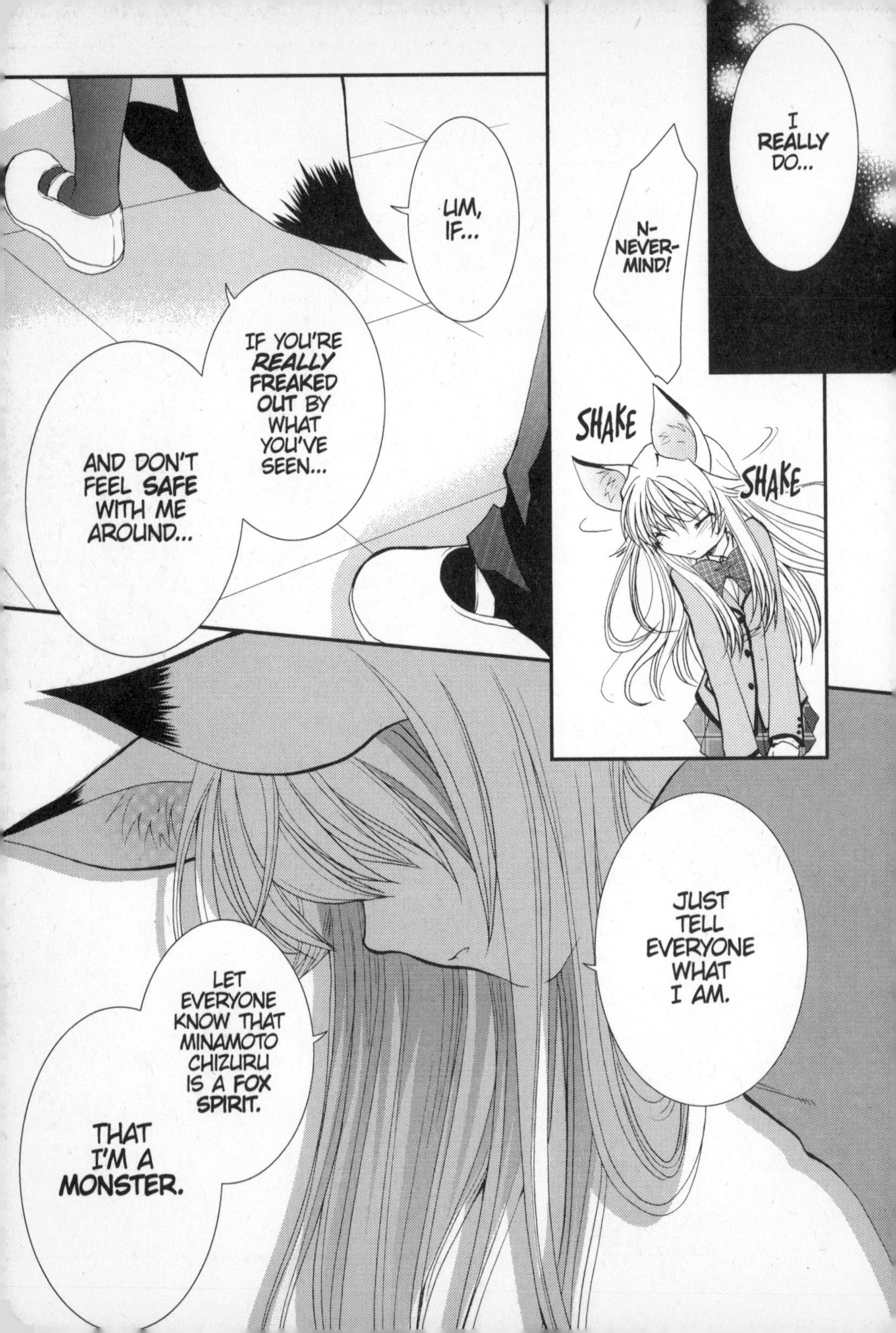
I REALLY DO...
N-NEVERMIND!
SHAKE
SHAKE
UM, IF...
IF YOU'RE *REALLY* FREAKED OUT BY WHAT YOU'VE SEEN...
AND DON'T FEEL **SAFE** WITH ME AROUND...
JUST TELL EVERYONE WHAT I AM.
LET EVERYONE KNOW THAT MINAMOTO CHIZURU IS A FOX SPIRIT.
THAT I'M A MONSTER.

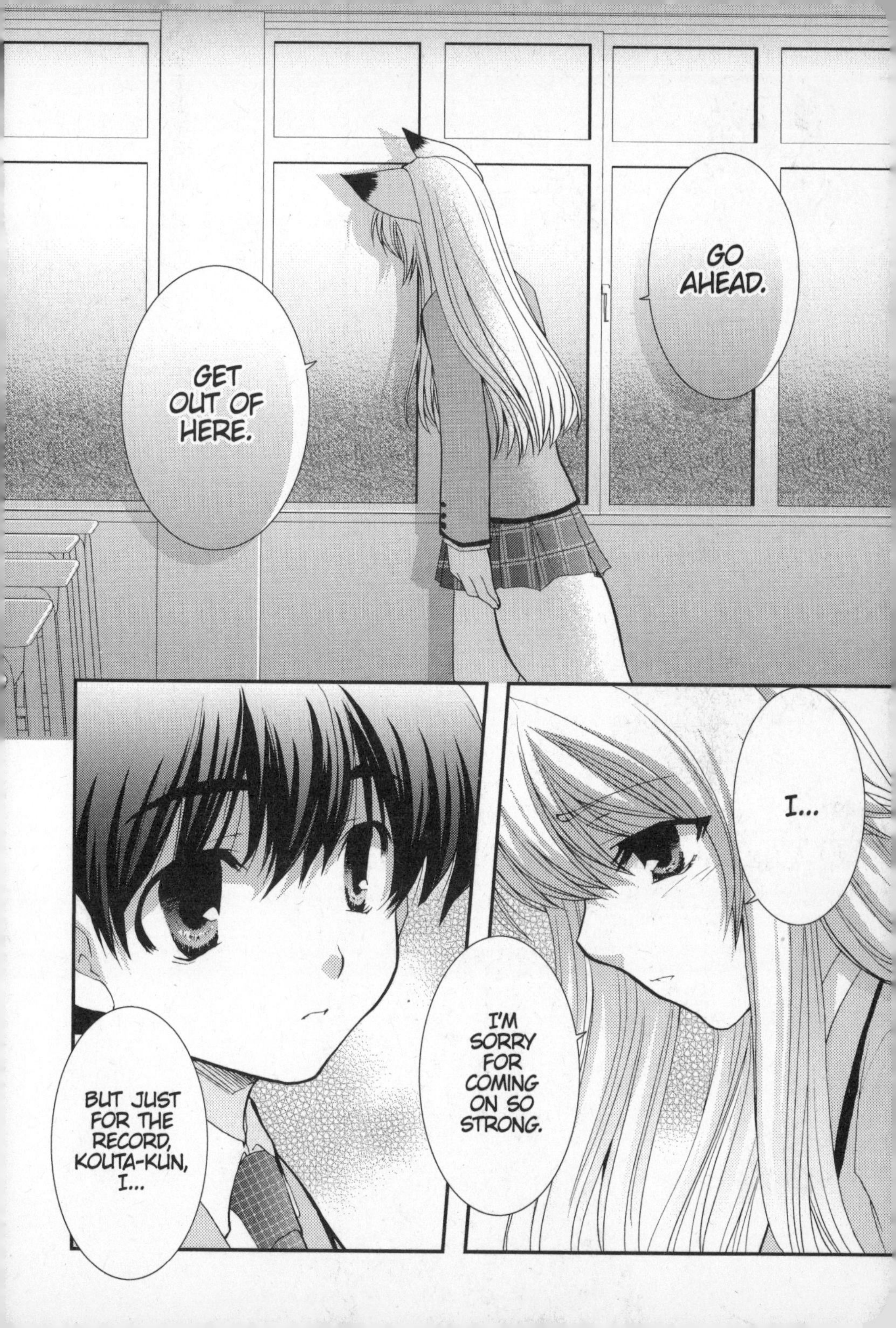
GO AHEAD.
GET OUT OF HERE.
I...
I'M SORRY FOR COMING ON SO STRONG.
BUT JUST FOR THE RECORD, KOUTA-KUN, I...

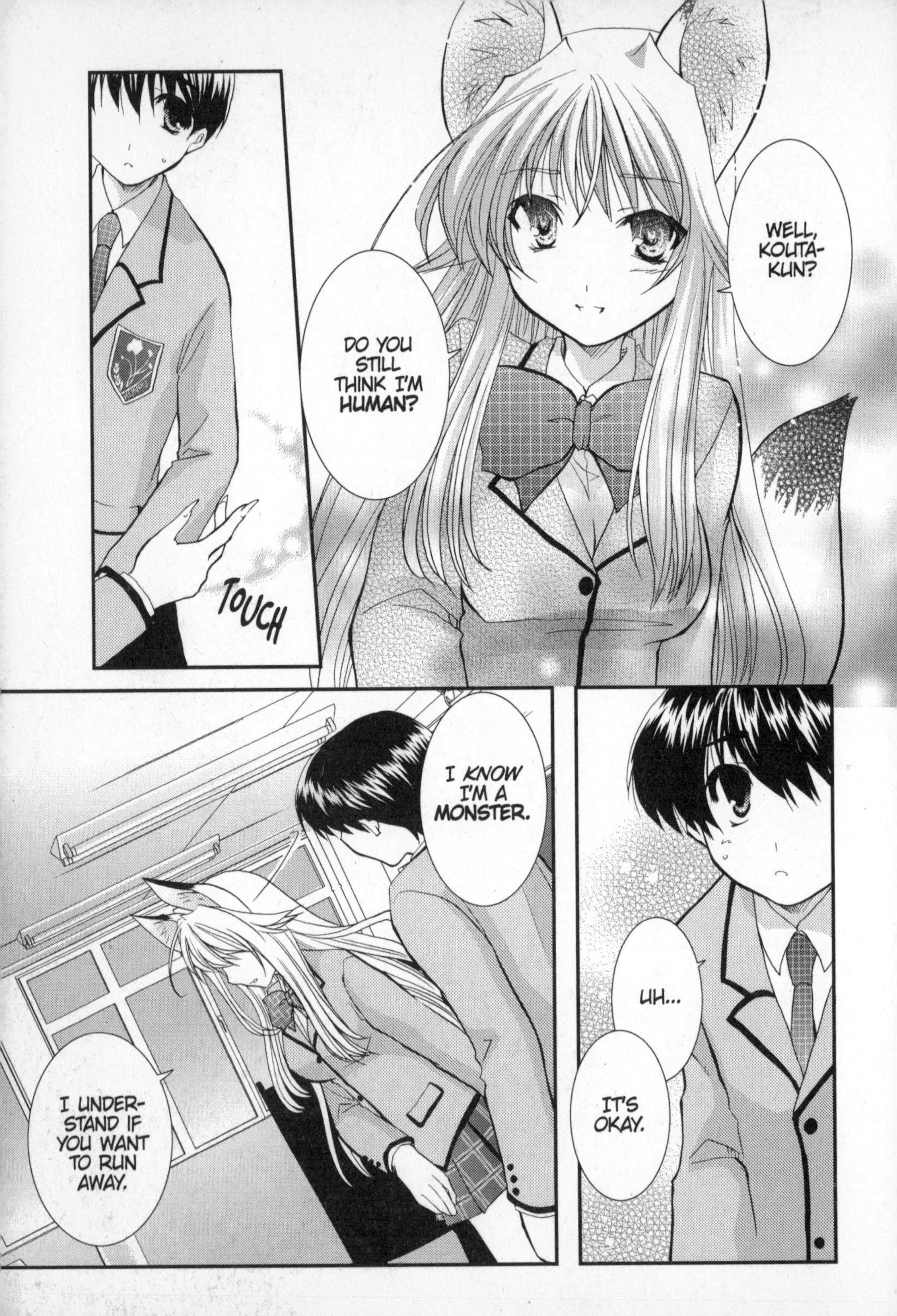
WELL, KOUTA-KUN?
DO YOU STILL THINK I'M HUMAN?
TOUCH
UH...
IT'S OKAY.
I *KNOW* I'M A MONSTER.
I UNDER-STAND IF YOU WANT TO RUN AWAY.

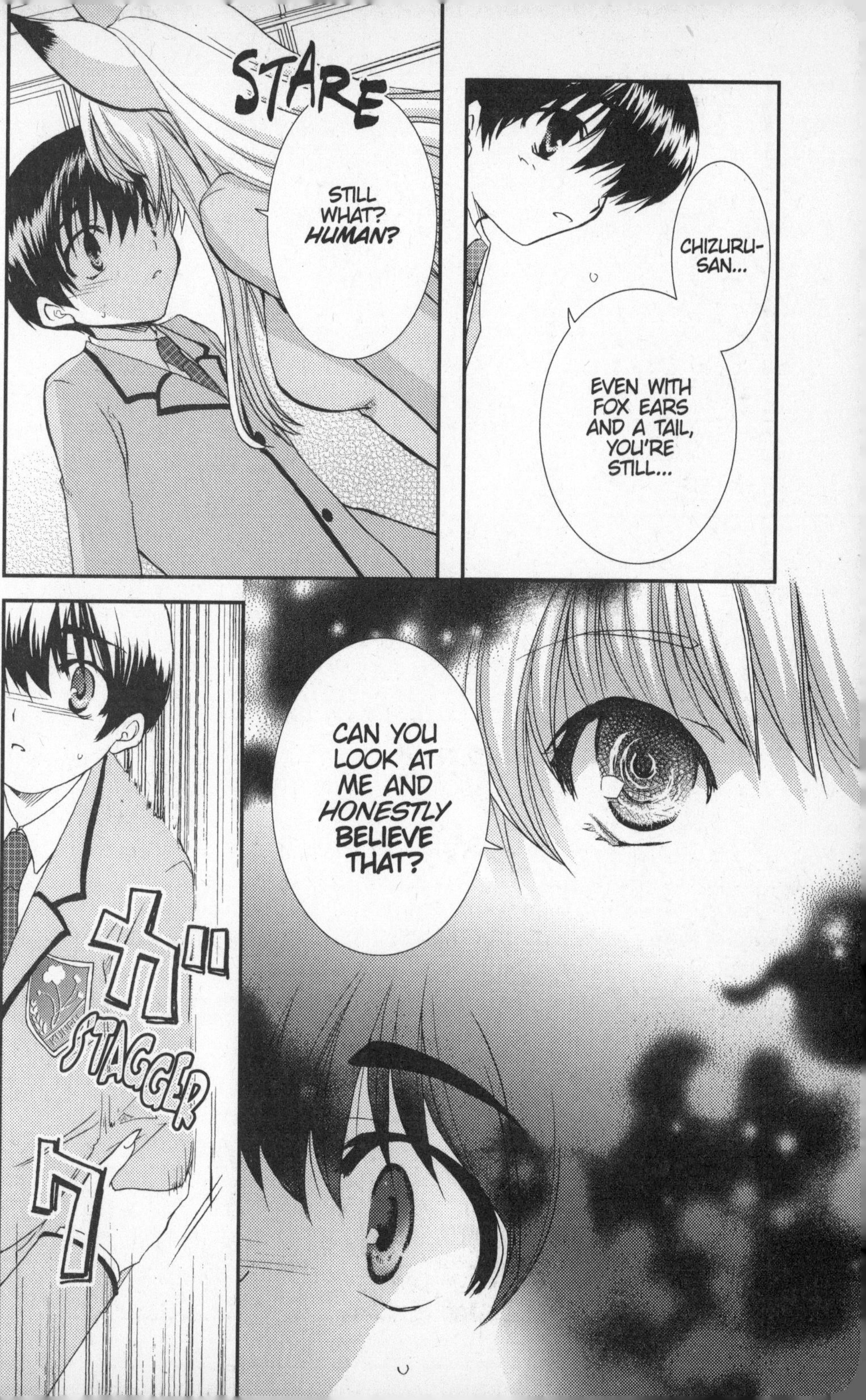
CHIZURU-SAN...
EVEN WITH FOX EARS AND A TAIL, YOU'RE STILL...
STARE
STILL WHAT? *HUMAN?*
CAN YOU LOOK AT ME AND *HONESTLY* BELIEVE THAT?
STAGGER

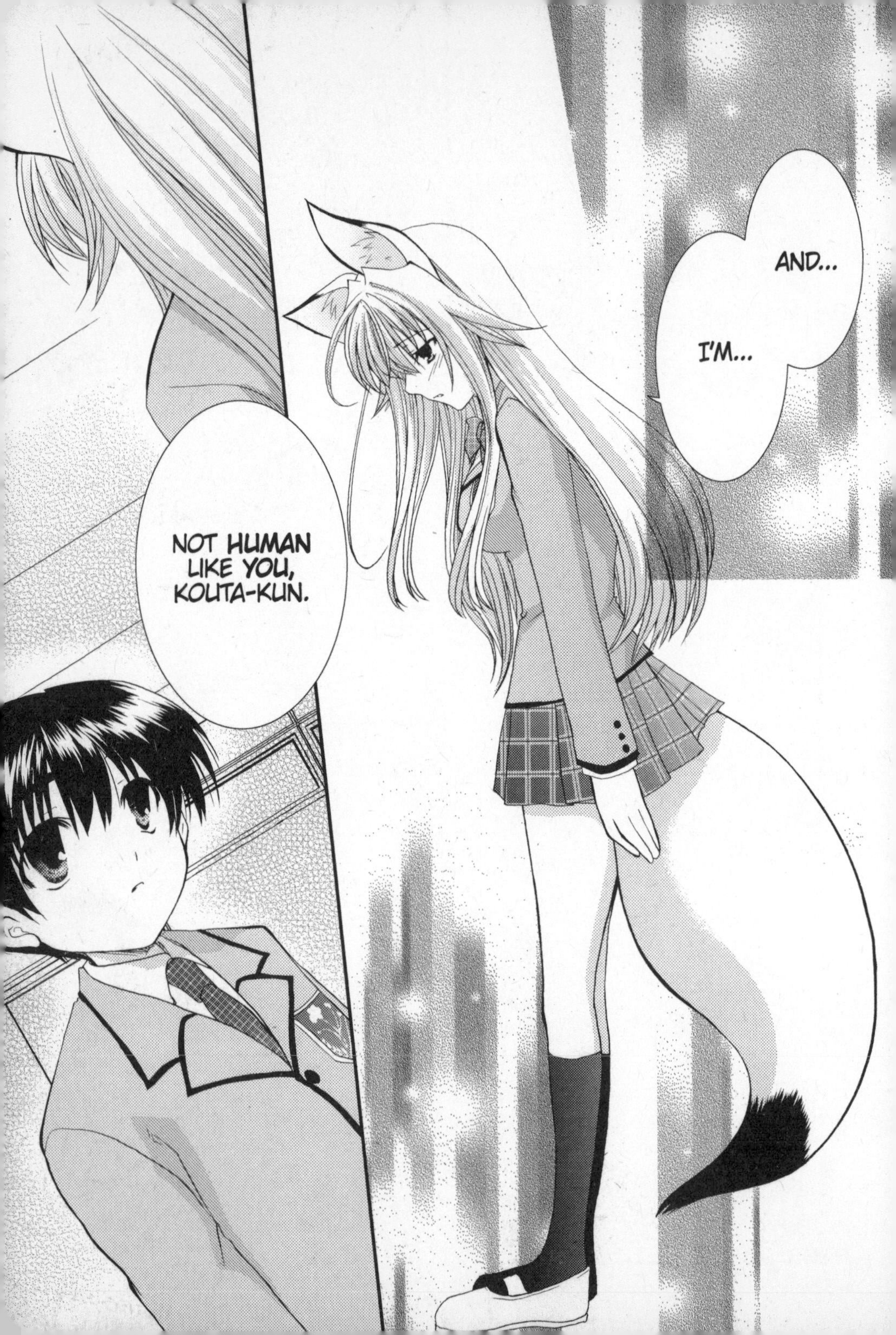
AND...
I'M...
NOT HUMAN LIKE YOU, KOUTA-KUN.

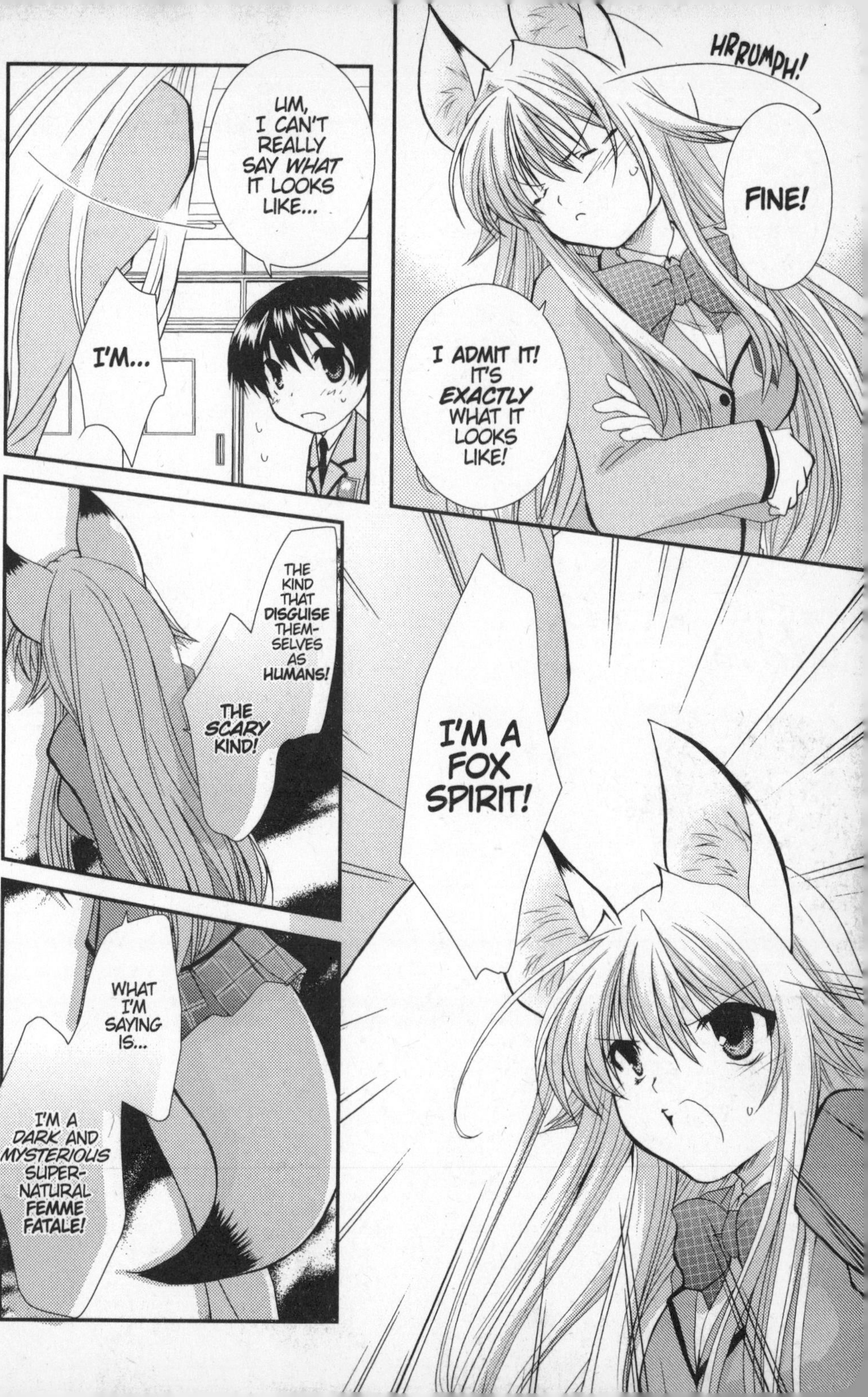
HRRUMPH!
FINE!
I ADMIT IT! IT'S *EXACTLY* WHAT IT LOOKS LIKE!
UM, I CAN'T REALLY SAY *WHAT* IT LOOKS LIKE...
I'M...
I'M A FOX SPIRIT!
THE KIND THAT DISGUISE THEM-SELVES AS HUMANS!
THE *SCARY* KIND!
WHAT I'M SAYING IS...
I'M A *DARK AND MYSTERIOUS* SUPER-NATURAL FEMME FATALE!

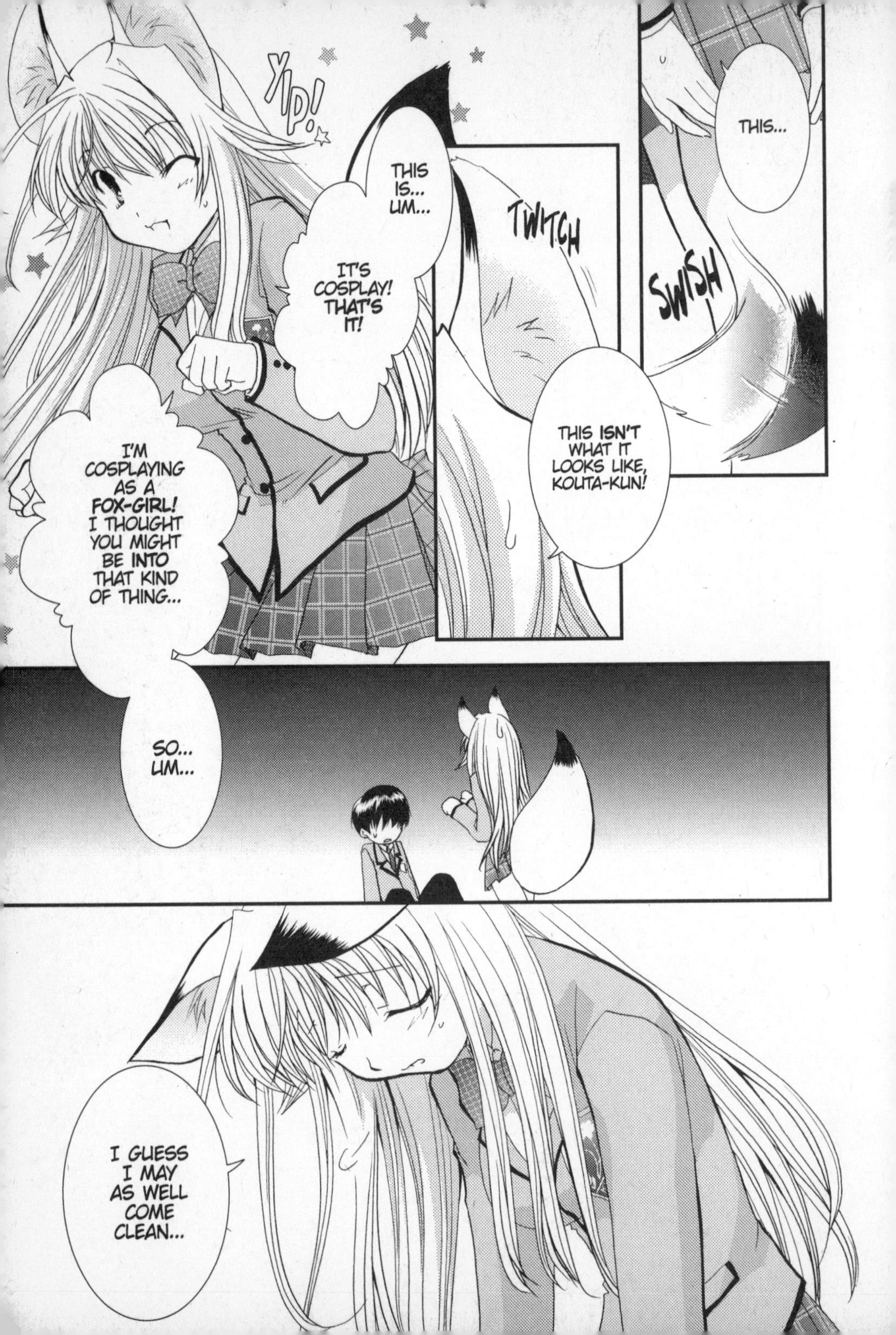
THIS...
SWISH
TWITCH
THIS ISN'T WHAT IT LOOKS LIKE, KOUTA-KUN!
YIP!
THIS IS... UM...
IT'S COSPLAY! THAT'S IT!
I'M COSPLAYING AS A FOX-GIRL! I THOUGHT YOU MIGHT BE INTO THAT KIND OF THING...
SO... UM...
I GUESS I MAY AS WELL COME CLEAN...

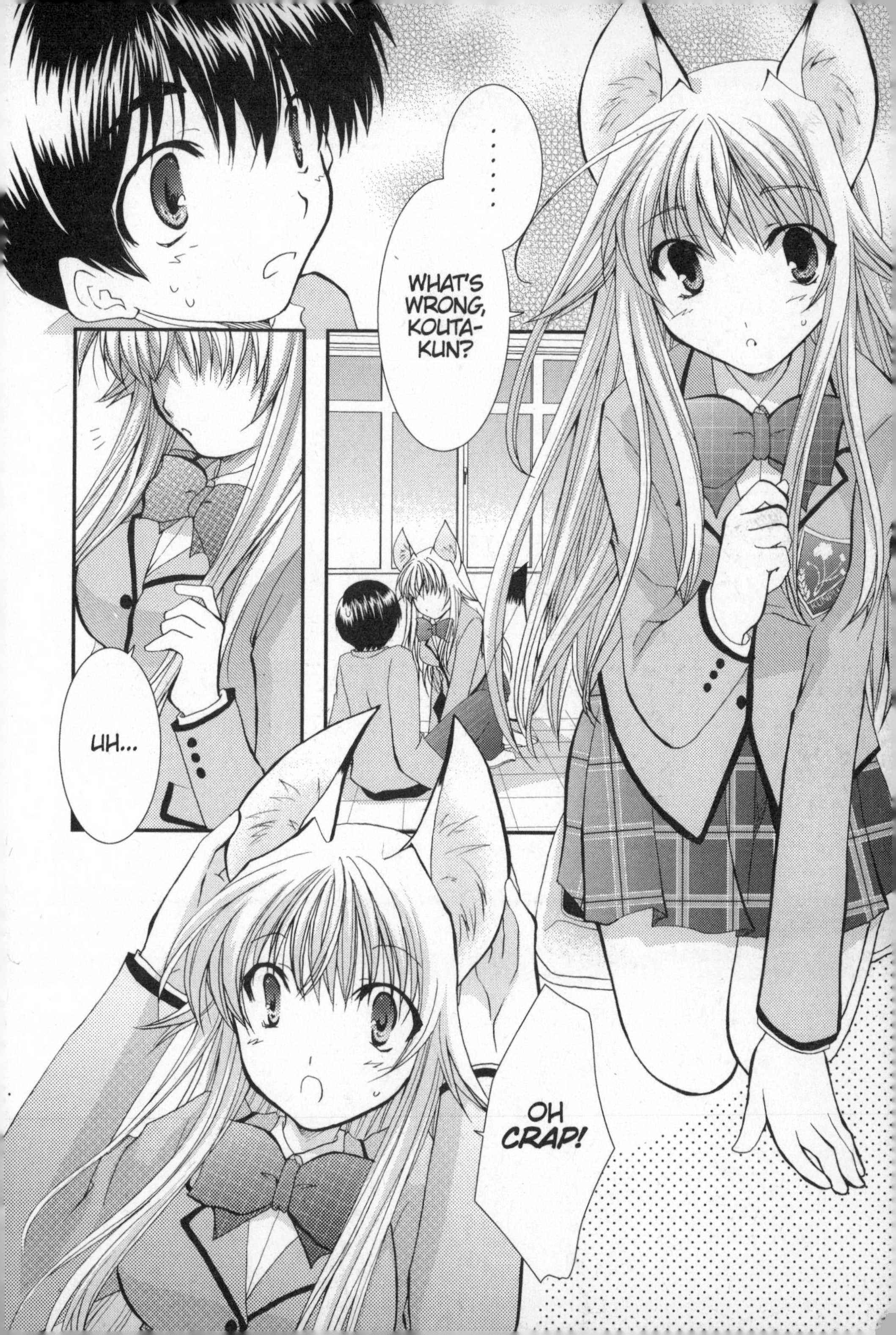
......
WHAT'S WRONG, KOUTA-KUN?
UH...
OH CRAP!

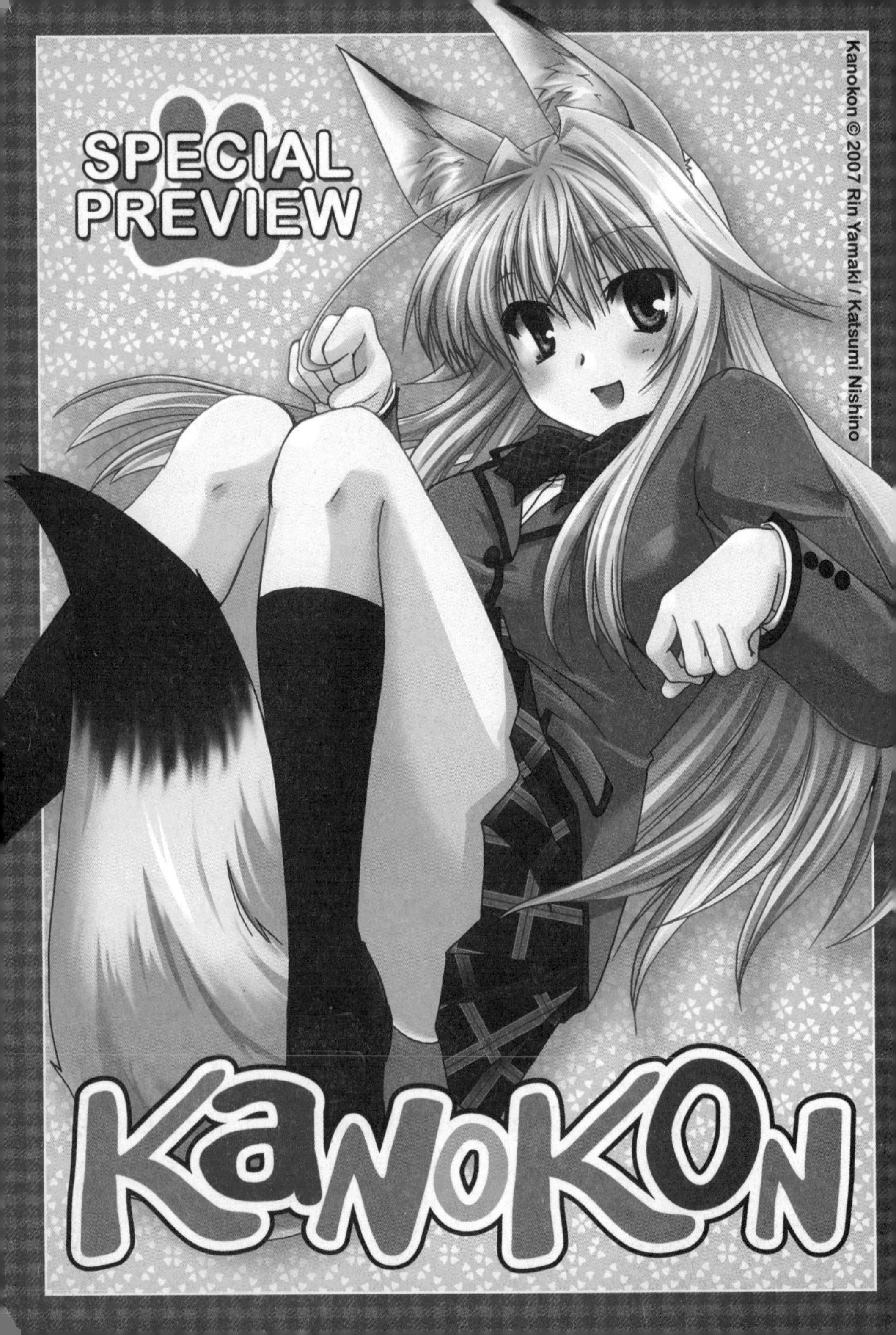
SPECIAL
PREVIEW
KANOKON
Kanokon © 2007 Rin Yamaki / Katsumi Nishino

COMING SOON

AUGUST 2013
Crimson Empire Vol. 2

SEPTEMBER 2013
Alice in the Country of Clover:
Cheshire Cat Waltz Vol. 6

OCTOBER 2013
Alice in the Country of Joker:
Circus and Liars Game Vol. 3

NOVEMBER 2013
Alice in the Country of Hearts:
The Mad Hatter's Late Night
Tea Party Vol. 1

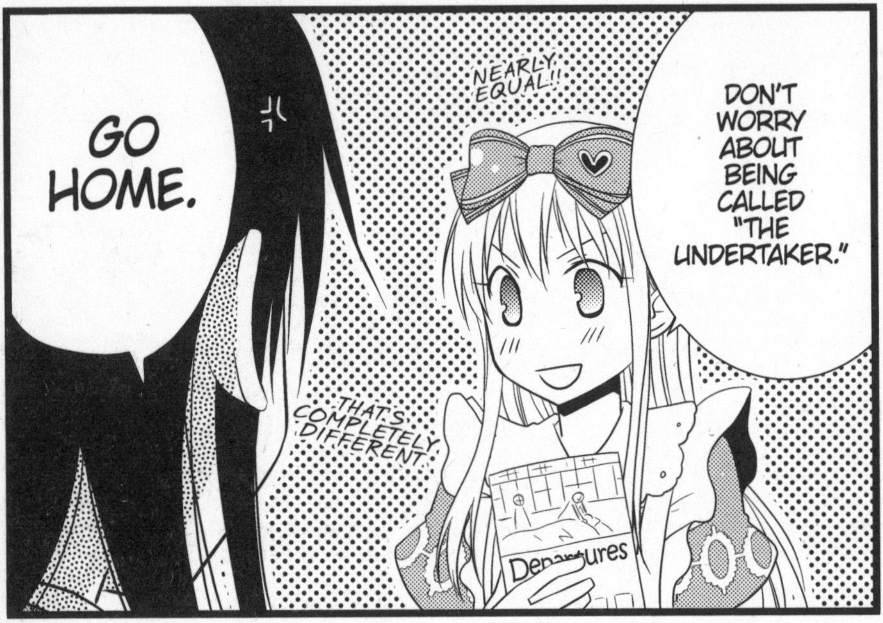
DON'T WORRY ABOUT BEING CALLED "THE UNDERTAKER."
NEARLY EQUAL!!
GO HOME.
THAT'S COMPLETELY DIFFERENT.
Departures

Deep Appreciation!

I've been under your care a lot.
QuinRose

Thank you for your help!
Assistant

Thank you for everything.
Friends and Acquaintances

And most importantly,
thank you to everyone
who picked up this book!
The Readers

Thank you very much!

THE CLOCKMAKER'S STORY: POST-MORTEM

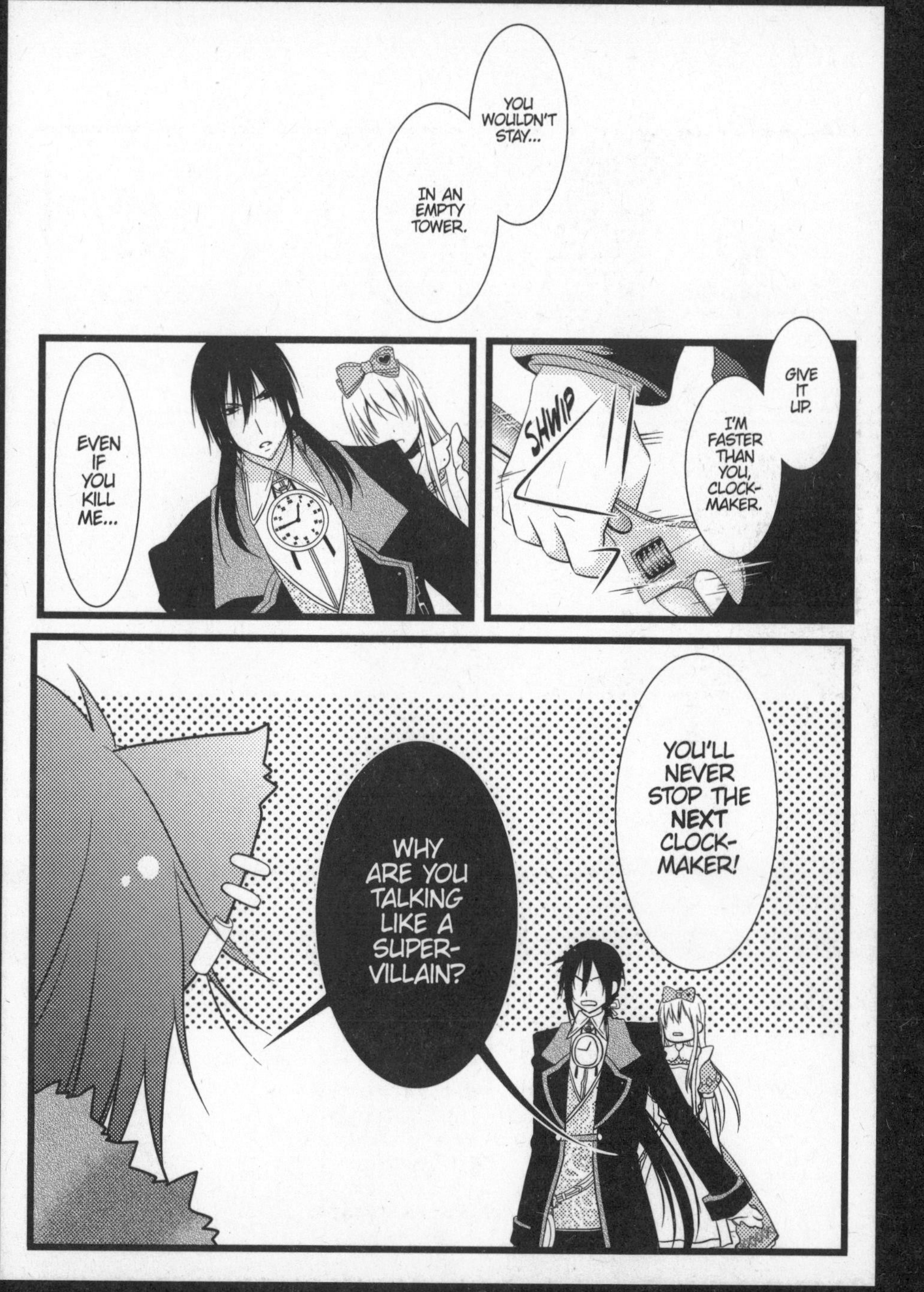
YOU WOULDN'T STAY...
IN AN EMPTY TOWER.
GIVE IT UP.
SHWIP
I'M FASTER THAN YOU, CLOCK-MAKER.
EVEN IF YOU KILL ME...
YOU'LL NEVER STOP THE NEXT CLOCK-MAKER!
WHY ARE YOU TALKING LIKE A SUPER-VILLAIN?

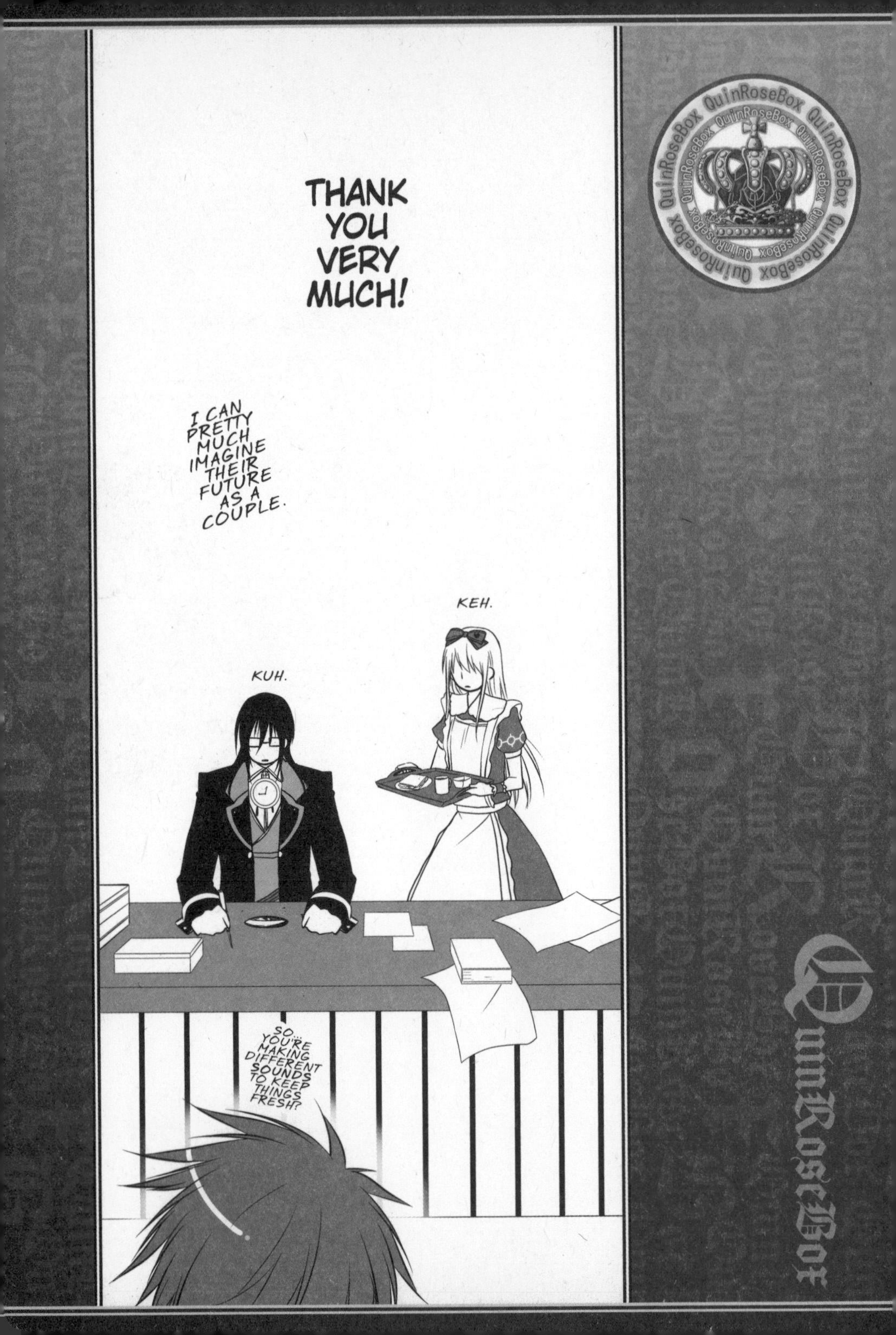
THANK YOU VERY MUCH!
I CAN PRETTY MUCH IMAGINE THEIR FUTURE AS A COUPLE.
KEH.
KUH.
SO... YOU'RE MAKING DIFFERENT SOUNDS TO KEEP THINGS FRESH?

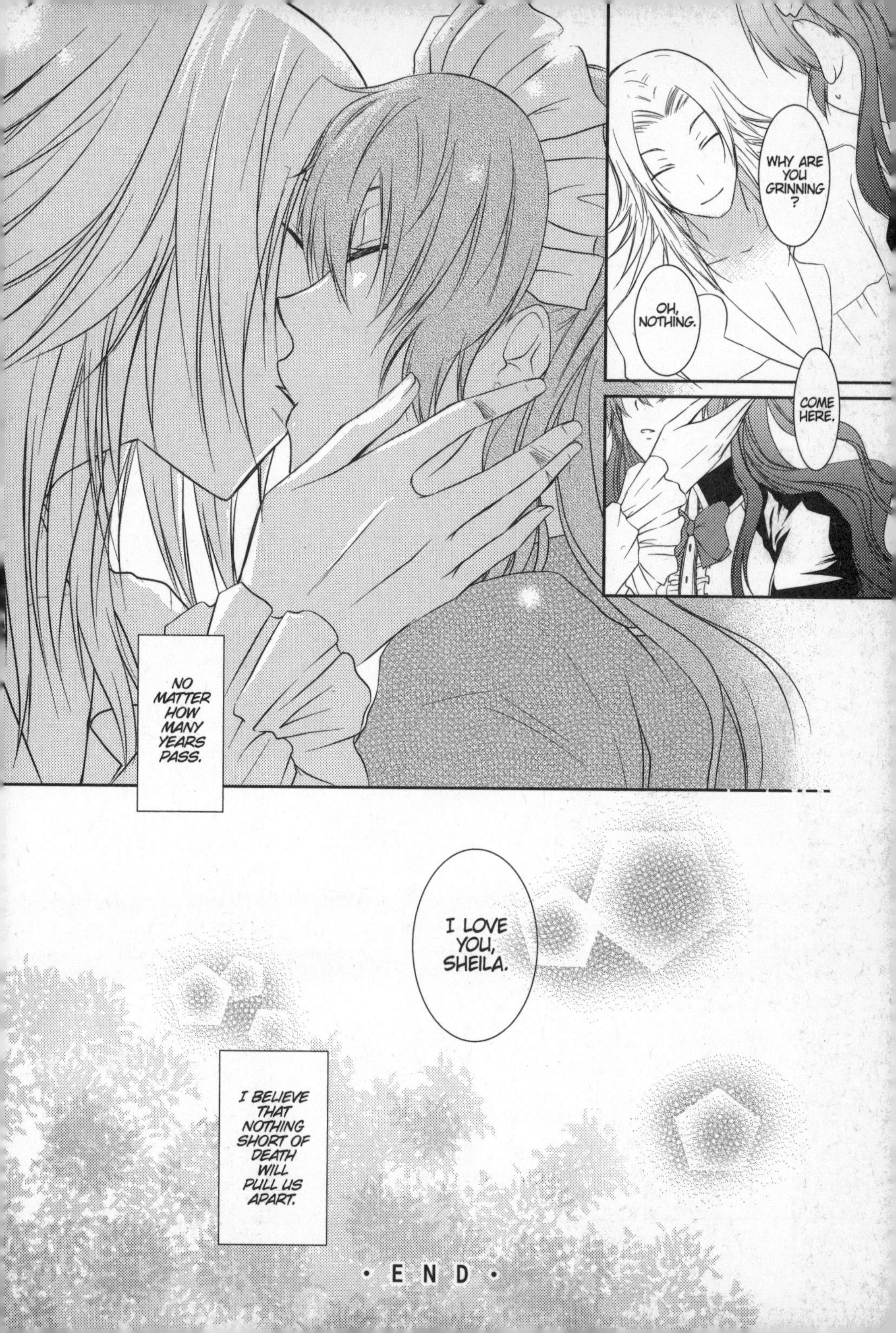
WHY ARE YOU GRINNING?
OH, NOTHING.
COME HERE.
NO MATTER HOW MANY YEARS PASS.
I LOVE YOU, SHEILA.
I BELIEVE THAT NOTHING SHORT OF DEATH WILL PULL US APART.
• END •

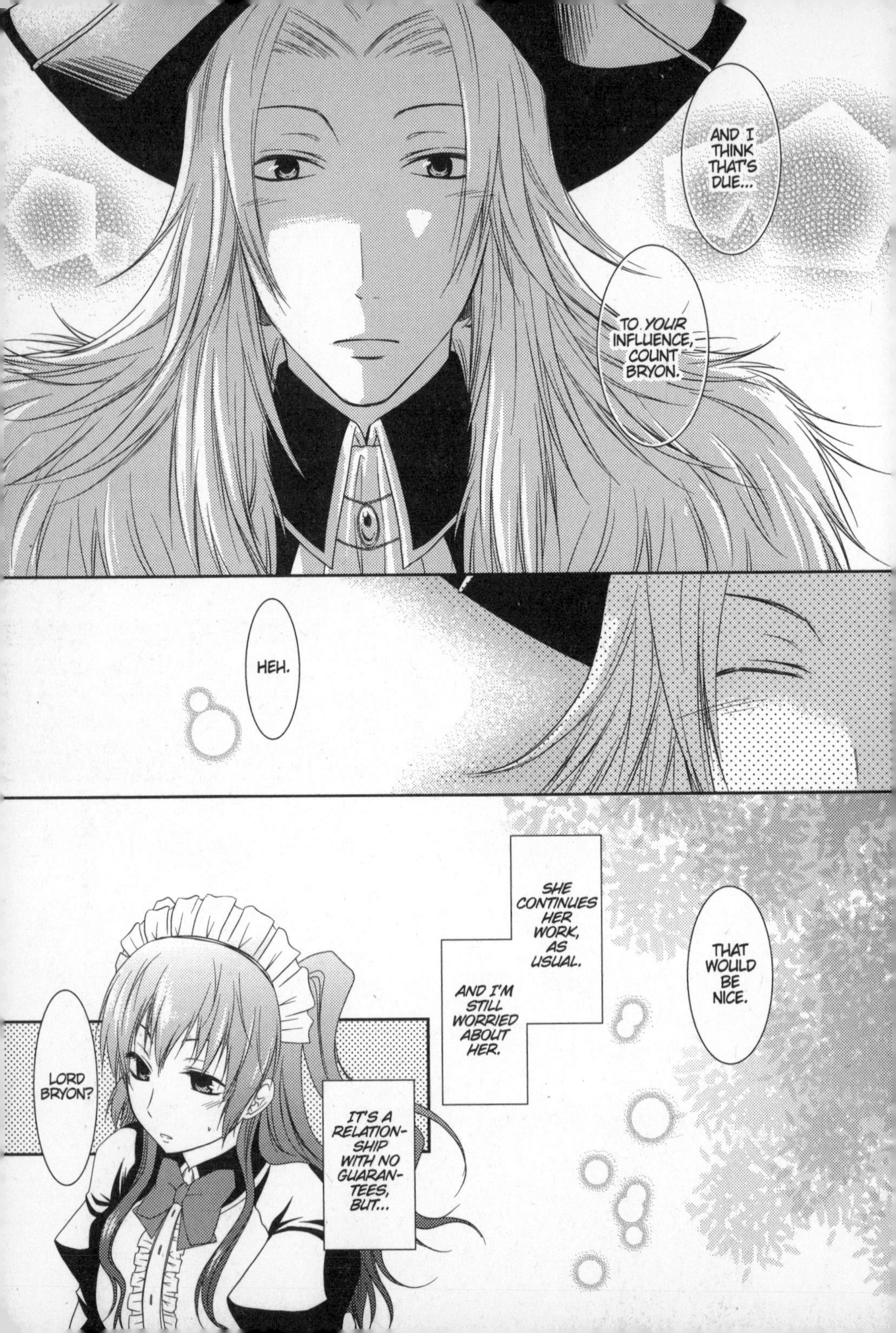
AND I THINK THAT'S DUE...
TO YOUR INFLUENCE, COUNT BRYON.
HEH.
THAT WOULD BE NICE.
SHE CONTINUES HER WORK, AS USUAL.
AND I'M STILL WORRIED ABOUT HER.
IT'S A RELATIONSHIP WITH NO GUARANTEES, BUT...
LORD BRYON?

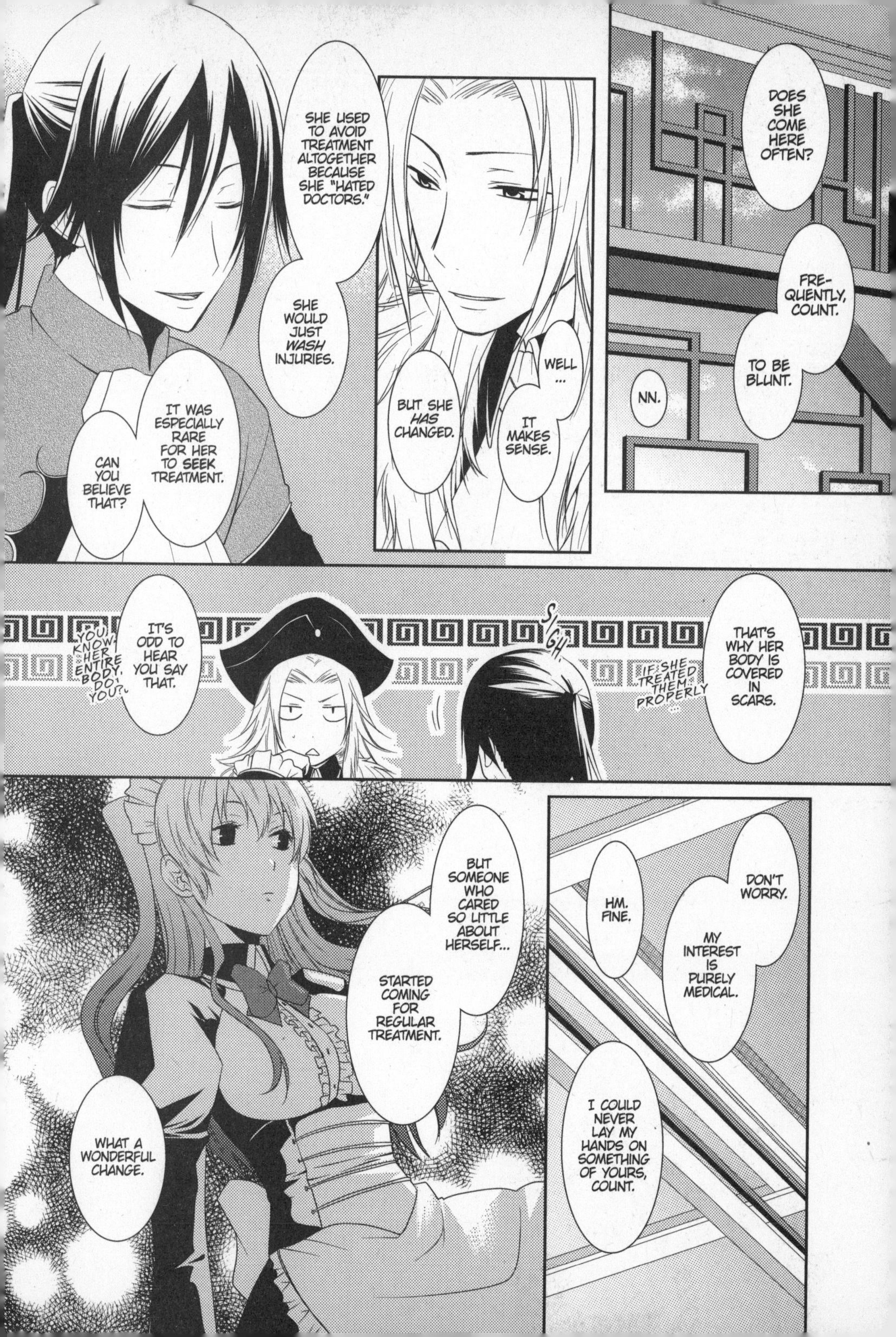
DOES SHE COME HERE OFTEN?
FRE-QUENTLY, COUNT.
TO BE BLUNT.
NN.
WELL ...
IT MAKES SENSE.
BUT SHE *HAS* CHANGED.
SHE USED TO AVOID TREATMENT ALTOGETHER BECAUSE SHE "HATED DOCTORS."
SHE WOULD JUST *WASH* INJURIES.
IT WAS ESPECIALLY RARE FOR HER TO SEEK TREATMENT.
CAN YOU BELIEVE THAT?
THAT'S WHY HER BODY IS COVERED IN SCARS.
IF SHE TREATED THEM PROPERLY ...
SIGH
IT'S ODD TO HEAR YOU SAY THAT.
YOU KNOW HER ENTIRE BODY, DO YOU?
DON'T WORRY.
MY INTEREST IS PURELY MEDICAL.
HM. FINE.
I COULD NEVER LAY MY HANDS ON SOMETHING OF YOURS, COUNT.
BUT SOMEONE WHO CARED SO LITTLE ABOUT HERSELF...
STARTED COMING FOR REGULAR TREATMENT.
WHAT A WONDERFUL CHANGE.

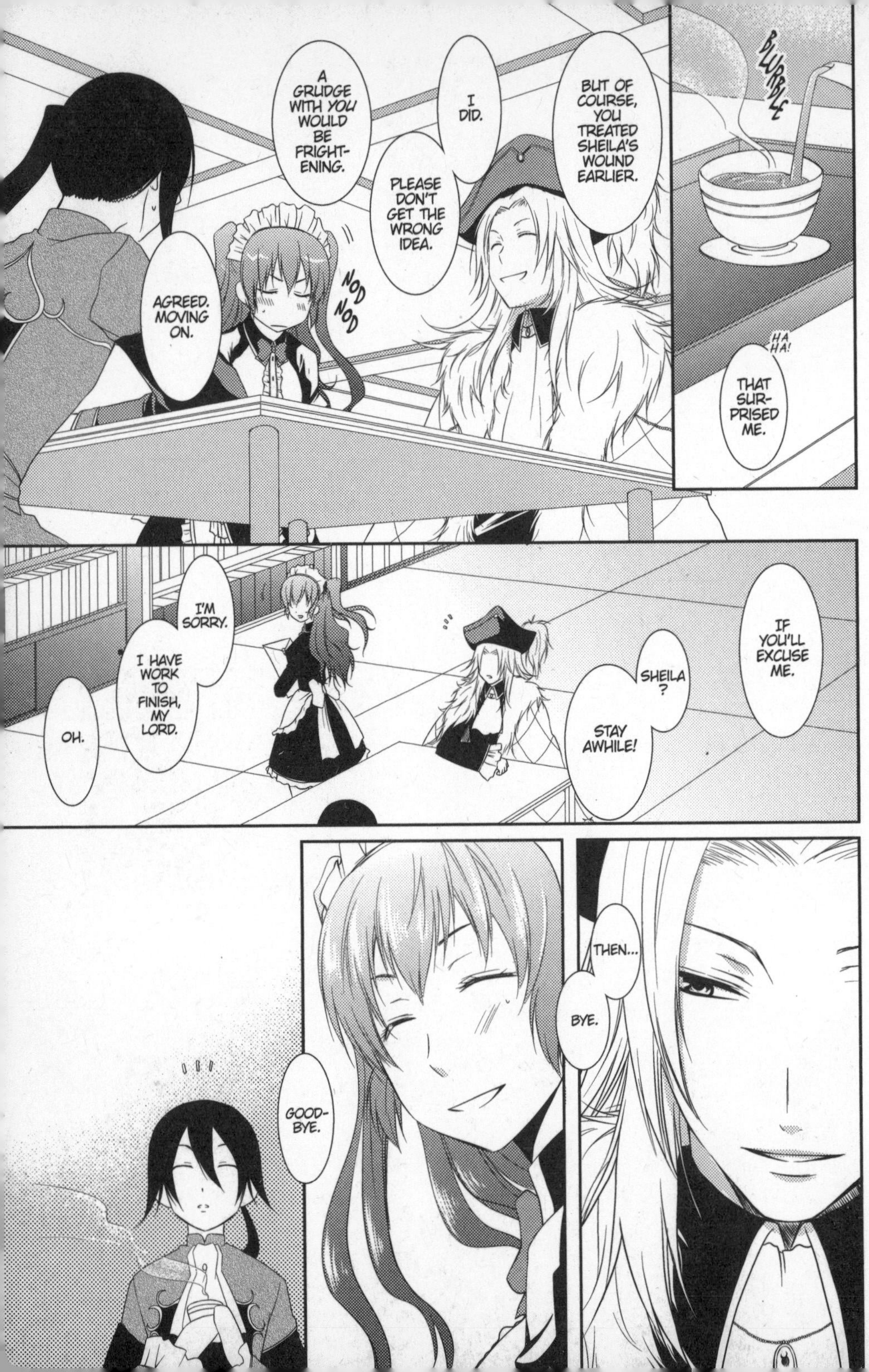
BLURBLE
HA HA!
THAT SURPRISED ME.
BUT OF COURSE, YOU TREATED SHEILA'S WOUND EARLIER.
I DID.
PLEASE DON'T GET THE WRONG IDEA.
A GRUDGE WITH YOU WOULD BE FRIGHTENING.
NOD NOD
AGREED. MOVING ON.
IF YOU'LL EXCUSE ME.
SHEILA?
STAY AWHILE!
I'M SORRY.
I HAVE WORK TO FINISH, MY LORD.
OH.
THEN...
BYE.
GOOD-BYE.

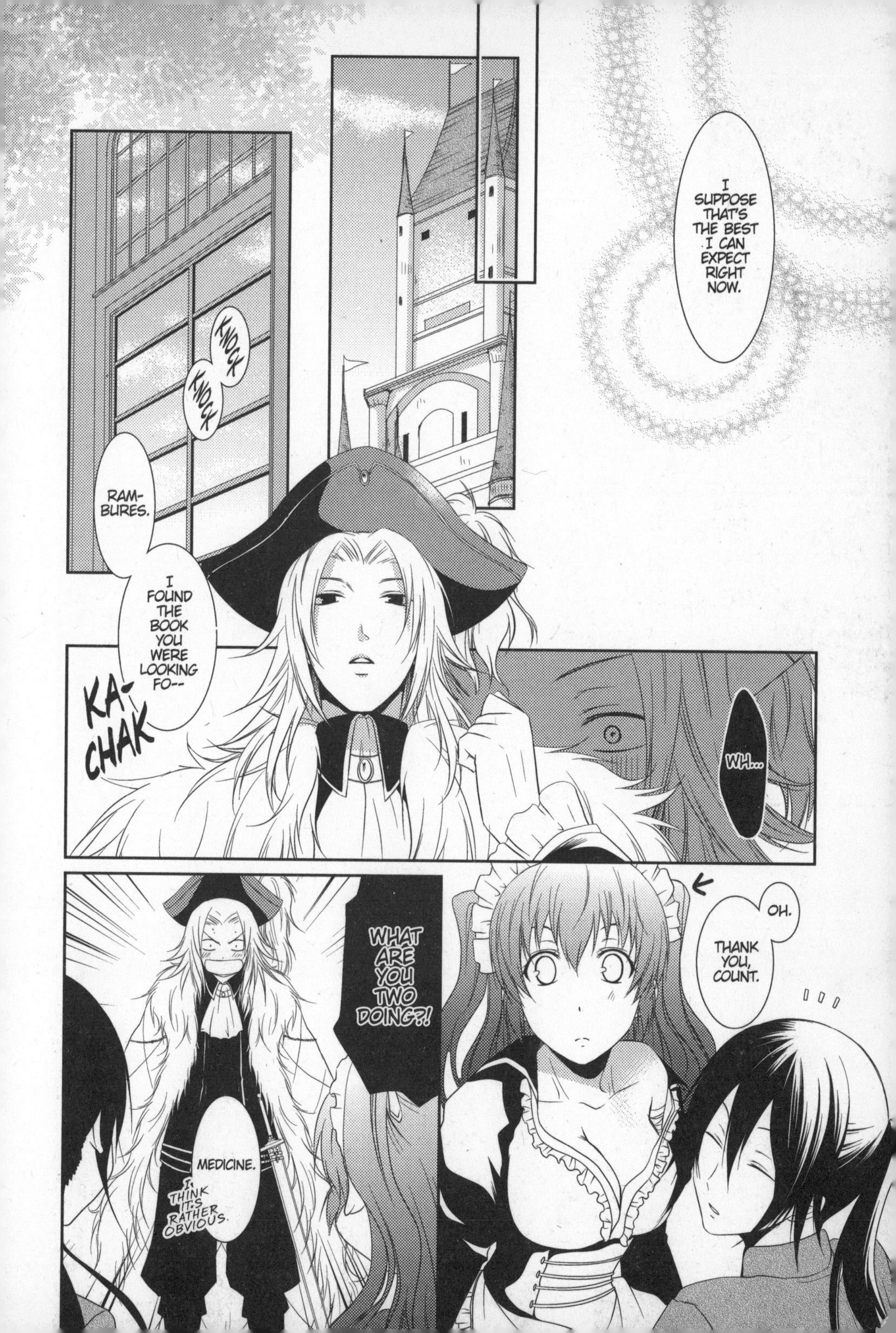
I SUPPOSE THAT'S THE BEST I CAN EXPECT RIGHT NOW.
KNOCK KNOCK
RAMBURES.
I FOUND THE BOOK YOU WERE LOOKING FO--
KA-CHAK
WH...
OH.
THANK YOU, COUNT.
WHAT ARE YOU TWO DOING?!
MEDICINE.
I THINK IT'S RATHER OBVIOUS.

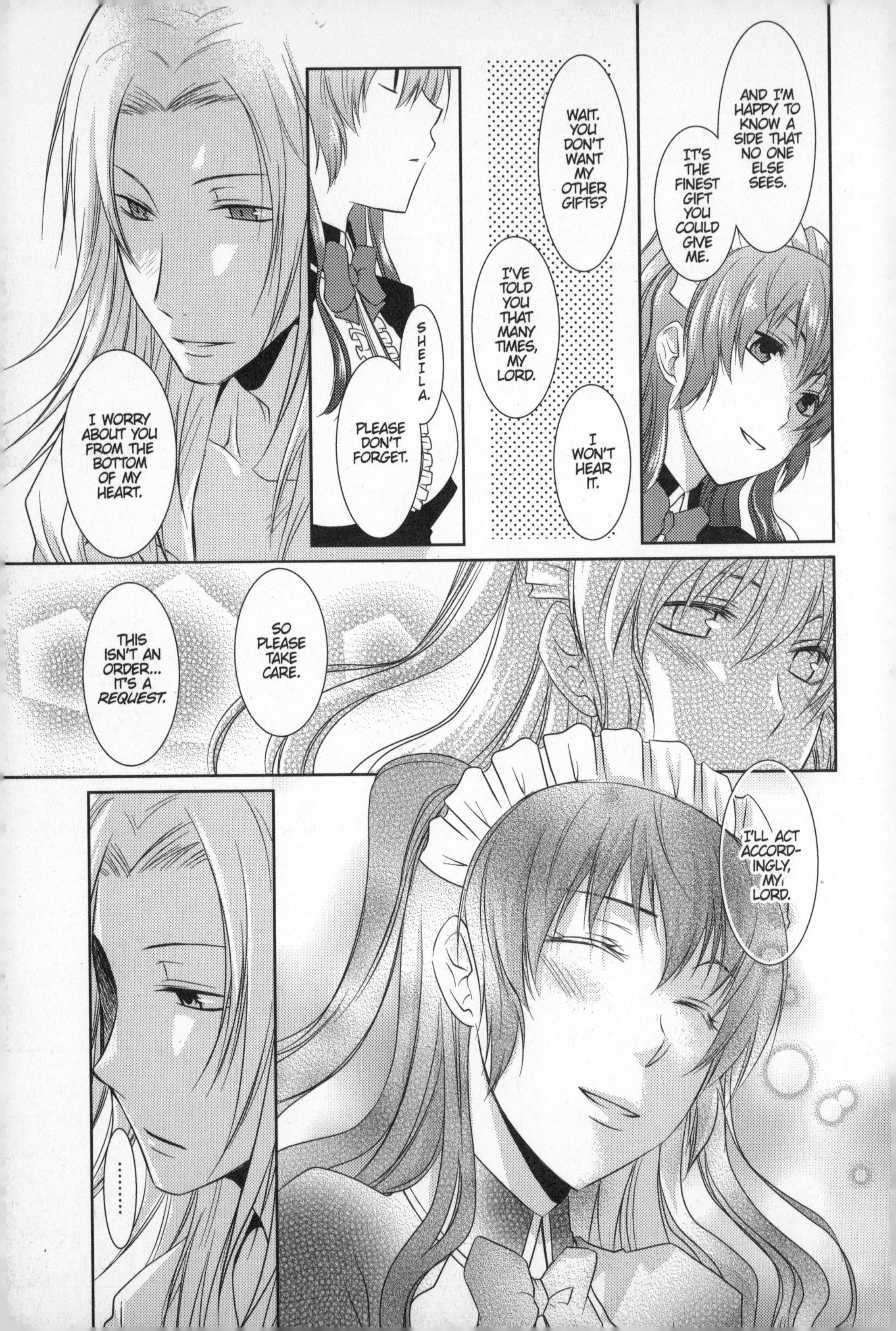
AND I'M HAPPY TO KNOW A SIDE THAT NO ONE ELSE SEES.
IT'S THE FINEST GIFT YOU COULD GIVE ME.
WAIT. YOU DON'T WANT MY OTHER GIFTS?
I'VE TOLD YOU THAT MANY TIMES, MY LORD.
I WON'T HEAR IT.
SHEILA.
PLEASE DON'T FORGET.
I WORRY ABOUT YOU FROM THE BOTTOM OF MY HEART.
SO PLEASE TAKE CARE.
THIS ISN'T AN ORDER... IT'S A *REQUEST.*
I'LL ACT ACCORDINGLY, MY LORD.
......

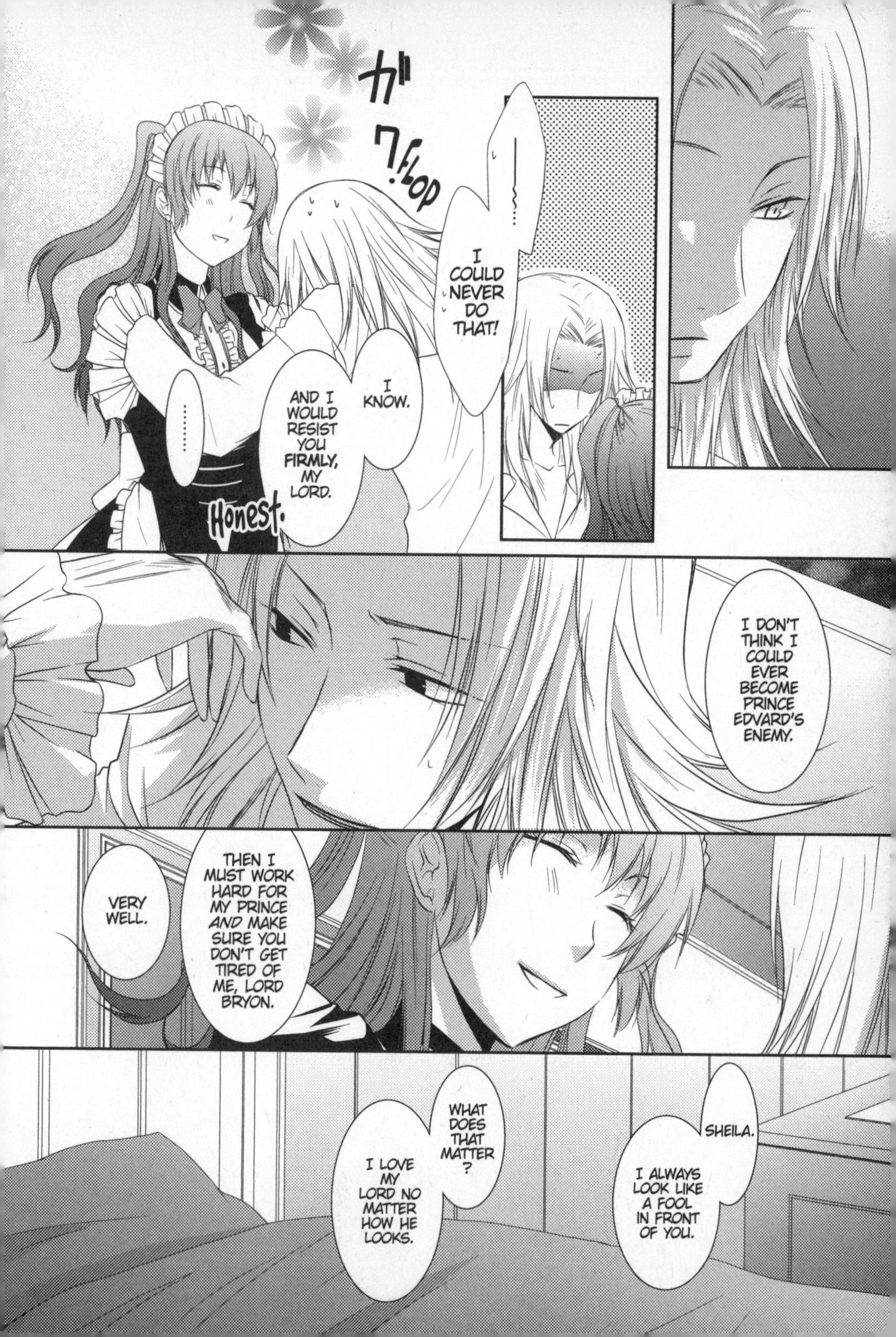

—...!
I COULD NEVER DO THAT!
FLOP
I KNOW.
AND I WOULD RESIST YOU FIRMLY, MY LORD.
......
Honest.
I DON'T THINK I COULD EVER BECOME PRINCE EDVARD'S ENEMY.
THEN I MUST WORK HARD FOR MY PRINCE AND MAKE SURE YOU DON'T GET TIRED OF ME, LORD BRYON.
VERY WELL.
SHEILA.
I ALWAYS LOOK LIKE A FOOL IN FRONT OF YOU.
WHAT DOES THAT MATTER?
I LOVE MY LORD NO MATTER HOW HE LOOKS.

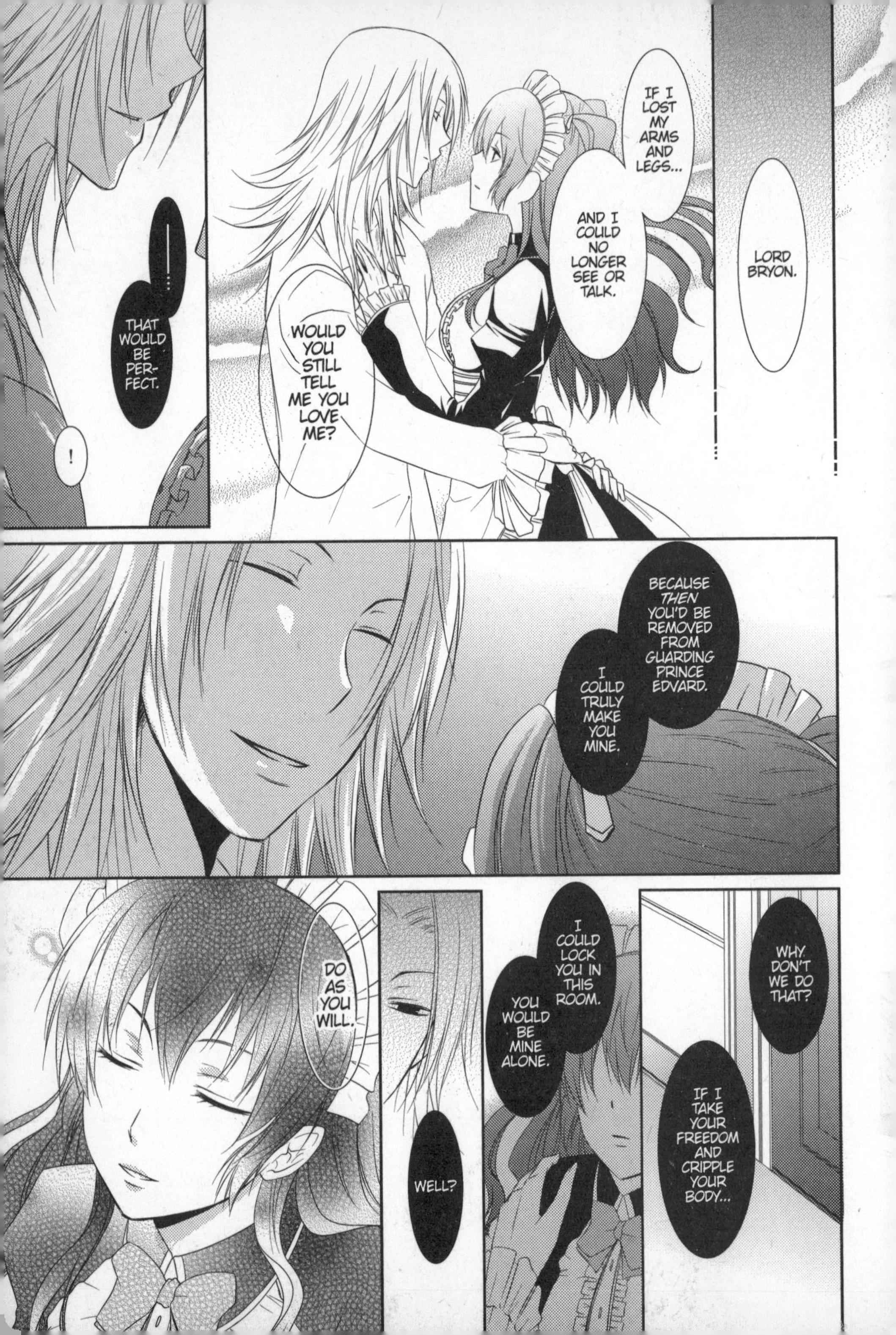
LORD BRYON.
IF I LOST MY ARMS AND LEGS...
AND I COULD NO LONGER SEE OR TALK.
WOULD YOU STILL TELL ME YOU LOVE ME?
!...
THAT WOULD BE PERFECT.
!
BECAUSE *THEN* YOU'D BE REMOVED FROM GUARDING PRINCE EDVARD.
I COULD TRULY MAKE YOU MINE.
WHY DON'T WE DO THAT?
IF I TAKE YOUR FREEDOM AND CRIPPLE YOUR BODY...
I COULD LOCK YOU IN THIS ROOM.
YOU WOULD BE MINE ALONE.
WELL?
DO AS YOU WILL.

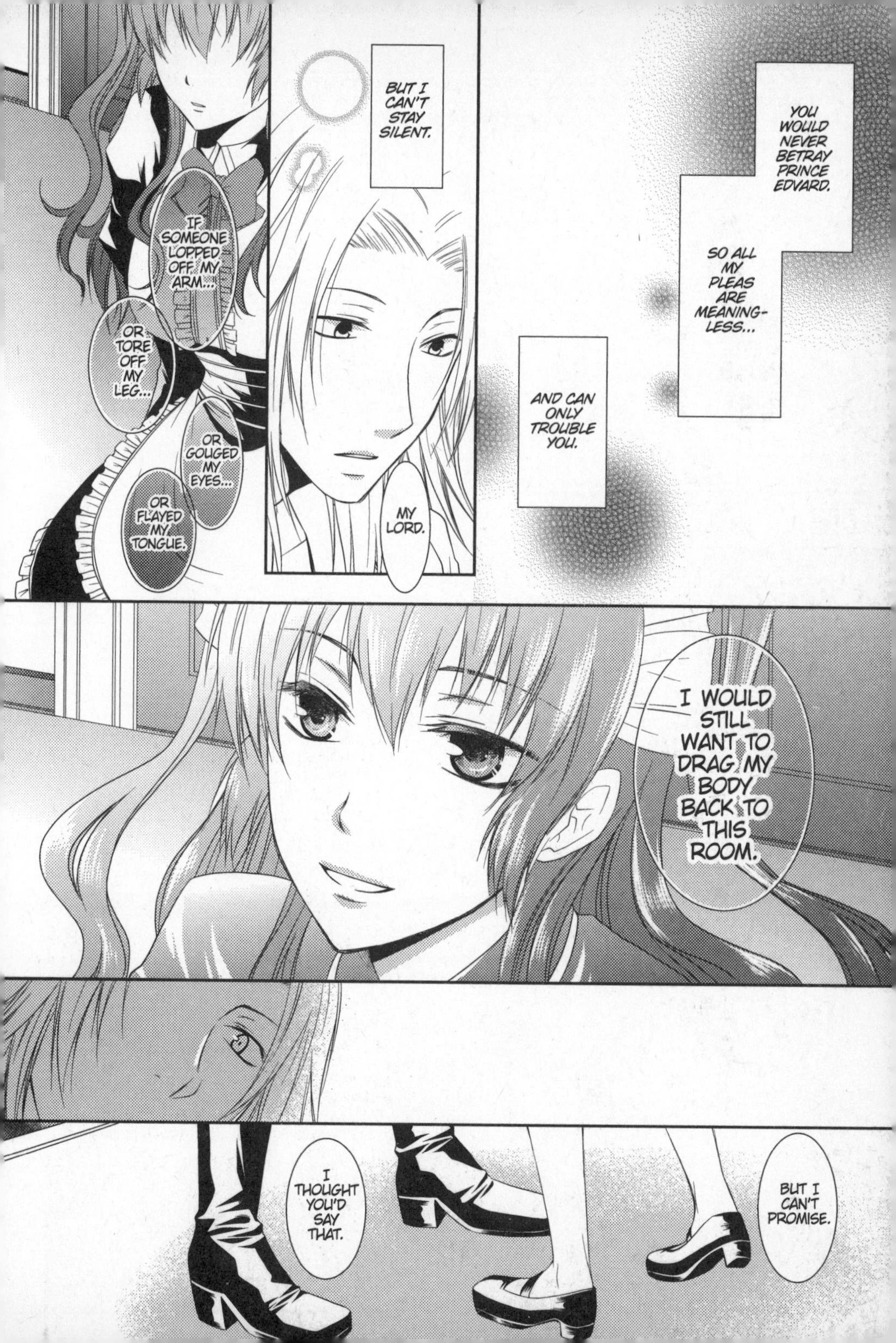
YOU WOULD NEVER BETRAY PRINCE EDVARD.
SO ALL MY PLEAS ARE MEANING-LESS...
AND CAN ONLY TROUBLE YOU.
BUT I CAN'T STAY SILENT.
MY LORD.
IF SOMEONE LOPPED OFF MY ARM...
OR TORE OFF MY LEG...
OR GOUGED MY EYES...
OR FLAYED MY TONGUE.
I WOULD STILL WANT TO DRAG MY BODY BACK TO THIS ROOM.
BUT I CAN'T PROMISE.
I THOUGHT YOU'D SAY THAT.

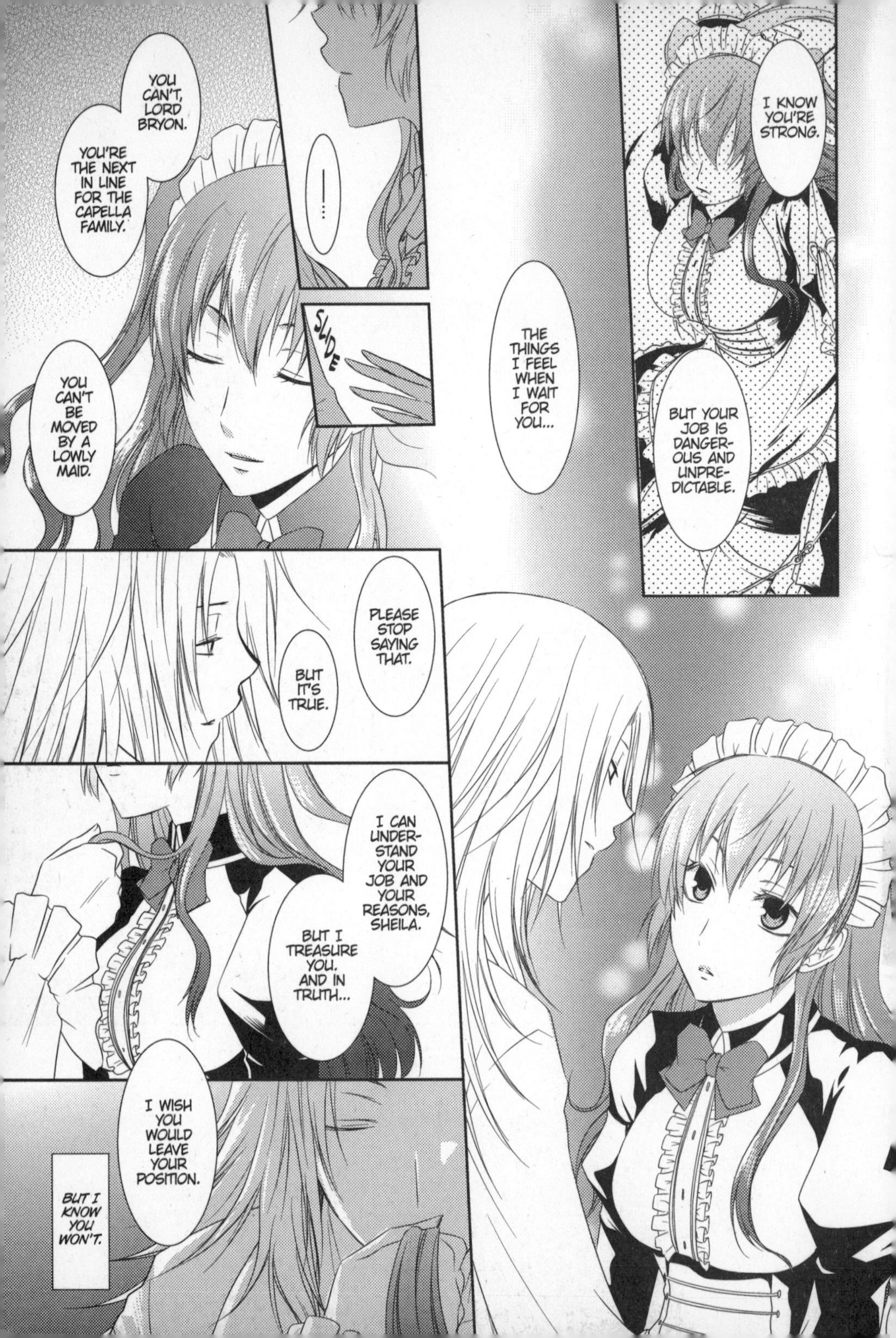
I KNOW YOU'RE STRONG.
BUT YOUR JOB IS DANGEROUS AND UNPREDICTABLE.
THE THINGS I FEEL WHEN I WAIT FOR YOU...
...!
SLIDE
YOU CAN'T, LORD BRYON.
YOU'RE THE NEXT IN LINE FOR THE CAPELLA FAMILY.
YOU CAN'T BE MOVED BY A LOWLY MAID.
PLEASE STOP SAYING THAT.
BUT IT'S TRUE.
I CAN UNDERSTAND YOUR JOB AND YOUR REASONS, SHEILA.
BUT I TREASURE YOU. AND IN TRUTH...
I WISH YOU WOULD LEAVE YOUR POSITION.
BUT I KNOW YOU WON'T.

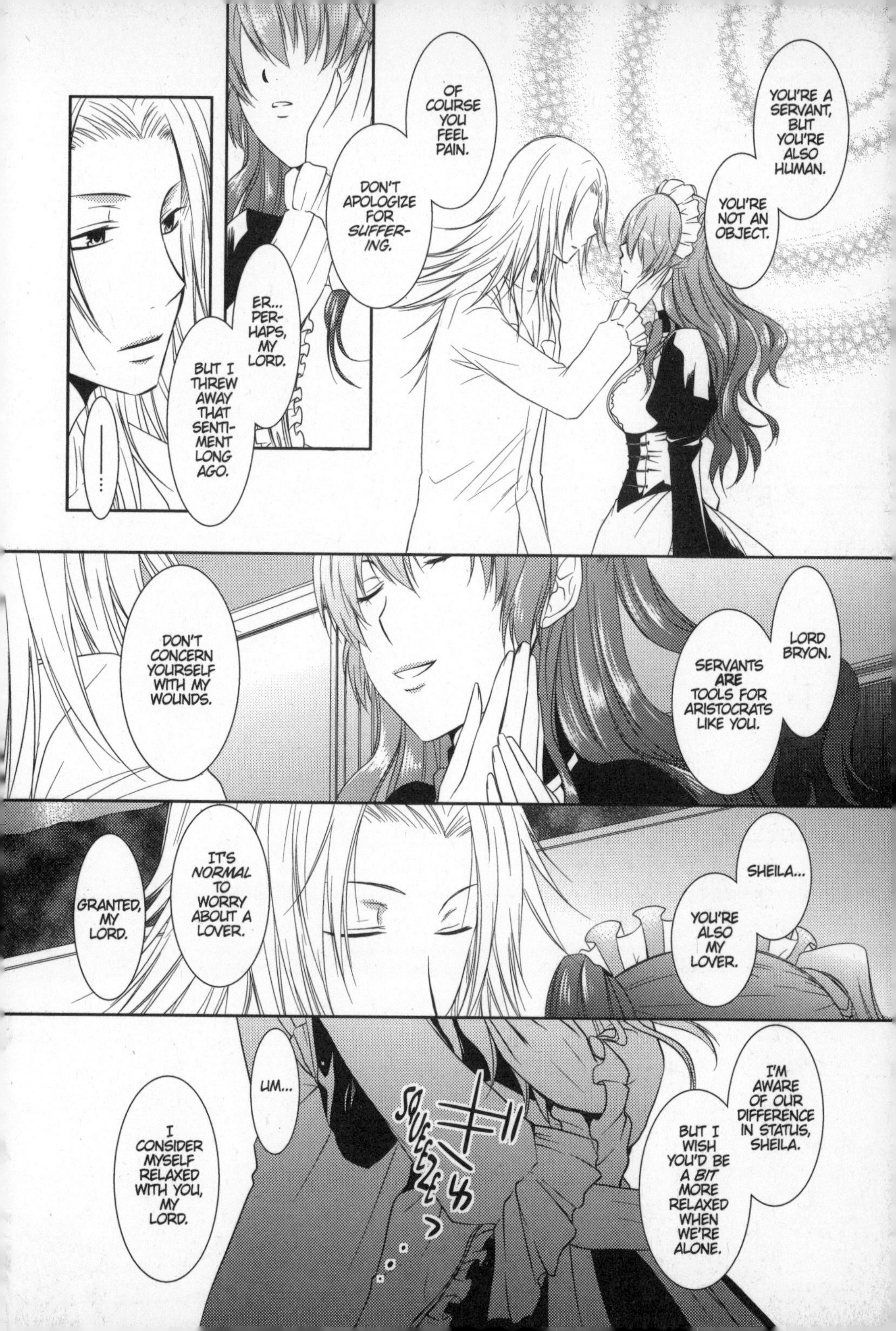
YOU'RE A SERVANT, BUT YOU'RE ALSO HUMAN.
YOU'RE NOT AN OBJECT.
OF COURSE YOU FEEL PAIN.
DON'T APOLOGIZE FOR *SUFFERING.*
ER... PERHAPS, MY LORD.
BUT I THREW AWAY THAT SENTIMENT LONG AGO.
......
LORD BRYON.
SERVANTS **ARE** TOOLS FOR ARISTOCRATS LIKE YOU.
DON'T CONCERN YOURSELF WITH MY WOUNDS.
SHEILA...
YOU'RE ALSO MY LOVER.
IT'S *NORMAL* TO WORRY ABOUT A LOVER.
GRANTED, MY LORD.
I'M AWARE OF OUR DIFFERENCE IN STATUS, SHEILA.
BUT I WISH YOU'D BE A *BIT* MORE RELAXED WHEN WE'RE ALONE.
SQUEEZE
UM...
I CONSIDER MYSELF RELAXED WITH YOU, MY LORD.

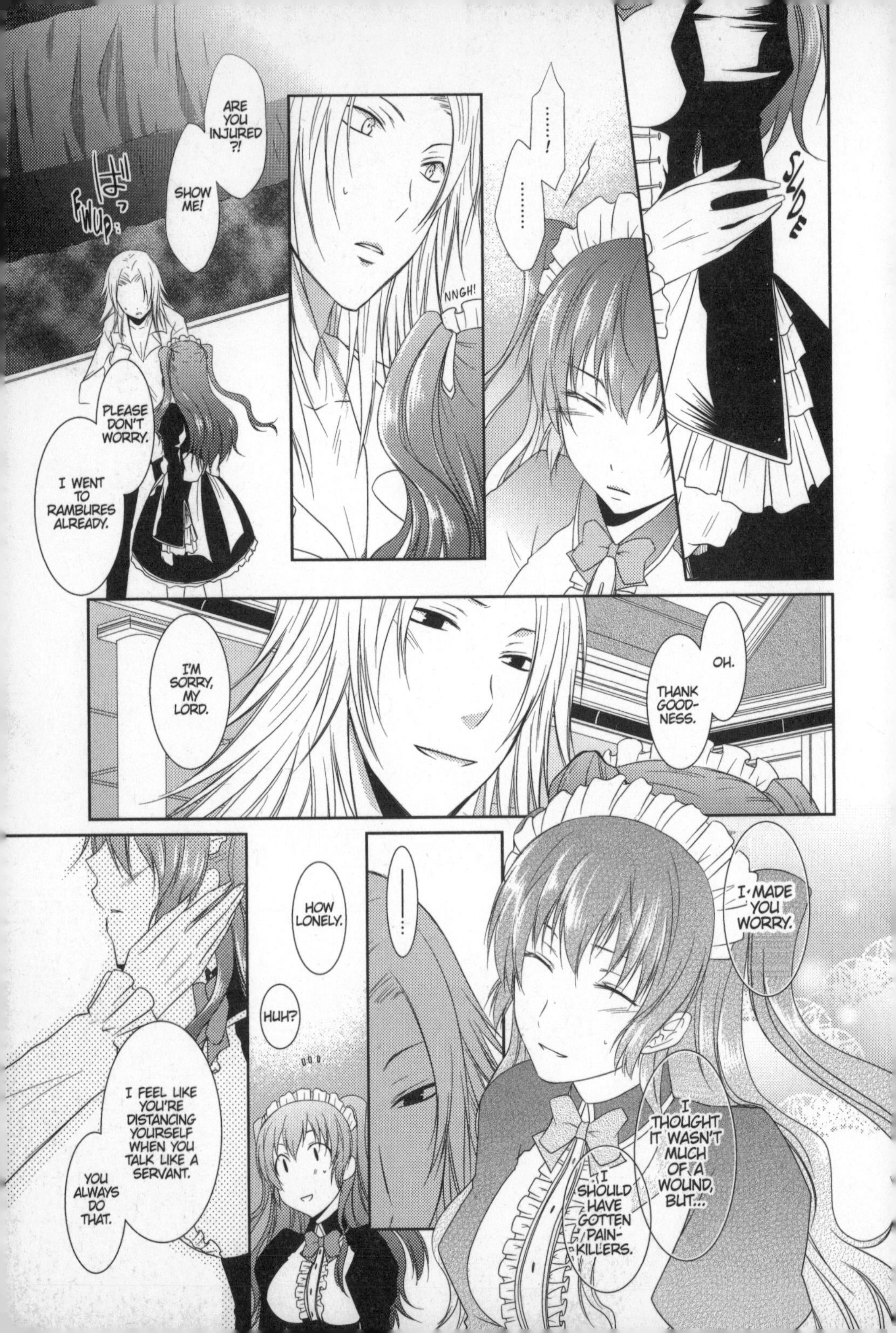
SLIDE
......!
......
NNGH!
ばっ
FWUP
ARE YOU INJURED?!
SHOW ME!
PLEASE DON'T WORRY.
I WENT TO RAMBURES ALREADY.
OH.
THANK GOODNESS.
I'M SORRY, MY LORD.
I MADE YOU WORRY.
I THOUGHT IT WASN'T MUCH OF A WOUND, BUT...
I SHOULD HAVE GOTTEN PAIN-KILLERS.
...!!
HOW LONELY.
HUH?
I FEEL LIKE YOU'RE DISTANCING YOURSELF WHEN YOU TALK LIKE A SERVANT.
YOU ALWAYS DO THAT.

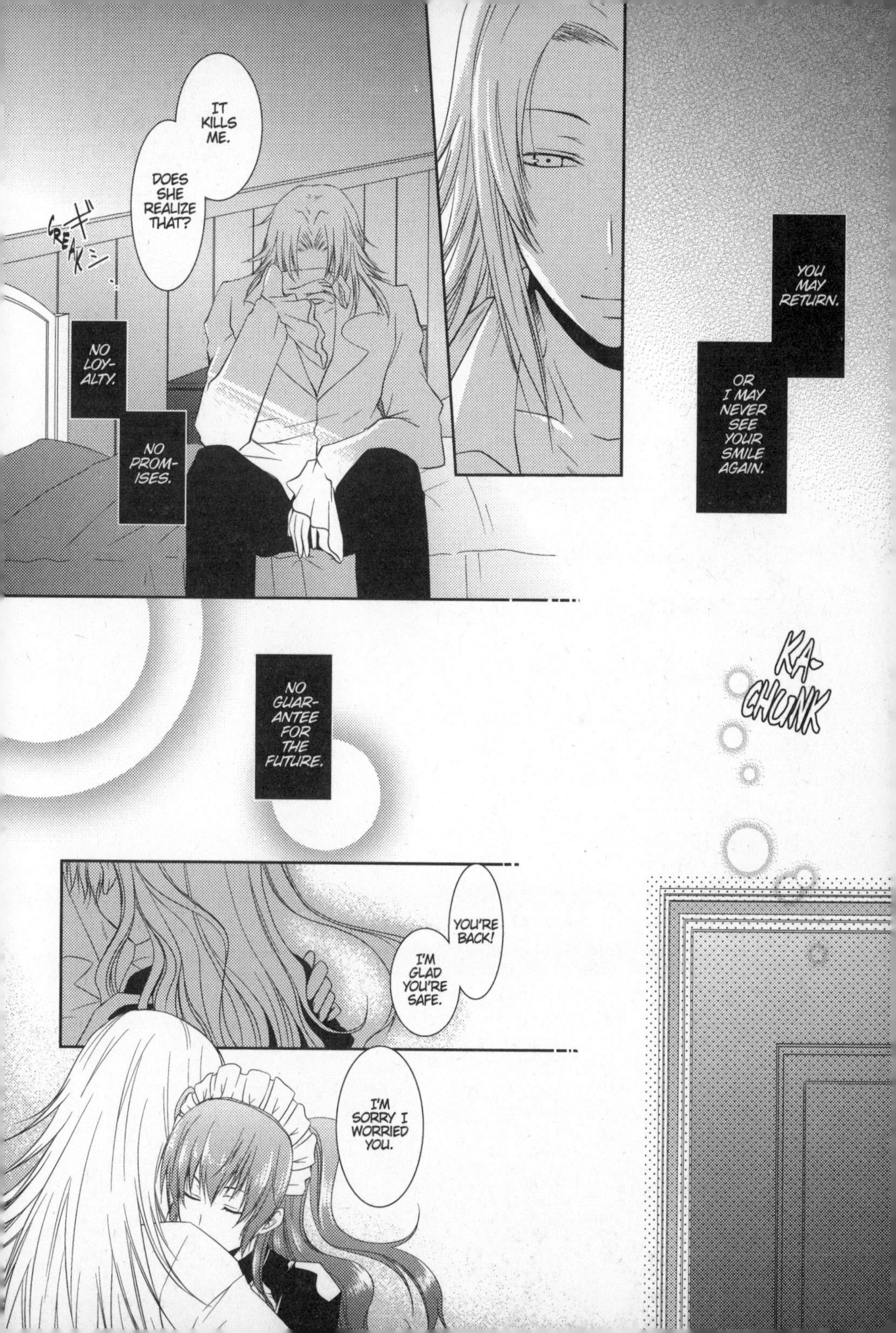
YOU MAY RETURN.
OR I MAY NEVER SEE YOUR SMILE AGAIN.
IT KILLS ME.
DOES SHE REALIZE THAT?
CREAK
NO LOY-ALTY.
NO PROMISES.
KA-CHUNK
NO GUARANTEE FOR THE FUTURE.
YOU'RE BACK!
I'M GLAD YOU'RE SAFE.
I'M SORRY I WORRIED YOU.

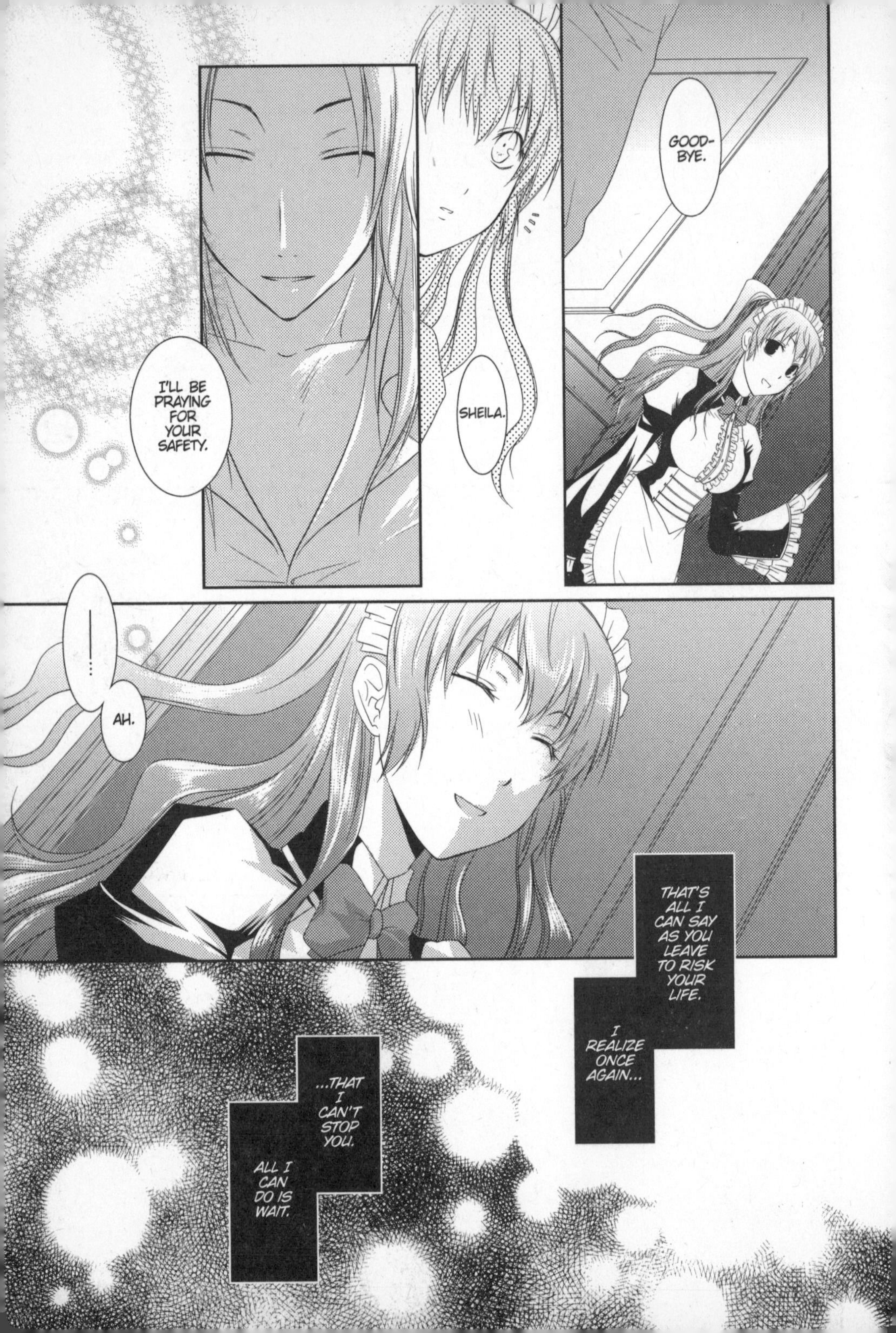
GOOD-BYE.
SHEILA.
I'LL BE PRAYING FOR YOUR SAFETY.
!...
AH.
THAT'S ALL I CAN SAY AS YOU LEAVE TO RISK YOUR LIFE.
I REALIZE ONCE AGAIN...
...THAT I CAN'T STOP YOU.
ALL I CAN DO IS WAIT.

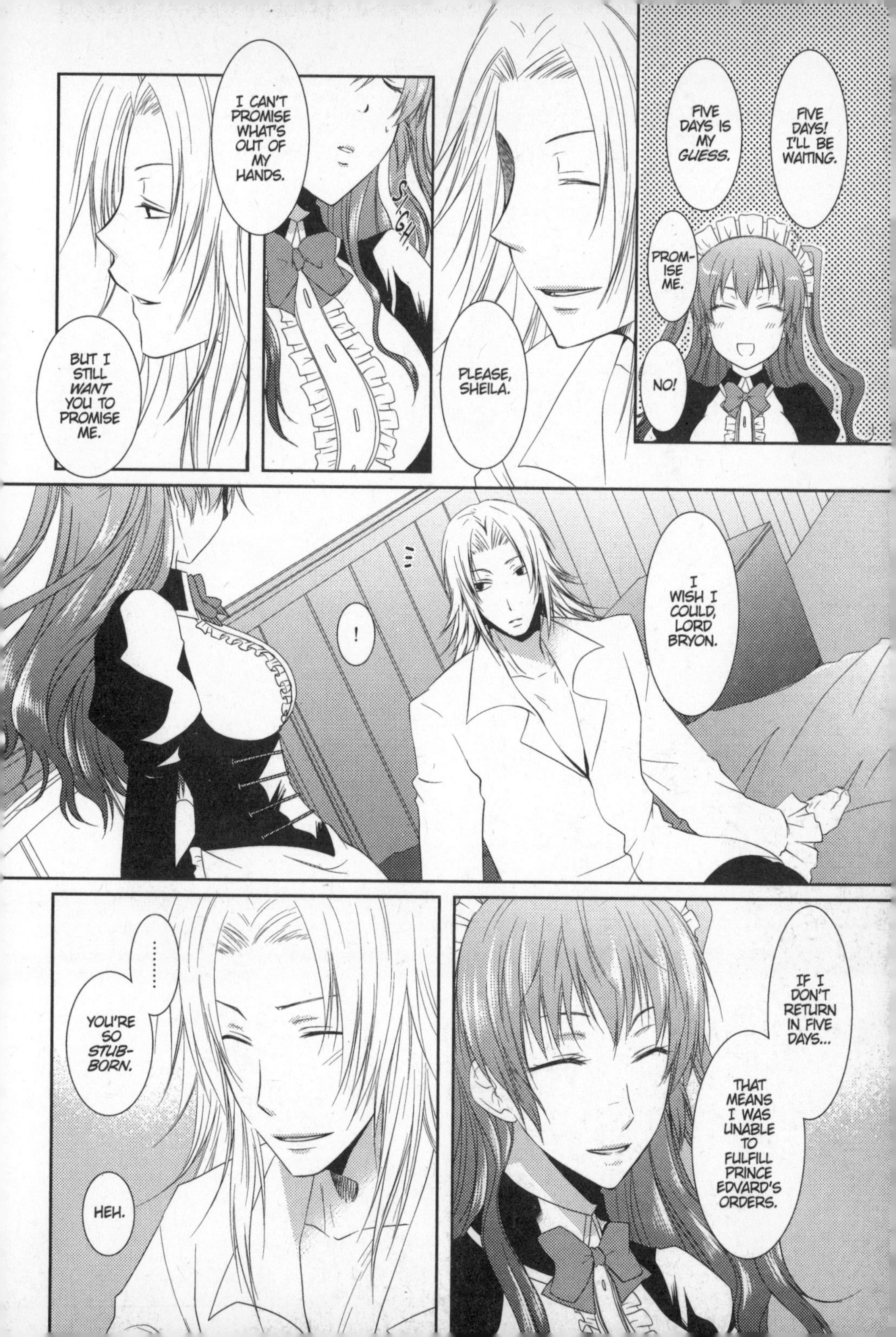

FIVE DAYS! I'LL BE WAITING.
FIVE DAYS IS MY GUESS.
PROMISE ME.
NO!
PLEASE, SHEILA.
I CAN'T PROMISE WHAT'S OUT OF MY HANDS.
SIGH
BUT I STILL WANT YOU TO PROMISE ME.
I WISH I COULD, LORD BRYON.
!
IF I DON'T RETURN IN FIVE DAYS...
THAT MEANS I WAS UNABLE TO FULFILL PRINCE EDVARD'S ORDERS.
......
YOU'RE SO STUBBORN.
HEH.

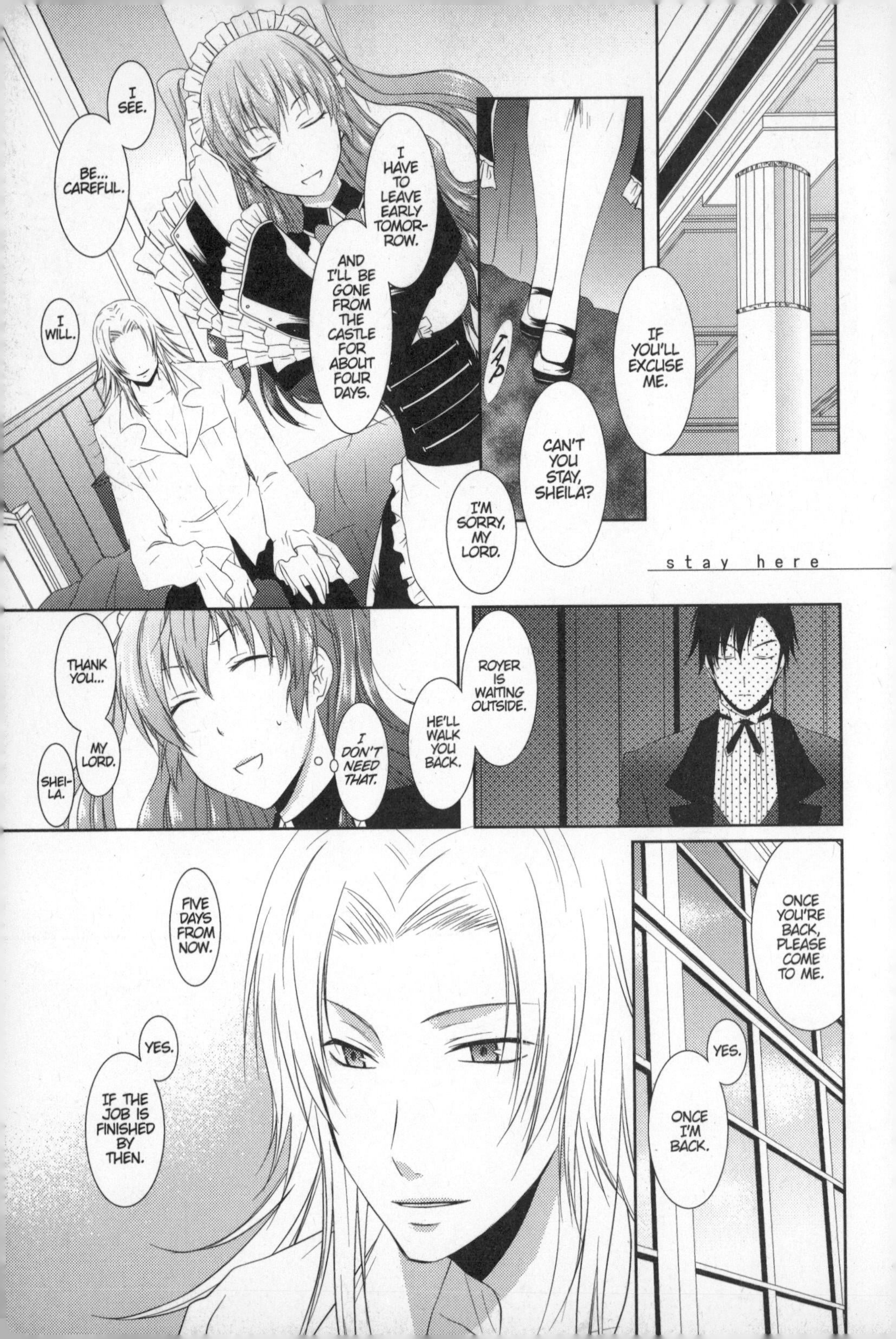
IF YOU'LL EXCUSE ME.
TAP
CAN'T YOU STAY, SHEILA?
I'M SORRY, MY LORD.
I HAVE TO LEAVE EARLY TOMORROW.
AND I'LL BE GONE FROM THE CASTLE FOR ABOUT FOUR DAYS.
I SEE.
BE... CAREFUL.
I WILL.
stay here
ROYER IS WAITING OUTSIDE.
HE'LL WALK YOU BACK.
I DON'T NEED THAT.
THANK YOU...
MY LORD.
SHEI-LA.
ONCE YOU'RE BACK, PLEASE COME TO ME.
YES.
ONCE I'M BACK.
FIVE DAYS FROM NOW.
YES.
IF THE JOB IS FINISHED BY THEN.

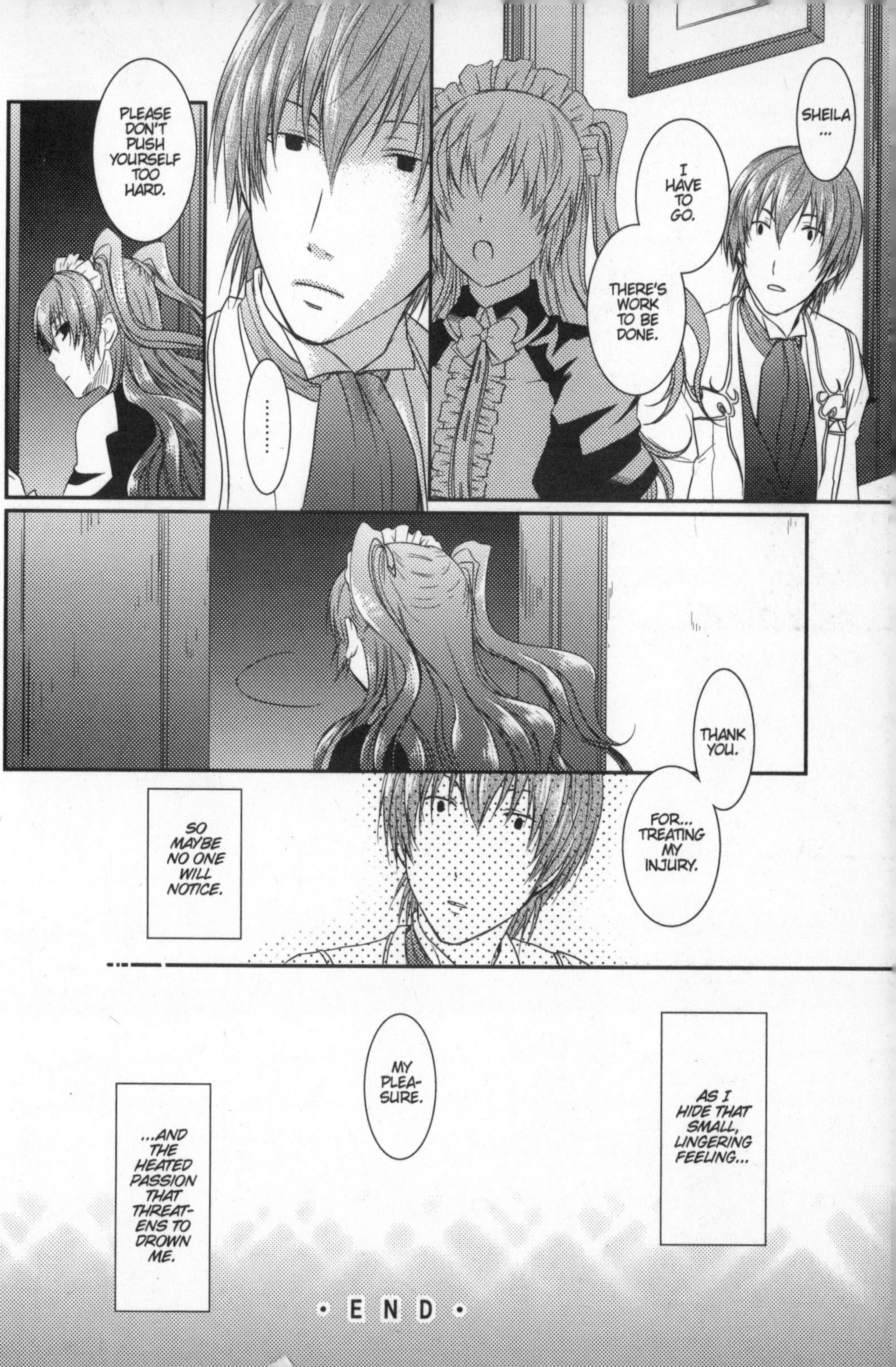
SHEILA...
I HAVE TO GO.
THERE'S WORK TO BE DONE.
......
PLEASE DON'T PUSH YOURSELF TOO HARD.
THANK YOU.
FOR... TREATING MY INJURY.
SO MAYBE NO ONE WILL NOTICE.
AS I HIDE THAT SMALL, LINGERING FEELING...
MY PLEASURE.
...AND THE HEATED PASSION THAT THREATEN-ENS TO DROWN ME.
• E N D •

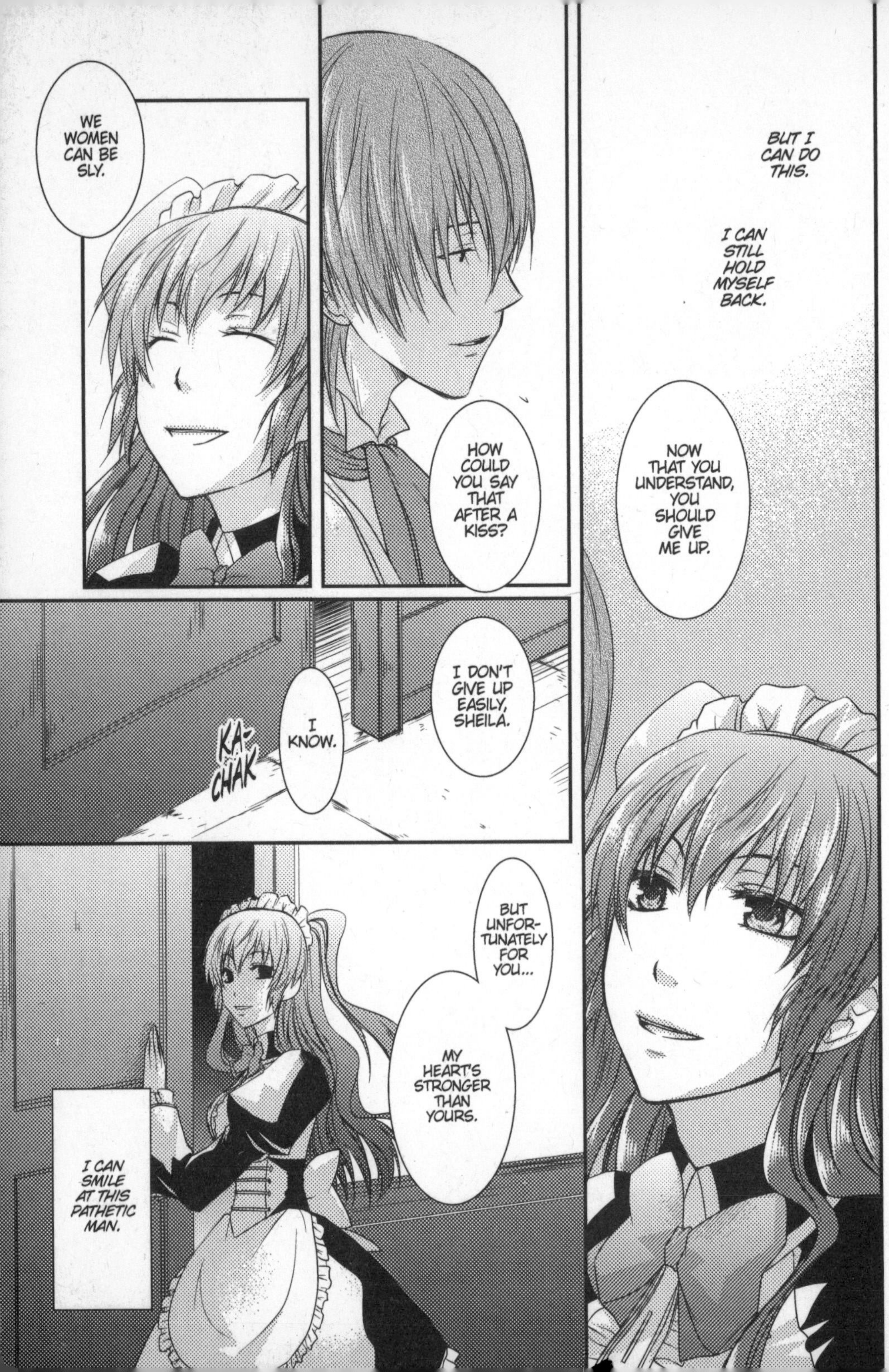
BUT I CAN DO THIS.
I CAN STILL HOLD MYSELF BACK.
NOW THAT YOU UNDERSTAND, YOU SHOULD GIVE ME UP.
HOW COULD YOU SAY THAT AFTER A KISS?
WE WOMEN CAN BE SLY.
I DON'T GIVE UP EASILY, SHEILA.
I KNOW.
KA-CHAK
BUT UNFOR-TUNATELY FOR YOU...
MY HEART'S STRONGER THAN YOURS.
I CAN SMILE AT THIS PATHETIC MAN.

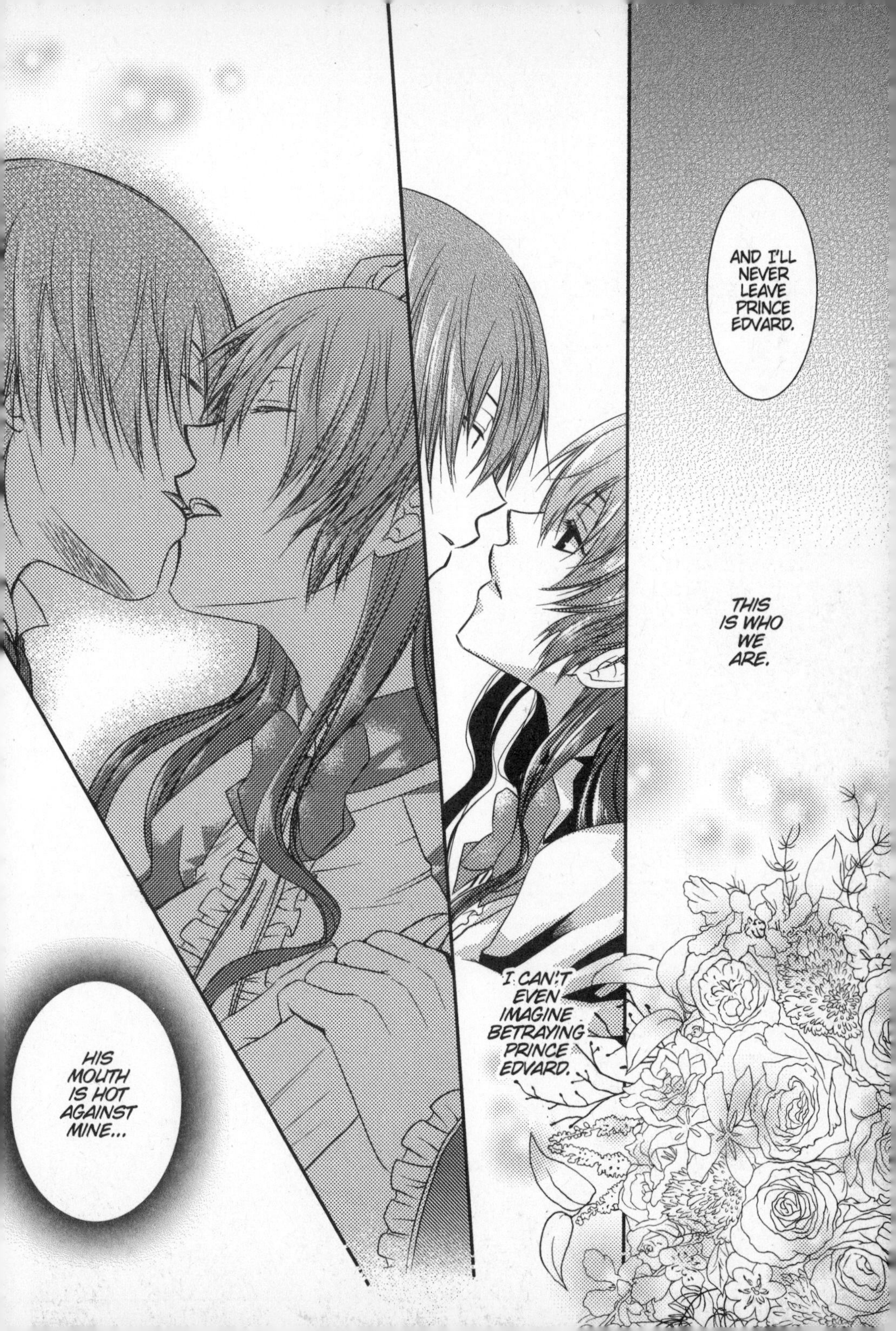
AND I'LL NEVER LEAVE PRINCE EDVARD.
THIS IS WHO WE ARE.
I CAN'T EVEN IMAGINE BETRAYING PRINCE EDVARD.
HIS MOUTH IS HOT AGAINST MINE...

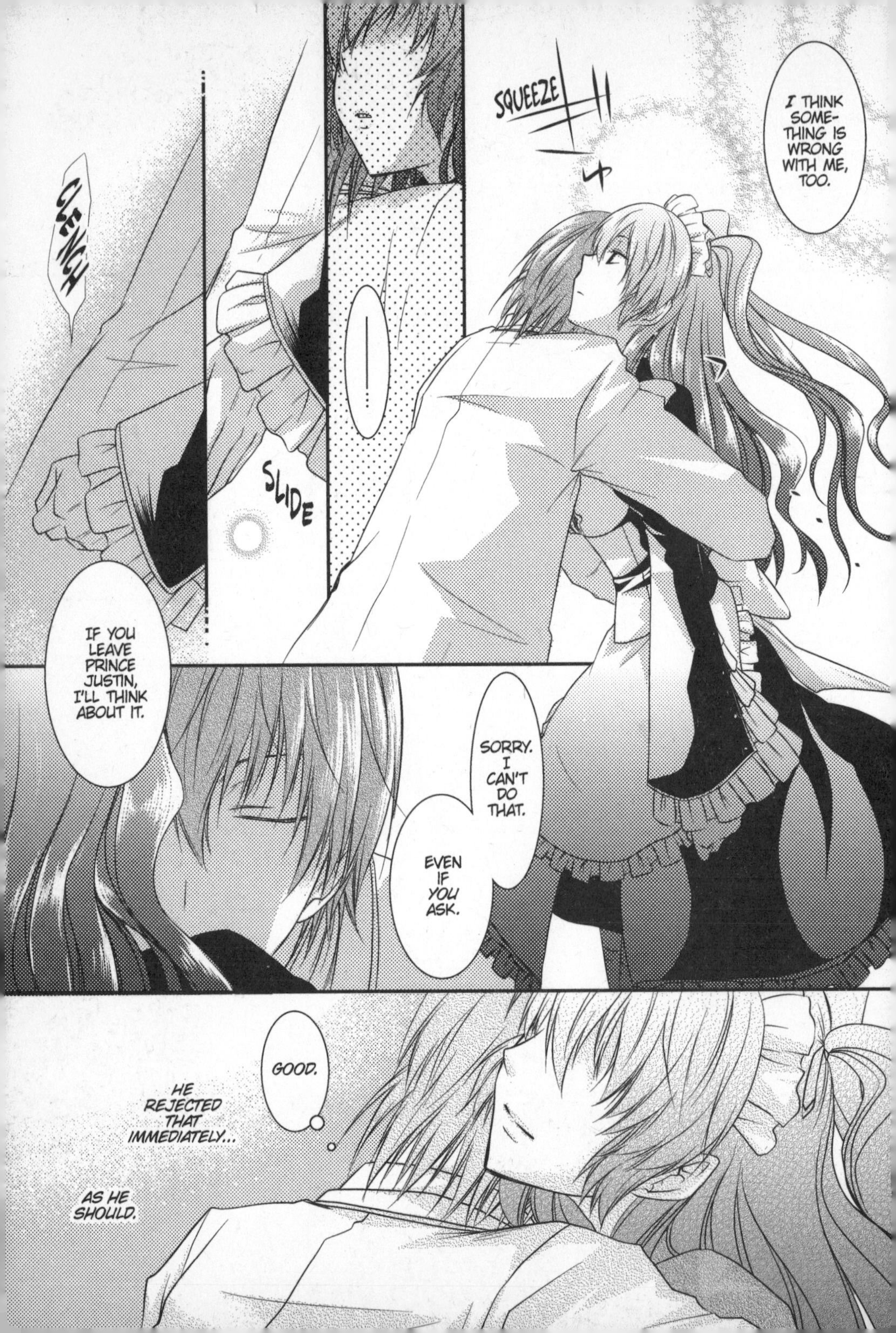
I THINK SOMETHING IS WRONG WITH ME, TOO.
SQUEEZE
!
SLIDE
CLENCH
IF YOU LEAVE PRINCE JUSTIN, I'LL THINK ABOUT IT.
SORRY. I CAN'T DO THAT.
EVEN IF YOU ASK.
GOOD.
HE REJECTED THAT IMMEDIATELY...
AS HE SHOULD.

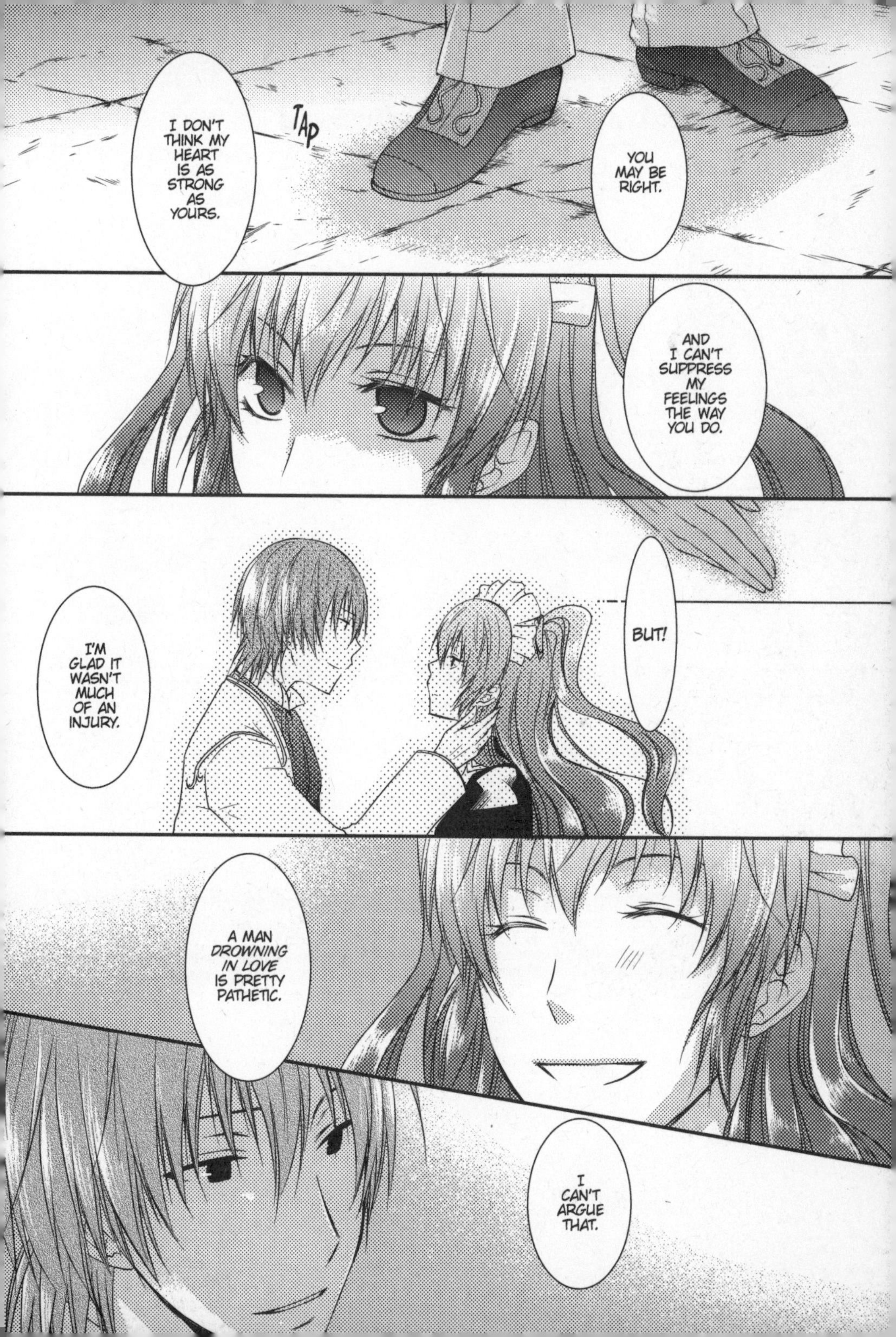
YOU MAY BE RIGHT.
TAP
I DON'T THINK MY HEART IS AS STRONG AS YOURS.
AND I CAN'T SUPPRESS MY FEELINGS THE WAY YOU DO.
BUT!
I'M GLAD IT WASN'T MUCH OF AN INJURY.
A MAN *DROWNING IN LOVE* IS PRETTY PATHETIC.
I CAN'T ARGUE THAT.

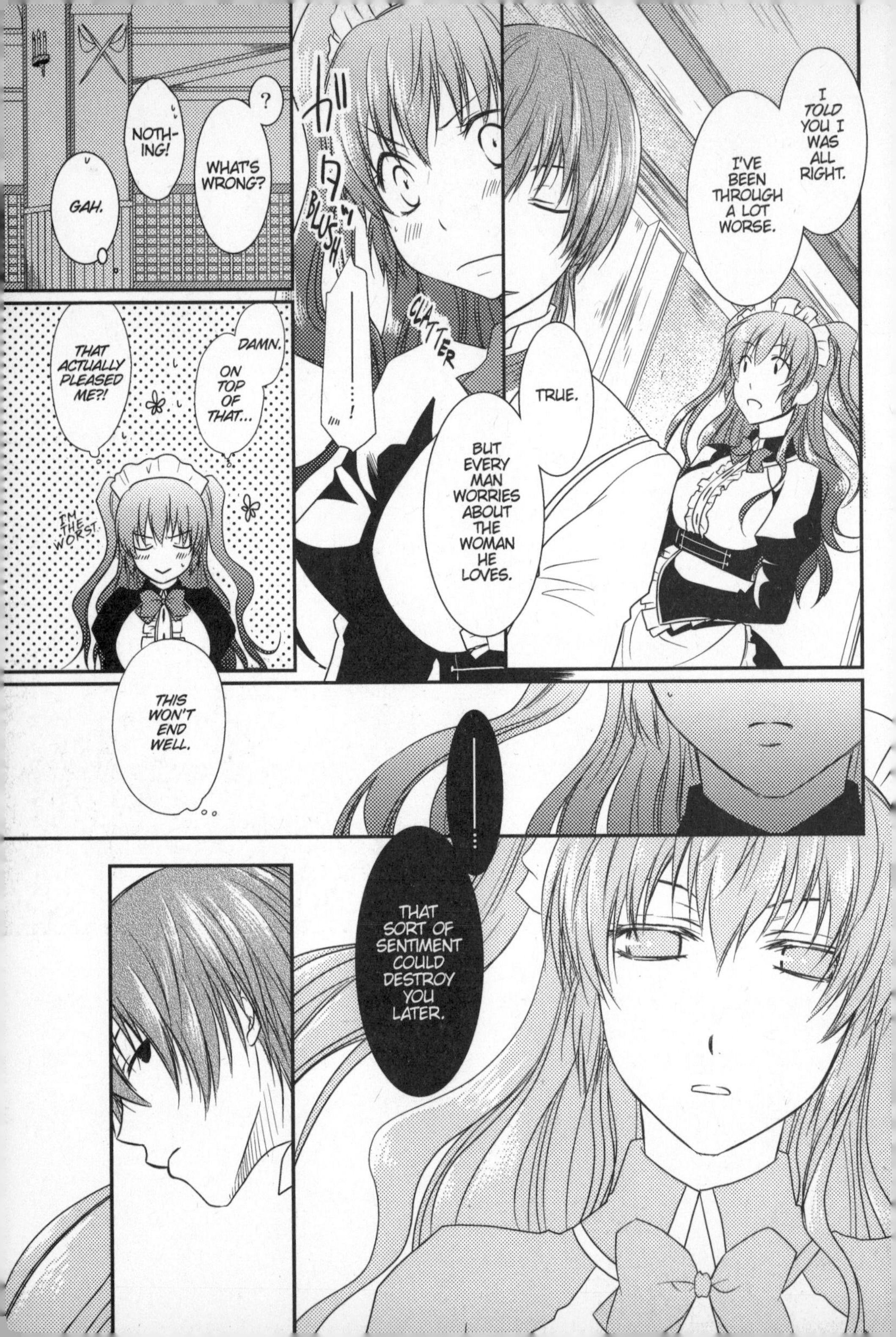
I TOLD YOU I WAS ALL RIGHT.
I'VE BEEN THROUGH A LOT WORSE.
TRUE.
BUT EVERY MAN WORRIES ABOUT THE WOMAN HE LOVES.
BLUSH
CLATTER
...!
?
WHAT'S WRONG?
NOTHING!
GAH.
DAMN. ON TOP OF THAT...
THAT ACTUALLY PLEASED ME?!
I'M THE WORST.
THIS WON'T END WELL.
——...
THAT SORT OF SENTIMENT COULD DESTROY YOU LATER.

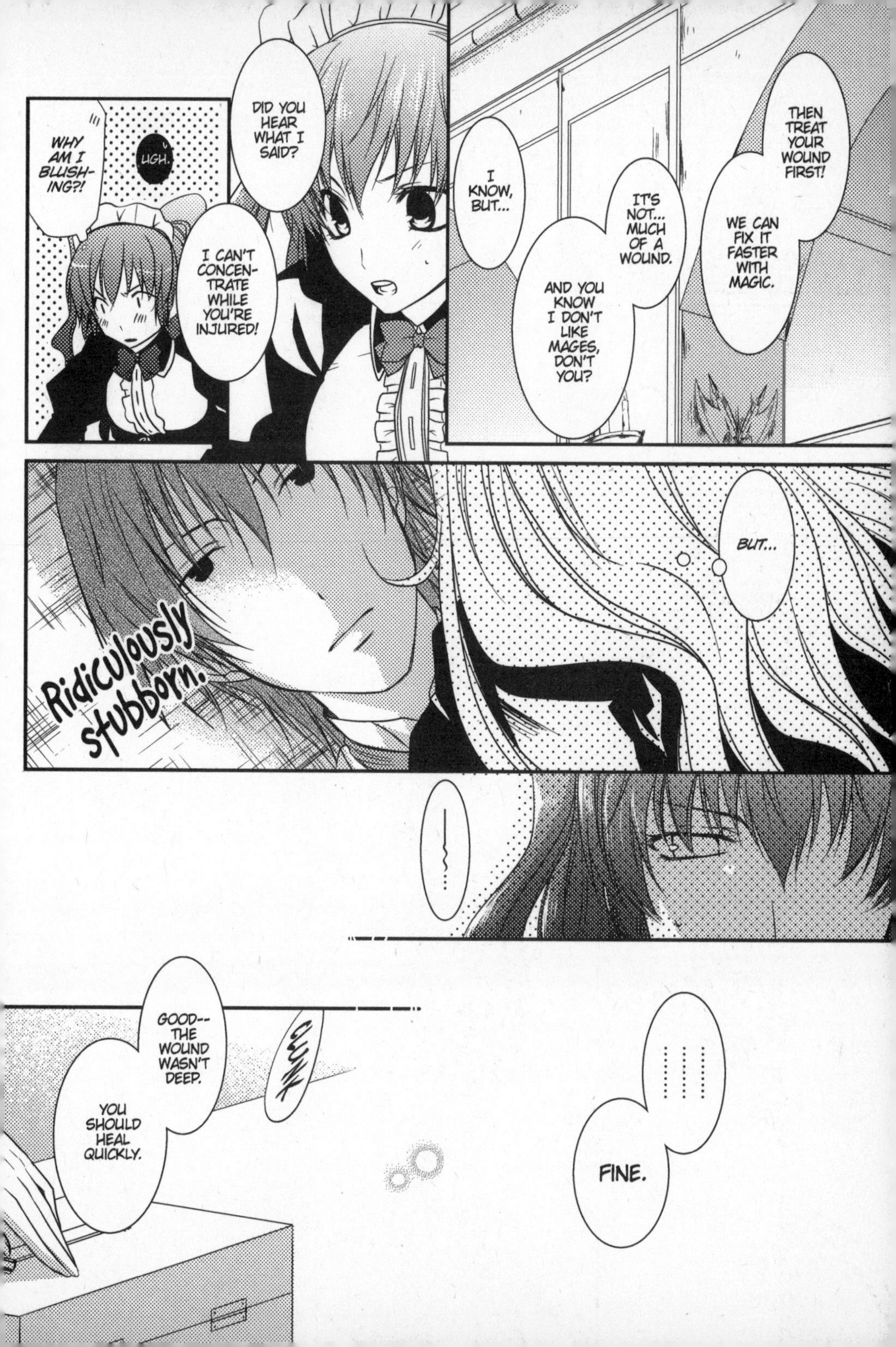
THEN TREAT YOUR WOUND FIRST!
WE CAN FIX IT FASTER WITH MAGIC.
IT'S NOT... MUCH OF A WOUND.
AND YOU KNOW I DON'T LIKE MAGES, DON'T YOU?
I KNOW, BUT...
DID YOU HEAR WHAT I SAID?
I CAN'T CONCENTRATE WHILE YOU'RE INJURED!
UGH.
WHY AM I BLUSHING?!
BUT...
Ridiculously stubborn.
......
FINE.
CLUNK
GOOD-- THE WOUND WASN'T DEEP.
YOU SHOULD HEAL QUICKLY.

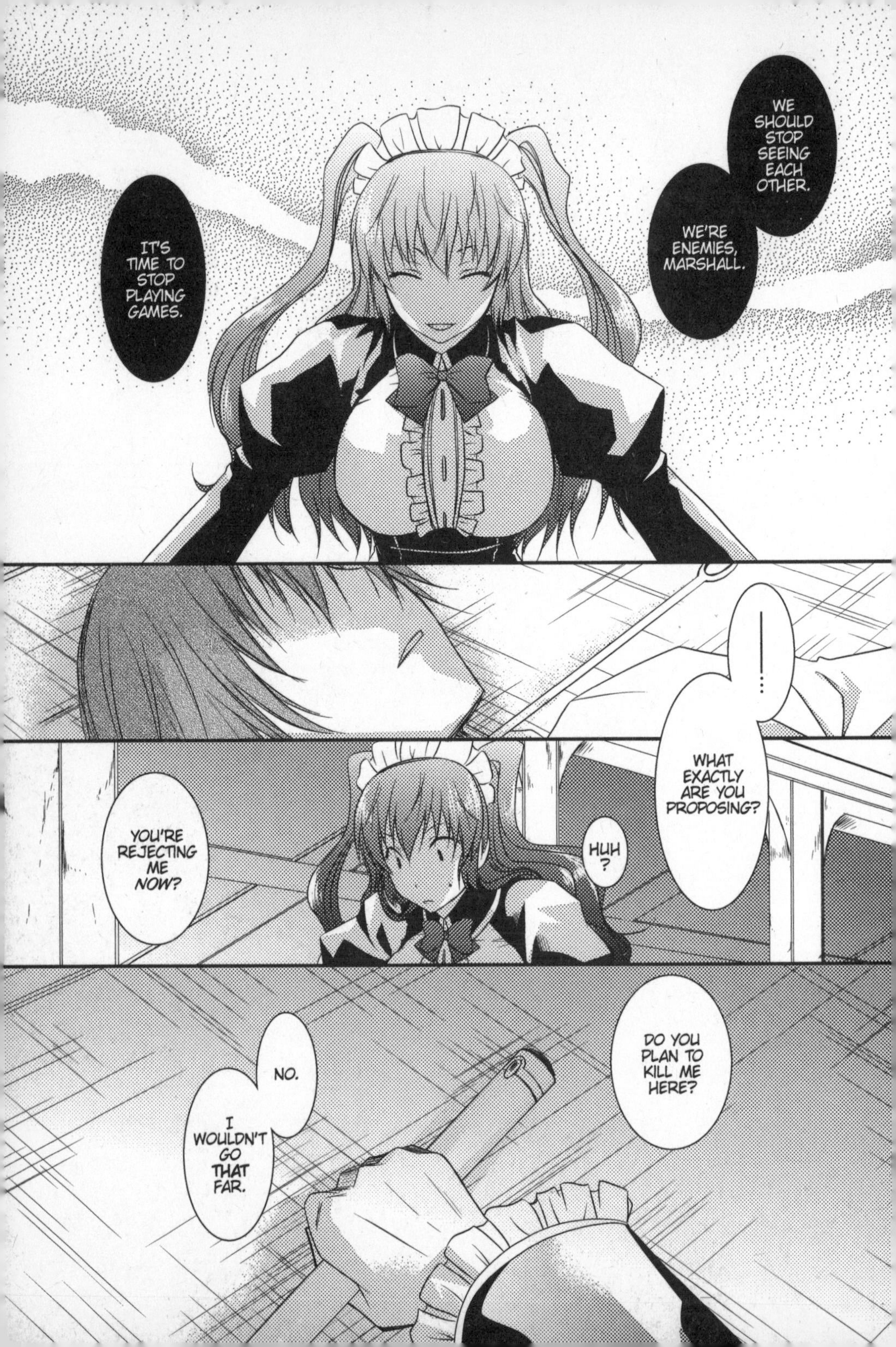
WE SHOULD STOP SEEING EACH OTHER.
WE'RE ENEMIES, MARSHALL.
IT'S TIME TO STOP PLAYING GAMES.
—…
WHAT EXACTLY ARE YOU PROPOSING?
HUH?
YOU'RE REJECTING ME *NOW*?
DO YOU PLAN TO KILL ME HERE?
NO.
I WOULDN'T GO THAT FAR.

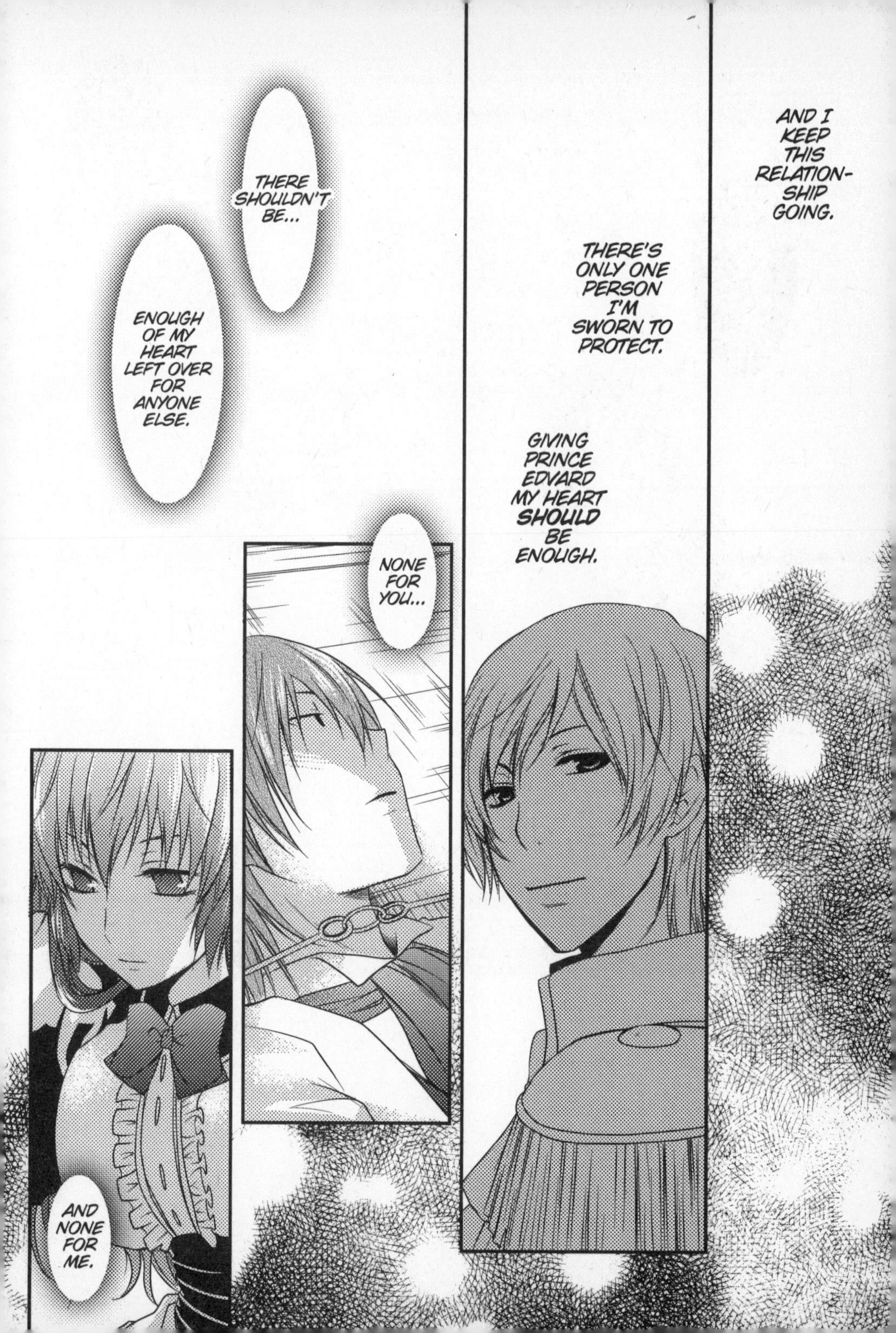
AND I KEEP THIS RELATION-SHIP GOING.
THERE'S ONLY ONE PERSON I'M SWORN TO PROTECT.
GIVING PRINCE EDVARD MY HEART **SHOULD** BE ENOUGH.
THERE SHOULDN'T BE...
ENOUGH OF MY HEART LEFT OVER FOR ANYONE ELSE.
NONE FOR YOU...
AND NONE FOR ME.

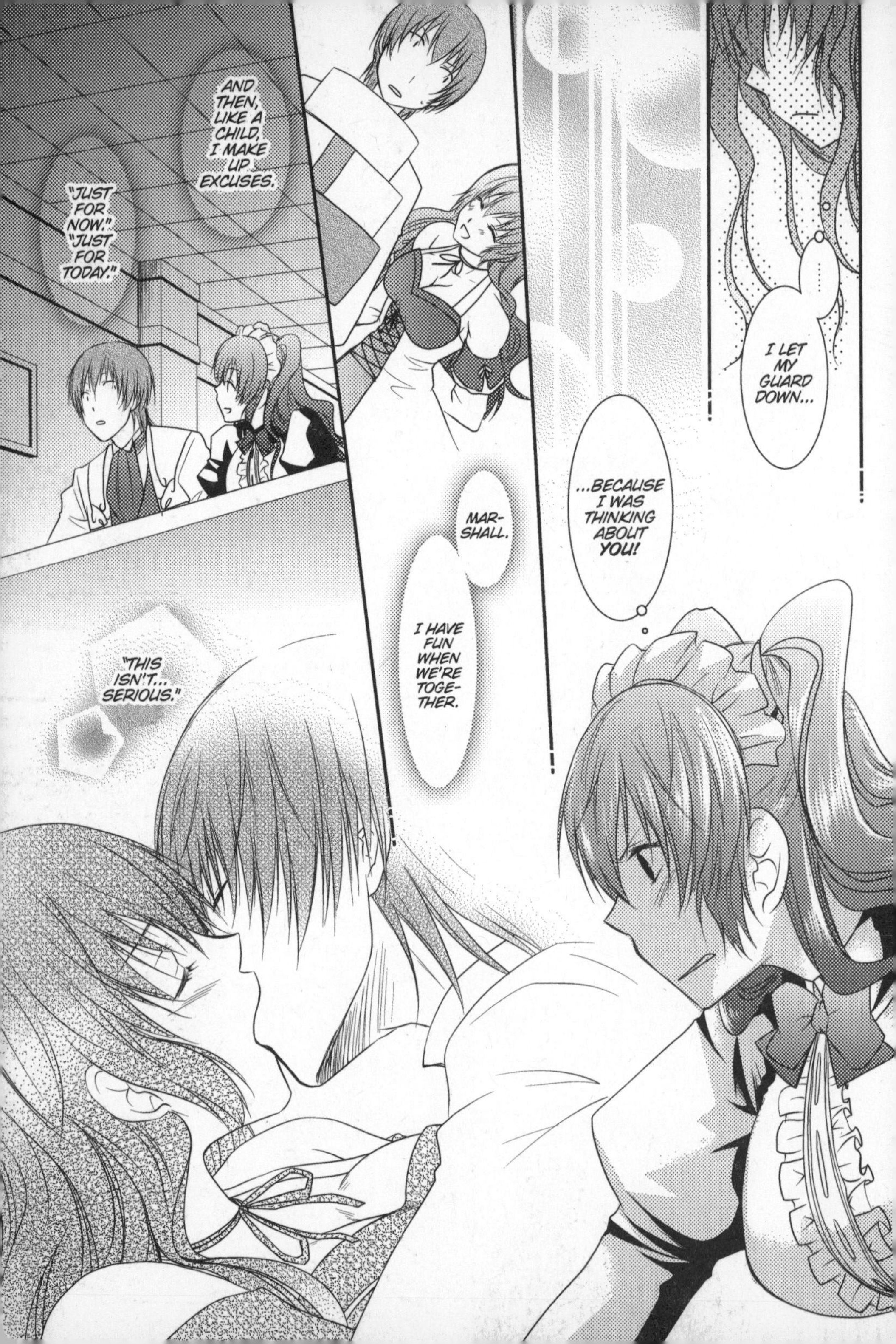
I LET MY GUARD DOWN...
...BECAUSE I WAS THINKING ABOUT YOU!
MARSHALL.
I HAVE FUN WHEN WE'RE TOGETHER.
AND THEN, LIKE A CHILD, I MAKE UP EXCUSES.
"JUST FOR NOW." "JUST FOR TODAY."
"THIS ISN'T... SERIOUS."

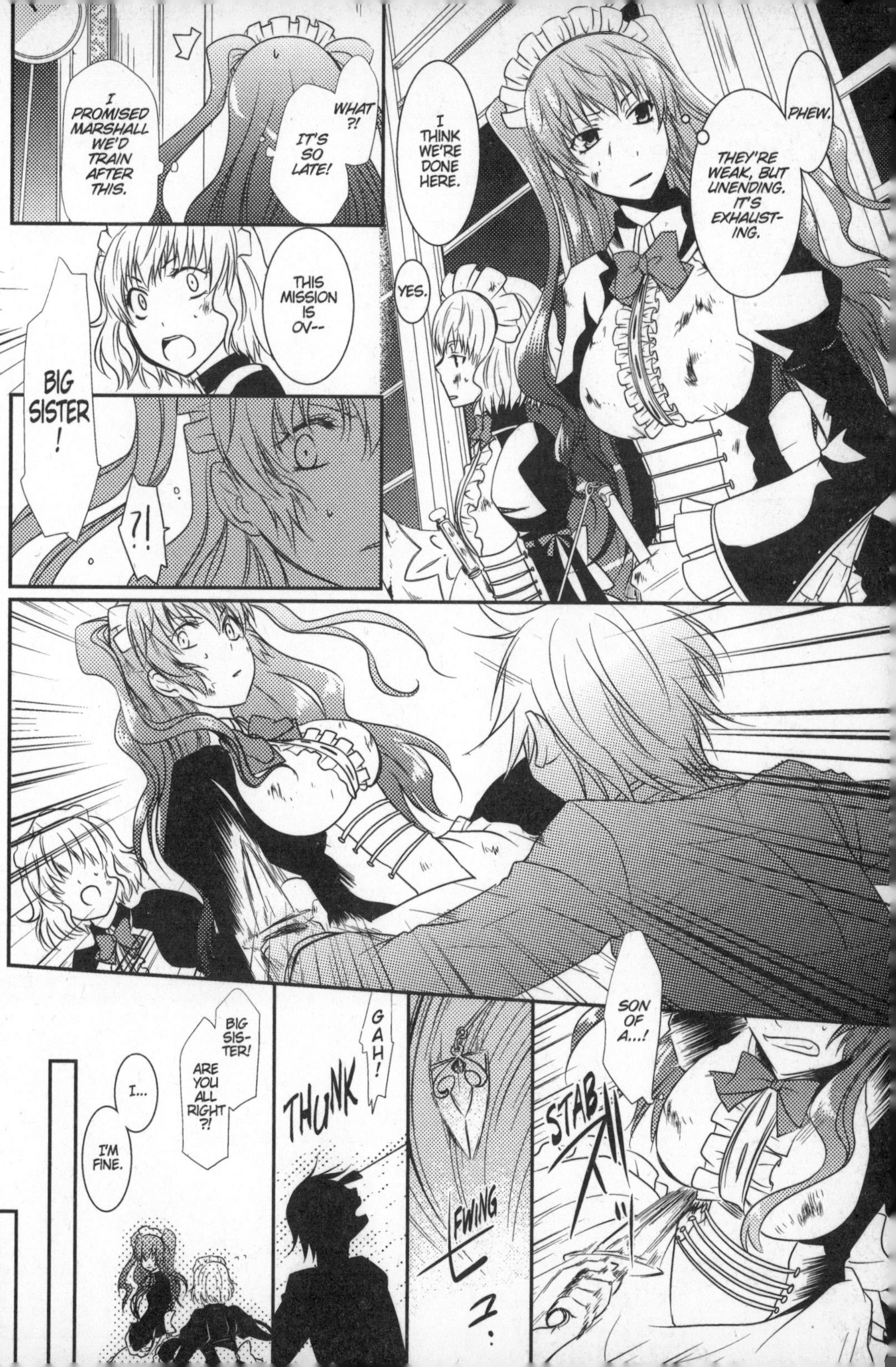
PHEW.
THEY'RE WEAK, BUT UNENDING. IT'S EXHAUST-ING.
I THINK WE'RE DONE HERE.
YES.
WHAT?! IT'S SO LATE!
I PROMISED MARSHALL WE'D TRAIN AFTER THIS.
THIS MISSION IS OV--
BIG SISTER!
?!
SON OF A...!
STAB
FWING
GAH!
THUNK
BIG SIS-TER! ARE YOU ALL RIGHT?!
I...
I'M FINE.

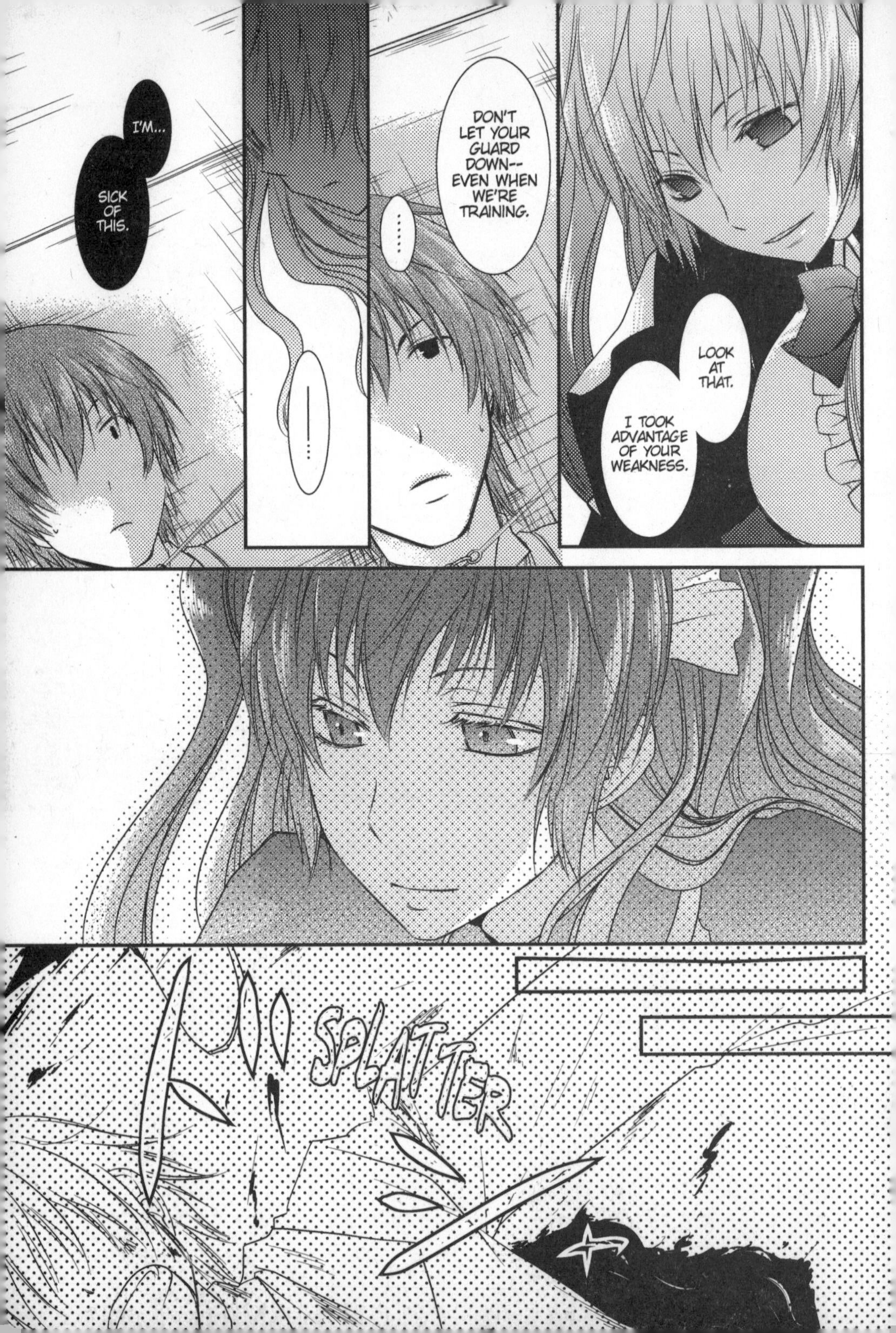
LOOK AT THAT.
I TOOK ADVANTAGE OF YOUR WEAKNESS.
DON'T LET YOUR GUARD DOWN-- EVEN WHEN WE'RE TRAINING.
......
--!...
I'M...
SICK OF THIS.
SPLATTER

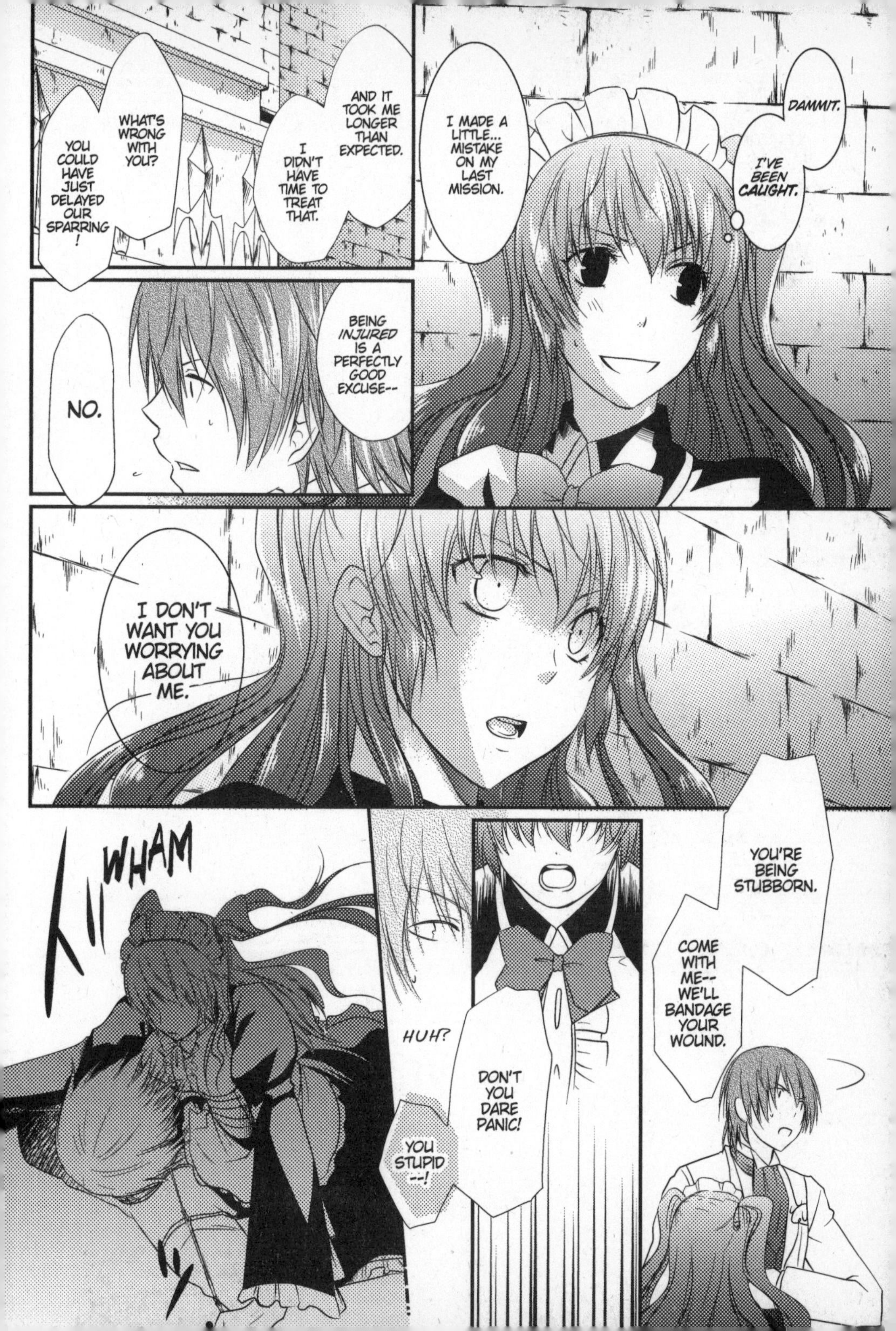
DAMMIT.
I'VE BEEN CAUGHT.
I MADE A LITTLE... MISTAKE ON MY LAST MISSION.
AND IT TOOK ME LONGER THAN EXPECTED.
I DIDN'T HAVE TIME TO TREAT THAT.
WHAT'S WRONG WITH YOU?
YOU COULD HAVE JUST DELAYED OUR SPARRING!
BEING INJURED IS A PERFECTLY GOOD EXCUSE--
NO.
I DON'T WANT YOU WORRYING ABOUT ME.
YOU'RE BEING STUBBORN.
COME WITH ME-- WE'LL BANDAGE YOUR WOUND.
DON'T YOU DARE PANIC!
HUH?
YOU STUPID--!
WHAM

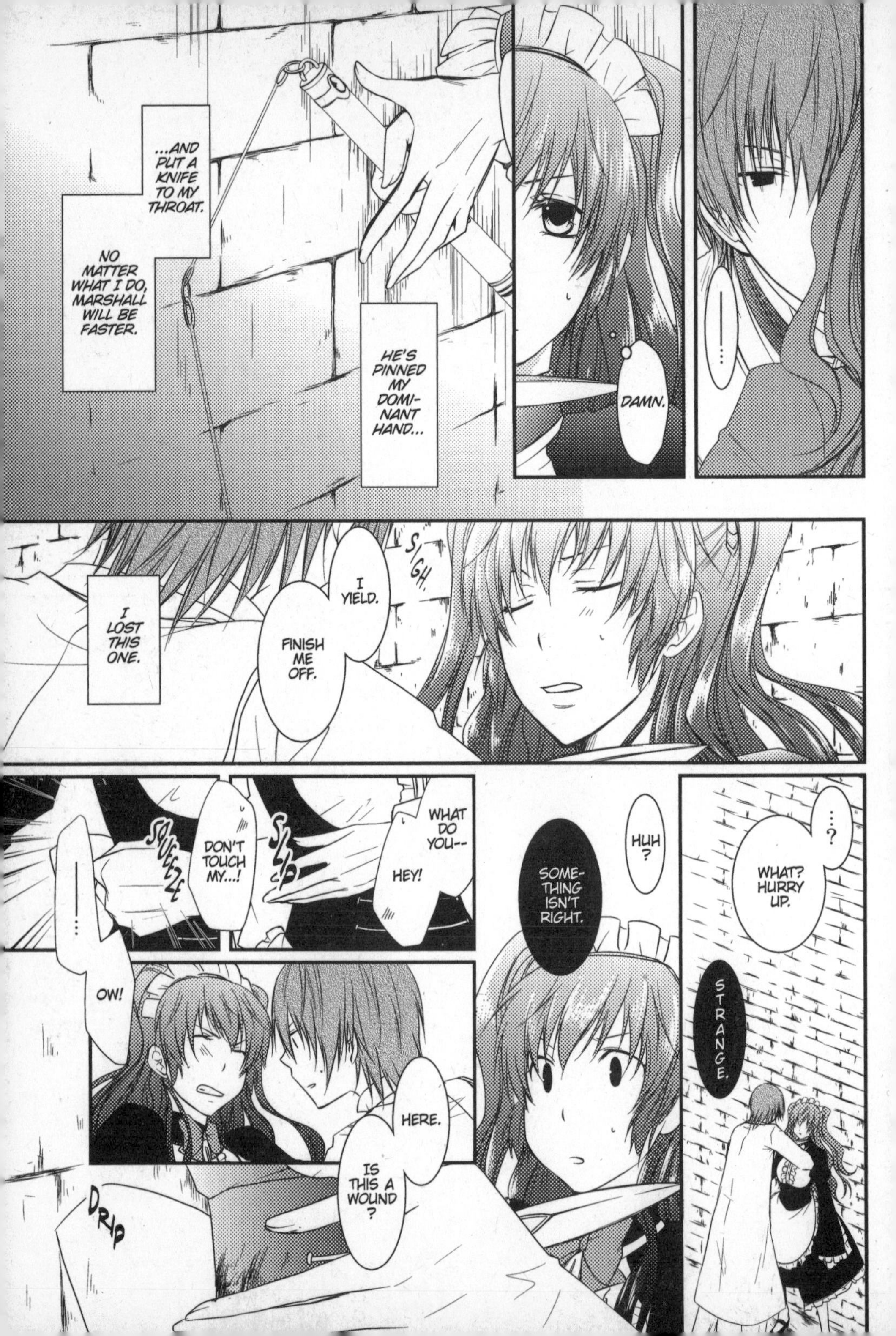
......
DAMN.
HE'S PINNED MY DOMI-NANT HAND...
...AND PUT A KNIFE TO MY THROAT.
NO MATTER WHAT I DO, MARSHALL WILL BE FASTER.
SIGH.
I YIELD.
FINISH ME OFF.
I LOST THIS ONE.
...?
WHAT? HURRY UP.
STRANGE.
HUH?
SOME-THING ISN'T RIGHT.
WHAT DO YOU--
HEY!
SLIP
DON'T TOUCH MY...!
SQUEEZE
......
OW!
HERE.
IS THIS A WOUND?
DRIP

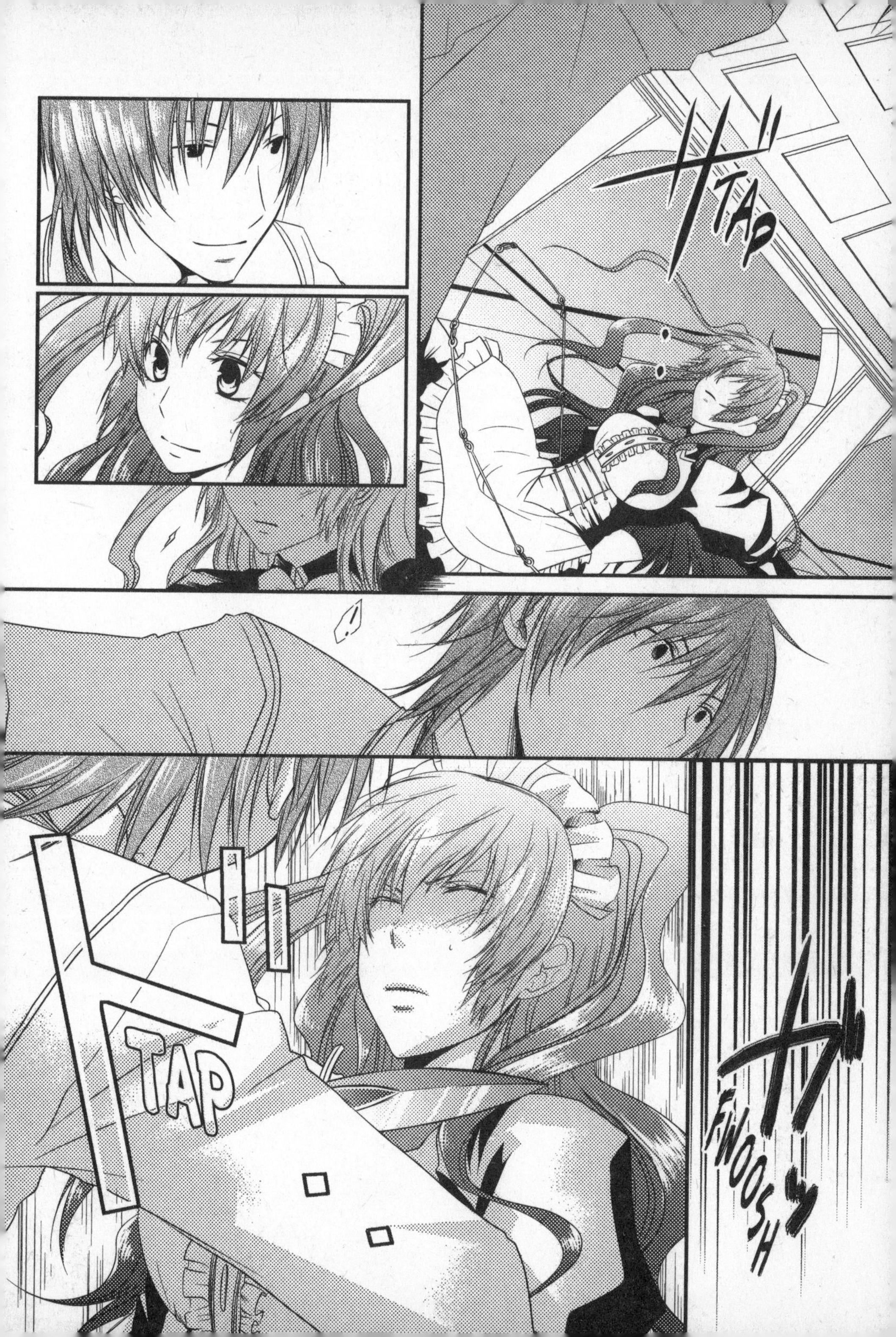
TAP
!
FWOOSH
TAP

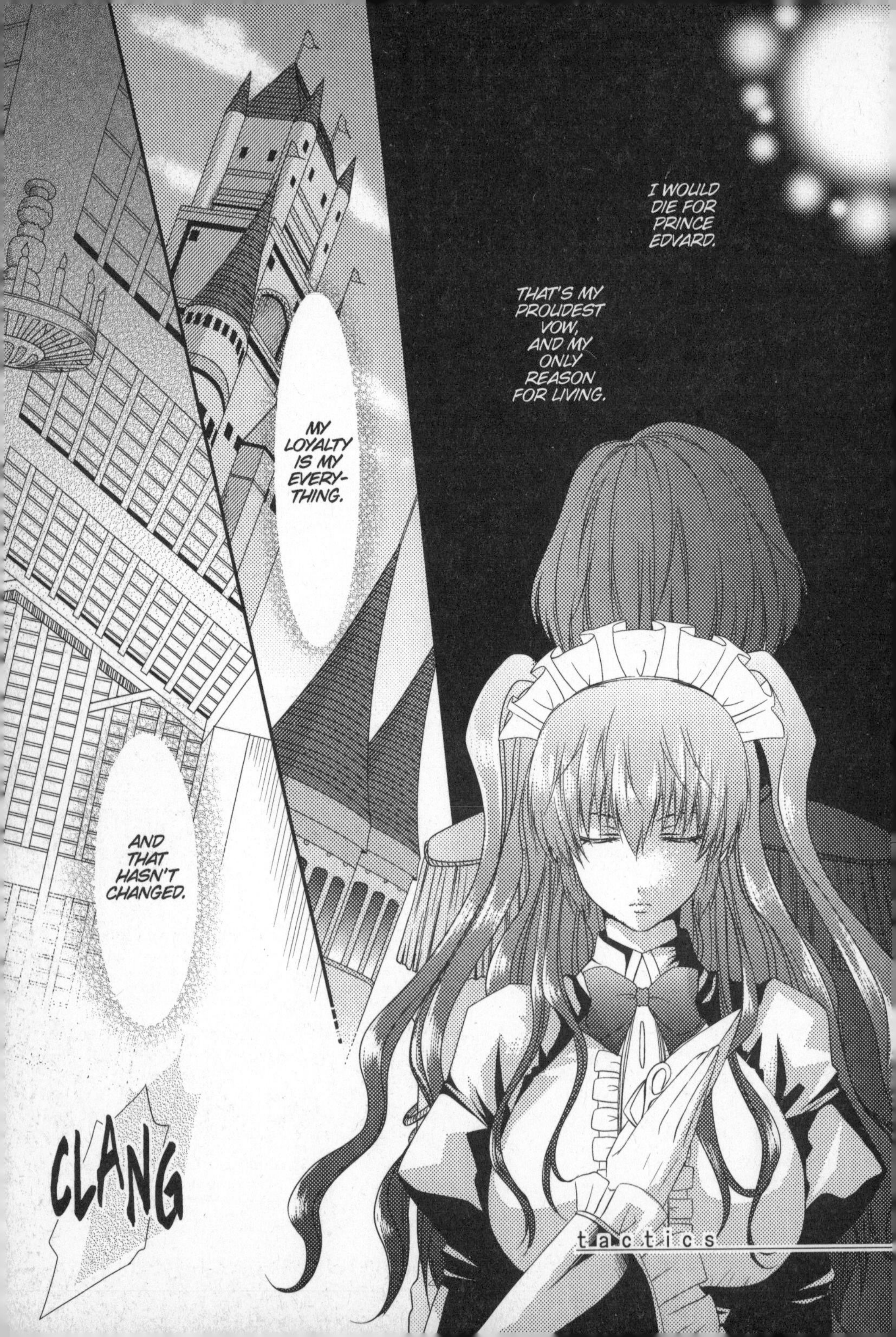
I WOULD DIE FOR PRINCE EDVARD.
THAT'S MY PROUDEST VOW, AND MY ONLY REASON FOR LIVING.
MY LOYALTY IS MY EVERY-THING.
AND THAT HASN'T CHANGED.
CLANG
tactics

Crimson Empire Character Information

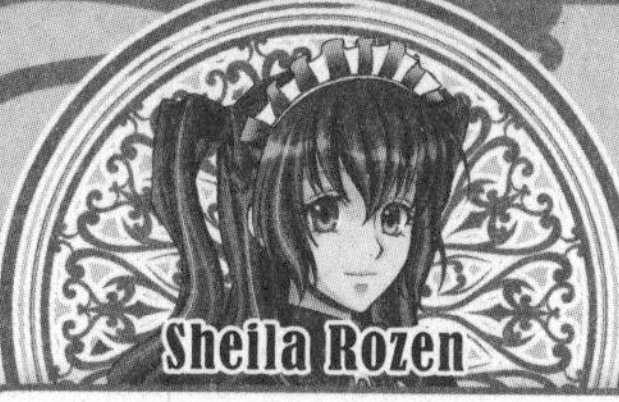

Sheila Rozen

The intensely loyal head maid to Prince Edvard—and his secret bodyguard. She's a skilled leader and shrewdly political, in addition to being fierce in combat. She doesn't hide her roots as a slave.

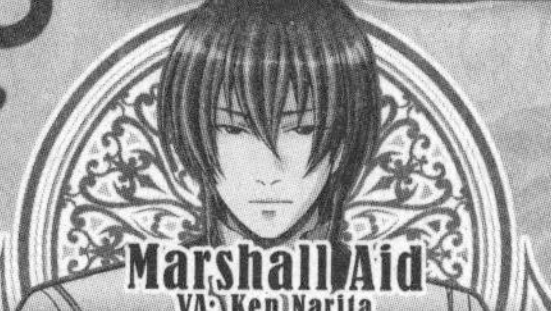

Marshall Aid

VA: Ken Narita

Prince Justin's head servant. He argues with Sheila in public but doesn't dislike her. In private, they're intimate enough to spar peacefully.

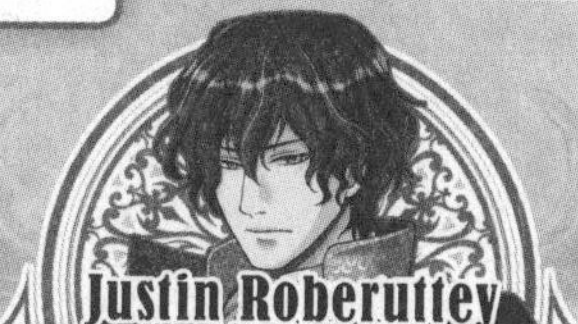

Justin Roberuttey

VA: Daisuke Hirakawa

The eldest prince, and Edvard's older brother. Since his mother is of lower status, Justin falls below his younger brother in line for the throne.

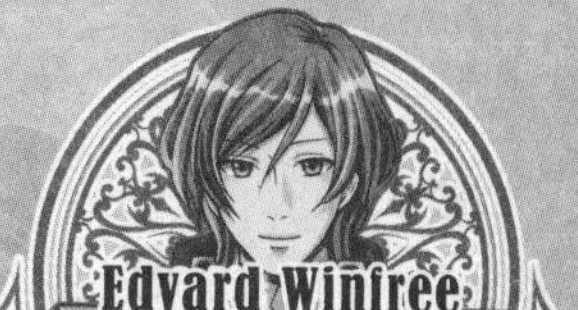

Edvard Winfree

VA: Kenichi Suzumura

Sheila's master. While friendly and regal on the surface, he's very condescending. He thinks of Sheila as more than a subordinate and loves her more than his own family... or so he *claims*.

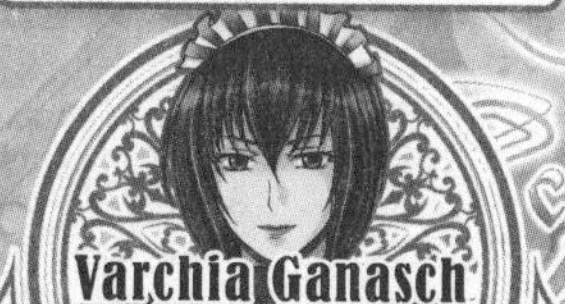

Varchia Ganasch

VA: Mitsuki Saiga

Varchia, the vice-maid, is a close friend of Sheila's, and is a former slave. Her actions and words are always painfully neutral. She's trustworthy and helps Sheila in both public and private.

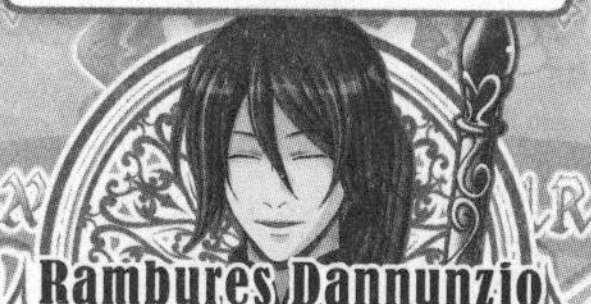

Rambures Dannunzio

VA: Taniyama Kisho

A commoner who was knighted after saving the king. He loves to lurk in his room and brew concoctions—which often stink and explode—instead of interacting with the nobility.

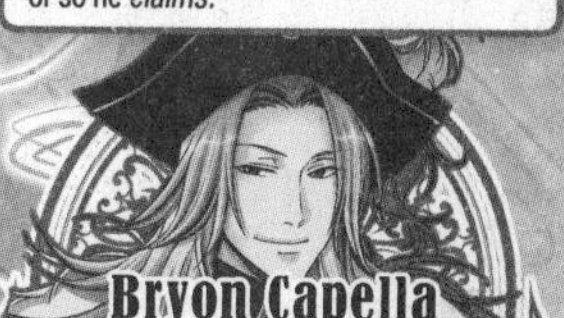

Bryon Capella

VA: Tatsuhisa Suzuki

Son of the marquis who one day will inherit the position and become an important pillar of the country. He seems cheerful and carefree, but rather guarded. Like his sister, he adores Sheila.

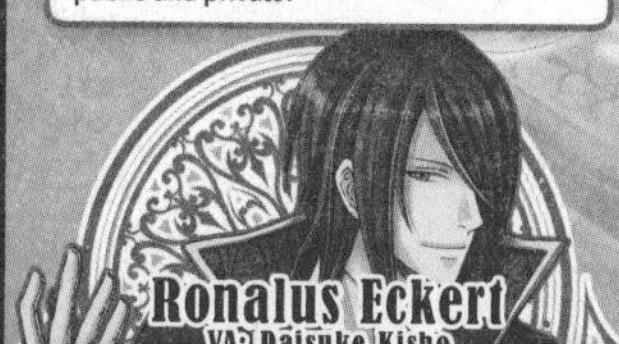

Ronalus Eckert

VA: Daisuke Kisho

Another guest in the royal castle, Ronalus is the servant to the Queen of Luxonne. Although he enjoys a higher status by serving the queen, he has a good relationship with other servants. His role is to monitor Meissen.

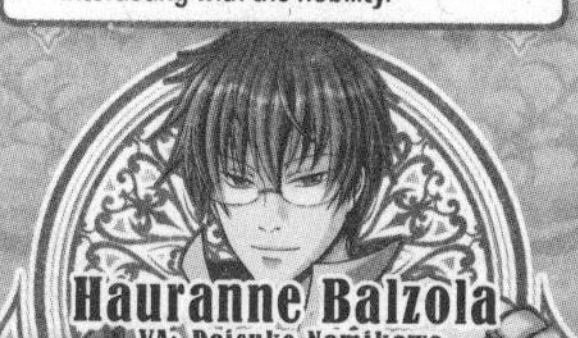

Hauranne Balzola

VA: Daisuke Namikawa

A wizard staying in the royal castle who is treated as a guest, but he's been in the castle longer than anyone. He's lived a *long* life...and his real age doesn't match his looks.

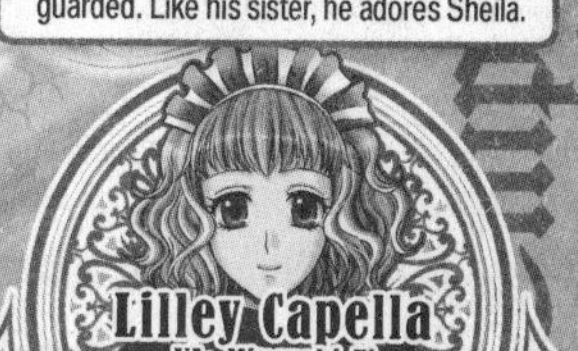

Lilley Capella

VA: Miyazaki Ui

Another battle maid, but of noble birth, Lilley is fiercely loyal to Sheila. She has innate skill, and her strength is second only to Sheila's. She and her brother Bryon are very close.

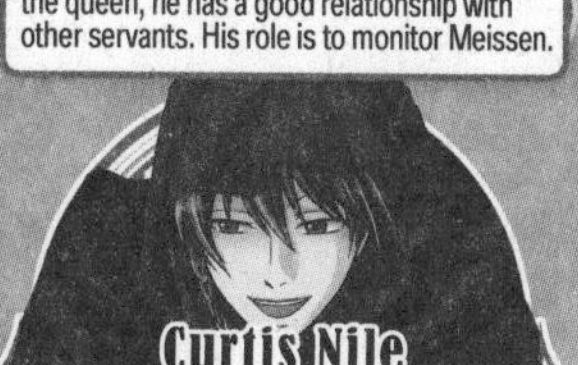

Curtis Nile

VA: Akira Ishida

A deadly assassin who specializes in poisons. He raised Sheila, and nearly killed her with his vicious training. Ever since, their relationship has been strained, to say the least.

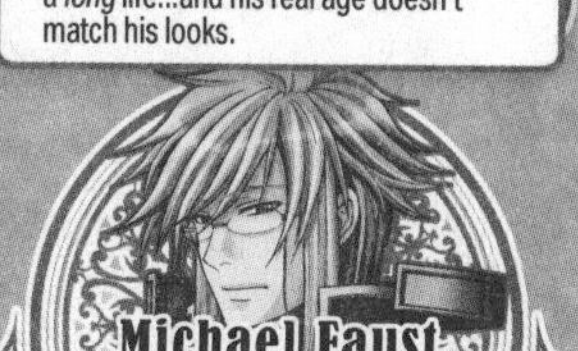

Michael Faust

VA: Hikaru Midorikawa

A demon who made a contract with Meissen. He's dangerously strong, monologues frequently, and is oddly nervous. His mental instability feeds his pessimism.

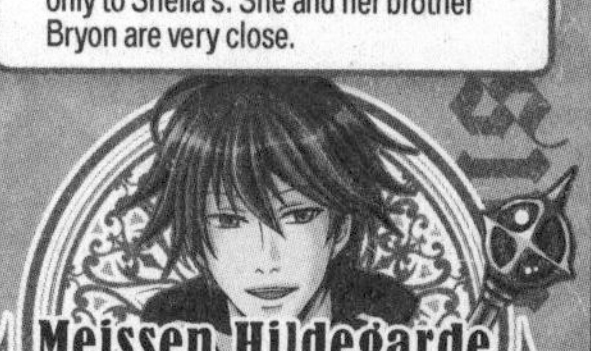

Meissen Hildegarde

VA: Hiro Shimono

Meissen has a tendency to wander, and he's traveled all over the world. His ladykiller persona hides a powerful wizard. He's searching for the truth and is trying to become a sage...supposedly.

CRIMSON EMPIRE
クリムゾン・エンパイア
~Circumstances to serve a noble~

We devote our life proudly.
my life for you. For all you.

Quin Rose 2008

- STORY -

The setting is a country of aristocrats: a tributary nation for Luxonne. *Crimson Empire* is a love adventure game about a maid, Sheila, who works in the luxurious royal castle. But behind the lavish façade, the castle is home to a savage—and bloody—political war.

Strong and skilled, Sheila uses her position as a maid to hide her true profession: bodyguard to Prince Edvard. Sheila carries a dark past of enslavement and murder. Now she survives day to day, with only a small wish in her heart.

While navigating the power struggle between Prince Edvard and his brother, the deceptive Prince Justin, Sheila must understand and use the dangerous people who surround her. But although a brilliant fighter and tactician, Sheila is unskilled when it comes to love and friendships. Such a gap between her power and her heart could lead to a dire ending indeed!

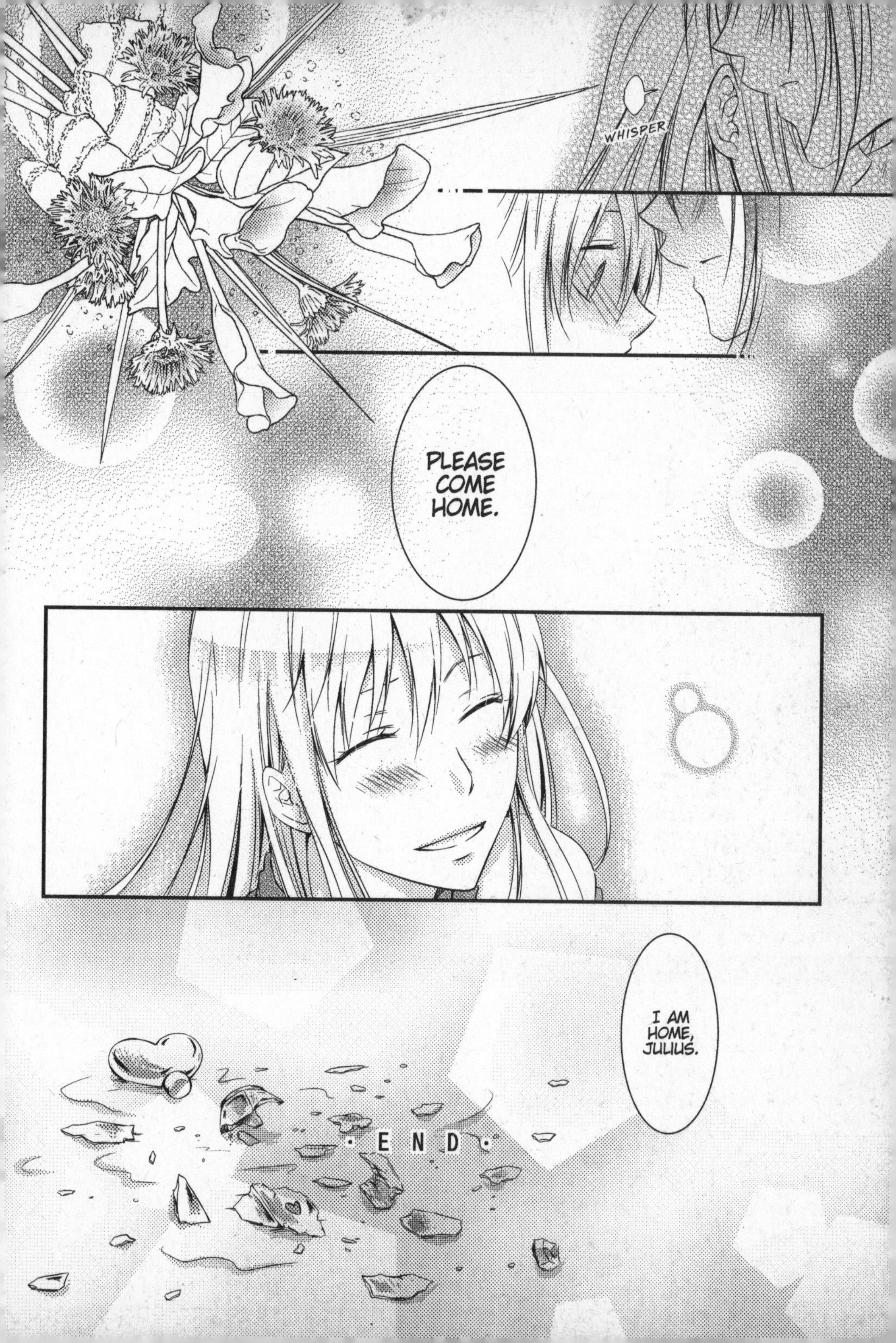
WHISPER
PLEASE COME HOME.
I AM HOME, JULIUS.
· E N D ·

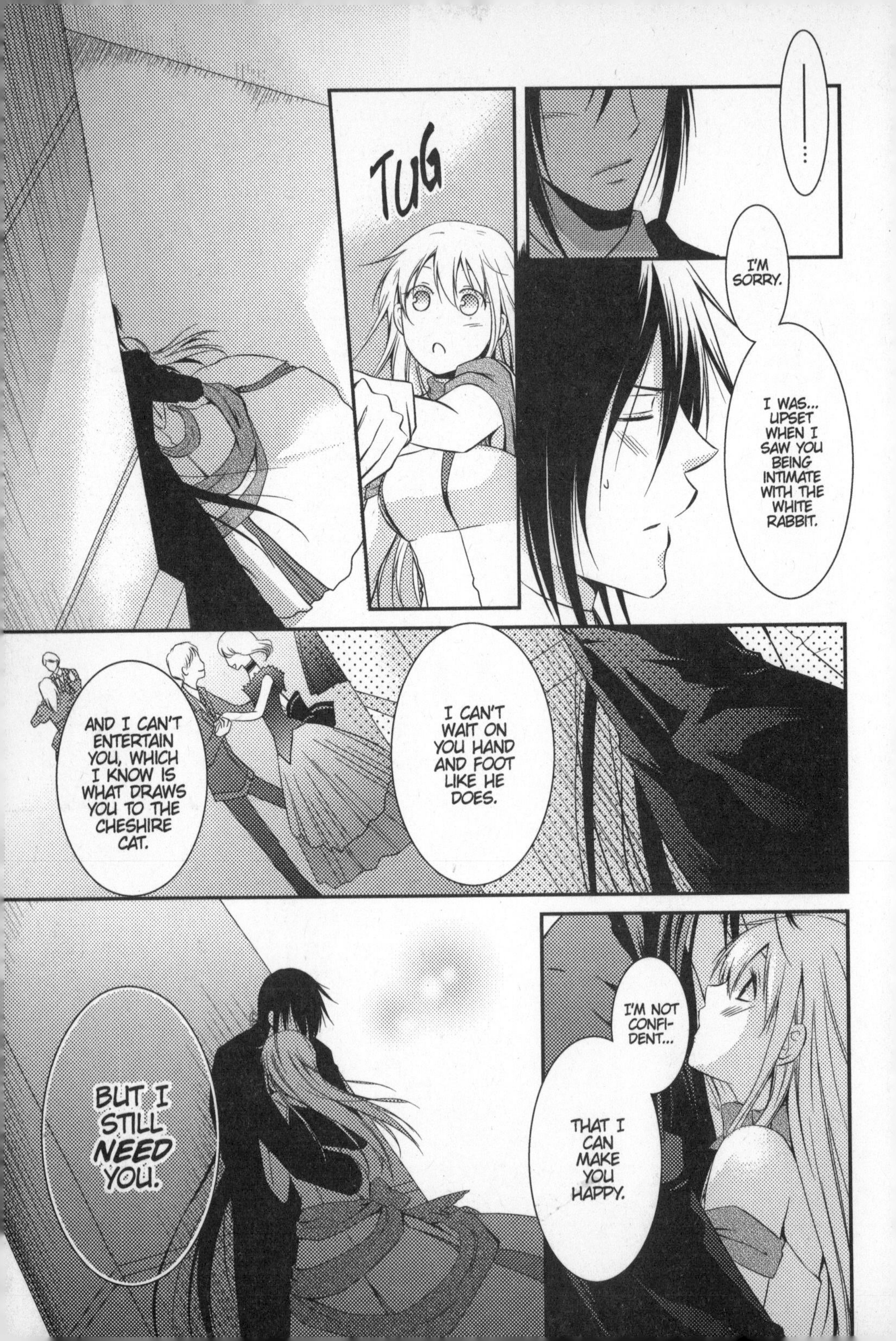
—...!
I'M SORRY.
I WAS... UPSET WHEN I SAW YOU BEING INTIMATE WITH THE WHITE RABBIT.
TUG
I CAN'T WAIT ON YOU HAND AND FOOT LIKE HE DOES.
AND I CAN'T ENTERTAIN YOU, WHICH I KNOW IS WHAT DRAWS YOU TO THE CHESHIRE CAT.
I'M NOT CONFIDENT...
THAT I CAN MAKE YOU HAPPY.
BUT I STILL **NEED** YOU.

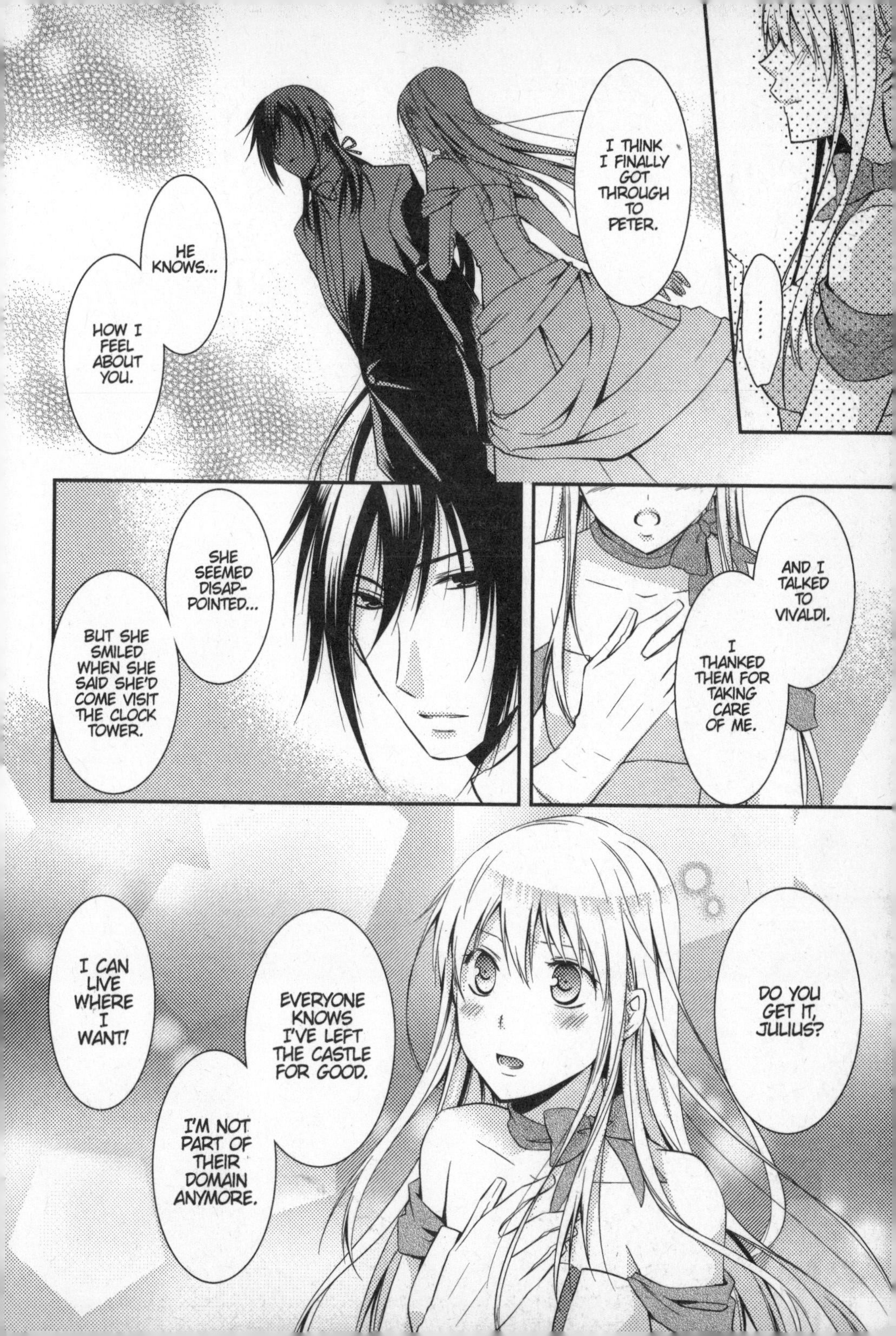
I THINK I FINALLY GOT THROUGH TO PETER.
......
HE KNOWS...
HOW I FEEL ABOUT YOU.
AND I TALKED TO VIVALDI.
I THANKED THEM FOR TAKING CARE OF ME.
SHE SEEMED DISAP-POINTED...
BUT SHE SMILED WHEN SHE SAID SHE'D COME VISIT THE CLOCK TOWER.
DO YOU GET IT, JULIUS?
EVERYONE KNOWS I'VE LEFT THE CASTLE FOR GOOD.
I'M NOT PART OF THEIR DOMAIN ANYMORE.
I CAN LIVE WHERE I WANT!

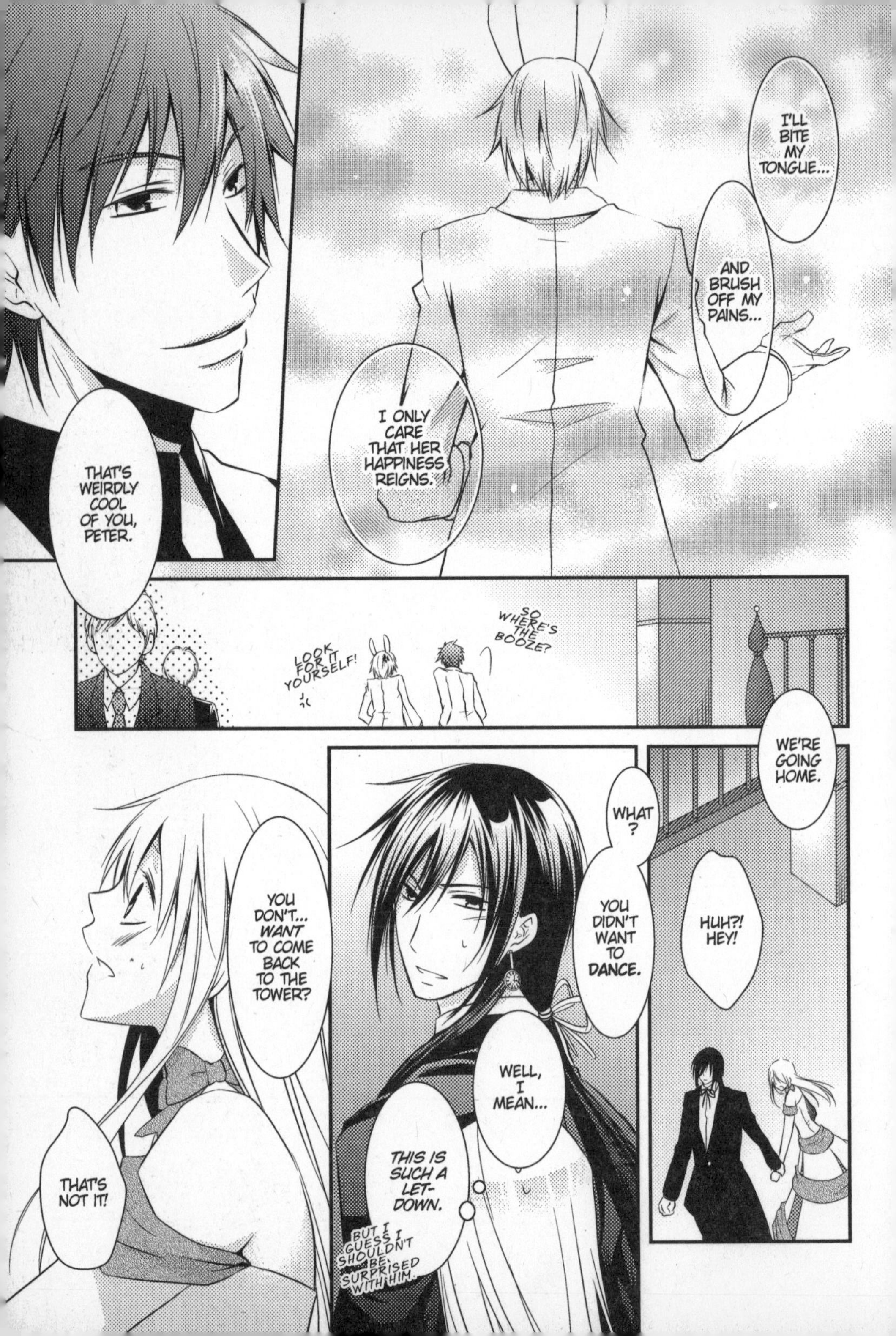
I'LL BITE MY TONGUE...
AND BRUSH OFF MY PAINS...
I ONLY CARE THAT HER HAPPINESS REIGNS.
THAT'S WEIRDLY COOL OF YOU, PETER.
SO WHERE'S THE BOOZE?
LOOK FOR IT YOURSELF!
WE'RE GOING HOME.
HUH?! HEY!
WHAT?
YOU DIDN'T WANT TO DANCE.
WELL, I MEAN...
THIS IS SUCH A LET-DOWN.
BUT I GUESS I SHOULDN'T BE SURPRISED WITH HIM.
YOU DON'T... WANT TO COME BACK TO THE TOWER?
THAT'S NOT IT!

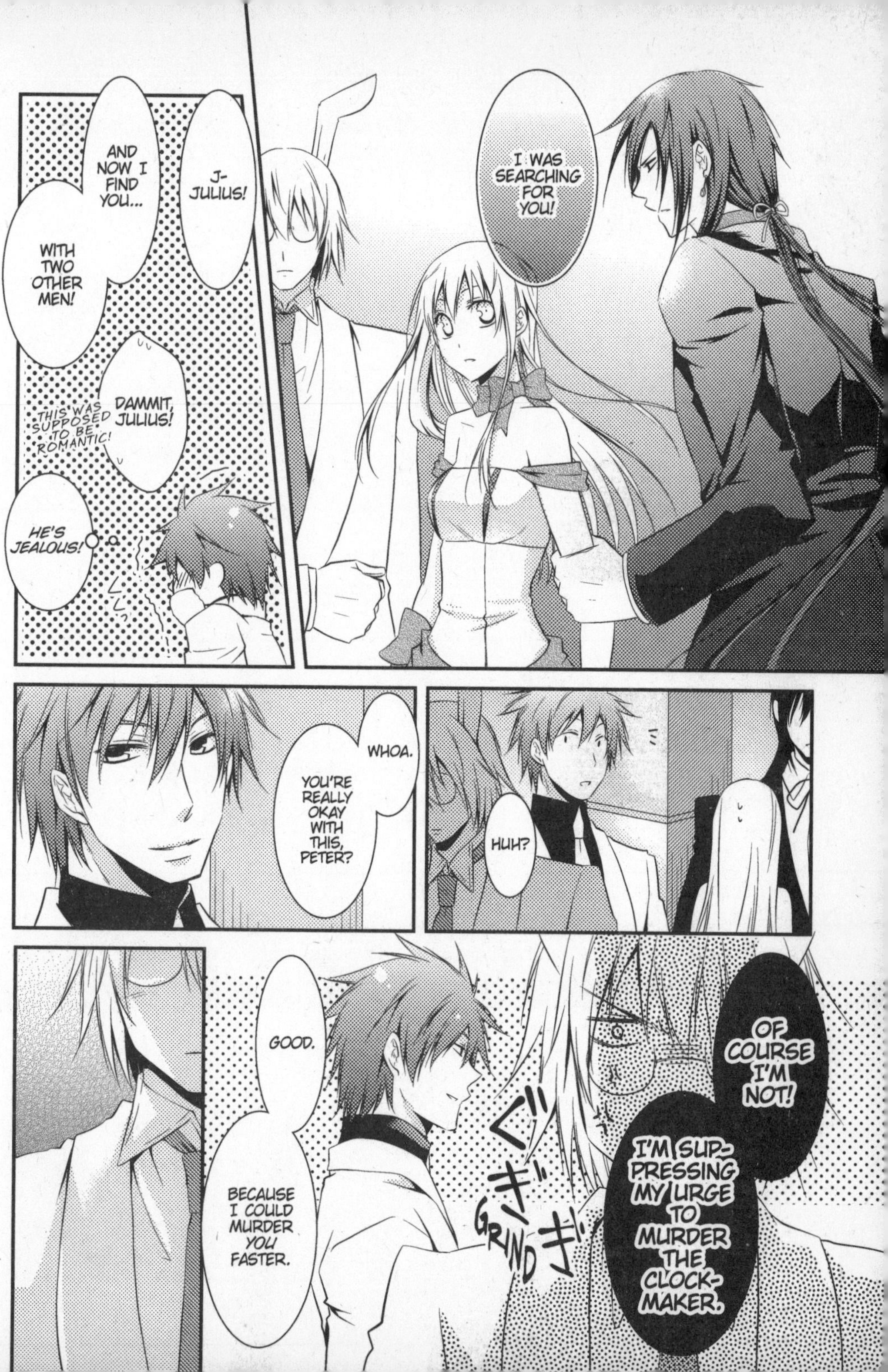
I WAS SEARCHING FOR YOU!
J-JULIUS!
AND NOW I FIND YOU...
WITH TWO OTHER MEN!
DAMMIT, JULIUS!
THIS WAS SUPPOSED TO BE ROMANTIC!
HE'S JEALOUS!
HUH?
WHOA.
YOU'RE REALLY OKAY WITH THIS, PETER?
OF COURSE I'M NOT!
I'M SUP-PRESSING MY URGE TO MURDER THE CLOCK-MAKER.
GRIND
GOOD.
BECAUSE I COULD MURDER YOU FASTER.

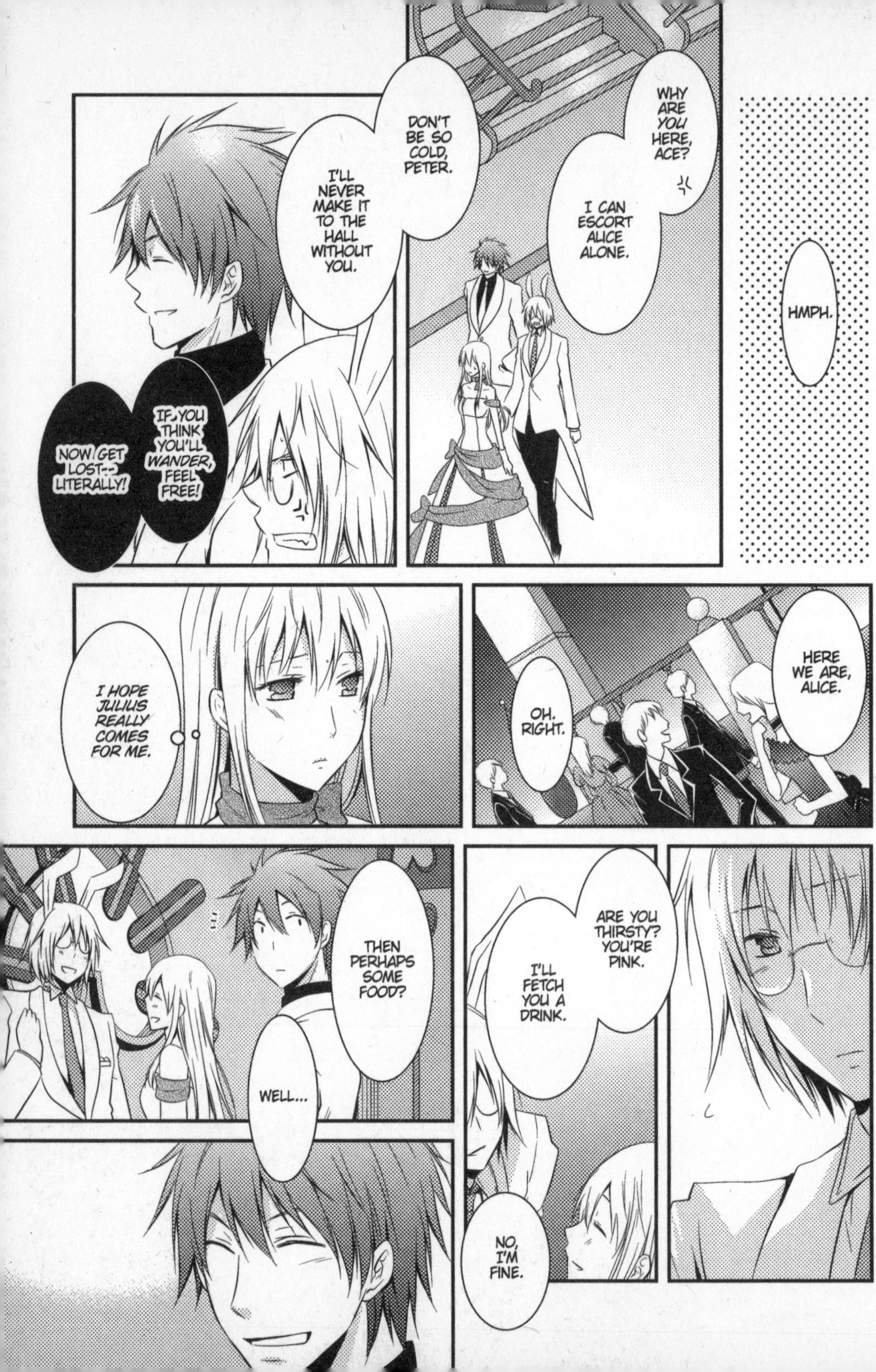
HMPH.
WHY ARE YOU HERE, ACE?
I CAN ESCORT ALICE ALONE.
DON'T BE SO COLD, PETER.
I'LL NEVER MAKE IT TO THE HALL WITHOUT YOU.
IF YOU THINK YOU'LL WANDER, FEEL FREE!
NOW GET LOST-- LITERALLY!
HERE WE ARE, ALICE.
OH. RIGHT.
I HOPE JULIUS REALLY COMES FOR ME.
ARE YOU THIRSTY? YOU'RE PINK.
I'LL FETCH YOU A DRINK.
NO, I'M FINE.
THEN PERHAPS SOME FOOD?
WELL...

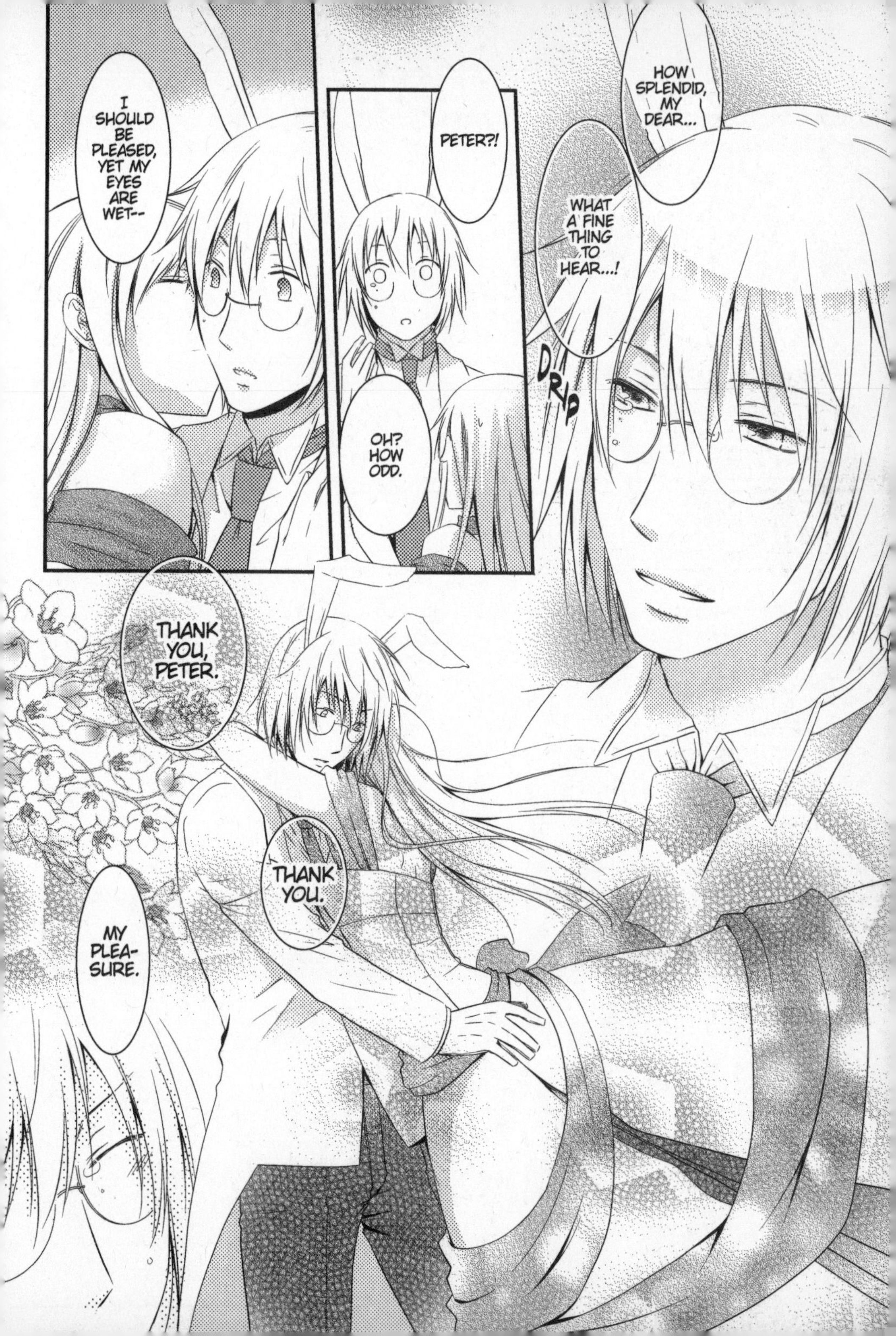
HOW SPLENDID, MY DEAR...
WHAT A FINE THING TO HEAR...!
DRIP
PETER?!
OH? HOW ODD.
I SHOULD BE PLEASED, YET MY EYES ARE WET--
THANK YOU, PETER.
THANK YOU.
MY PLEA-SURE.

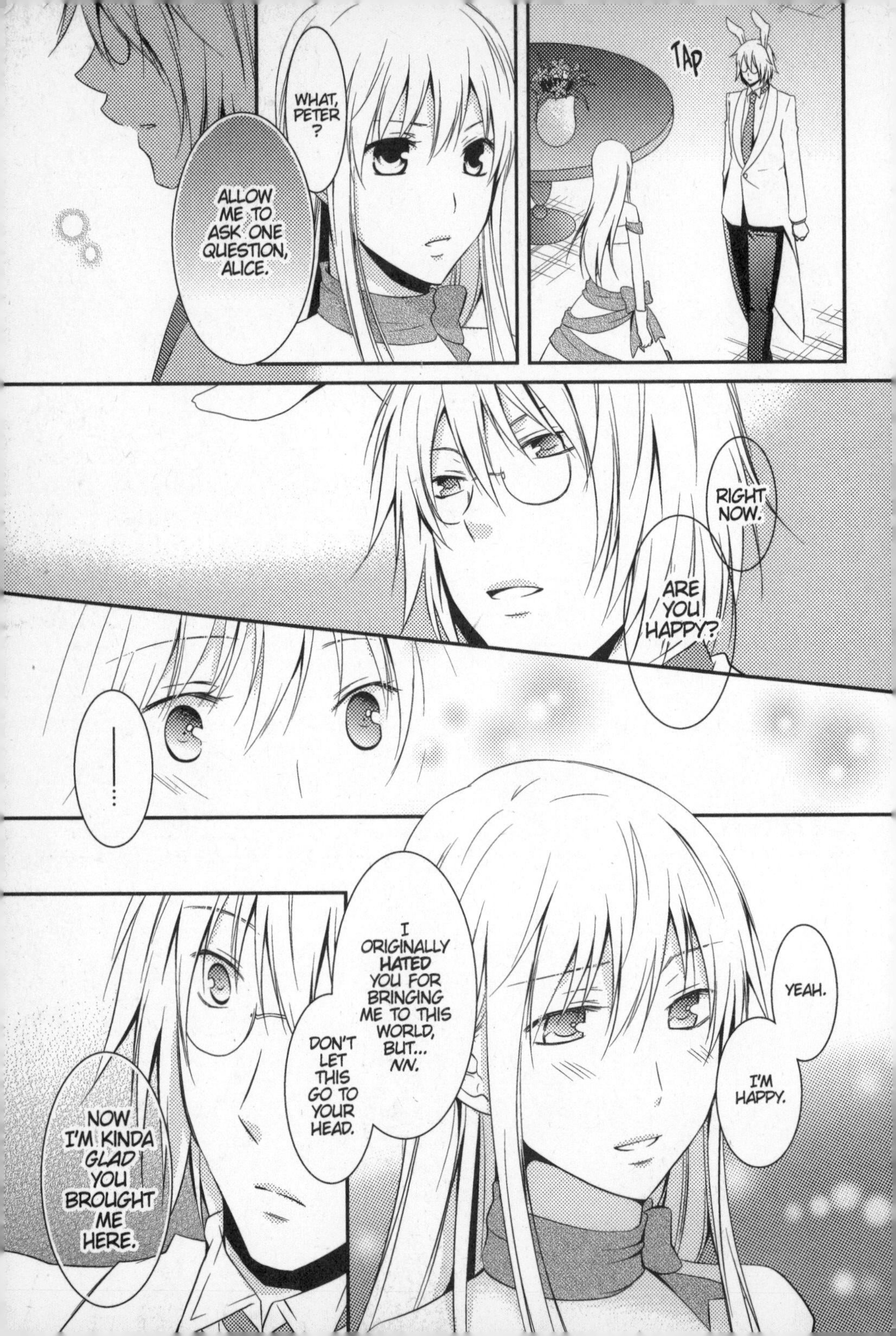
TAP
WHAT, PETER?
ALLOW ME TO ASK ONE QUESTION, ALICE.
RIGHT NOW.
ARE YOU HAPPY?
......
YEAH.
I'M HAPPY.
I ORIGINALLY HATED YOU FOR BRINGING ME TO THIS WORLD, BUT... NN.
DON'T LET THIS GO TO YOUR HEAD.
NOW I'M KINDA GLAD YOU BROUGHT ME HERE.

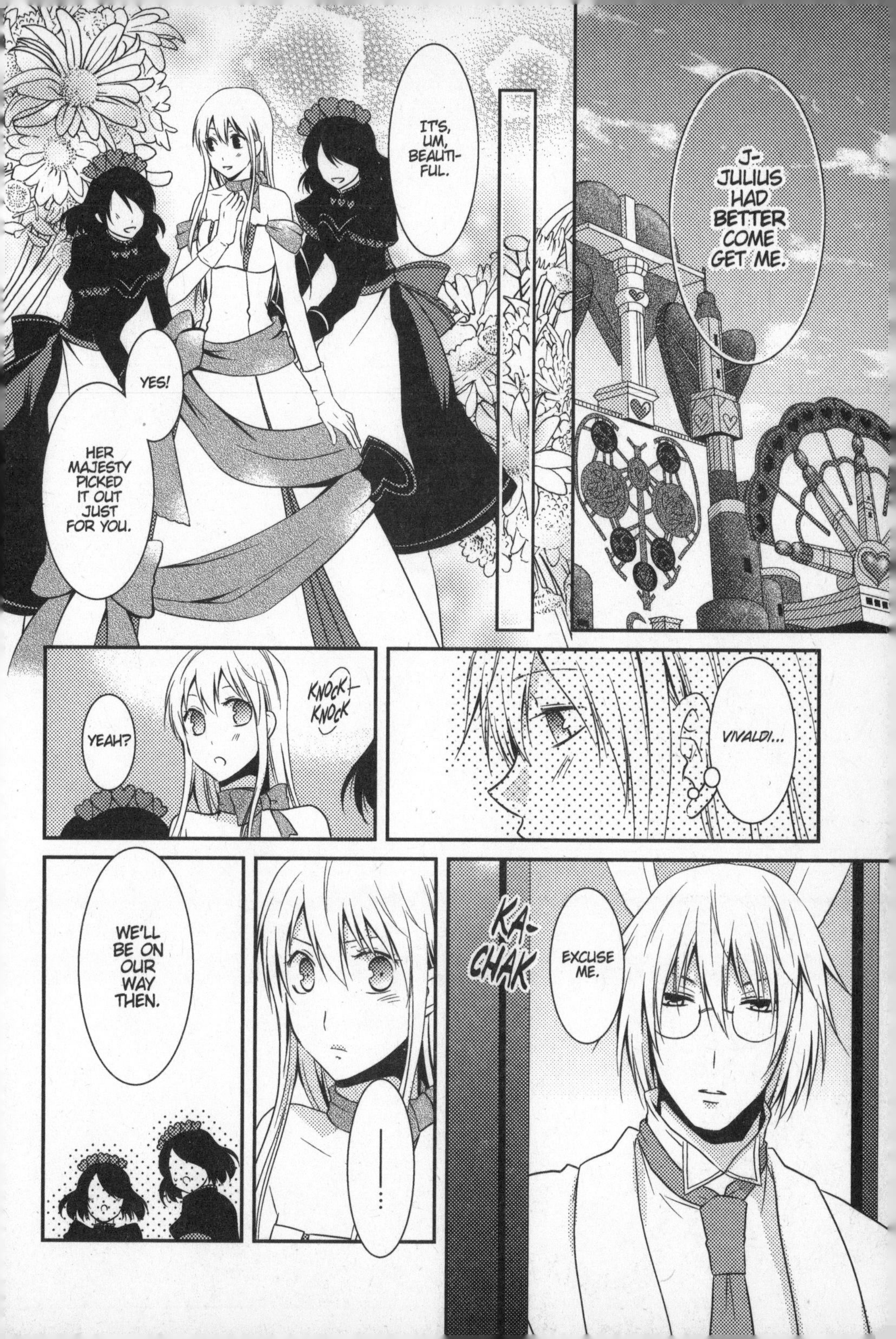
J-JULIUS HAD BETTER COME GET ME.
IT'S, UM, BEAUTIFUL.
YES!
HER MAJESTY PICKED IT OUT JUST FOR YOU.
VIVALDI...
KNOCK-KNOCK
YEAH?
KA-CHAK
EXCUSE ME.
......
WE'LL BE ON OUR WAY THEN.

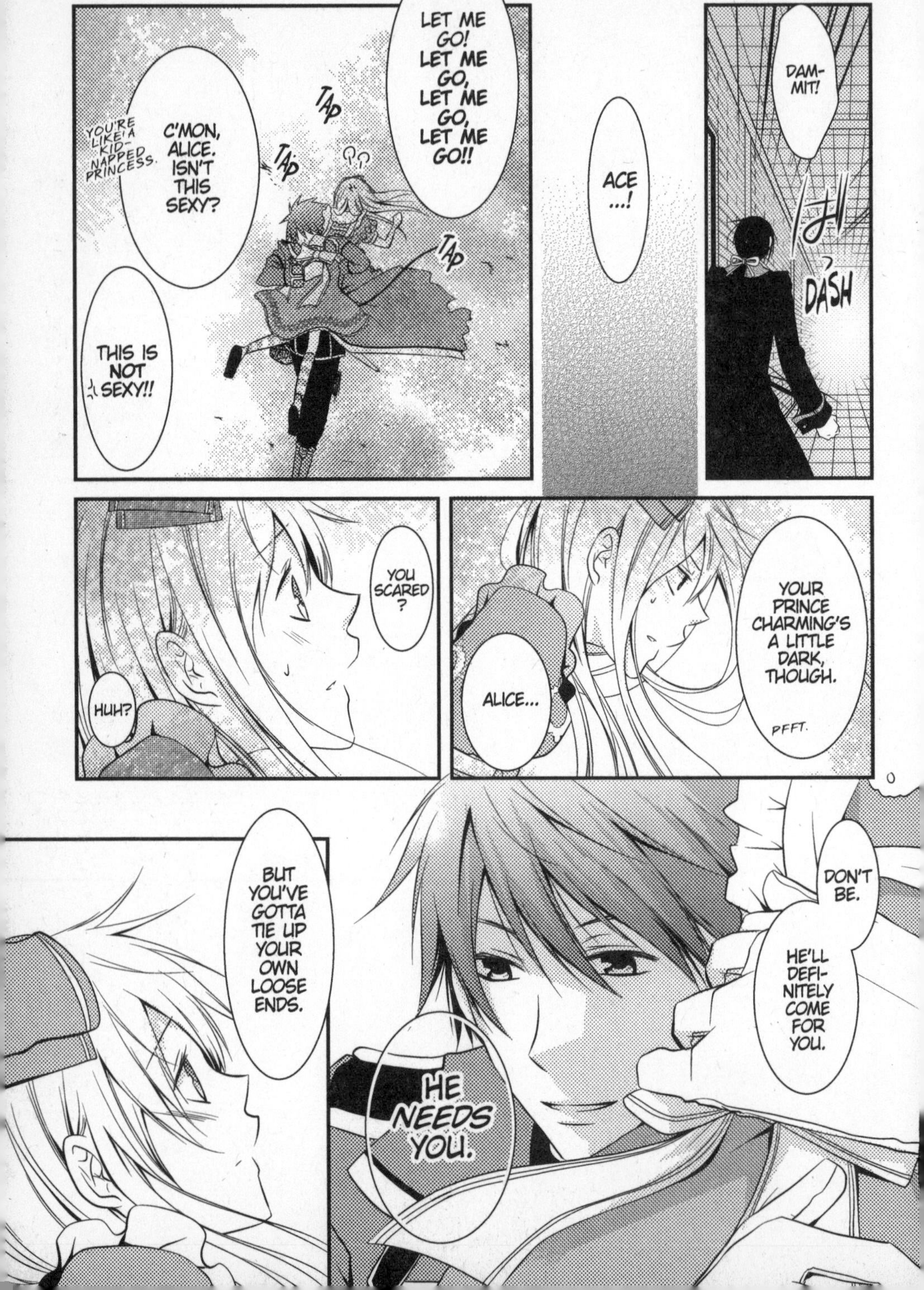
DAM-MIT!
DASH
ACE ...!
LET ME GO! LET ME GO, LET ME GO, LET ME GO!!
TAP
TAP
TAP
C'MON, ALICE. ISN'T THIS SEXY?
YOU'RE LIKE A KID-NAPPED PRINCESS.
THIS IS NOT SEXY!!
YOUR PRINCE CHARMING'S A LITTLE DARK, THOUGH.
PFFT.
ALICE...
YOU SCARED?
HUH?
DON'T BE.
HE'LL DEFINITELY COME FOR YOU.
HE NEEDS YOU.
BUT YOU'VE GOTTA TIE UP YOUR OWN LOOSE ENDS.

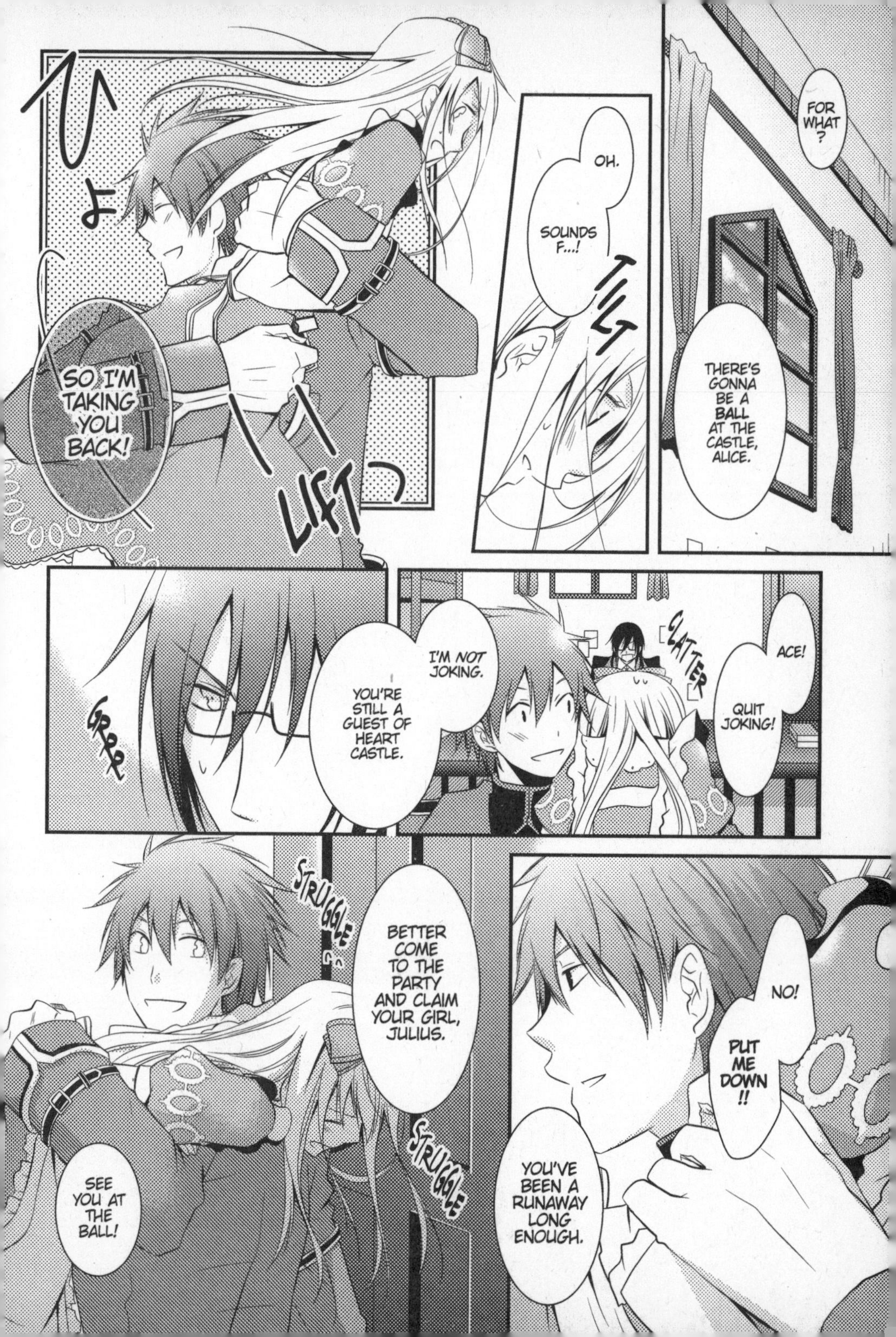
FOR WHAT?
THERE'S GONNA BE A BALL AT THE CASTLE, ALICE.
OH.
SOUNDS F...!
TILT
ひょ
LIFT
SO I'M TAKING YOU BACK!
ACE!
QUIT JOKING!
CLATTER
I'M NOT JOKING.
YOU'RE STILL A GUEST OF HEART CASTLE.
GRRR
NO!
PUT ME DOWN!!
YOU'VE BEEN A RUNAWAY LONG ENOUGH.
STRUGGLE
BETTER COME TO THE PARTY AND CLAIM YOUR GIRL, JULIUS.
STRUGGLE
SEE YOU AT THE BALL!

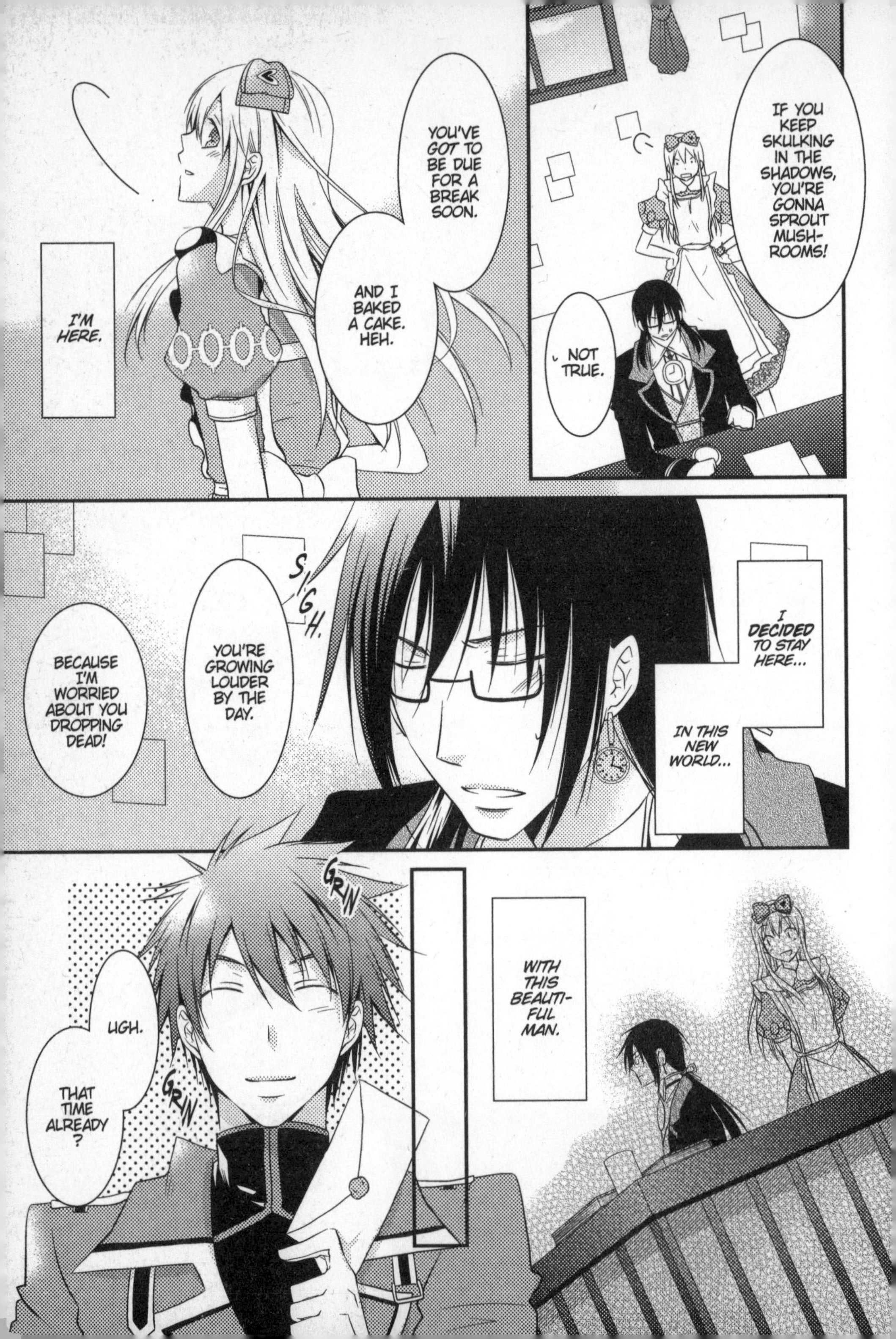
IF YOU KEEP SKULKING IN THE SHADOWS, YOU'RE GONNA SPROUT MUSH-ROOMS!
NOT TRUE.
YOU'VE GOT TO BE DUE FOR A BREAK SOON.
AND I BAKED A CAKE. HEH.
I'M HERE.
I DECIDED TO STAY HERE...
IN THIS NEW WORLD...
SIGH.
YOU'RE GROWING LOUDER BY THE DAY.
BECAUSE I'M WORRIED ABOUT YOU DROPPING DEAD!
WITH THIS BEAUTI-FUL MAN.
GRIN
GRIN
UGH.
THAT TIME ALREADY ?

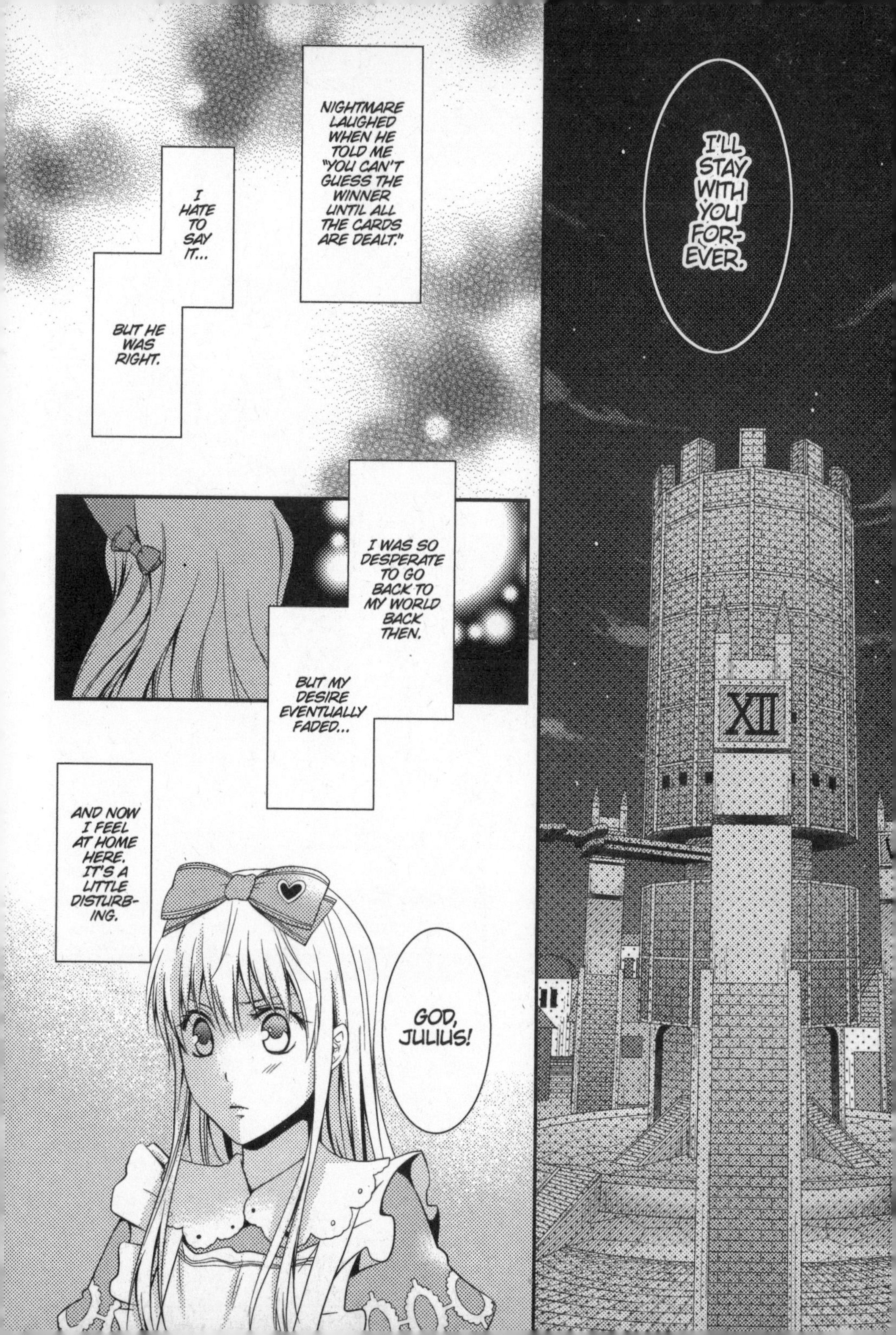
I'LL STAY WITH YOU FOR-EVER.
NIGHTMARE LAUGHED WHEN HE TOLD ME "YOU CAN'T GUESS THE WINNER UNTIL ALL THE CARDS ARE DEALT."
I HATE TO SAY IT...
BUT HE WAS RIGHT.
I WAS SO DESPERATE TO GO BACK TO MY WORLD BACK THEN.
BUT MY DESIRE EVENTUALLY FADED...
AND NOW I FEEL AT HOME HERE. IT'S A LITTLE DISTURB-ING.
GOD, JULIUS!

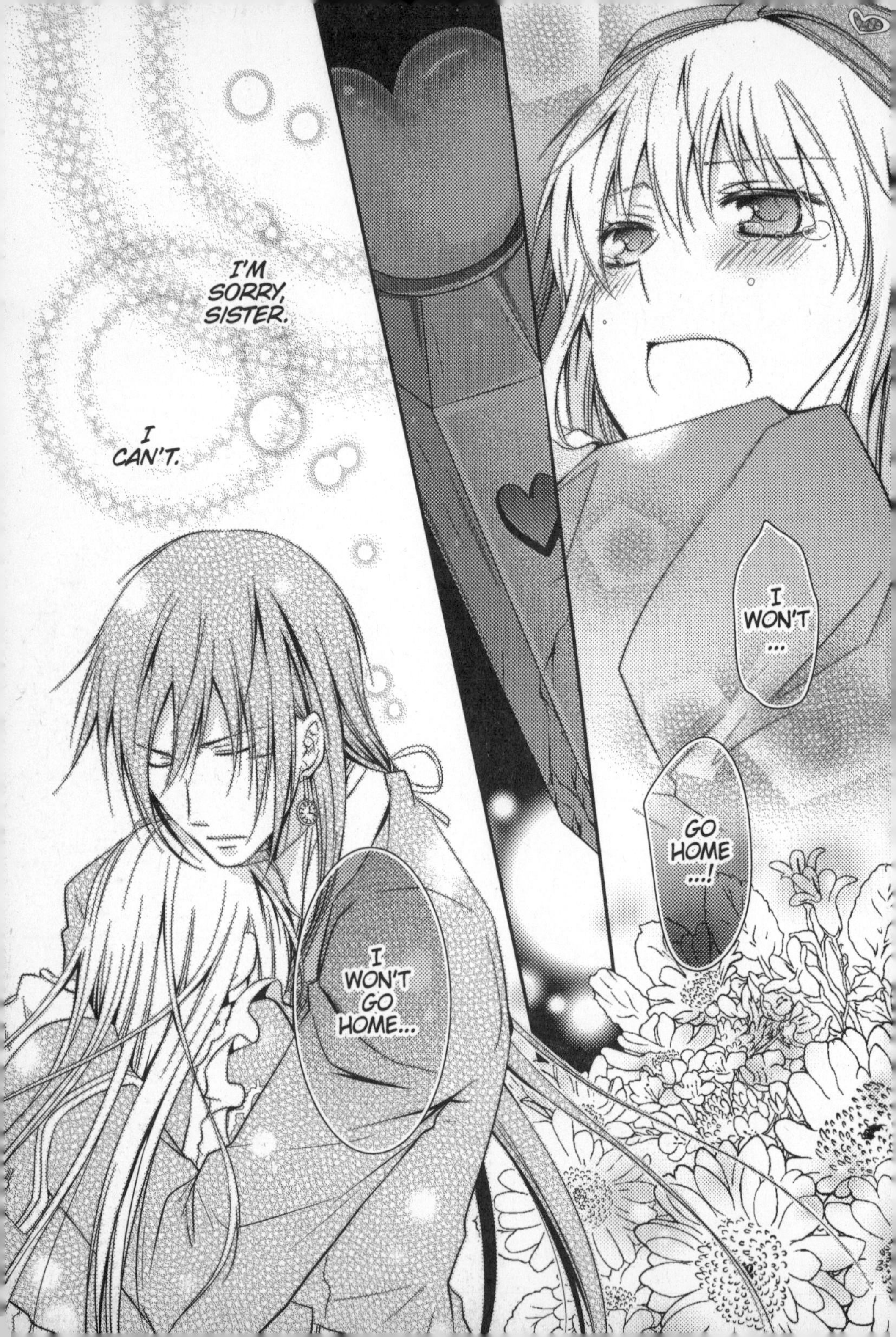
I WON'T ...
GO HOME ...!
I'M SORRY, SISTER.
I CAN'T.
I WON'T GO HOME...

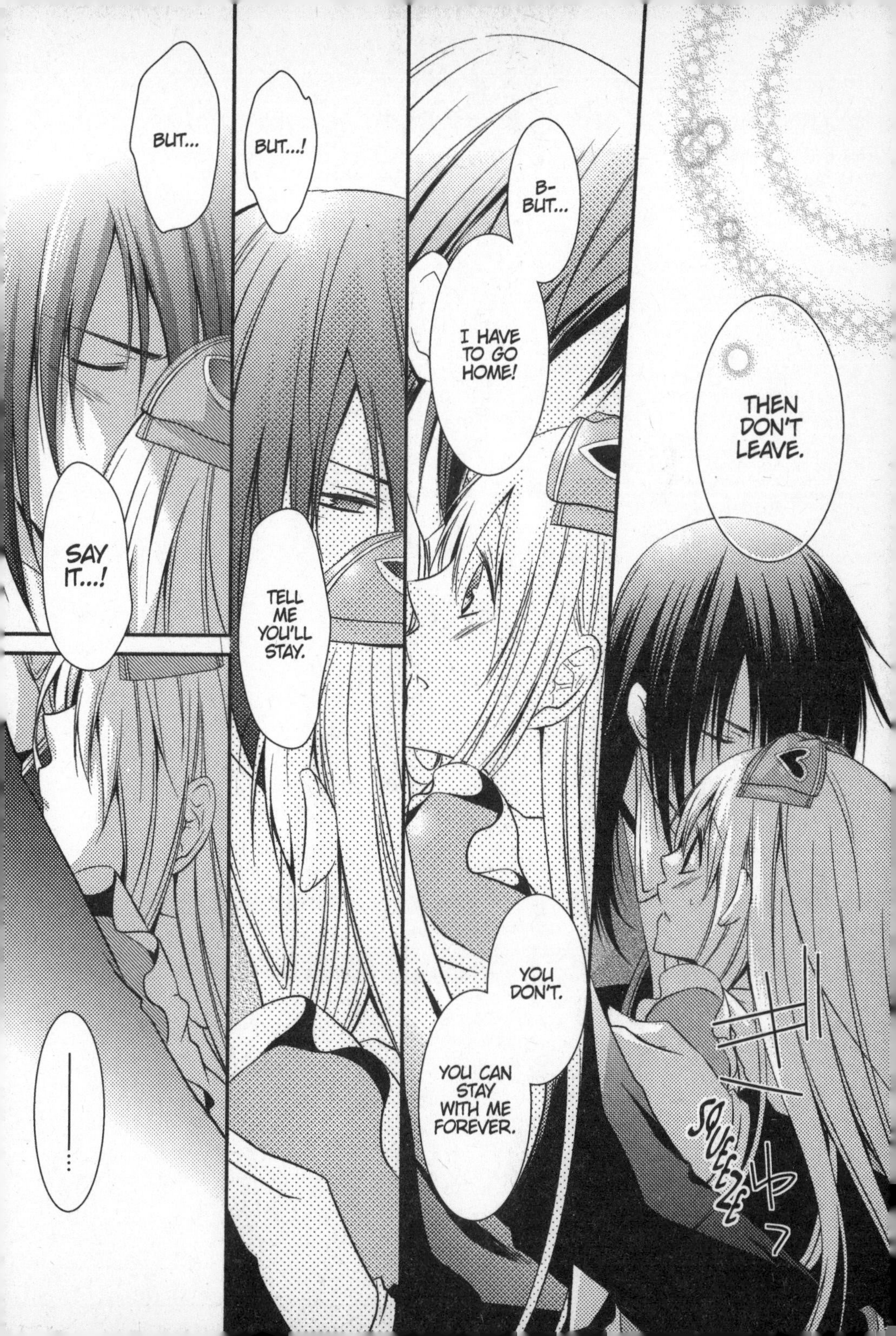
THEN DON'T LEAVE.
SQUEEZE
B-BUT...
I HAVE TO GO HOME!
YOU DON'T.
YOU CAN STAY WITH ME FOREVER.
BUT...!
TELL ME YOU'LL STAY.
BUT...
SAY IT...!
—...

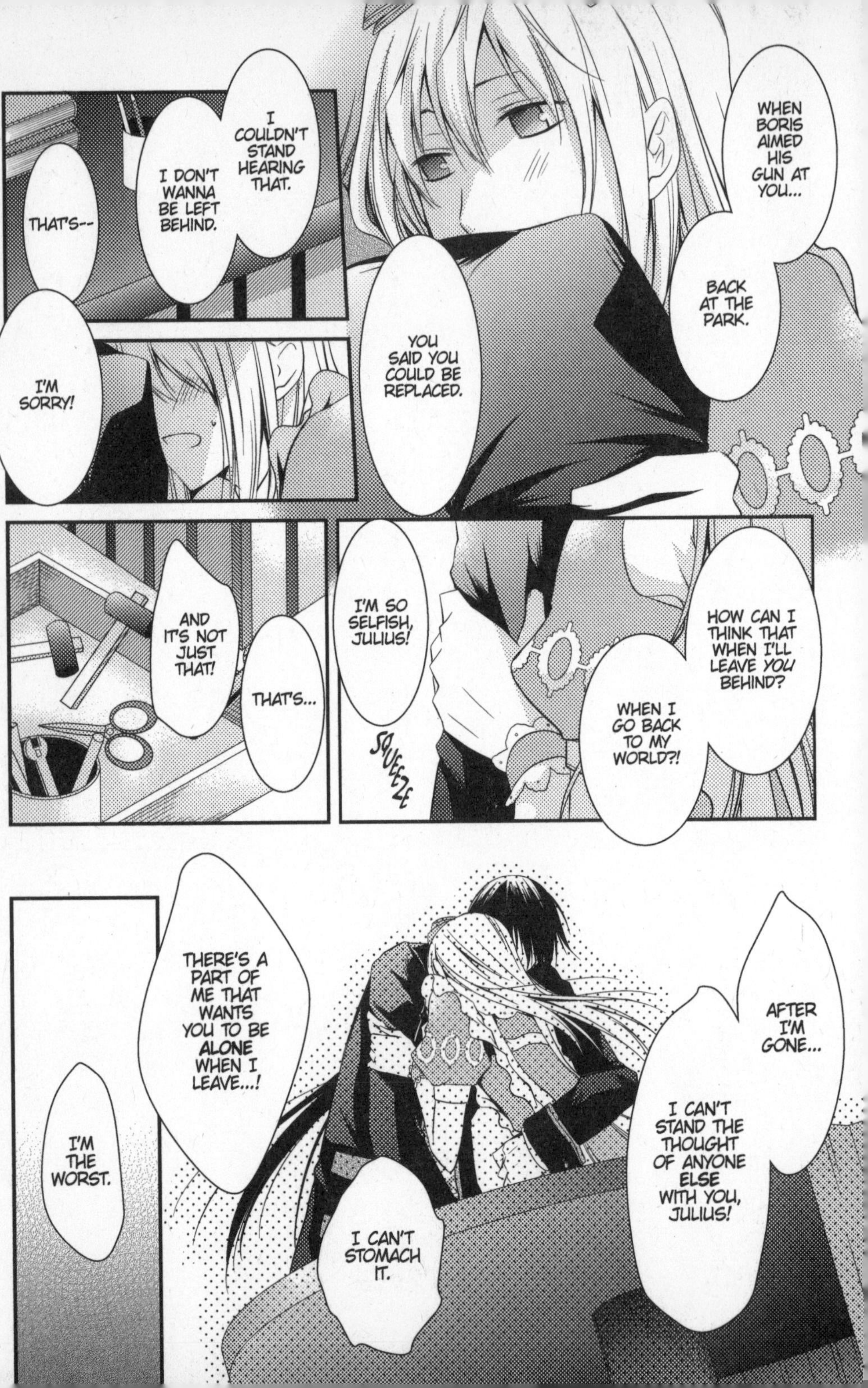
WHEN BORIS AIMED HIS GUN AT YOU...
BACK AT THE PARK.
YOU SAID YOU COULD BE REPLACED.
I COULDN'T STAND HEARING THAT.
I DON'T WANNA BE LEFT BEHIND.
THAT'S--
I'M SORRY!
HOW CAN I THINK THAT WHEN I'LL LEAVE *YOU* BEHIND?
WHEN I GO BACK TO MY WORLD?!
I'M SO SELFISH, JULIUS!
SQUEEZE
THAT'S...
AND IT'S NOT JUST THAT!
AFTER I'M GONE...
I CAN'T STAND THE THOUGHT OF ANYONE ELSE WITH YOU, JULIUS!
THERE'S A PART OF ME THAT WANTS YOU TO BE **ALONE** WHEN I LEAVE...!
I CAN'T STOMACH IT.
I'M THE WORST.

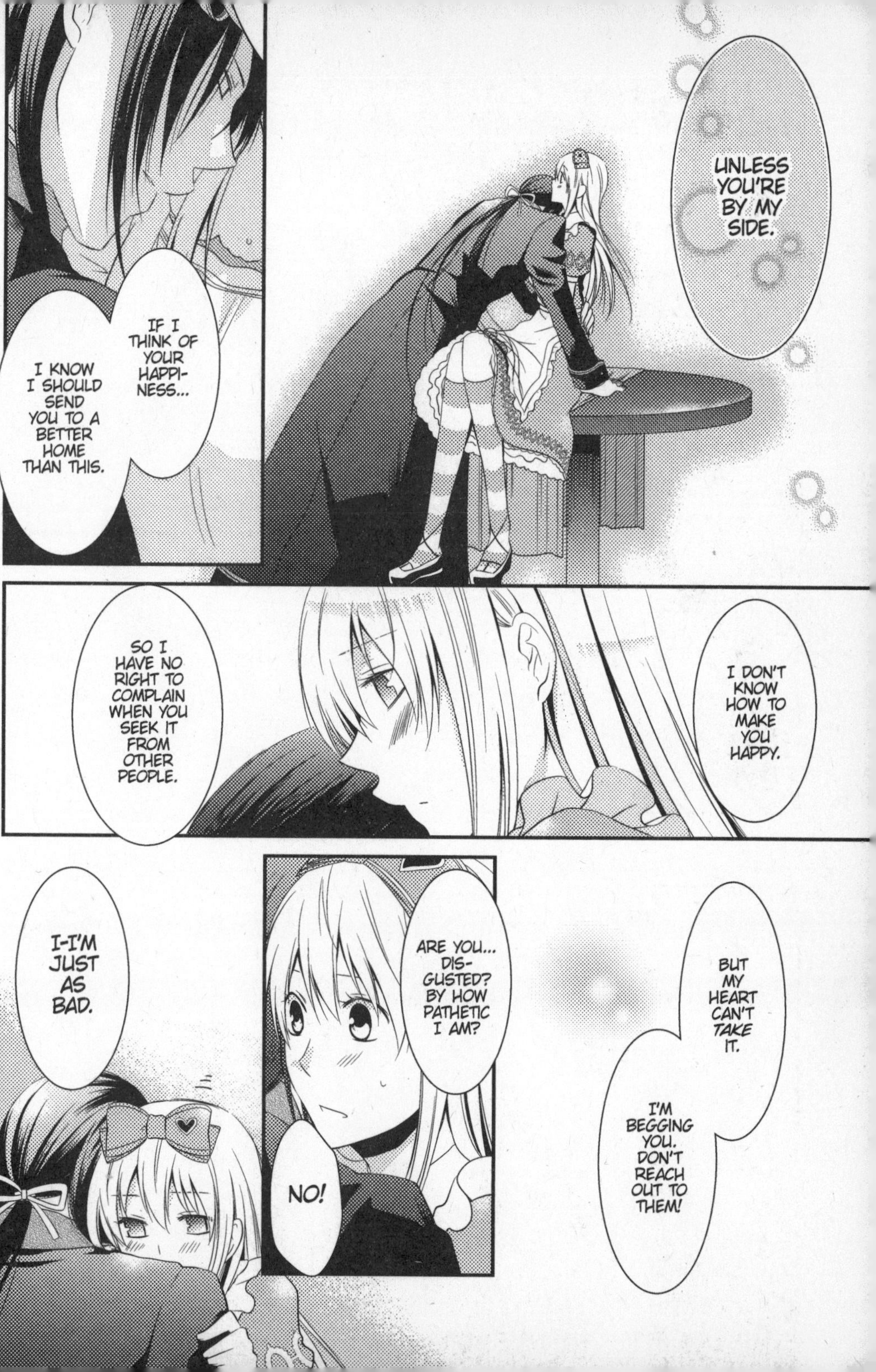
UNLESS YOU'RE BY MY SIDE.
IF I THINK OF YOUR HAPPINESS...
I KNOW I SHOULD SEND YOU TO A BETTER HOME THAN THIS.
I DON'T KNOW HOW TO MAKE YOU HAPPY.
SO I HAVE NO RIGHT TO COMPLAIN WHEN YOU SEEK IT FROM OTHER PEOPLE.
BUT MY HEART CAN'T *TAKE* IT.
I'M BEGGING YOU. DON'T REACH OUT TO THEM!
ARE YOU... DISGUSTED? BY HOW PATHETIC I AM?
NO!
I-I'M JUST AS BAD.

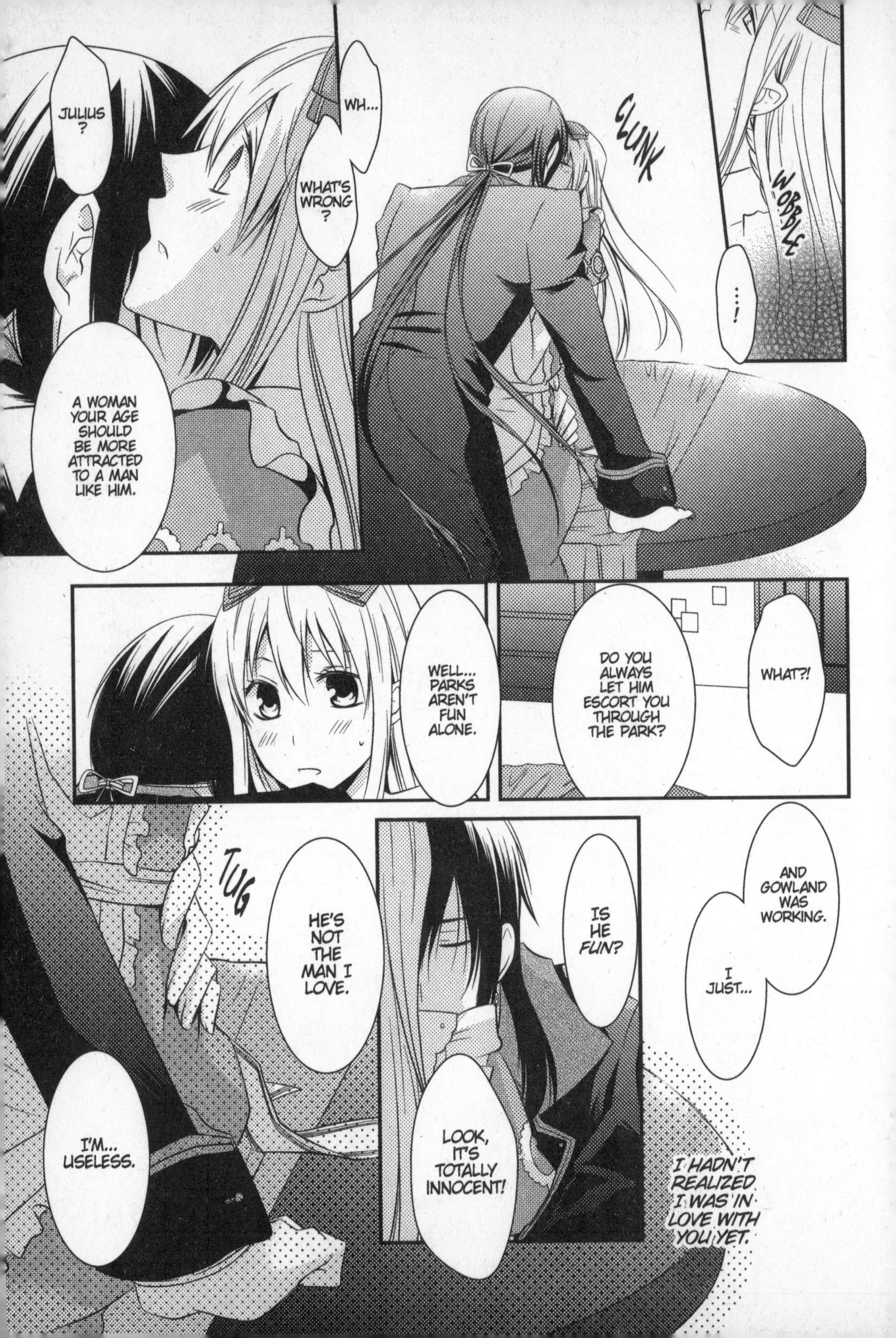
WOBBLE
...!
CLUNK
WH... WHAT'S WRONG?
JULIUS?
A WOMAN YOUR AGE SHOULD BE MORE ATTRACTED TO A MAN LIKE HIM.
WHAT?!
DO YOU ALWAYS LET HIM ESCORT YOU THROUGH THE PARK?
WELL... PARKS AREN'T FUN ALONE.
AND GOWLAND WAS WORKING.
I JUST...
IS HE *FUN*?
HE'S NOT THE MAN I LOVE.
LOOK, IT'S TOTALLY INNOCENT!
I HADN'T REALIZED I WAS IN LOVE WITH YOU YET.
TUG
I'M... USELESS.

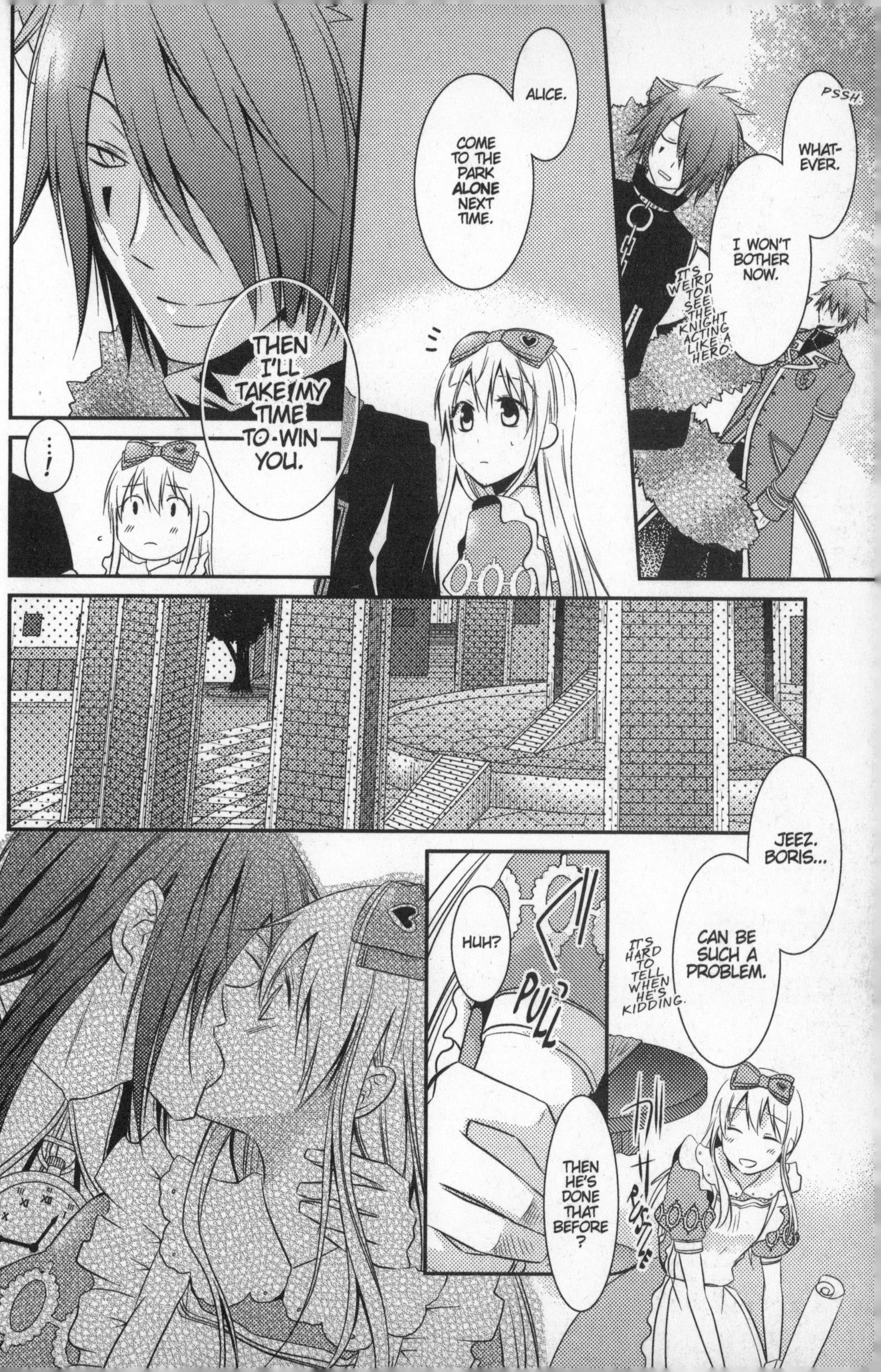
PSSH.
WHAT-EVER.
I WON'T BOTHER NOW.
IT'S WEIRD TO SEE THE KNIGHT ACTING LIKE A HERO.
ALICE.
COME TO THE PARK ALONE NEXT TIME.
THEN I'LL TAKE MY TIME TO WIN YOU.
...!
JEEZ. BORIS...
CAN BE SUCH A PROBLEM.
IT'S HARD TO TELL WHEN HE'S KIDDING.
RUSTLE
HUH?
PULL
THEN HE'S DONE THAT BEFORE?

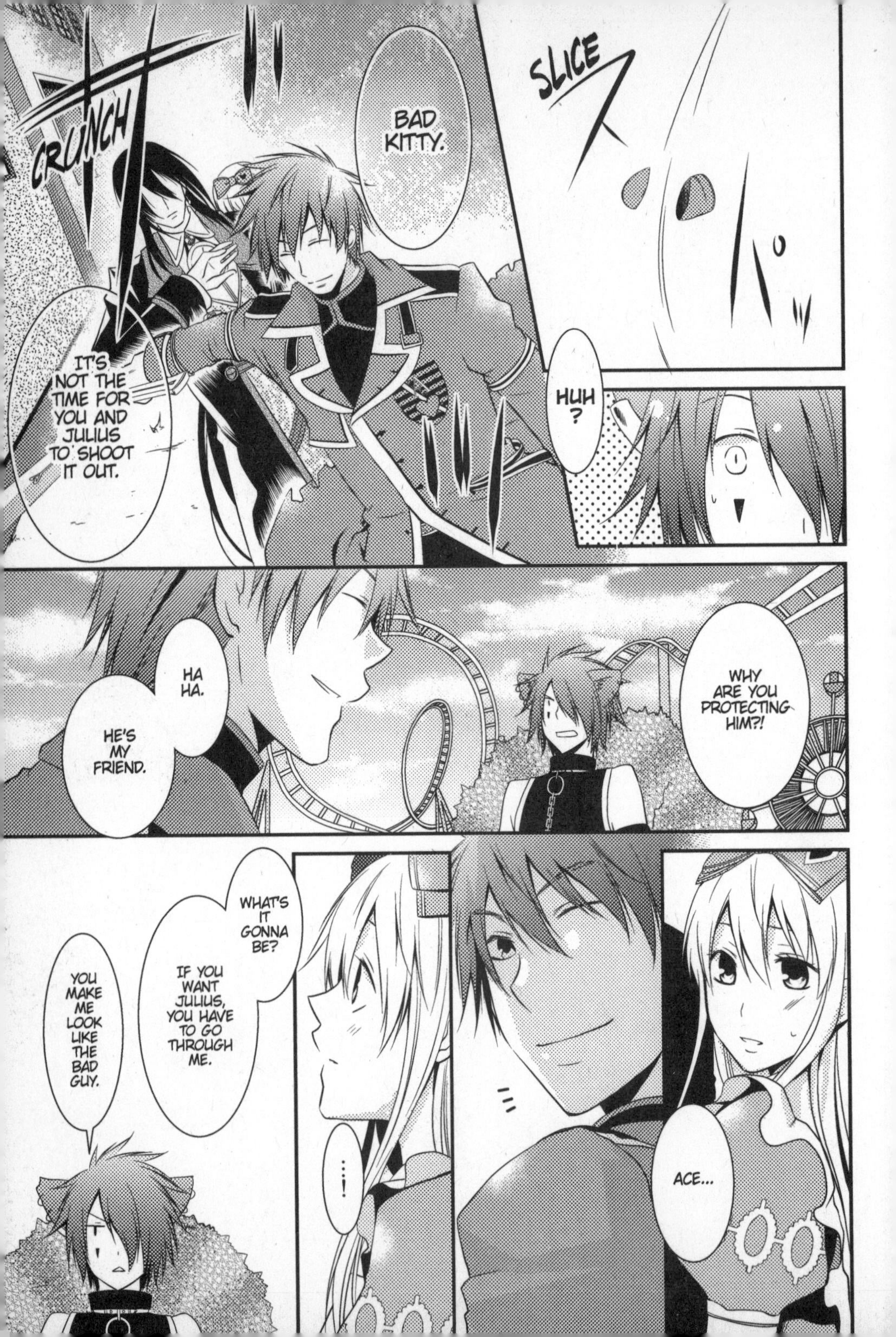
SLICE
HUH?
BAD KITTY.
CRUNCH
IT'S NOT THE TIME FOR YOU AND JULIUS TO SHOOT IT OUT.
WHY ARE YOU PROTECTING HIM?!
HA HA.
HE'S MY FRIEND.
ACE...
WHAT'S IT GONNA BE?
IF YOU WANT JULIUS, YOU HAVE TO GO THROUGH ME.
...!
YOU MAKE ME LOOK LIKE THE BAD GUY.

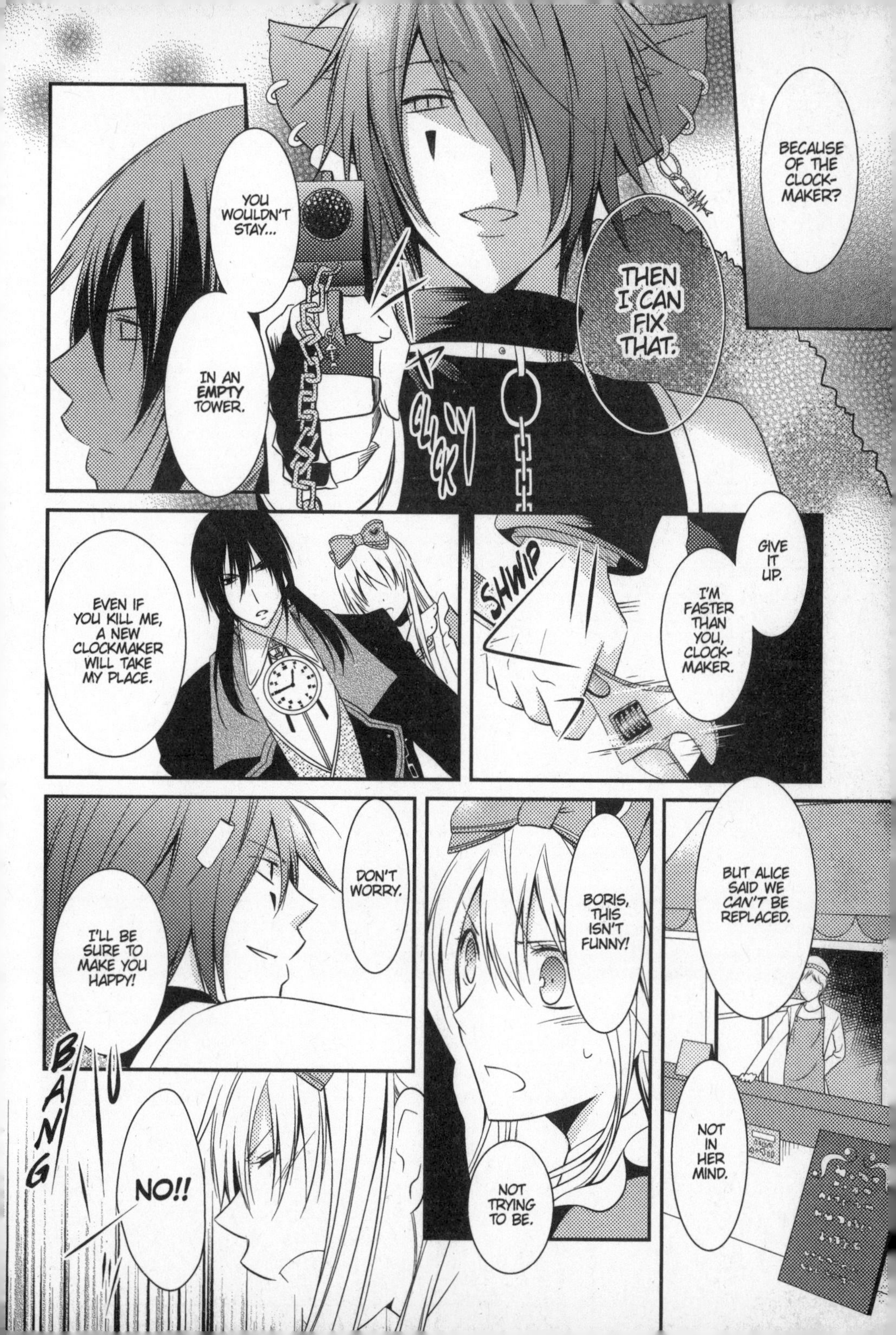

BECAUSE OF THE CLOCK-MAKER?
THEN I CAN FIX THAT.
YOU WOULDN'T STAY...
IN AN EMPTY TOWER.
CLICK
SHWIP
GIVE IT UP.
I'M FASTER THAN YOU, CLOCK-MAKER.
EVEN IF YOU KILL ME, A NEW CLOCKMAKER WILL TAKE MY PLACE.
BUT ALICE SAID WE *CAN'T* BE REPLACED.
NOT IN HER MIND.
BORIS, THIS ISN'T FUNNY!
NOT TRYING TO BE.
DON'T WORRY.
I'LL BE SURE TO MAKE YOU HAPPY!
BANG
NO!!

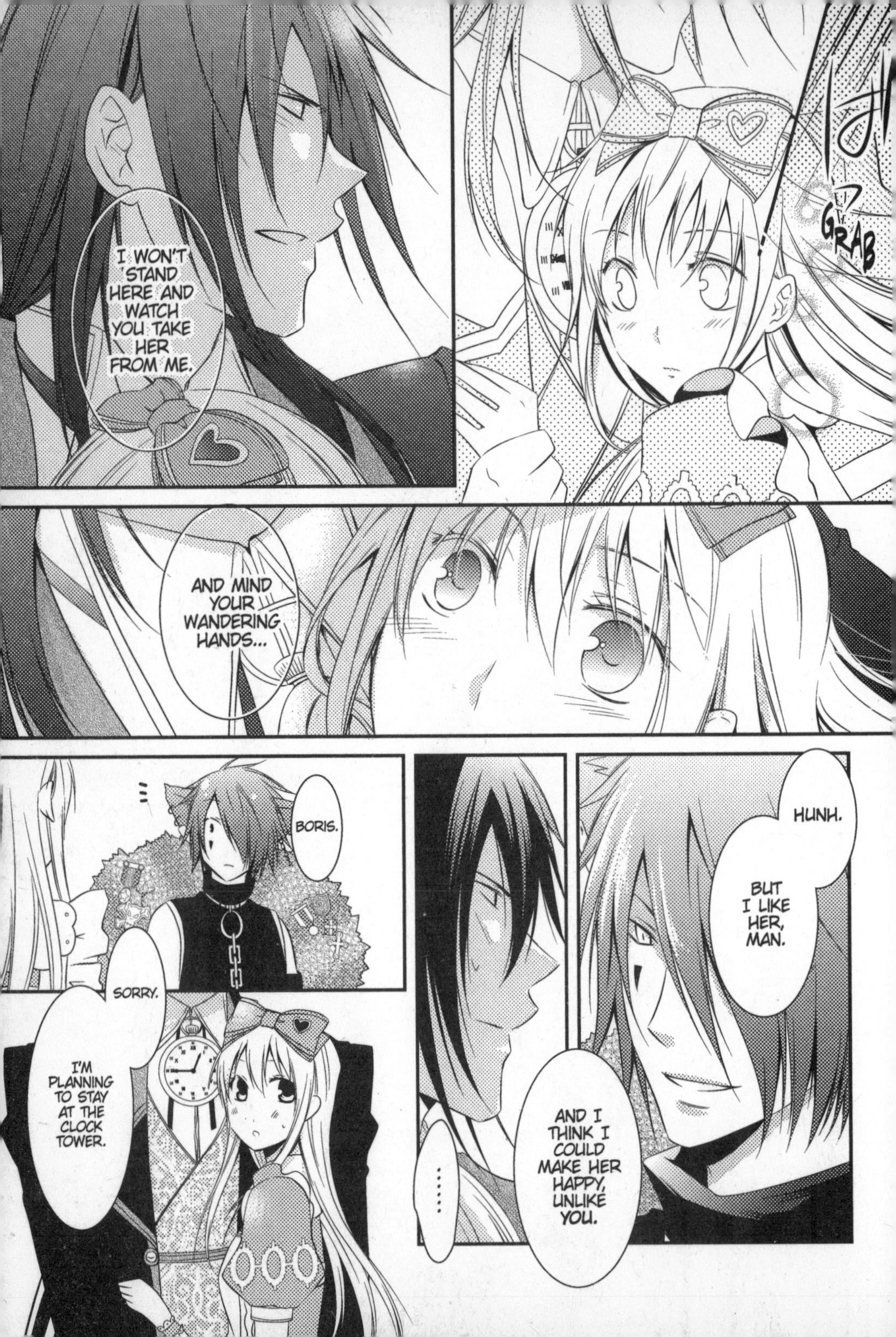
GRAB
I WON'T STAND HERE AND WATCH YOU TAKE HER FROM ME.
AND MIND YOUR WANDERING HANDS...
HUNH.
BUT I LIKE HER, MAN.
AND I THINK I COULD MAKE HER HAPPY, UNLIKE YOU.
......
BORIS.
SORRY.
I'M PLANNING TO STAY AT THE CLOCK TOWER.

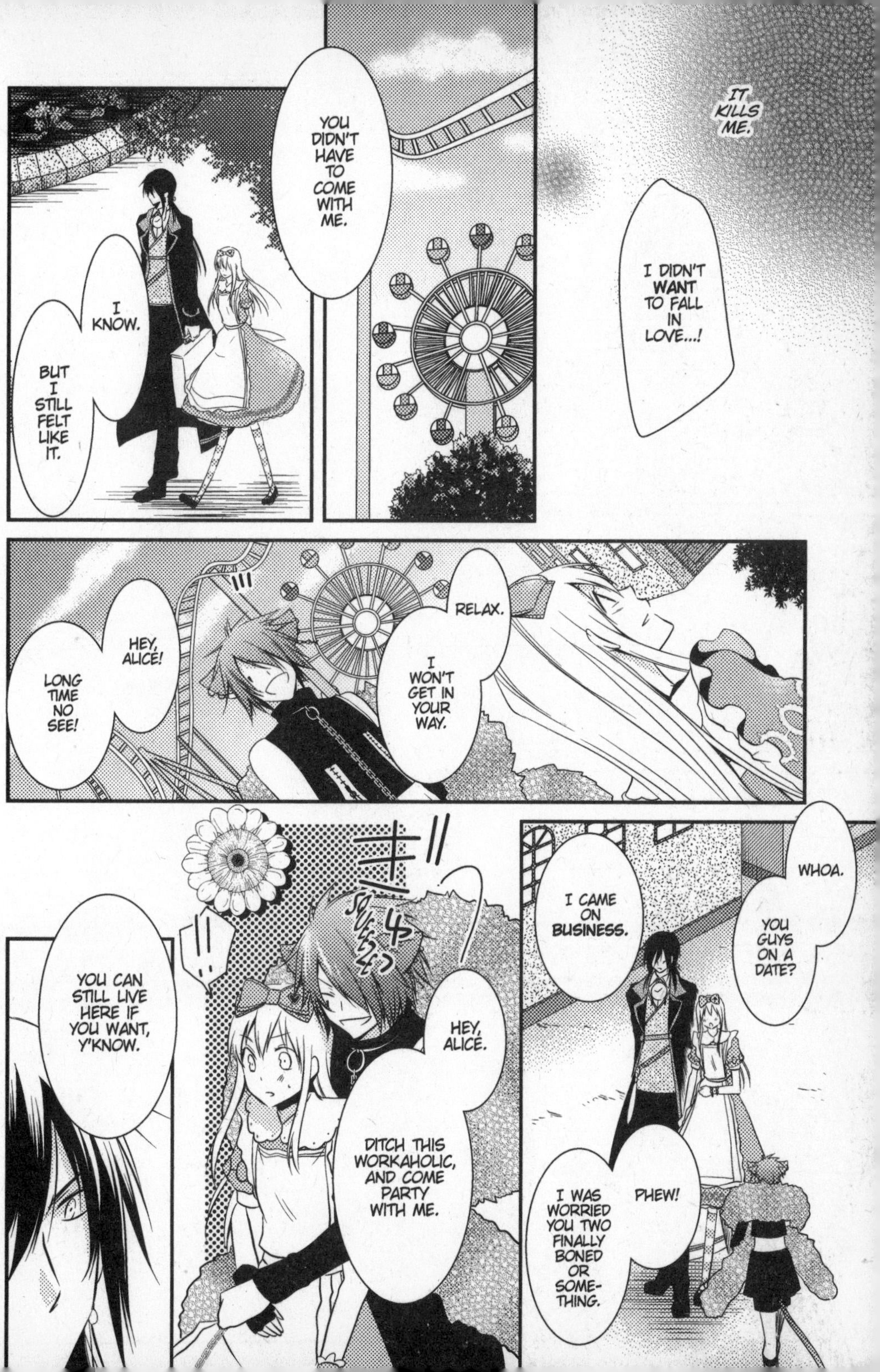
IT KILLS ME.
I DIDN'T WANT TO FALL IN LOVE...!
YOU DIDN'T HAVE TO COME WITH ME.
I KNOW.
BUT I STILL FELT LIKE IT.
RELAX.
I WON'T GET IN YOUR WAY.
HEY, ALICE!
LONG TIME NO SEE!
WHOA.
YOU GUYS ON A DATE?
I CAME ON BUSINESS.
PHEW!
I WAS WORRIED YOU TWO FINALLY BONED OR SOME-THING.
SQUEEZE
HEY, ALICE.
DITCH THIS WORKAHOLIC, AND COME PARTY WITH ME.
YOU CAN STILL LIVE HERE IF YOU WANT, Y'KNOW.

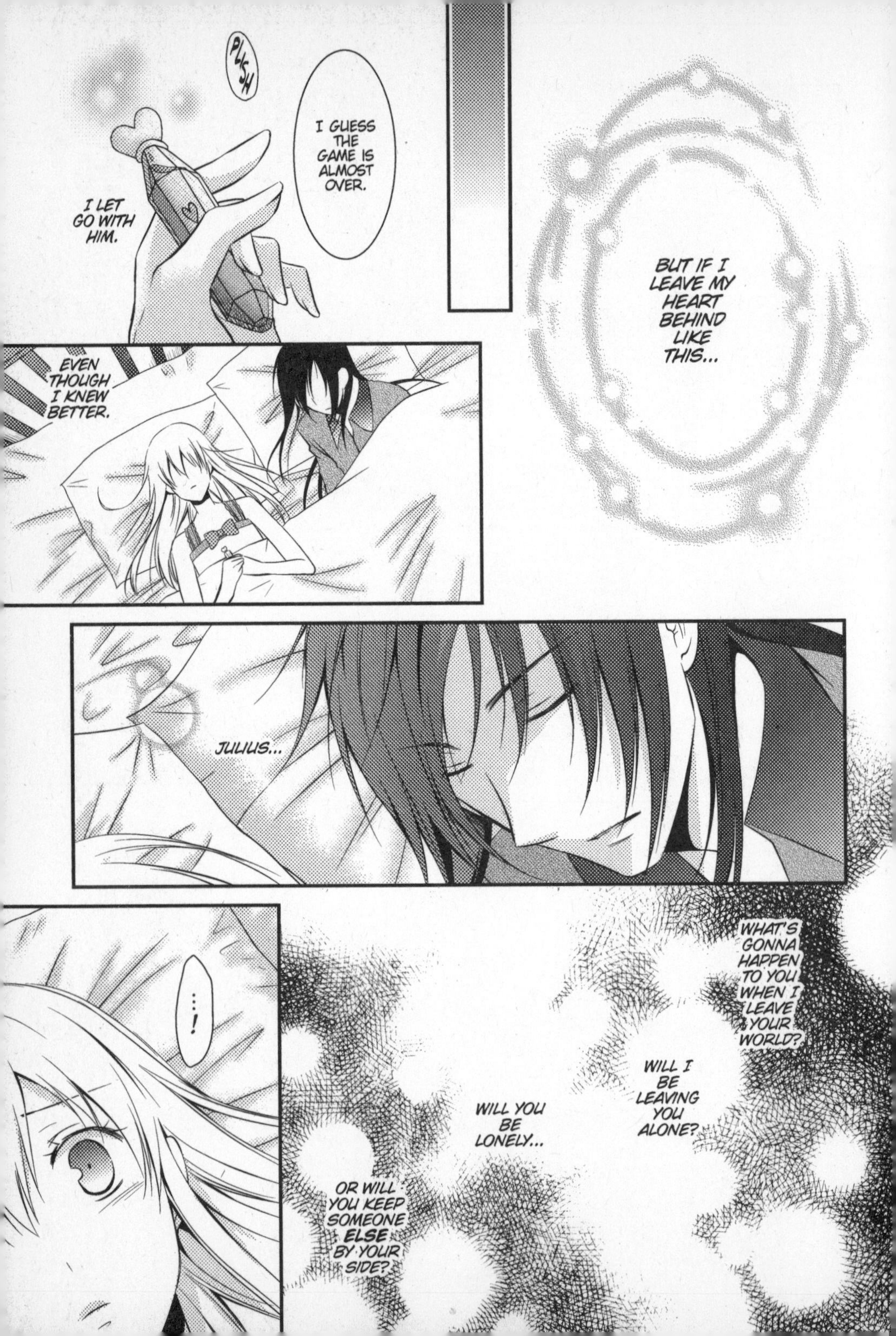
PLISH
I GUESS THE GAME IS ALMOST OVER.
I LET GO WITH HIM.
EVEN THOUGH I KNEW BETTER.
BUT IF I LEAVE MY HEART BEHIND LIKE THIS...
JULIUS...
WHAT'S GONNA HAPPEN TO YOU WHEN I LEAVE YOUR WORLD?
WILL I BE LEAVING YOU ALONE?
WILL YOU BE LONELY...
OR WILL YOU KEEP SOMEONE ELSE BY YOUR SIDE?
...!

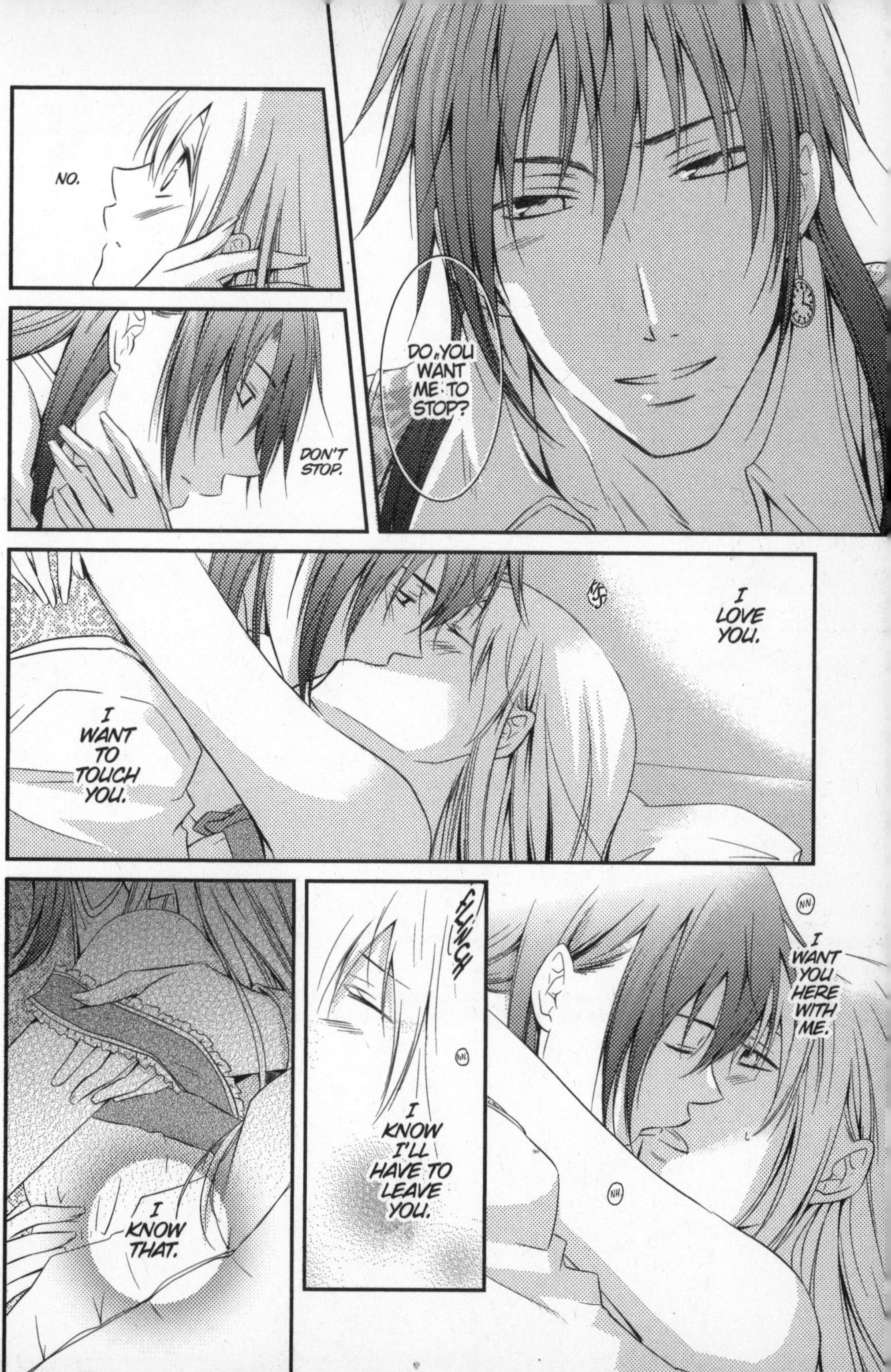
DO YOU WANT ME TO STOP?
NO.
DON'T STOP.
I LOVE YOU.
I WANT TO TOUCH YOU.
NN.
I WANT YOU HERE WITH ME.
FLINCH
NN.
I KNOW I'LL HAVE TO LEAVE YOU.
NH.
I KNOW THAT.

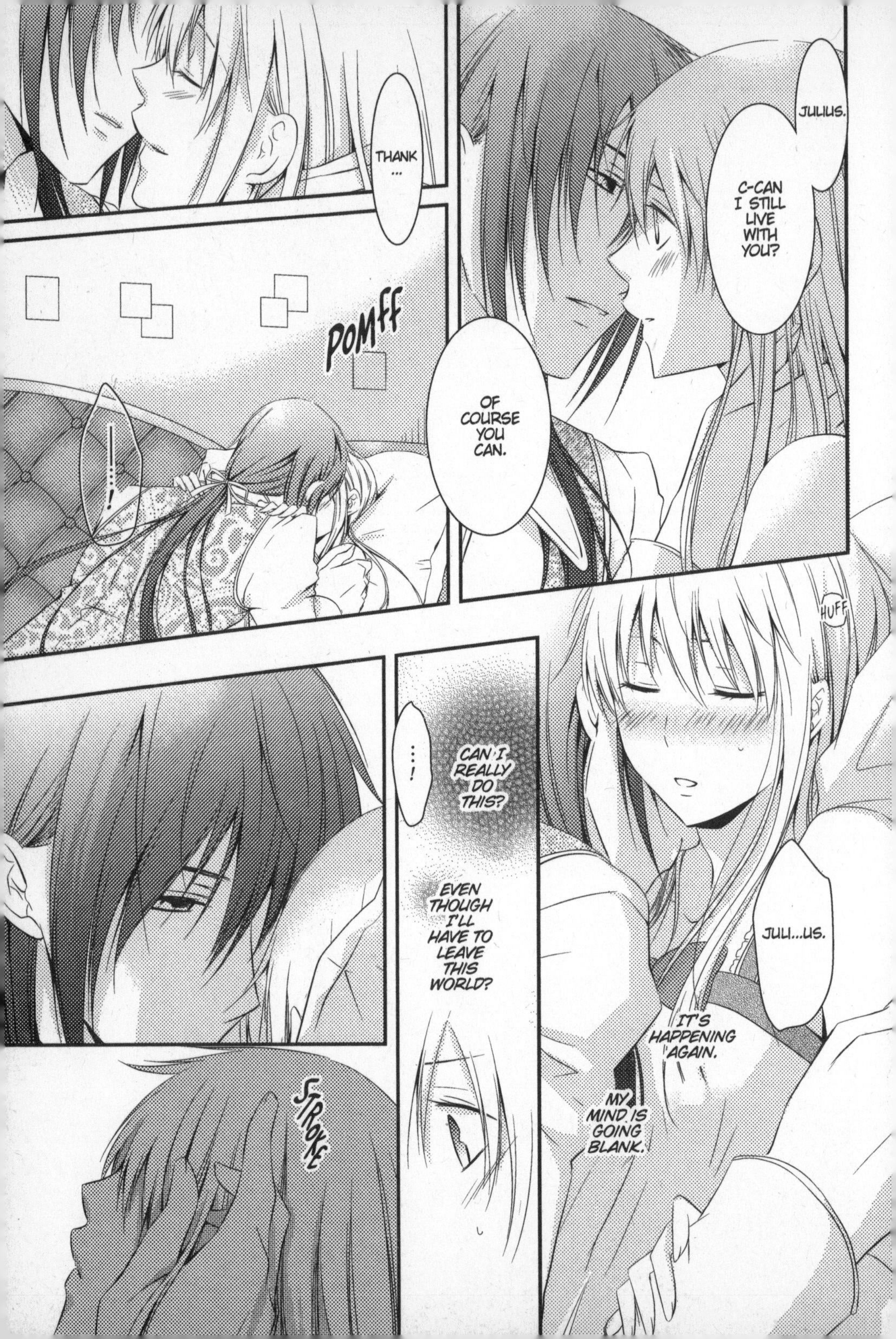
JULIUS.
C-CAN I STILL LIVE WITH YOU?
OF COURSE YOU CAN.
THANK ...
POMFF
......!
HUFF
JULI...US.
IT'S HAPPENING AGAIN.
MY MIND IS GOING BLANK.
...!
CAN I REALLY DO THIS?
EVEN THOUGH I'LL HAVE TO LEAVE THIS WORLD?
STROKE

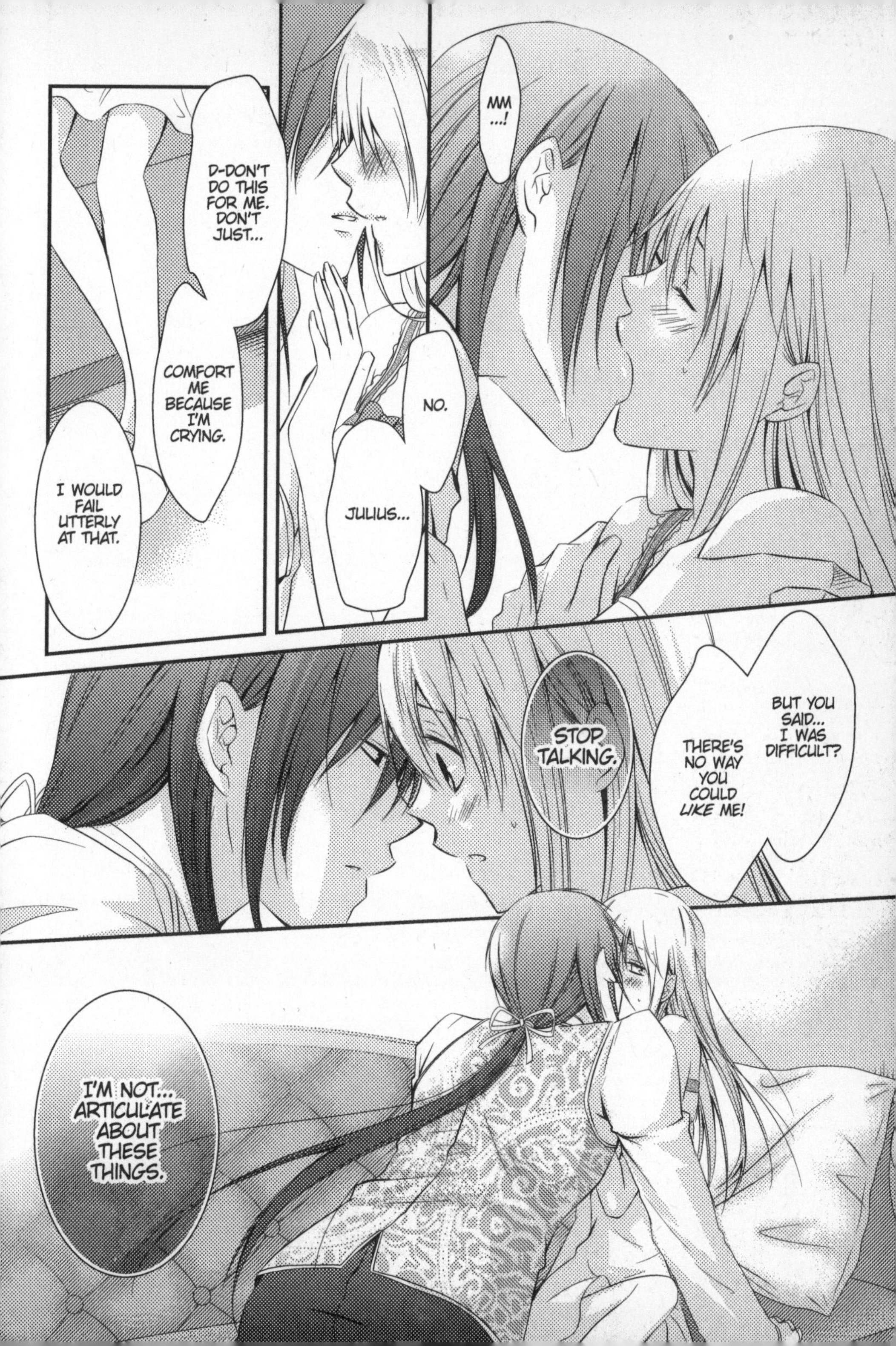
MM ...!
NO.
JULIUS...
D-DON'T DO THIS FOR ME. DON'T JUST...
COMFORT ME BECAUSE I'M CRYING.
I WOULD FAIL UTTERLY AT THAT.
BUT YOU SAID... I WAS DIFFICULT?
THERE'S NO WAY YOU COULD LIKE ME!
STOP TALKING.
I'M NOT... ARTICULATE ABOUT THESE THINGS.

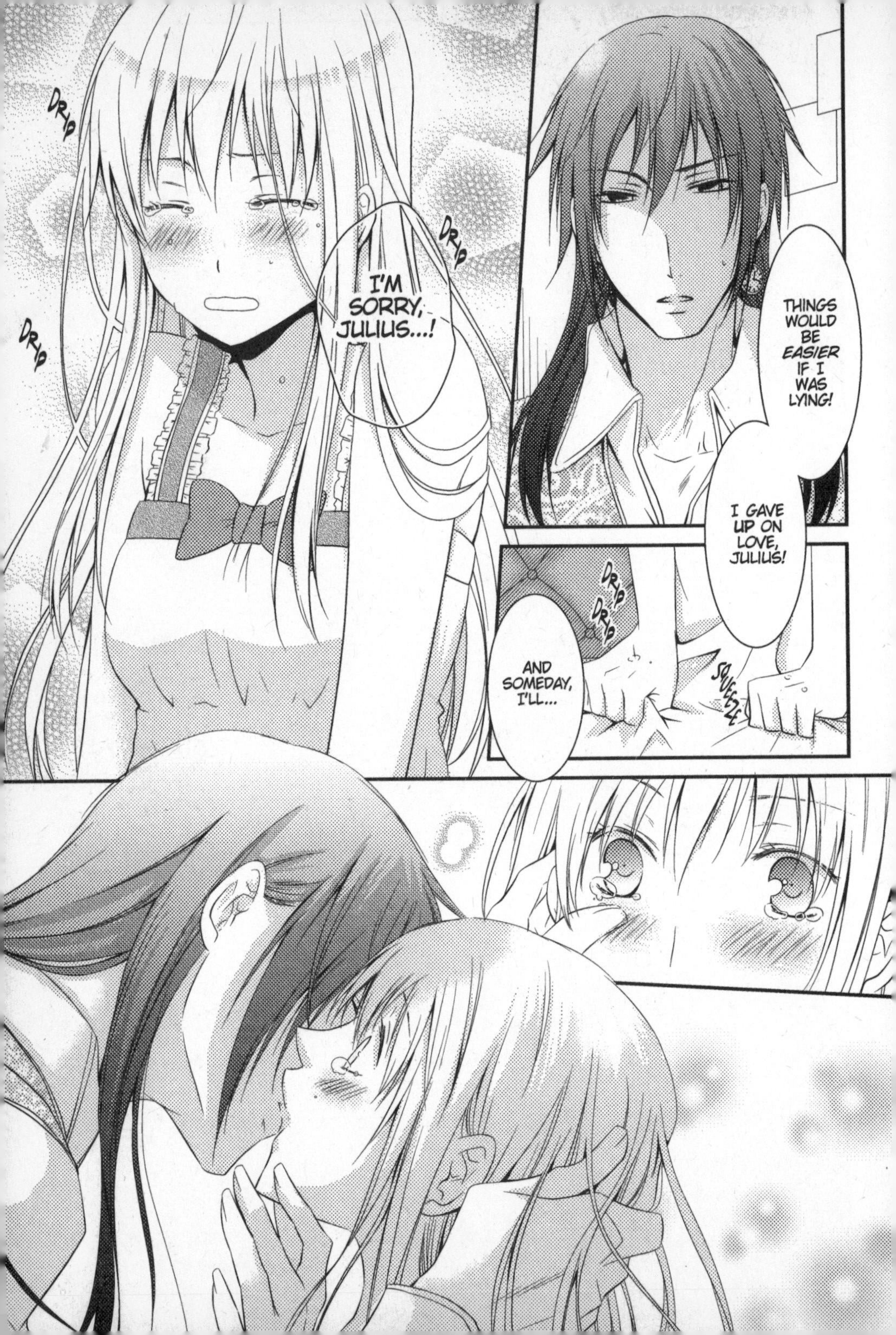
THINGS WOULD BE EASIER IF I WAS LYING!
I GAVE UP ON LOVE, JULIUS!
DRIP DRIP
SQUEEZE
AND SOMEDAY, I'LL...
DRIP
DRIP
DRIP
I'M SORRY, JULIUS...!

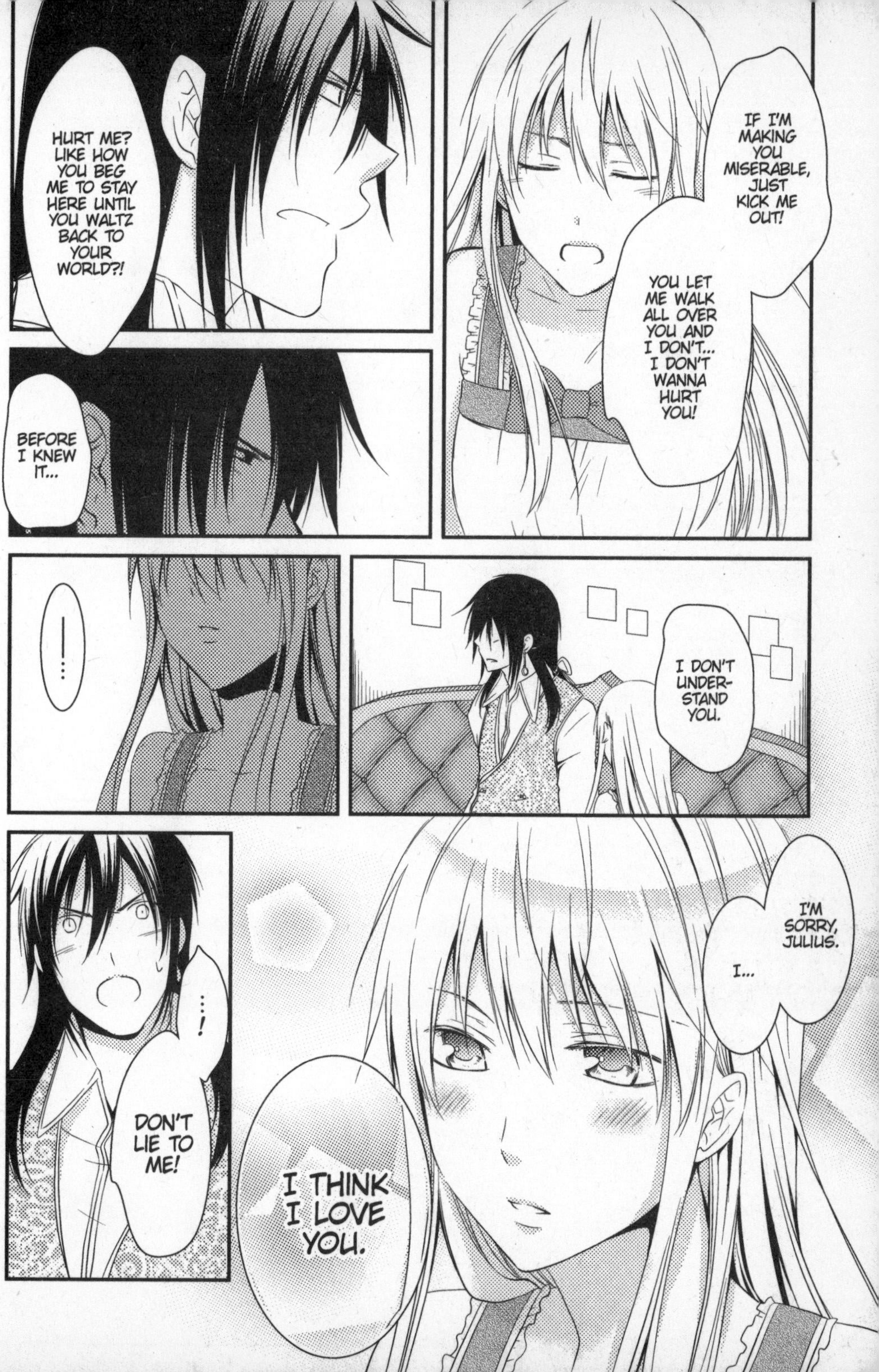
IF I'M MAKING YOU MISERABLE, JUST KICK ME OUT!
YOU LET ME WALK ALL OVER YOU AND I DON'T... I DON'T WANNA HURT YOU!
HURT ME? LIKE HOW YOU BEG ME TO STAY HERE UNTIL YOU WALTZ BACK TO YOUR WORLD?!
BEFORE I KNEW IT...
I DON'T UNDER-STAND YOU.
—!...
I'M SORRY, JULIUS.
I...
I THINK I LOVE YOU.
...!
DON'T LIE TO ME!

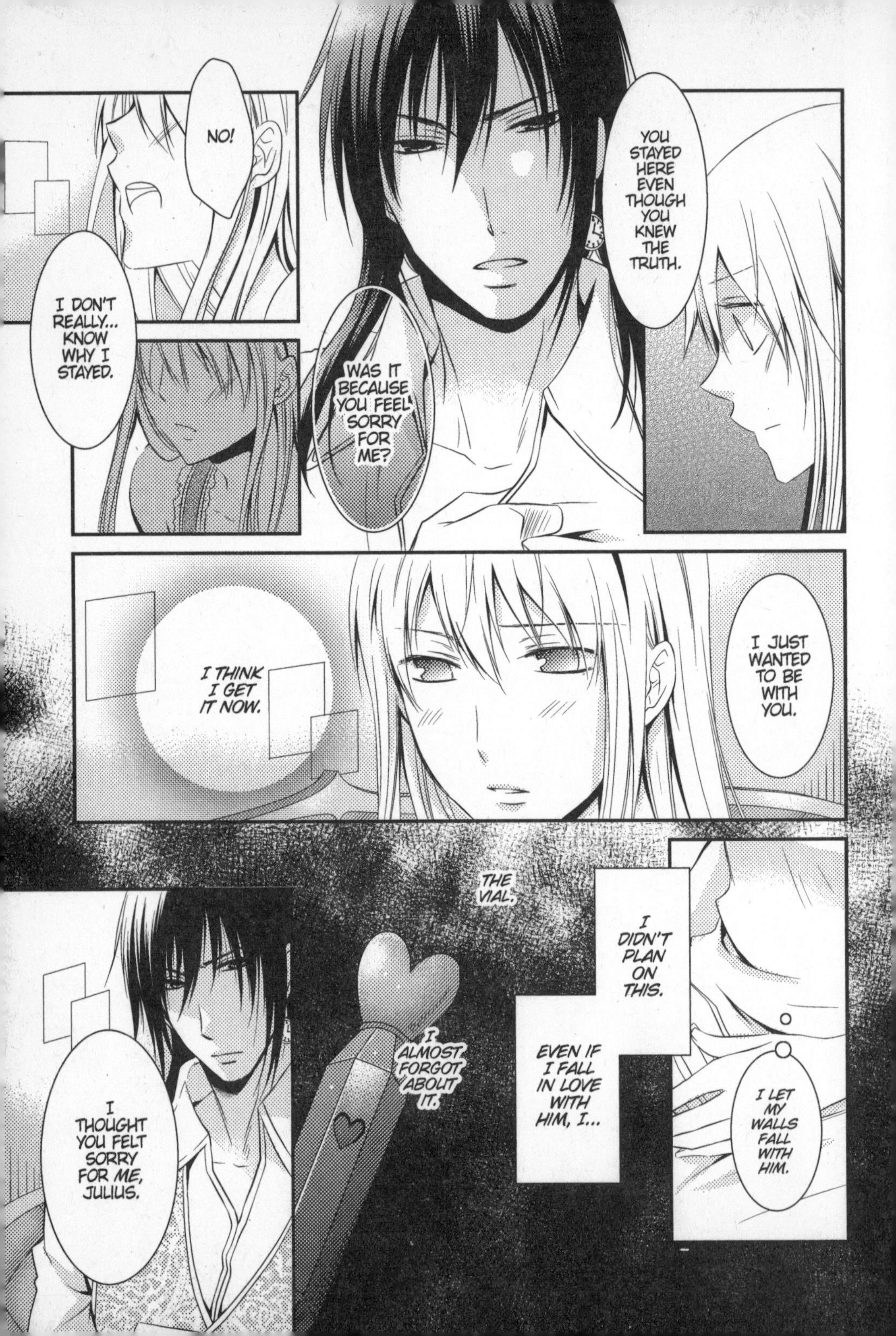
YOU STAYED HERE EVEN THOUGH YOU KNEW THE TRUTH.
WAS IT BECAUSE YOU FEEL SORRY FOR ME?
NO!
I DON'T REALLY... KNOW WHY I STAYED.
I JUST WANTED TO BE WITH YOU.
I THINK I GET IT NOW.
I DIDN'T PLAN ON THIS.
I LET MY WALLS FALL WITH HIM.
EVEN IF I FALL IN LOVE WITH HIM, I...
THE VIAL.
I ALMOST FORGOT ABOUT IT.
I THOUGHT YOU FELT SORRY FOR ME, JULIUS.

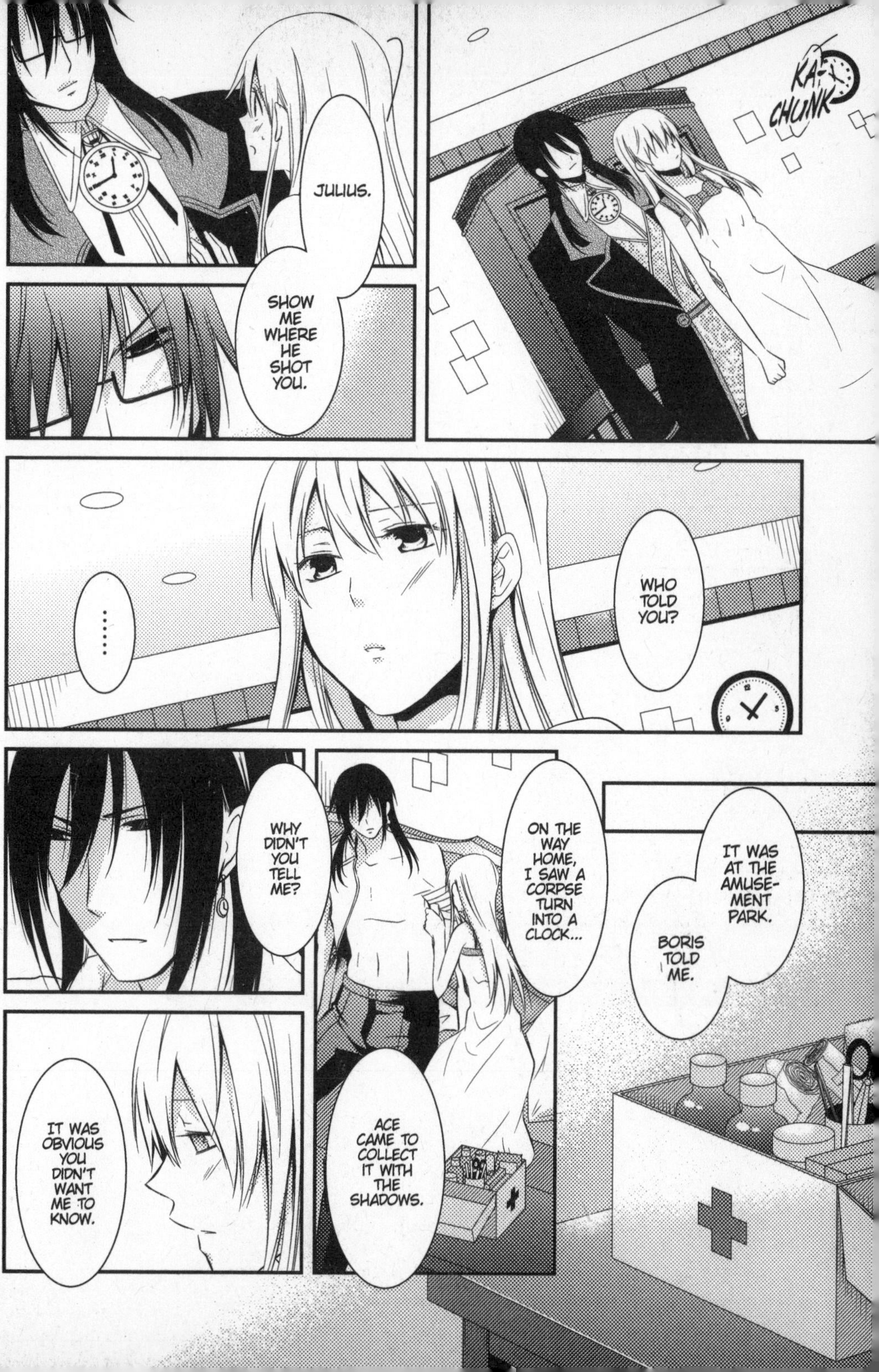
KA-CHUNK
JULIUS.
SHOW ME WHERE HE SHOT YOU.
WHO TOLD YOU?
......
IT WAS AT THE AMUSEMENT PARK.
BORIS TOLD ME.
ON THE WAY HOME, I SAW A CORPSE TURN INTO A CLOCK...
WHY DIDN'T YOU TELL ME?
ACE CAME TO COLLECT IT WITH THE SHADOWS.
IT WAS OBVIOUS YOU DIDN'T WANT ME TO KNOW.

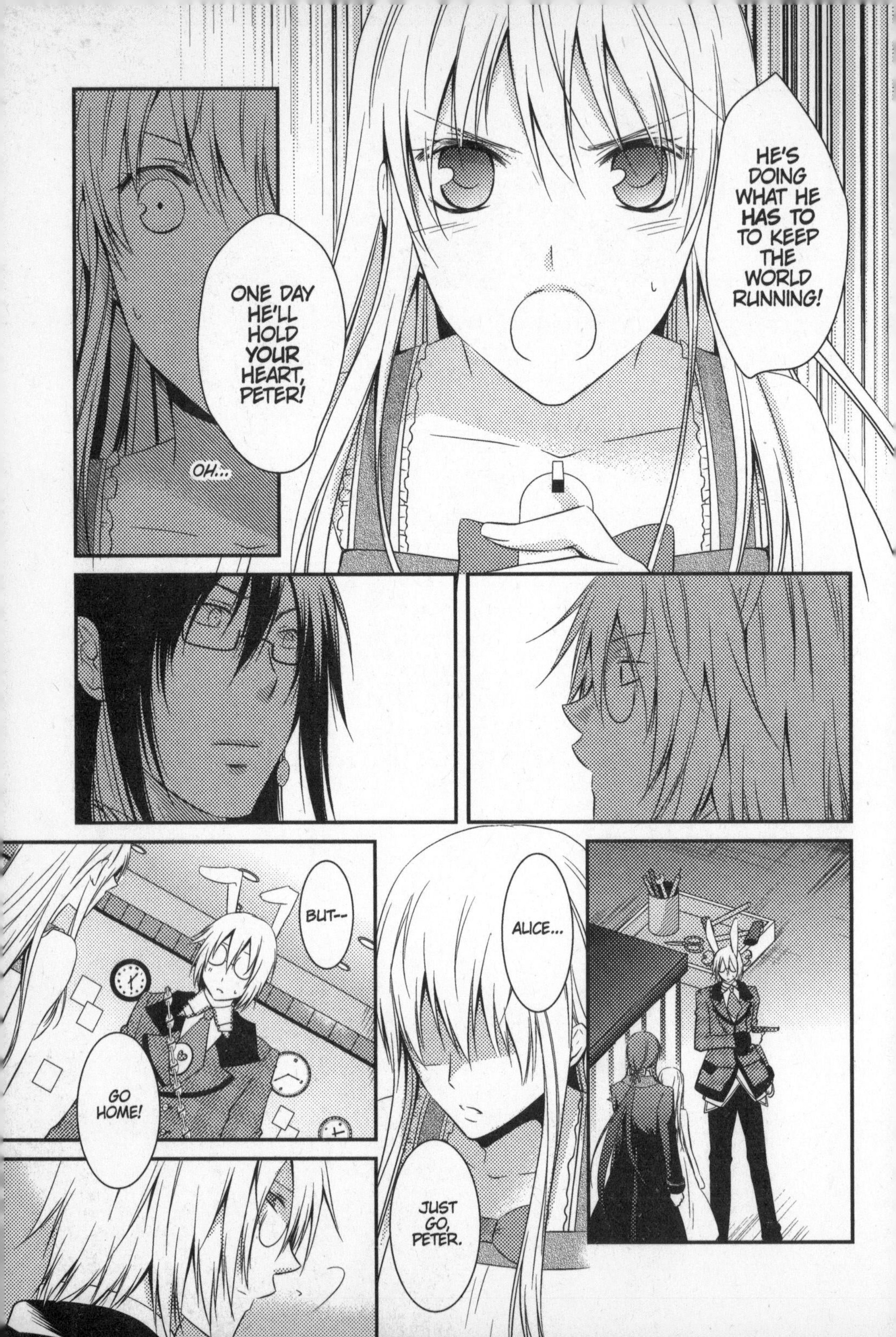
HE'S DOING WHAT HE HAS TO TO KEEP THE WORLD RUNNING!
ONE DAY HE'LL HOLD YOUR HEART, PETER!
OH...
ALICE...
JUST GO, PETER.
BUT--
GO HOME!

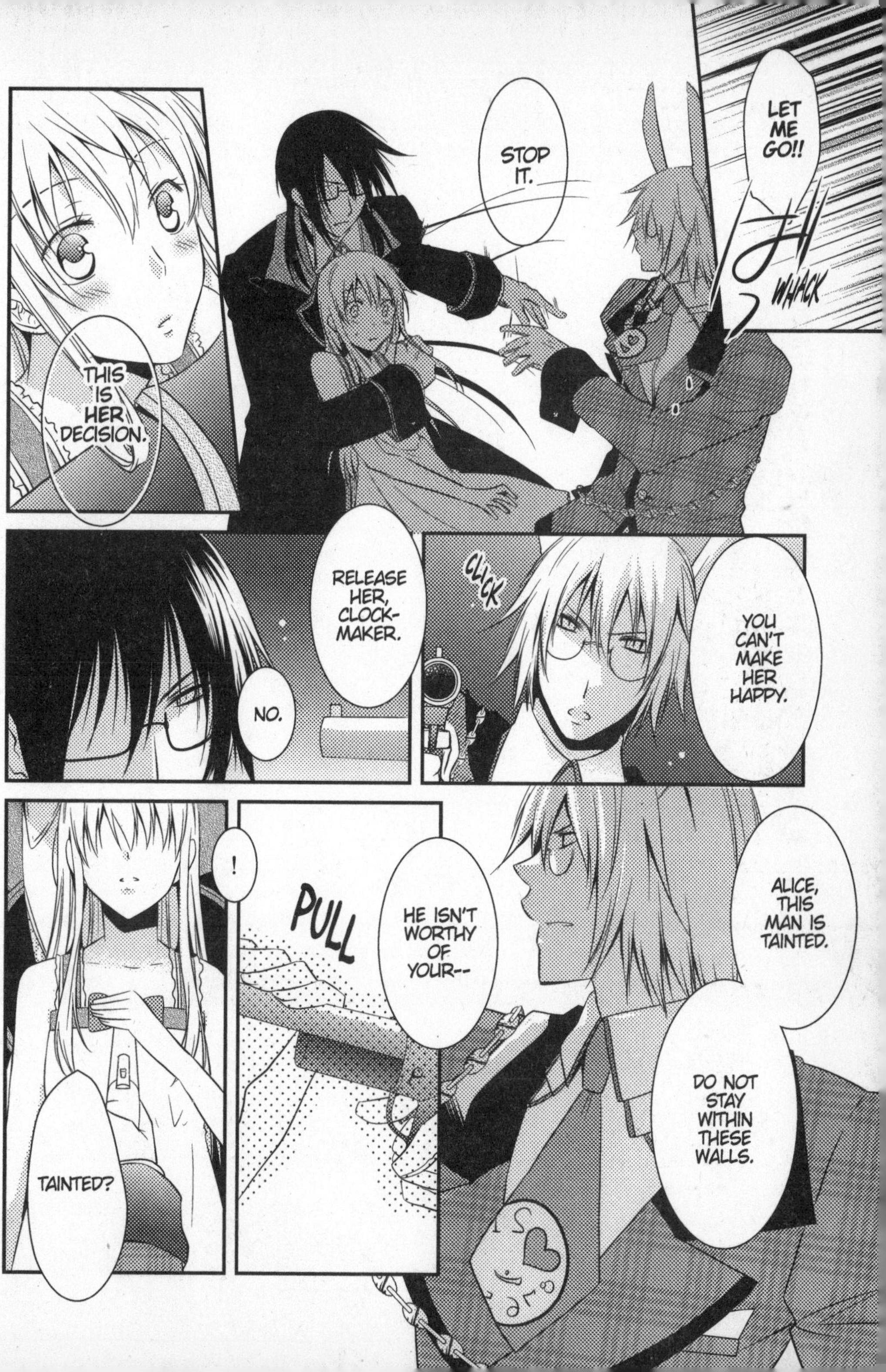
LET ME GO!!
WHACK
STOP IT.
THIS IS HER DECISION.
CLICK
YOU CAN'T MAKE HER HAPPY.
RELEASE HER, CLOCK-MAKER.
NO.
ALICE, THIS MAN IS TAINTED.
DO NOT STAY WITHIN THESE WALLS.
HE ISN'T WORTHY OF YOUR--
PULL
!
TAINTED?

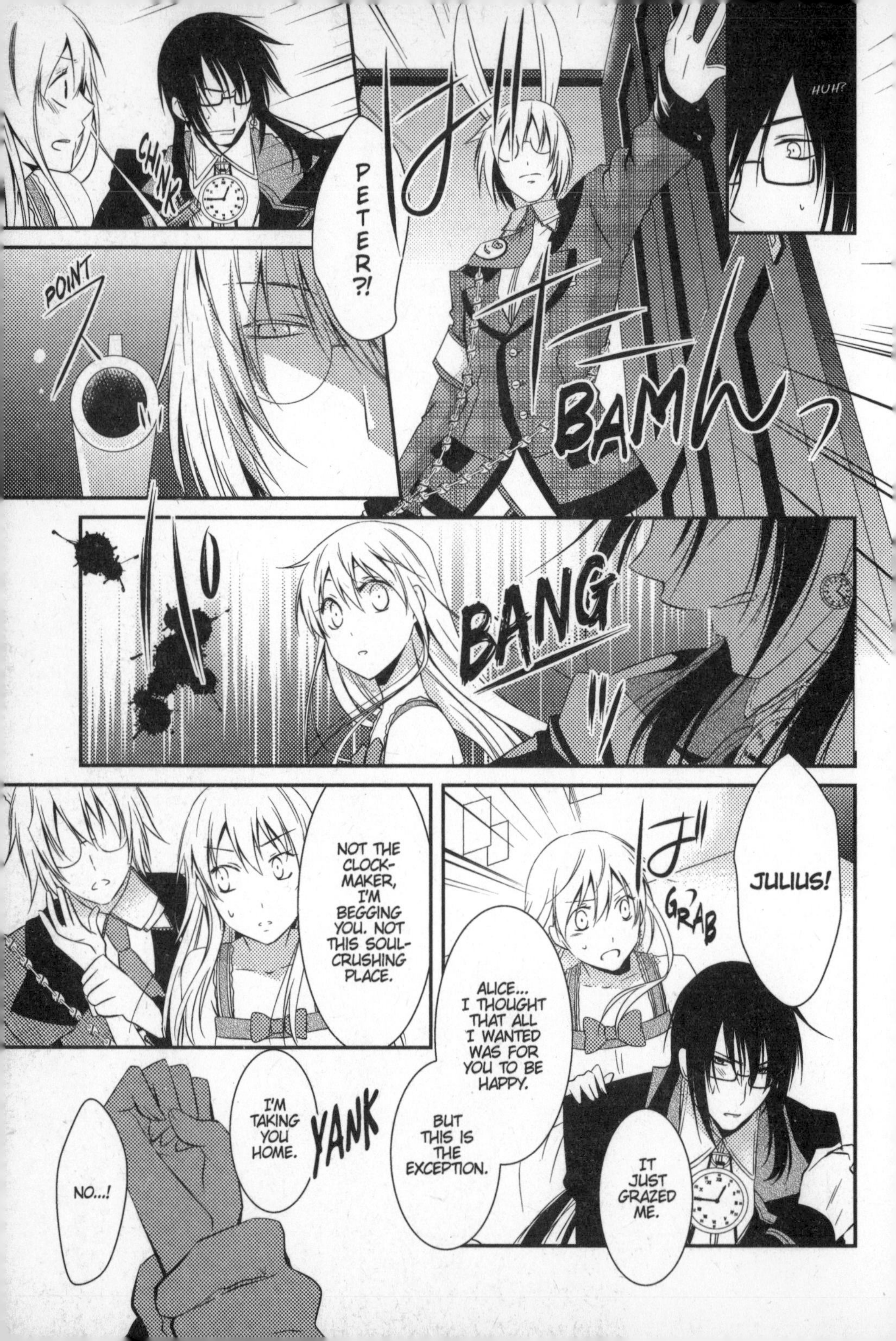
HUH?
PETER?!
CHINK
POINT
BAMh
BANG
JULIUS!
GRAB
IT JUST GRAZED ME.
NOT THE CLOCK-MAKER, I'M BEGGING YOU. NOT THIS SOUL-CRUSHING PLACE.
ALICE... I THOUGHT THAT ALL I WANTED WAS FOR YOU TO BE HAPPY.
BUT THIS IS THE EXCEPTION.
I'M TAKING YOU HOME.
YANK
NO...!

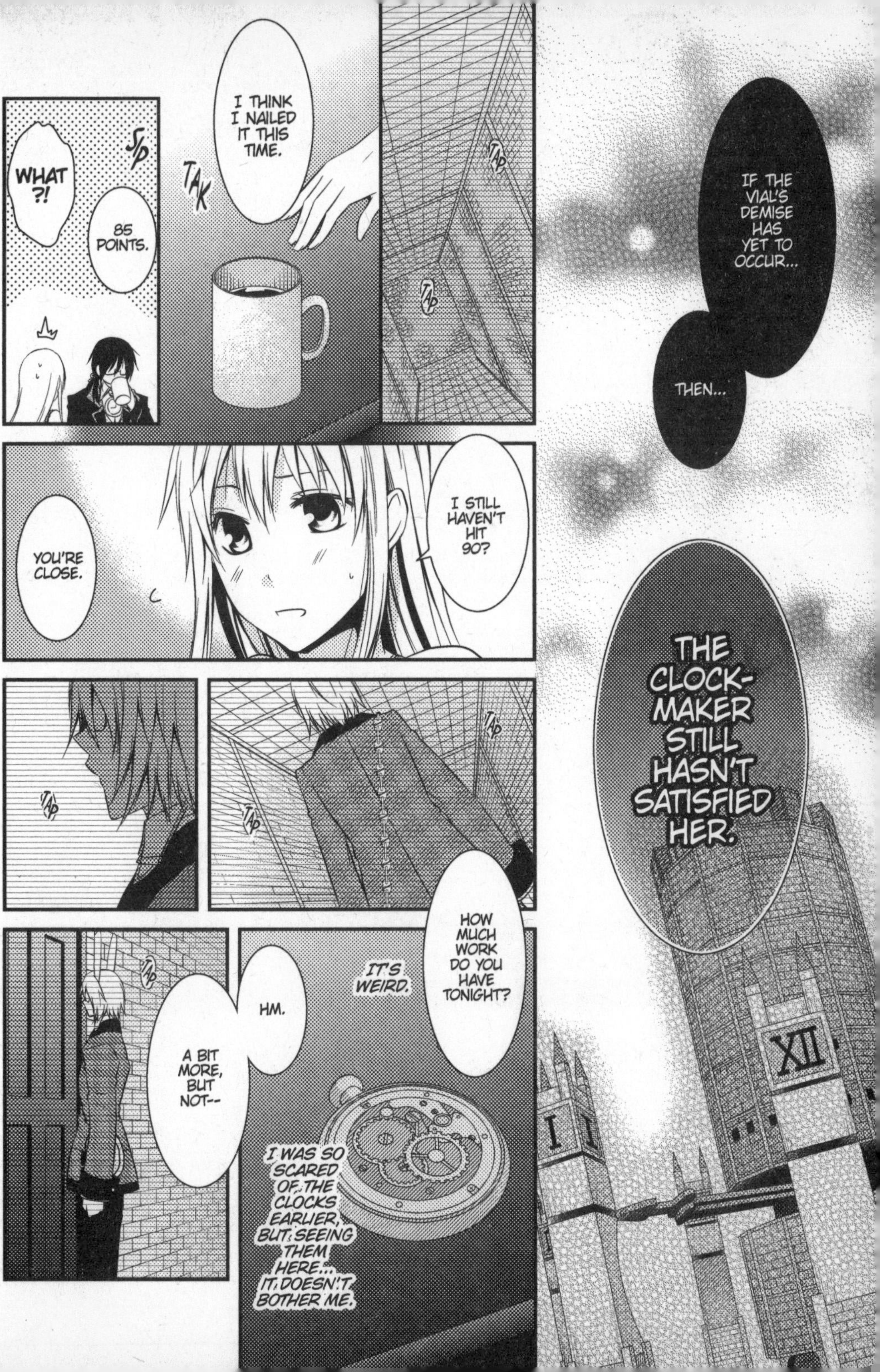
IF THE VIAL'S DEMISE HAS YET TO OCCUR...
THEN...
THE CLOCK-MAKER STILL HASN'T SATISFIED HER.
TAP
TAP
I THINK I NAILED IT THIS TIME.
TAK
SIP
85 POINTS.
WHAT ?!
I STILL HAVEN'T HIT 90?
YOU'RE CLOSE.
TAP
TAP
TAP
HOW MUCH WORK DO YOU HAVE TONIGHT?
IT'S WEIRD.
HM.
A BIT MORE, BUT NOT--
I WAS SO SCARED OF THE CLOCKS EARLIER, BUT SEEING THEM HERE... IT DOESN'T BOTHER ME.
TAP

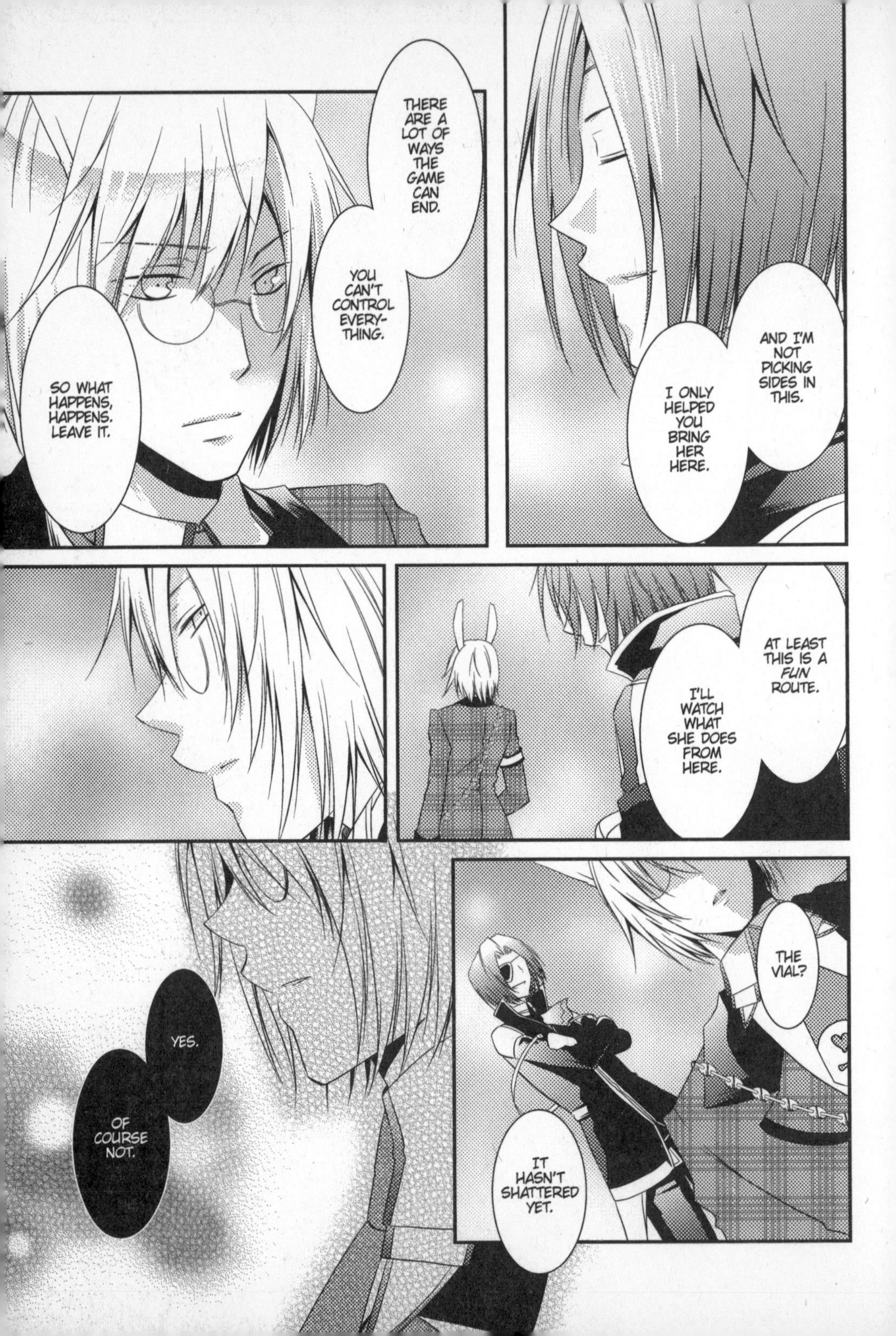
AND I'M NOT PICKING SIDES IN THIS.
I ONLY HELPED YOU BRING HER HERE.
THERE ARE A LOT OF WAYS THE GAME CAN END.
YOU CAN'T CONTROL EVERY-THING.
SO WHAT HAPPENS, HAPPENS. LEAVE IT.
AT LEAST THIS IS A *FUN* ROUTE.
I'LL WATCH WHAT SHE DOES FROM HERE.
THE VIAL?
IT HASN'T SHATTERED YET.
YES.
OF COURSE NOT.

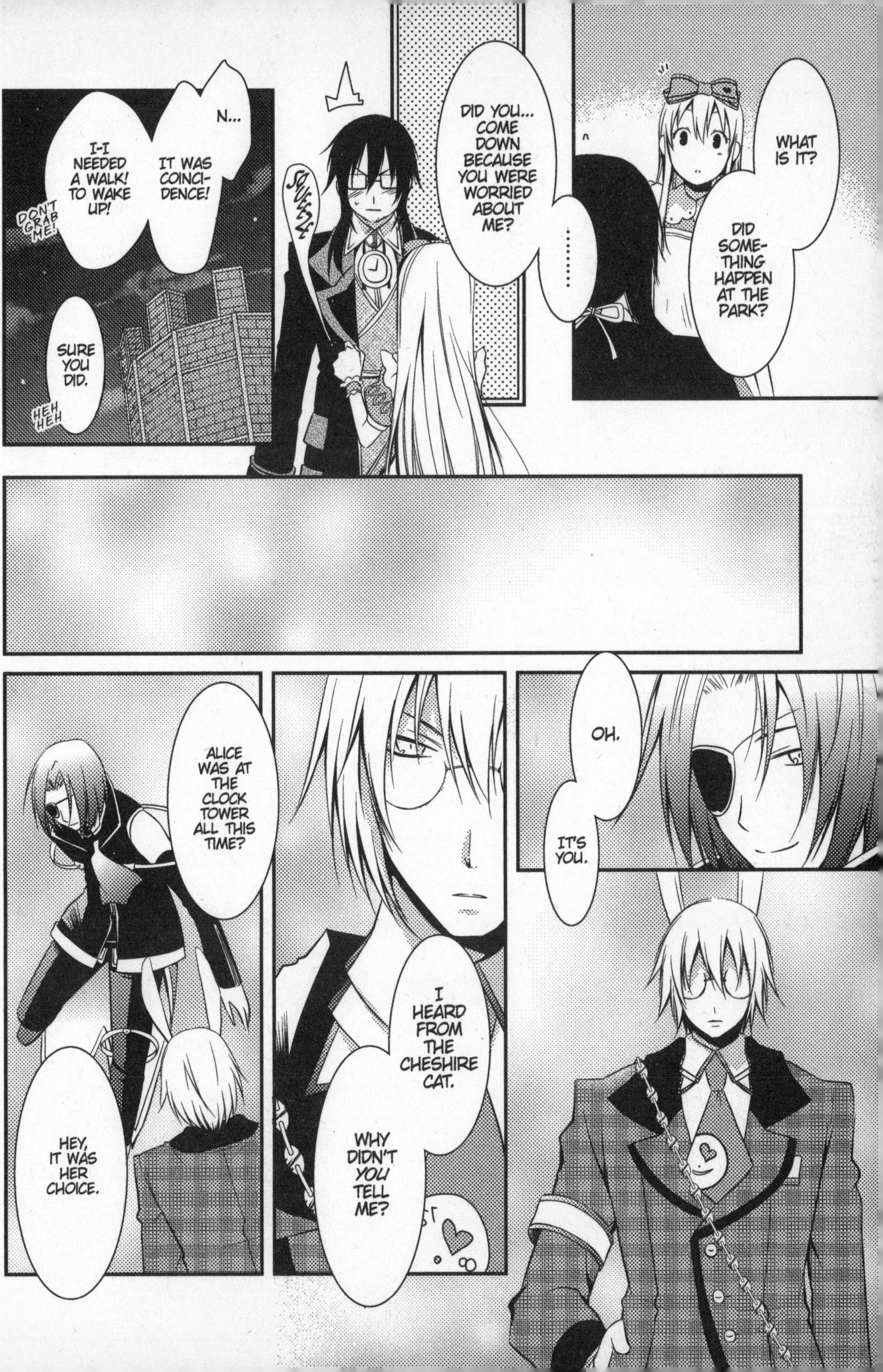
WHAT IS IT?
DID SOMETHING HAPPEN AT THE PARK?
......
DID YOU... COME DOWN BECAUSE YOU WERE WORRIED ABOUT ME?
SQUEEZE
N...
IT WAS COINCIDENCE!
I-I NEEDED A WALK! TO WAKE UP!
DON'T GRAB ME!
SURE YOU DID.
HEH HEH
OH.
IT'S YOU.
I HEARD FROM THE CHESHIRE CAT.
WHY DIDN'T YOU TELL ME?
ALICE WAS AT THE CLOCK TOWER ALL THIS TIME?
HEY, IT WAS HER CHOICE.

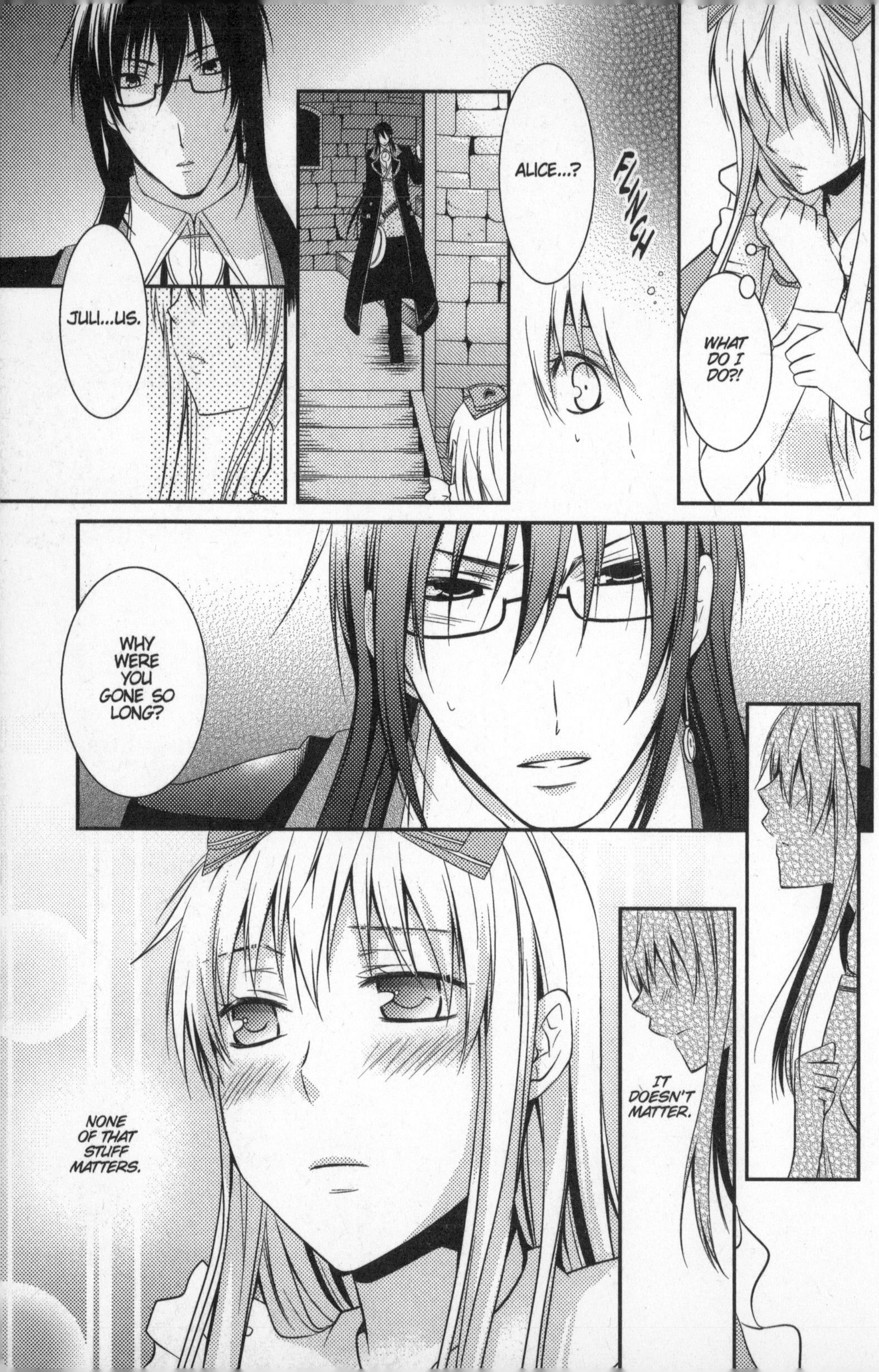
WHAT DO I DO?!
ALICE...?
FLINCH
JULI...US.
WHY WERE YOU GONE SO LONG?
IT DOESN'T MATTER.
NONE OF THAT STUFF MATTERS.

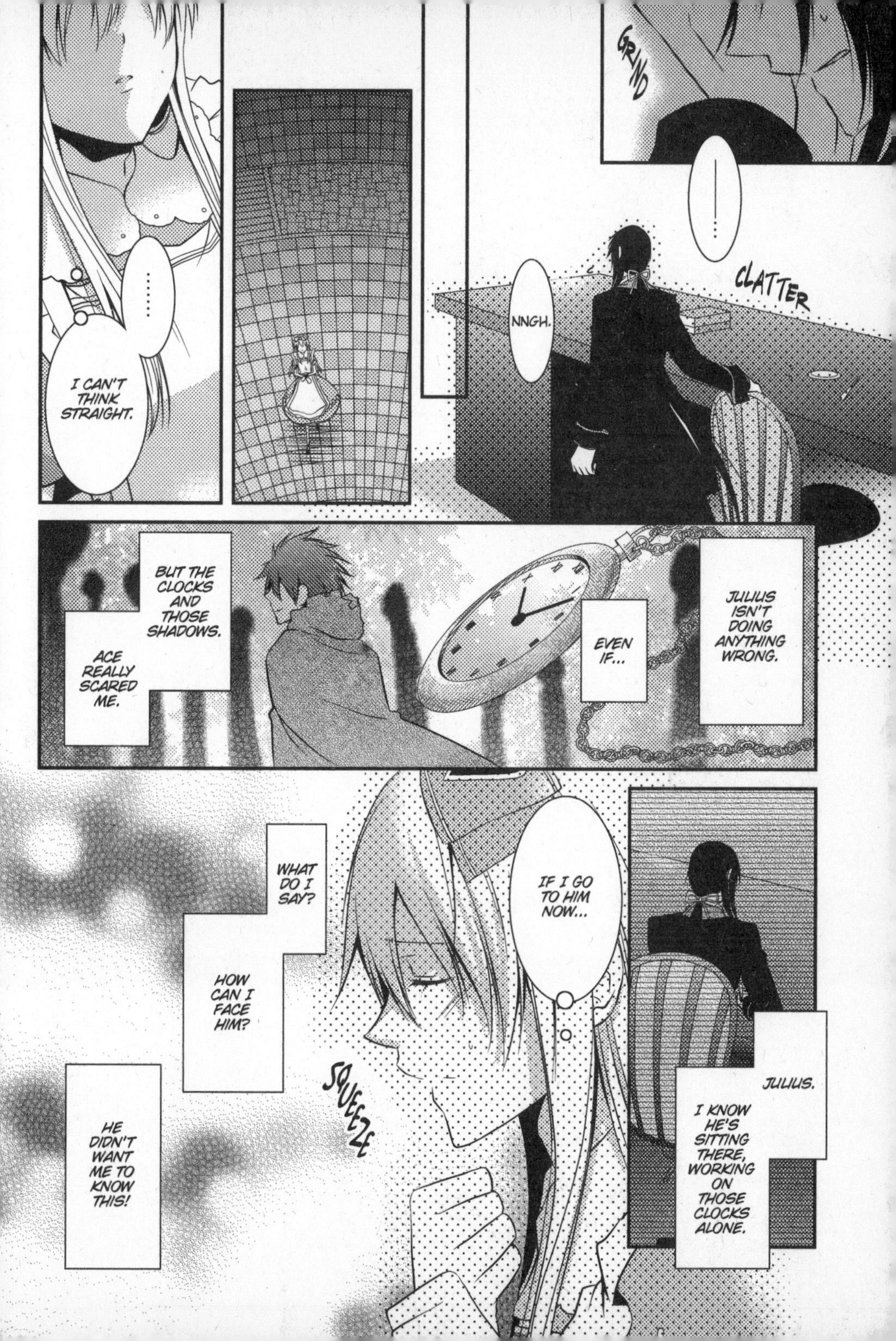
GRIND
......
CLATTER
NNGH.
......
I CAN'T THINK STRAIGHT.
JULIUS ISN'T DOING ANYTHING WRONG.
EVEN IF...
BUT THE CLOCKS AND THOSE SHADOWS.
ACE REALLY SCARED ME.
JULIUS.
I KNOW HE'S SITTING THERE, WORKING ON THOSE CLOCKS ALONE.
IF I GO TO HIM NOW...
WHAT DO I SAY?
HOW CAN I FACE HIM?
SQUEEZE
HE DIDN'T WANT ME TO KNOW THIS!

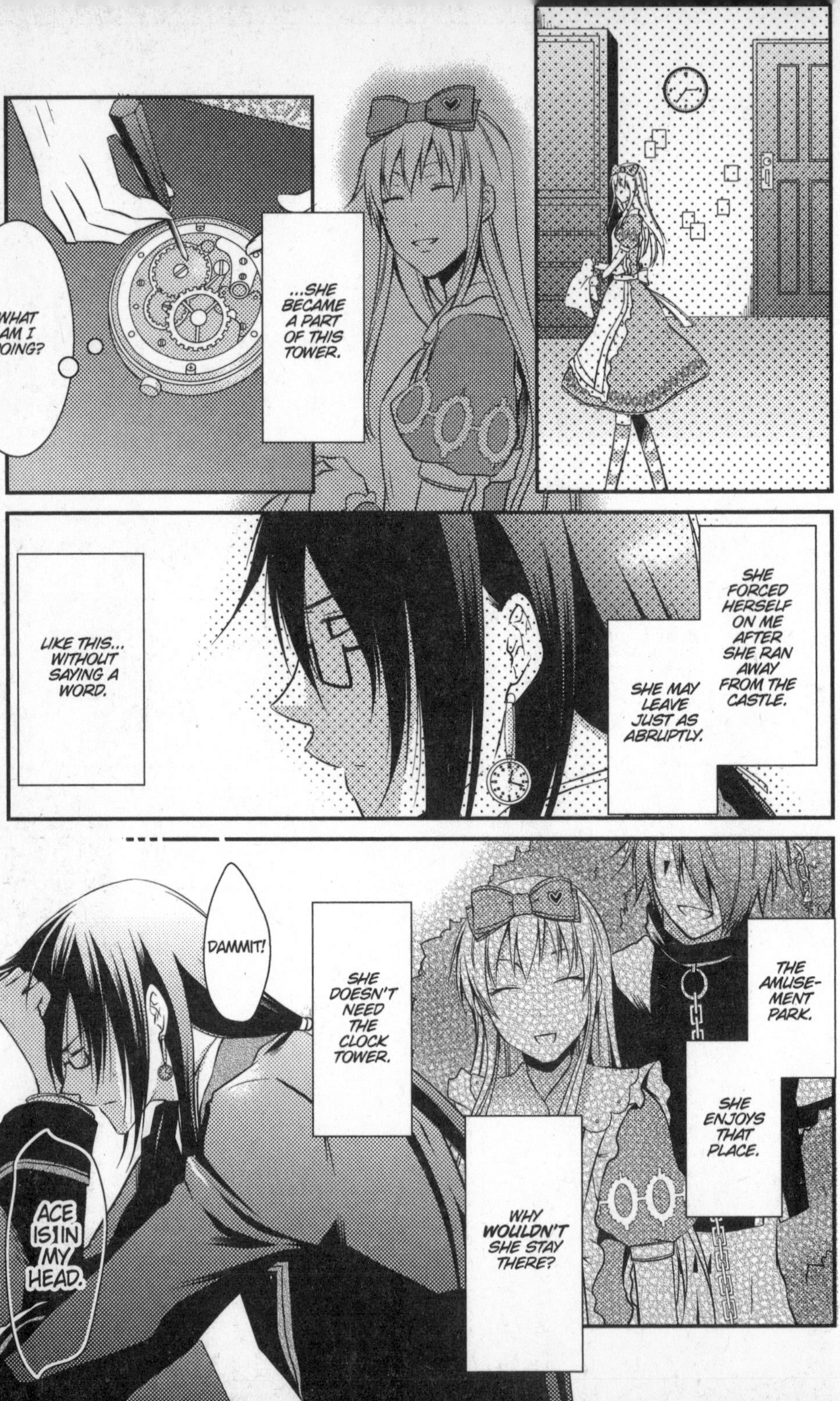
...SHE BECAME A PART OF THIS TOWER.
WHAT AM I DOING?
SHE FORCED HERSELF ON ME AFTER SHE RAN AWAY FROM THE CASTLE.
SHE MAY LEAVE JUST AS ABRUPTLY.
LIKE THIS... WITHOUT SAYING A WORD.
THE AMUSEMENT PARK.
SHE ENJOYS THAT PLACE.
WHY WOULDN'T SHE STAY THERE?
SHE DOESN'T NEED THE CLOCK TOWER.
DAMMIT!
ACE IS IN MY HEAD.

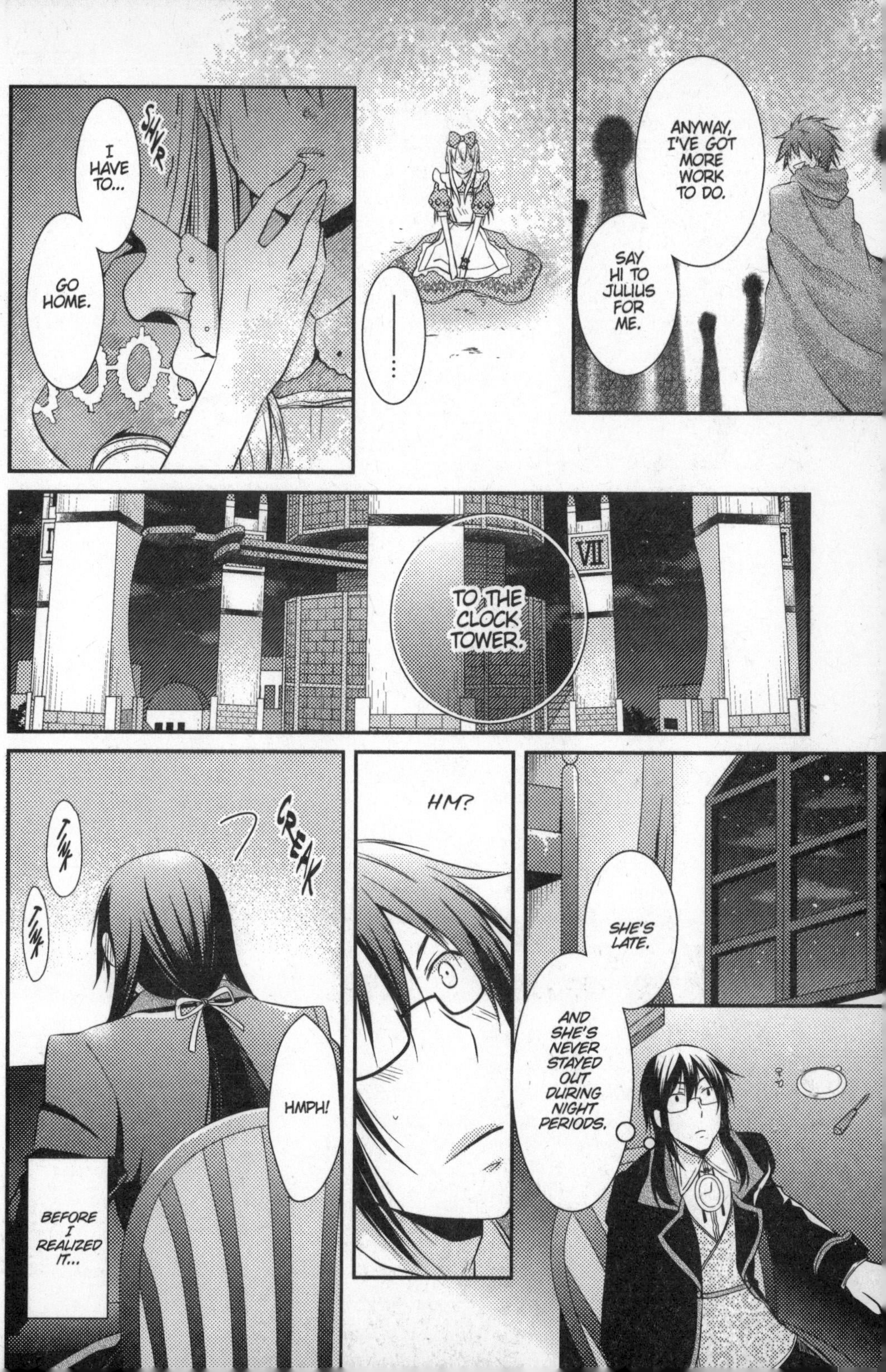
ANYWAY, I'VE GOT MORE WORK TO DO.
SAY HI TO JULIUS FOR ME.
—!…
SHVR
I HAVE TO...
GO HOME.
TO THE CLOCK TOWER.
SHE'S LATE.
AND SHE'S NEVER STAYED OUT DURING NIGHT PERIODS.
HM?
CREAK
TINK
TINK
HMPH!
BEFORE I REALIZED IT...

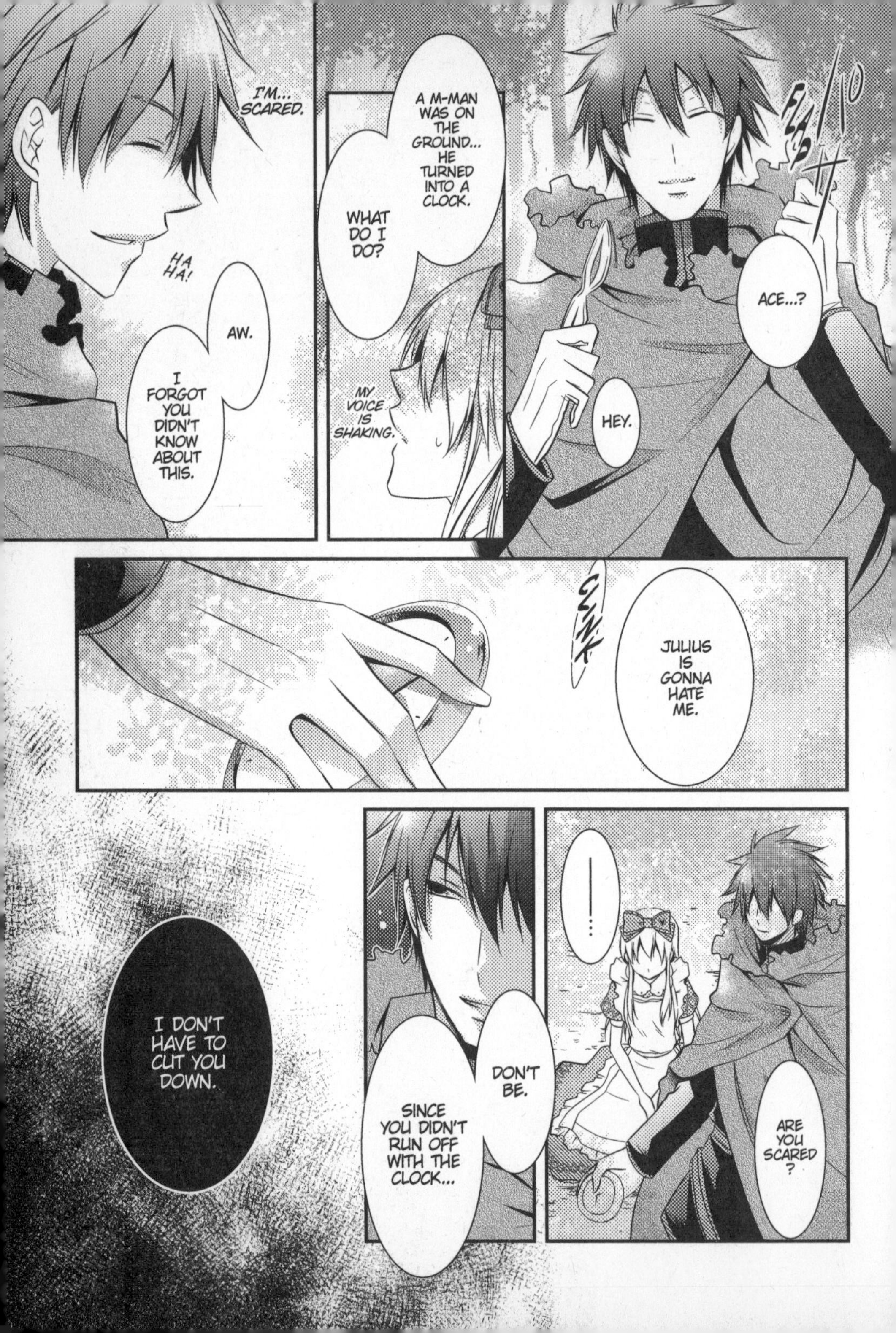
FLAP
ACE...?
HEY.
A M-MAN WAS ON THE GROUND... HE TURNED INTO A CLOCK.
WHAT DO I DO?
MY VOICE IS SHAKING.
I'M... SCARED.
HA HA!
AW.
I FORGOT YOU DIDN'T KNOW ABOUT THIS.
CLINK
JULIUS IS GONNA HATE ME.
...!
ARE YOU SCARED?
DON'T BE.
SINCE YOU DIDN'T RUN OFF WITH THE CLOCK...
I DON'T HAVE TO CUT YOU DOWN.

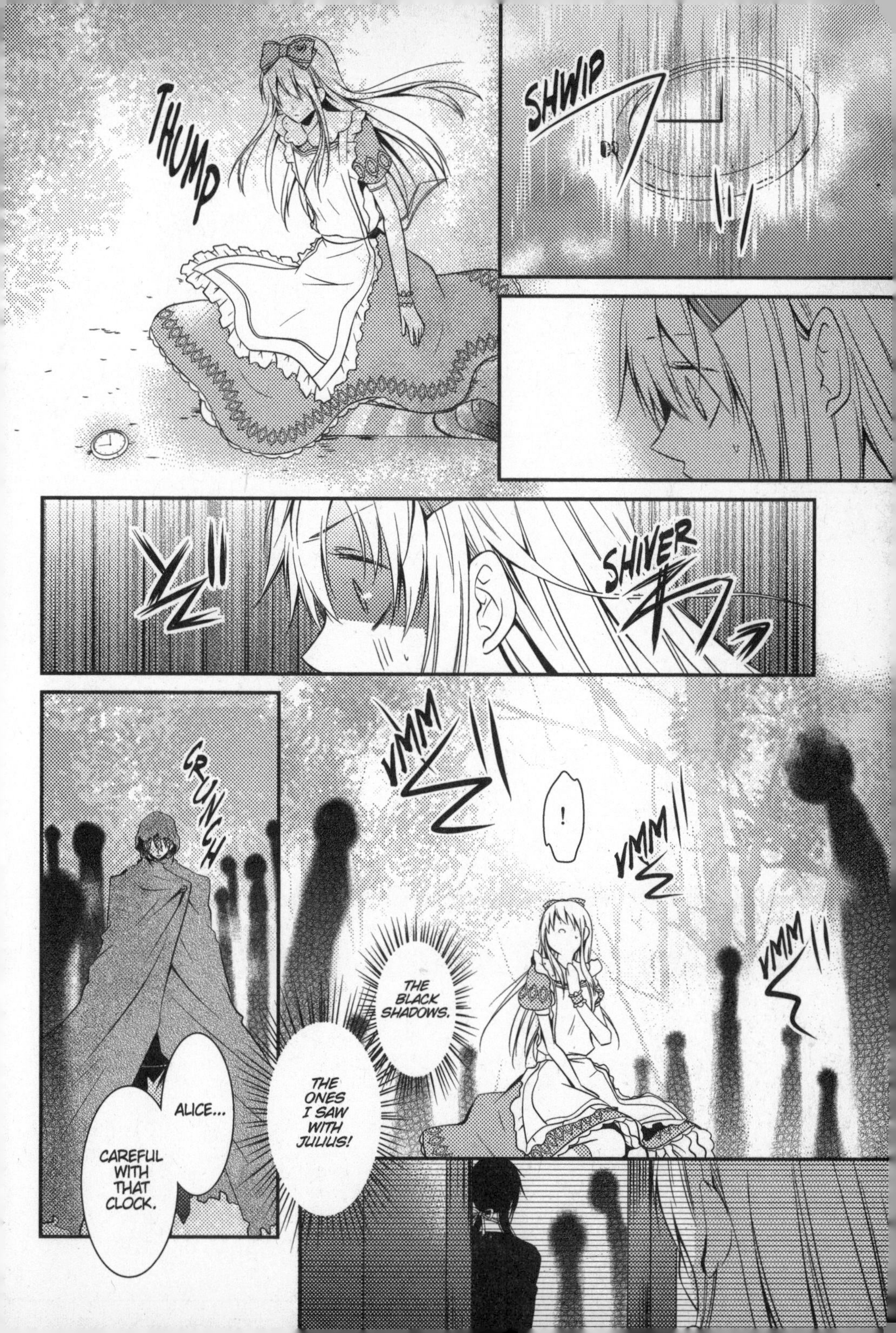
SHWIP
THUMP
SHIVER
VMM
!
VMM
VMM
THE BLACK SHADOWS.
THE ONES I SAW WITH JULIUS!
CRUNCH
ALICE...
CAREFUL WITH THAT CLOCK.

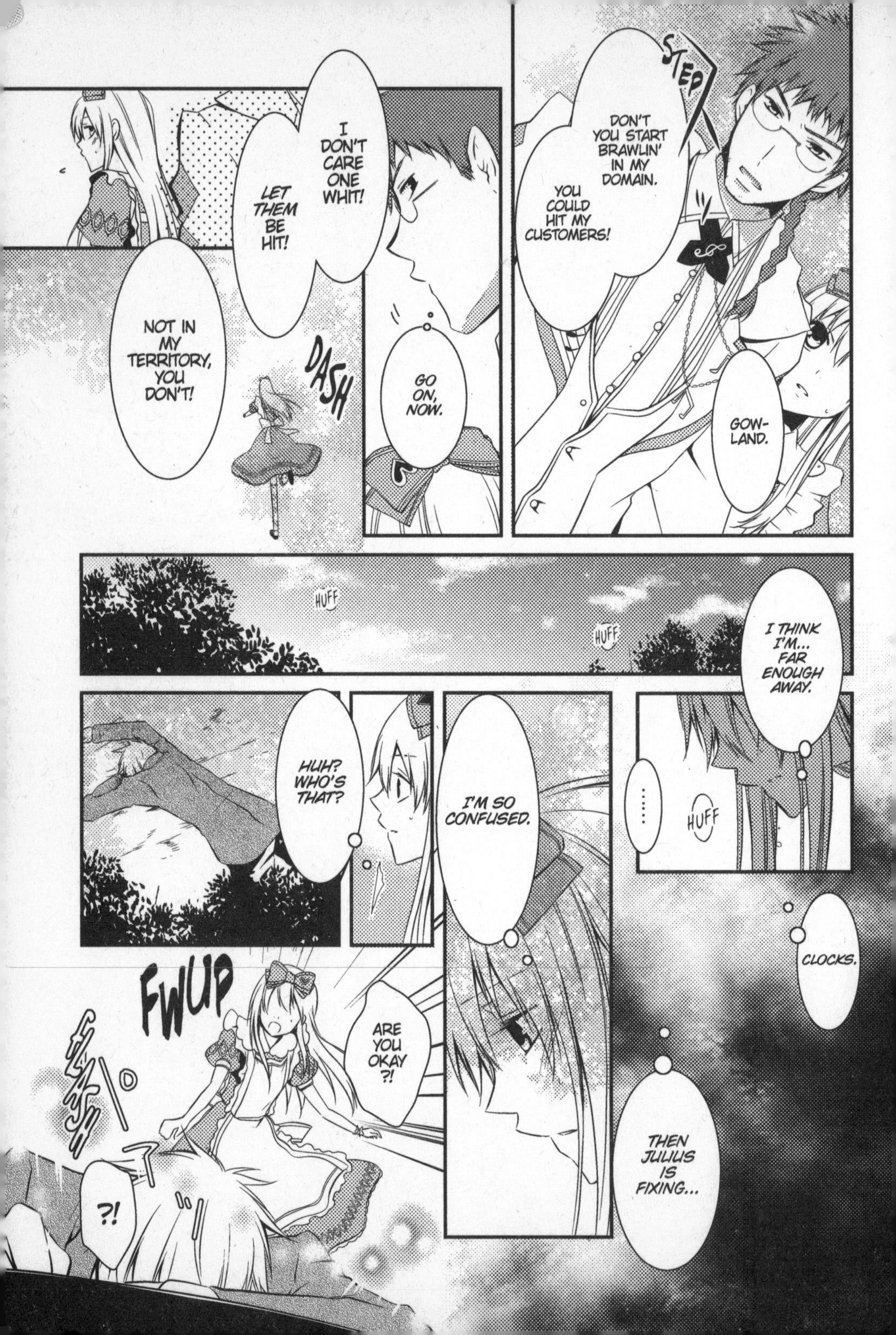
STEP
DON'T YOU START BRAWLIN' IN MY DOMAIN.
YOU COULD HIT MY CUSTOMERS!
GOW-LAND.
I DON'T CARE ONE WHIT!
LET THEM BE HIT!
GO ON, NOW.
NOT IN MY TERRITORY, YOU DON'T!
DASH
I THINK I'M... FAR ENOUGH AWAY.
HUFF
HUFF
......
HUFF
I'M SO CONFUSED.
HUH? WHO'S THAT?
THEN JULIUS IS FIXING...
CLOCKS.
FWUP
ARE YOU OKAY?!
FLASH
?!

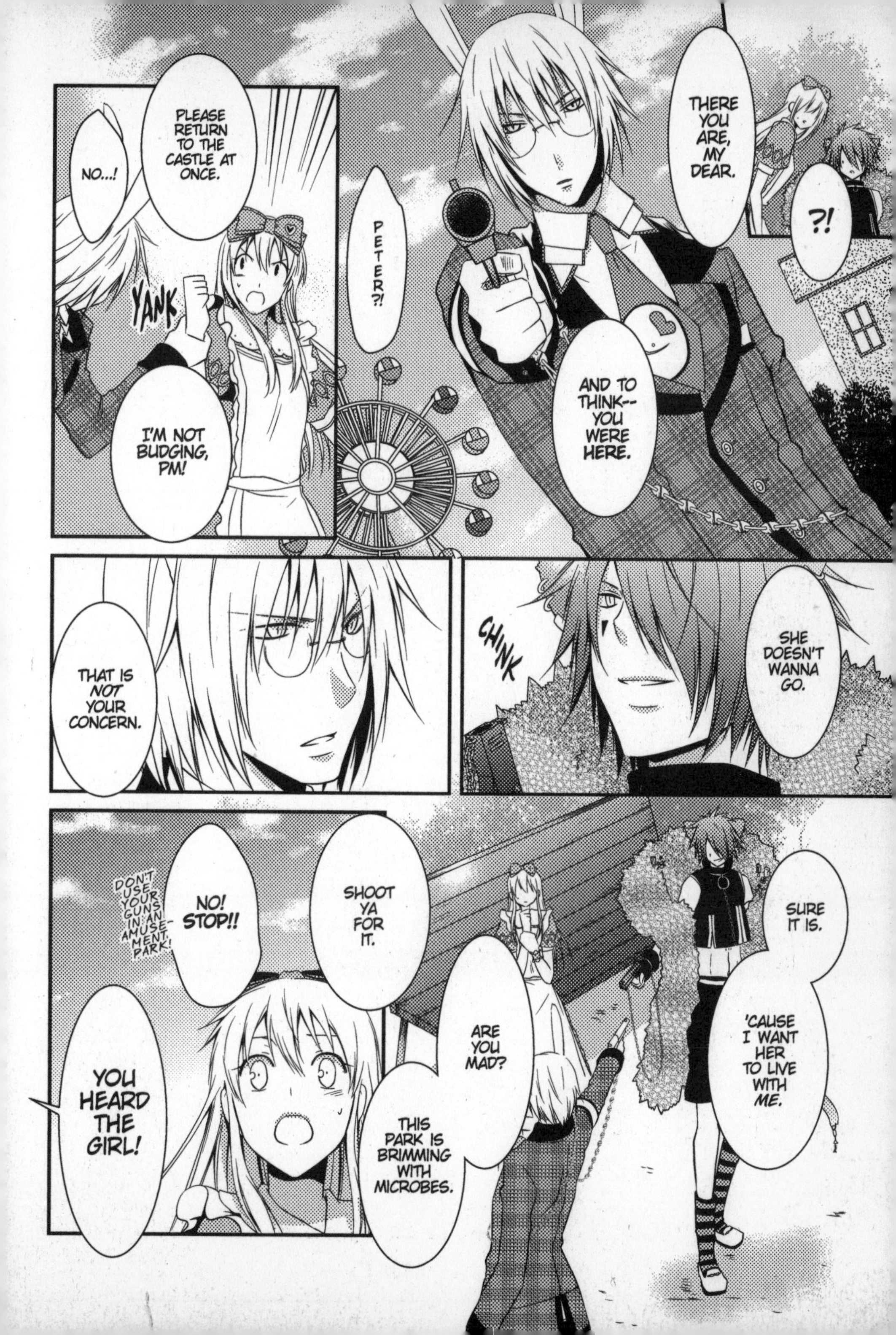
THERE YOU ARE, MY DEAR.
?!
AND TO THINK-- YOU WERE HERE.
PETER?!
PLEASE RETURN TO THE CASTLE AT ONCE.
NO...!
YANK
I'M NOT BUDGING, PM!
CHINK
SHE DOESN'T WANNA GO.
THAT IS *NOT* YOUR CONCERN.
SURE IT IS.
'CAUSE I WANT HER TO LIVE WITH *ME.*
SHOOT YA FOR IT.
ARE YOU MAD?
THIS PARK IS BRIMMING WITH MICROBES.
NO! STOP!!
DON'T USE YOUR GUNS IN AN AMUSEMENT PARK!
YOU HEARD THE GIRL!

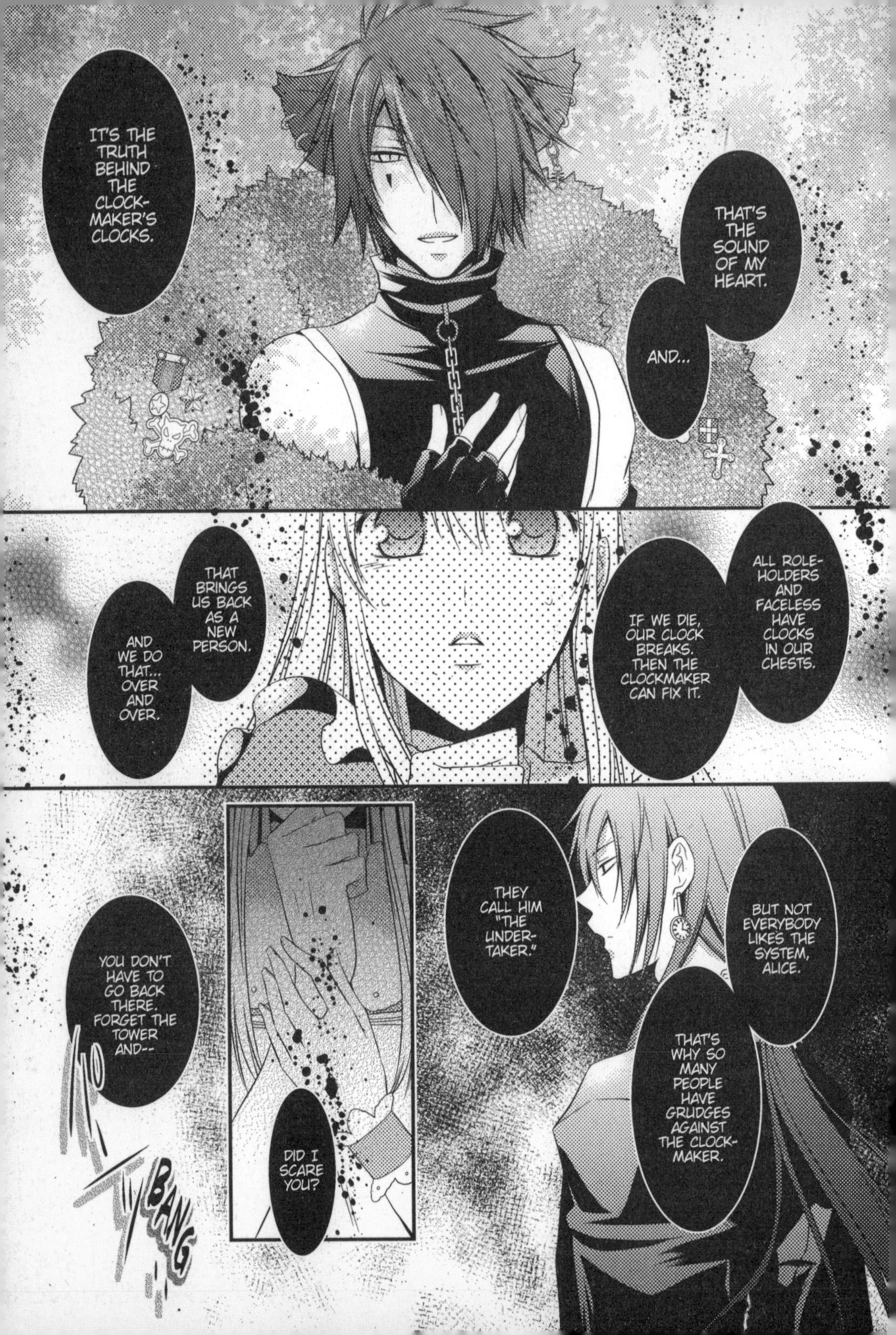
THAT'S THE SOUND OF MY HEART.
AND...
IT'S THE TRUTH BEHIND THE CLOCK-MAKER'S CLOCKS.
ALL ROLE-HOLDERS AND FACELESS HAVE CLOCKS IN OUR CHESTS.
IF WE DIE, OUR CLOCK BREAKS. THEN THE CLOCKMAKER CAN FIX IT.
THAT BRINGS US BACK AS A NEW PERSON.
AND WE DO THAT... OVER AND OVER.
BUT NOT EVERYBODY LIKES THE SYSTEM, ALICE.
THAT'S WHY SO MANY PEOPLE HAVE GRUDGES AGAINST THE CLOCK-MAKER.
THEY CALL HIM "THE UNDER-TAKER."
DID I SCARE YOU?
YOU DON'T HAVE TO GO BACK THERE. FORGET THE TOWER AND--
BANG

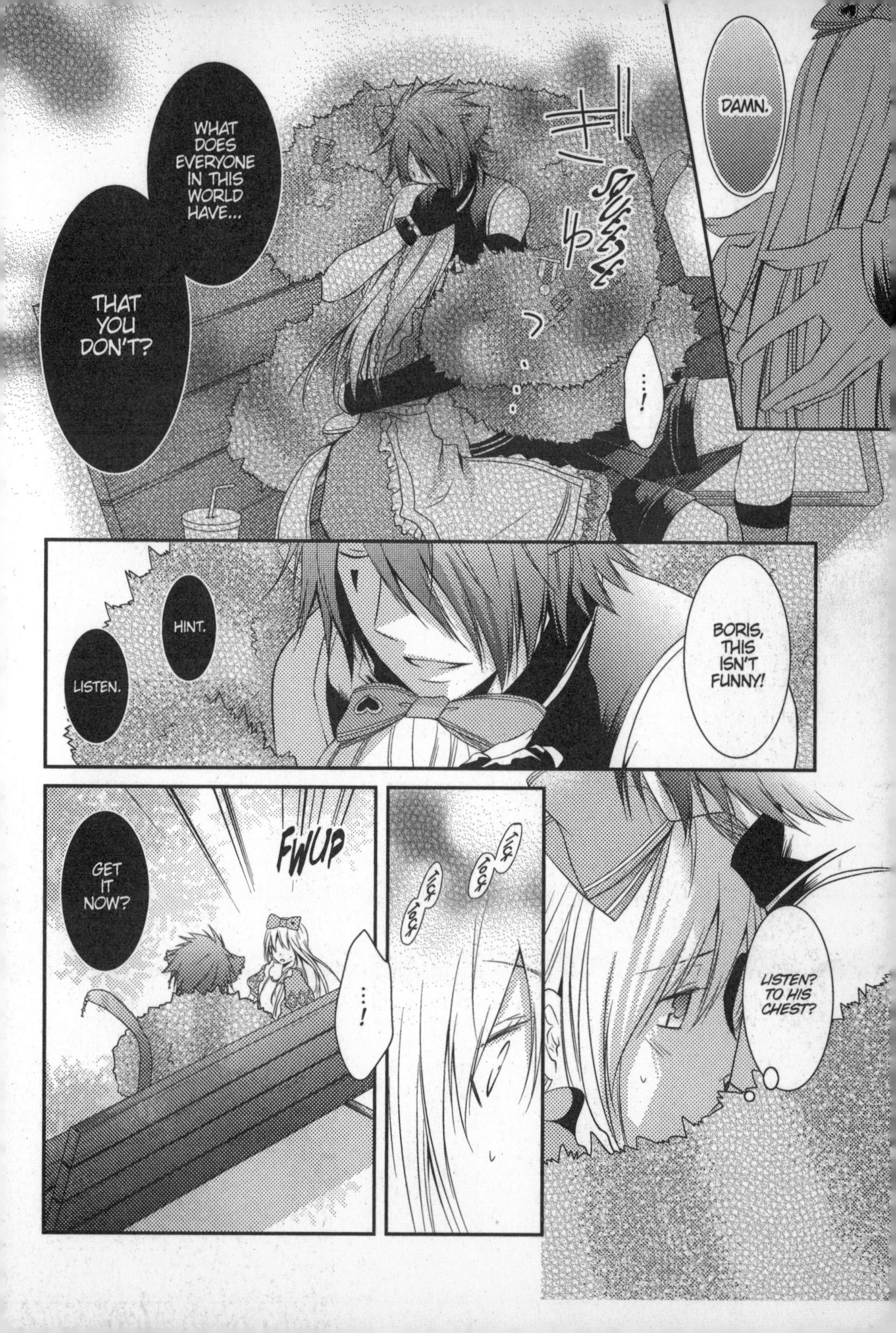
DAMN.
SQUEEZE
...!
WHAT DOES EVERYONE IN THIS WORLD HAVE...
THAT YOU DON'T?
BORIS, THIS ISN'T FUNNY!
HINT.
LISTEN.
LISTEN? TO HIS CHEST?
TICK TOCK
TICK TOCK
...!
FWUP
GET IT NOW?

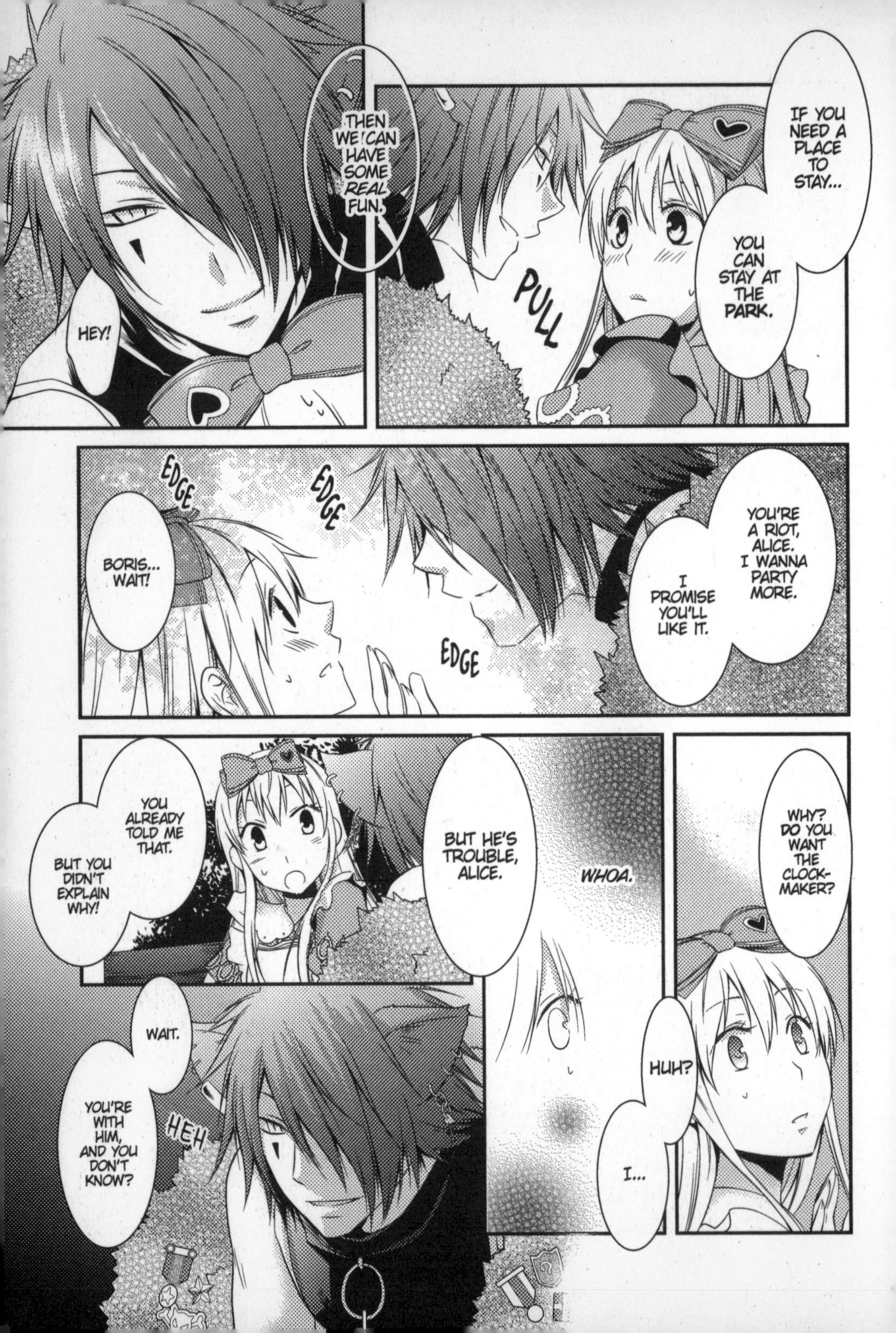
IF YOU NEED A PLACE TO STAY...
YOU CAN STAY AT THE PARK.
PULL
THEN WE CAN HAVE SOME *REAL* FUN.
HEY!
YOU'RE A RIOT, ALICE. I WANNA PARTY MORE.
I PROMISE YOU'LL LIKE IT.
EDGE
EDGE
EDGE
BORIS... WAIT!
WHY? DO YOU WANT THE CLOCK-MAKER?
HUH?
I...
BUT HE'S TROUBLE, ALICE.
WHOA.
YOU ALREADY TOLD ME THAT.
BUT YOU DIDN'T EXPLAIN WHY!
WAIT.
YOU'RE WITH HIM, AND YOU DON'T KNOW?
HEH

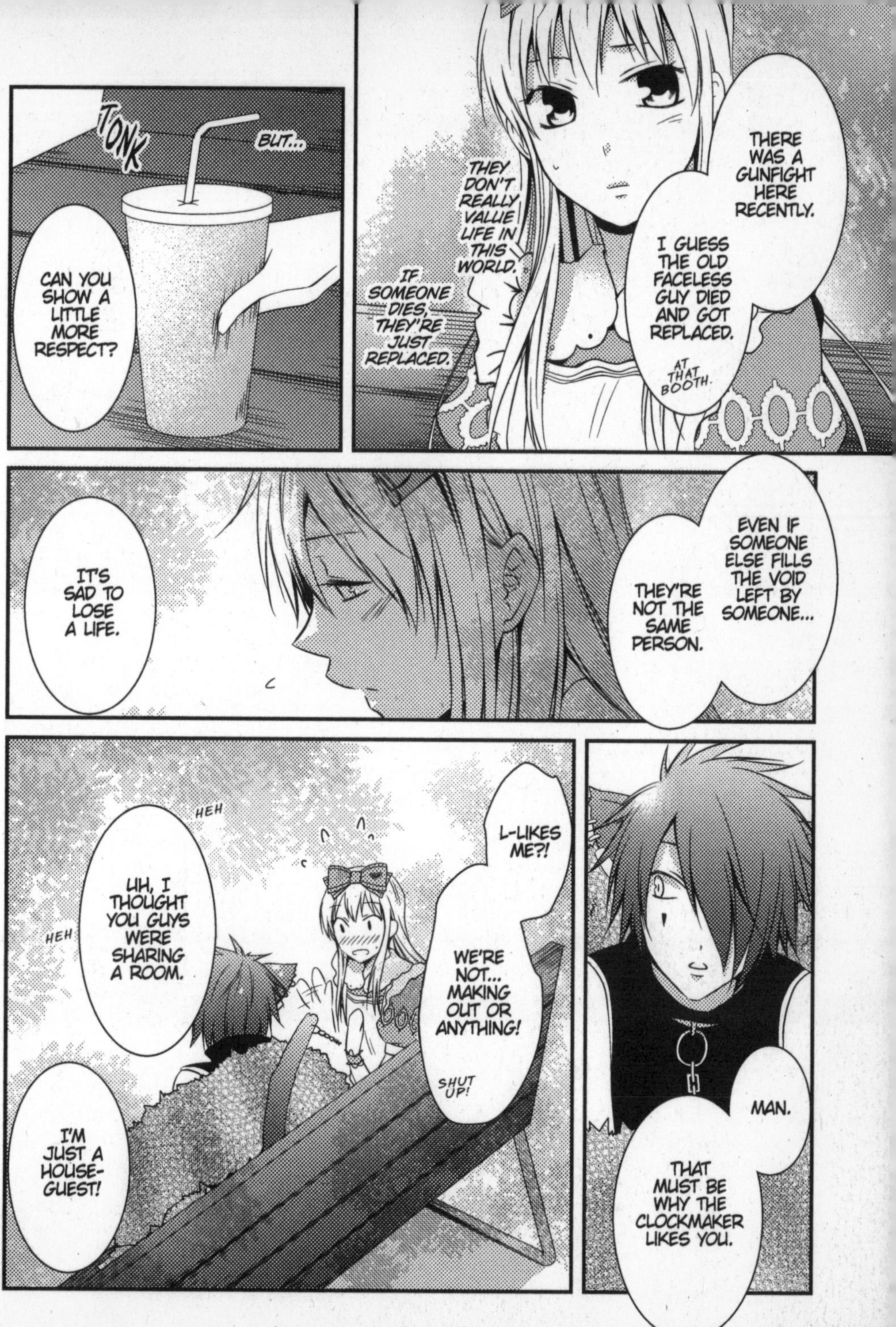
THERE WAS A GUNFIGHT HERE RECENTLY.
I GUESS THE OLD FACELESS GUY DIED AND GOT REPLACED.
AT THAT BOOTH.
THEY DON'T REALLY VALUE LIFE IN THIS WORLD.
IF SOMEONE DIES, THEY'RE JUST REPLACED.
TONK
BUT...
CAN YOU SHOW A LITTLE MORE RESPECT?
EVEN IF SOMEONE ELSE FILLS THE VOID LEFT BY SOMEONE...
THEY'RE NOT THE SAME PERSON.
IT'S SAD TO LOSE A LIFE.
MAN.
THAT MUST BE WHY THE CLOCKMAKER LIKES YOU.
L-LIKES ME?!
WE'RE NOT... MAKING OUT OR ANYTHING!
SHUT UP!
HEH
UH, I THOUGHT YOU GUYS WERE SHARING A ROOM.
HEH
I'M JUST A HOUSE-GUEST!

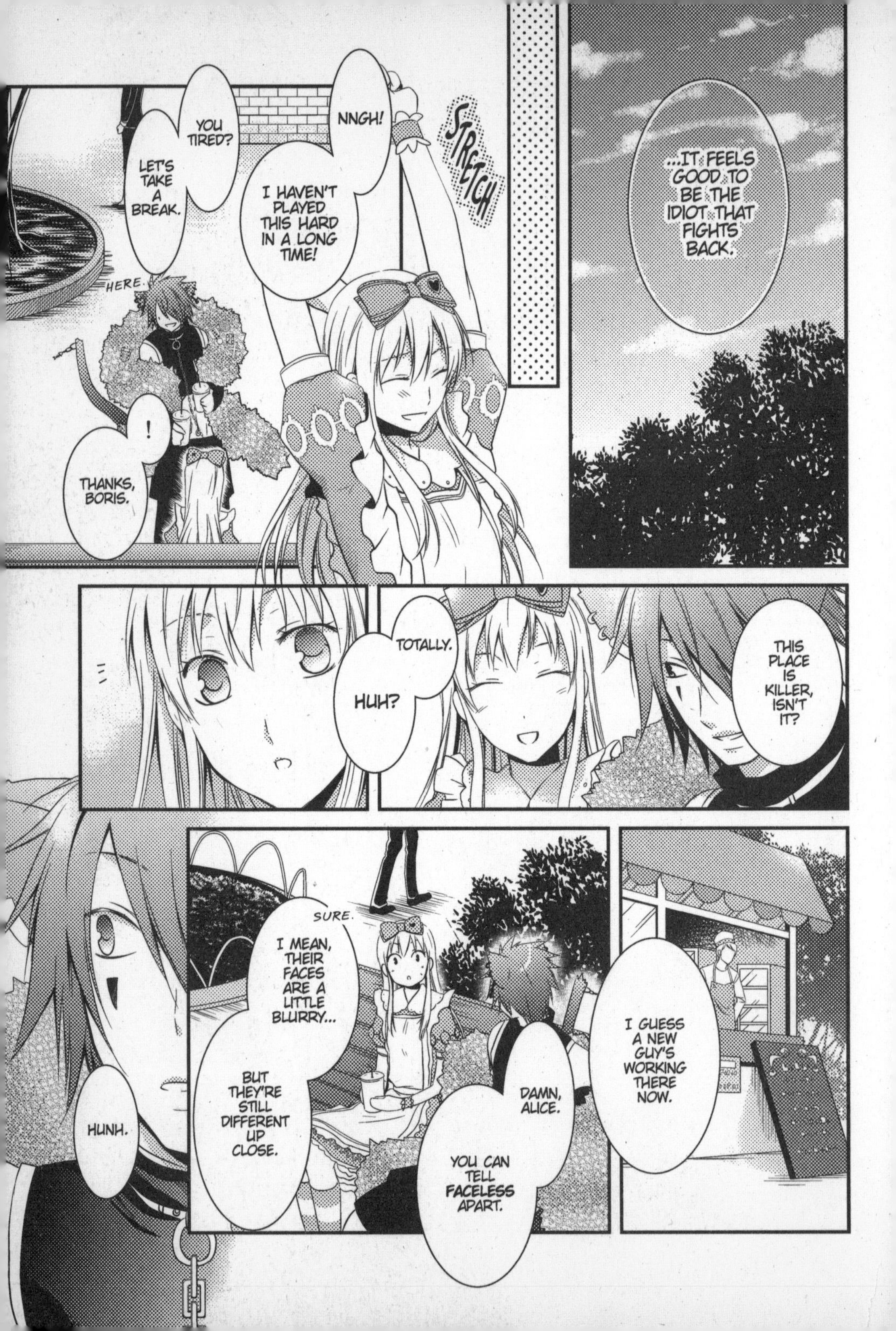
...IT FEELS GOOD TO BE THE IDIOT THAT FIGHTS BACK.
STRETCH
NNGH!
I HAVEN'T PLAYED THIS HARD IN A LONG TIME!
YOU TIRED?
LET'S TAKE A BREAK.
HERE.
!
THANKS, BORIS.
THIS PLACE IS KILLER, ISN'T IT?
TOTALLY.
HUH?
I GUESS A NEW GUY'S WORKING THERE NOW.
DAMN, ALICE.
YOU CAN TELL FACELESS APART.
SURE.
I MEAN, THEIR FACES ARE A LITTLE BLURRY...
BUT THEY'RE STILL DIFFERENT UP CLOSE.
HUNH.

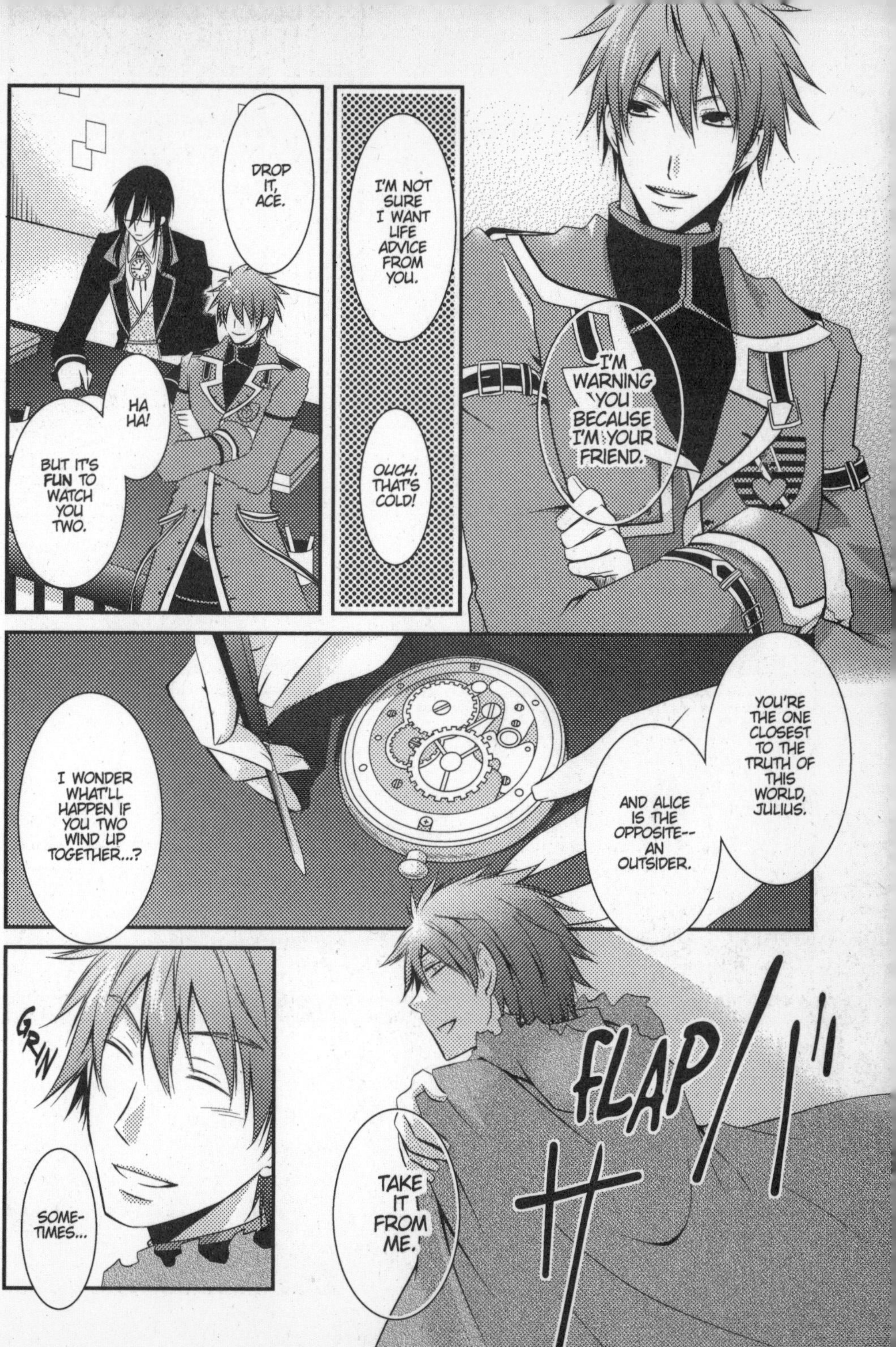
I'M WARNING YOU BECAUSE I'M YOUR FRIEND.
I'M NOT SURE I WANT LIFE ADVICE FROM YOU.
OUCH. THAT'S COLD!
DROP IT, ACE.
HA HA!
BUT IT'S FUN TO WATCH YOU TWO.
YOU'RE THE ONE CLOSEST TO THE TRUTH OF THIS WORLD, JULIUS.
AND ALICE IS THE OPPOSITE-- AN OUTSIDER.
I WONDER WHAT'LL HAPPEN IF YOU TWO WIND UP TOGETHER...?
FLAP
TAKE IT FROM ME.
GRIN
SOME-TIMES...

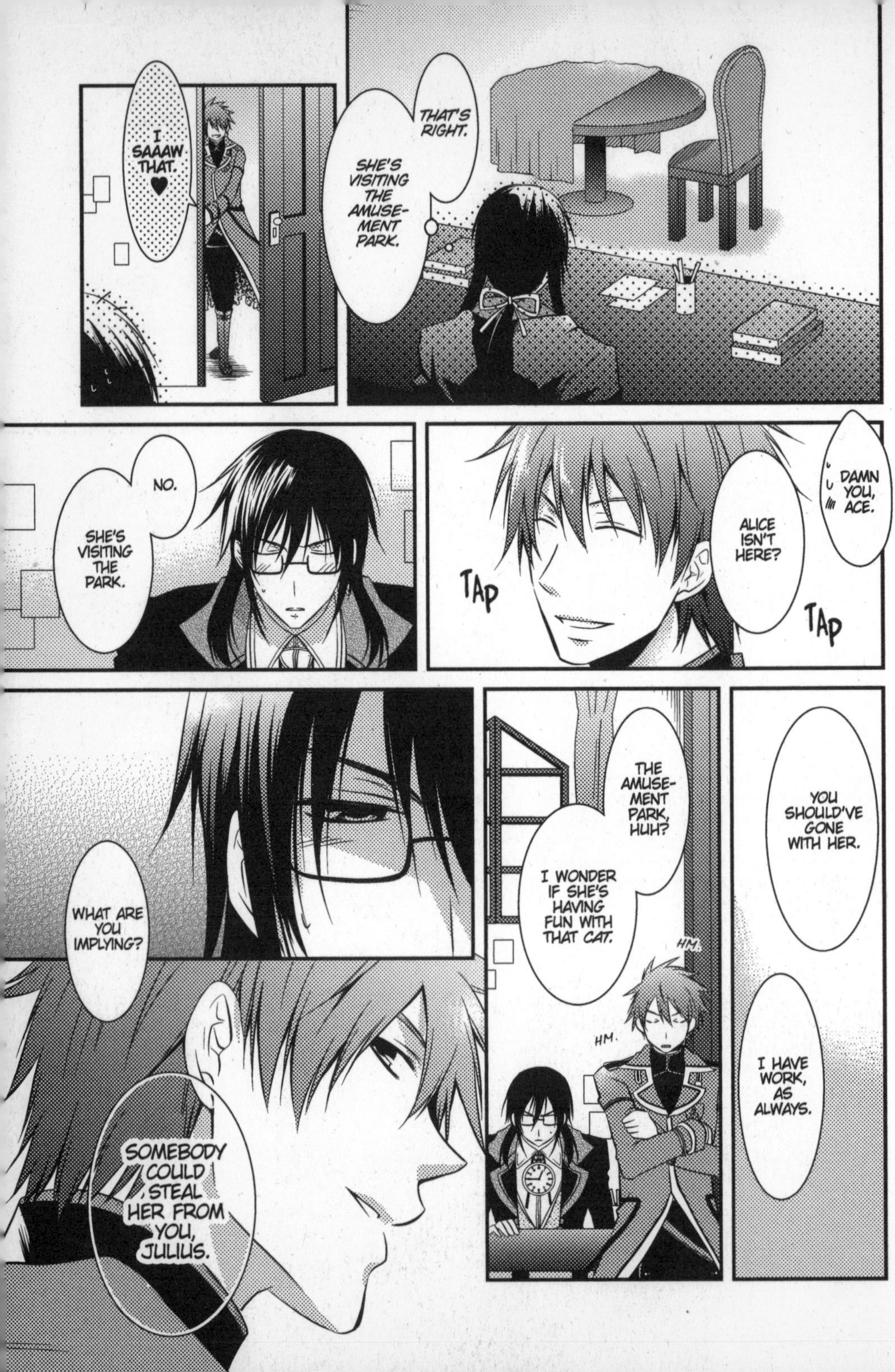
THAT'S RIGHT.
SHE'S VISITING THE AMUSEMENT PARK.
I SAAAW THAT. ♥
DAMN YOU, ACE.
ALICE ISN'T HERE?
TAP
TAP
NO.
SHE'S VISITING THE PARK.
YOU SHOULD'VE GONE WITH HER.
I HAVE WORK, AS ALWAYS.
THE AMUSEMENT PARK, HUH?
I WONDER IF SHE'S HAVING FUN WITH THAT CAT.
HM.
HM.
WHAT ARE YOU IMPLYING?
SOMEBODY COULD STEAL HER FROM YOU, JULIUS.

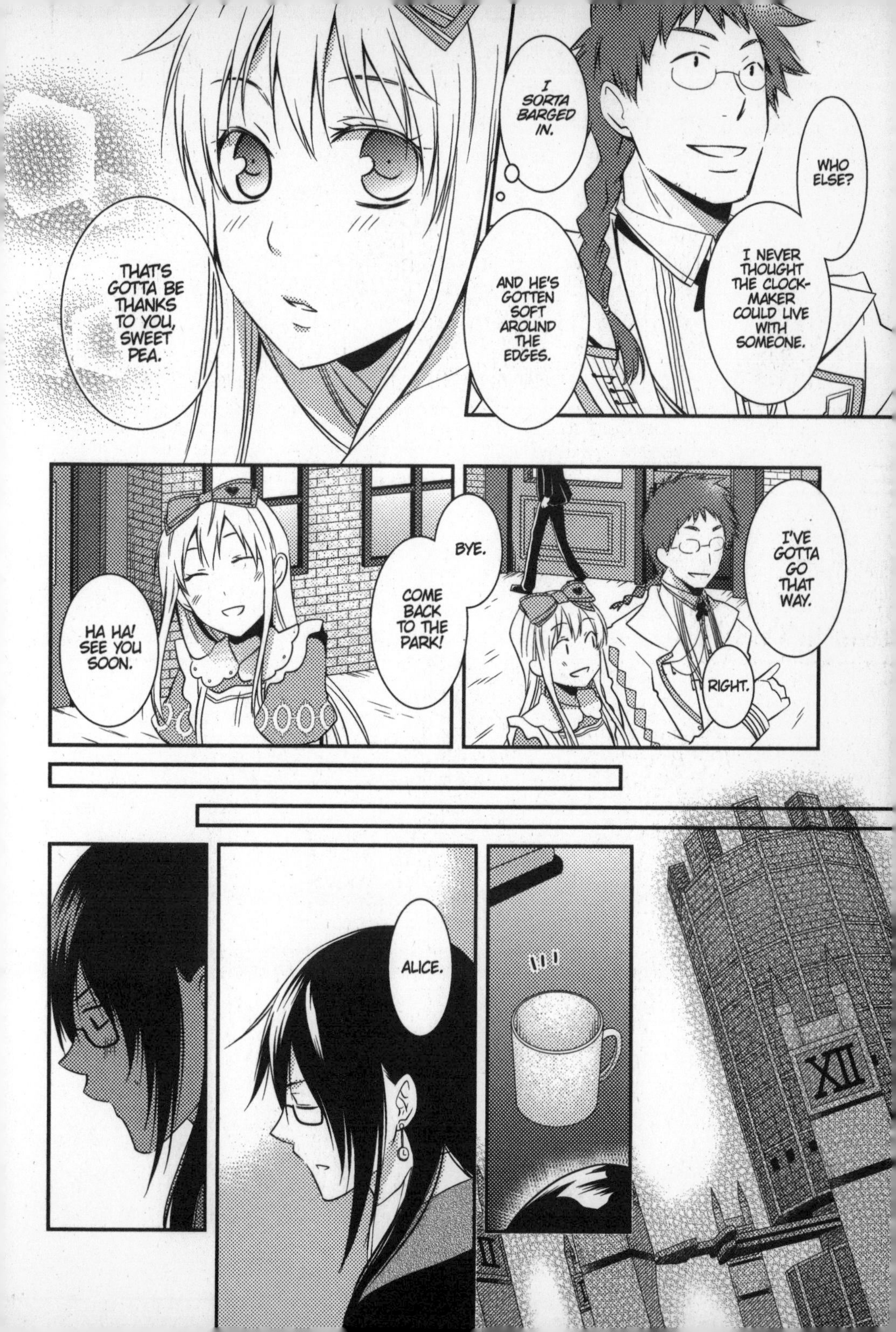
WHO ELSE?
I NEVER THOUGHT THE CLOCK-MAKER COULD LIVE WITH SOMEONE.
I SORTA BARGED IN.
AND HE'S GOTTEN SOFT AROUND THE EDGES.
THAT'S GOTTA BE THANKS TO YOU, SWEET PEA.
I'VE GOTTA GO THAT WAY.
RIGHT.
BYE.
COME BACK TO THE PARK!
HA HA! SEE YOU SOON.
XII
ALICE.

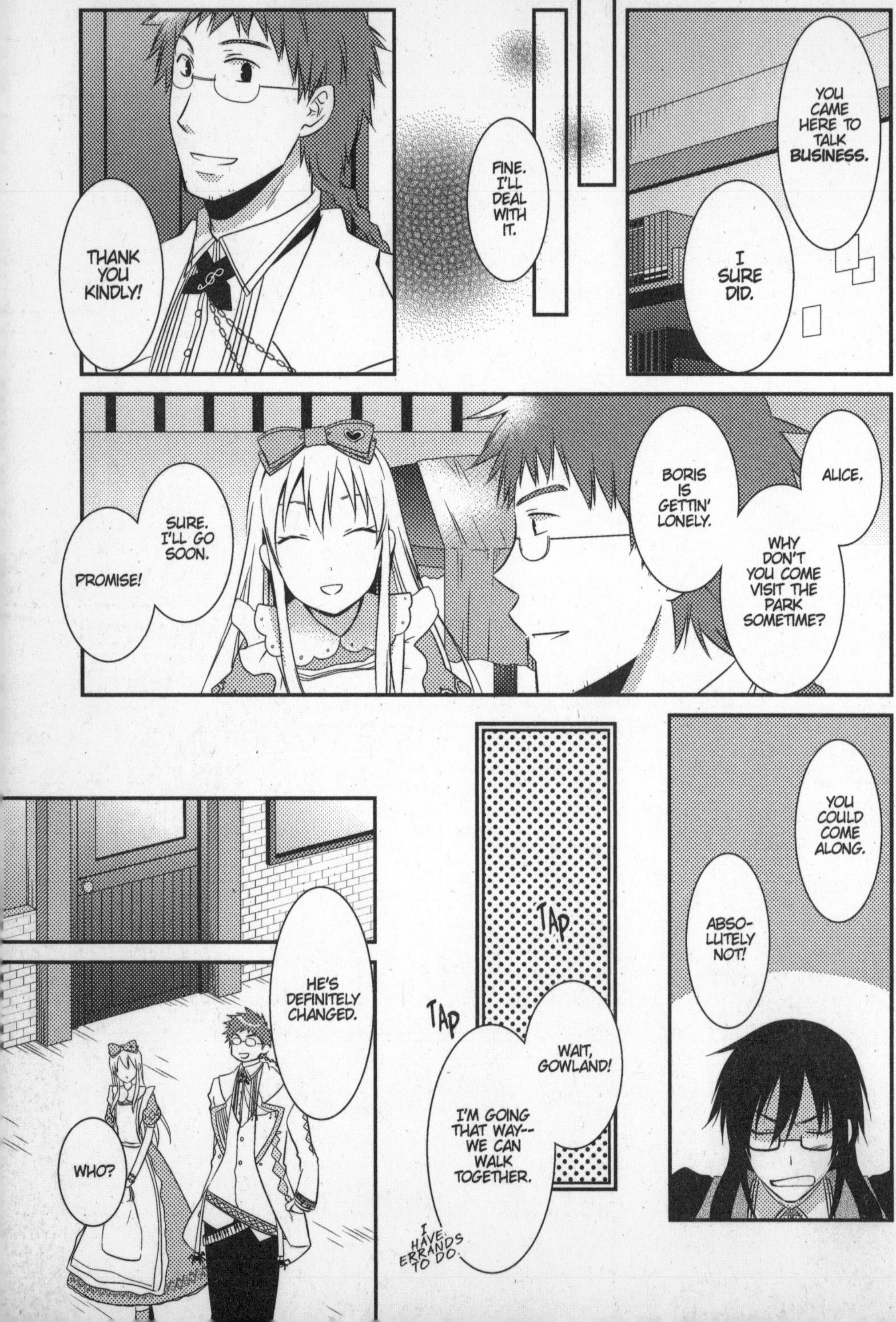
YOU CAME HERE TO TALK BUSINESS.
I SURE DID.
FINE. I'LL DEAL WITH IT.
THANK YOU KINDLY!
ALICE.
WHY DON'T YOU COME VISIT THE PARK SOMETIME?
BORIS IS GETTIN' LONELY.
SURE. I'LL GO SOON.
PROMISE!
YOU COULD COME ALONG.
ABSO-LUTELY NOT!
TAP
WAIT, GOWLAND!
I'M GOING THAT WAY-- WE CAN WALK TOGETHER.
I HAVE ERRANDS TO DO.
TAP
HE'S DEFINITELY CHANGED.
WHO?

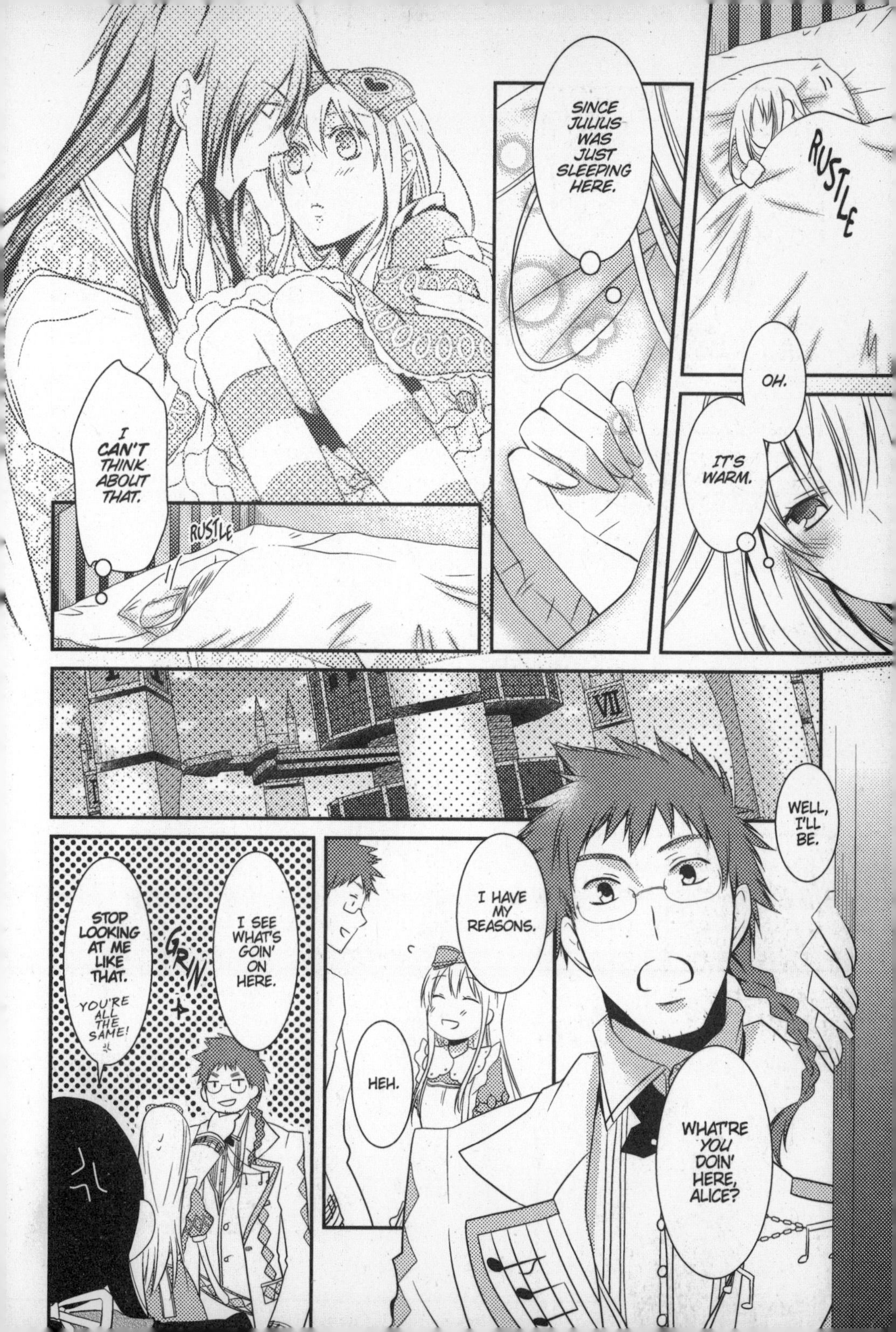
RUSTLE
SINCE JULIUS WAS JUST SLEEPING HERE.
OH.
IT'S WARM.
I CAN'T THINK ABOUT THAT.
RUSTLE
WELL, I'LL BE.
WHAT'RE YOU DOIN' HERE, ALICE?
I HAVE MY REASONS.
HEH.
I SEE WHAT'S GOIN' ON HERE.
GRIN
STOP LOOKING AT ME LIKE THAT.
YOU'RE ALL THE SAME!

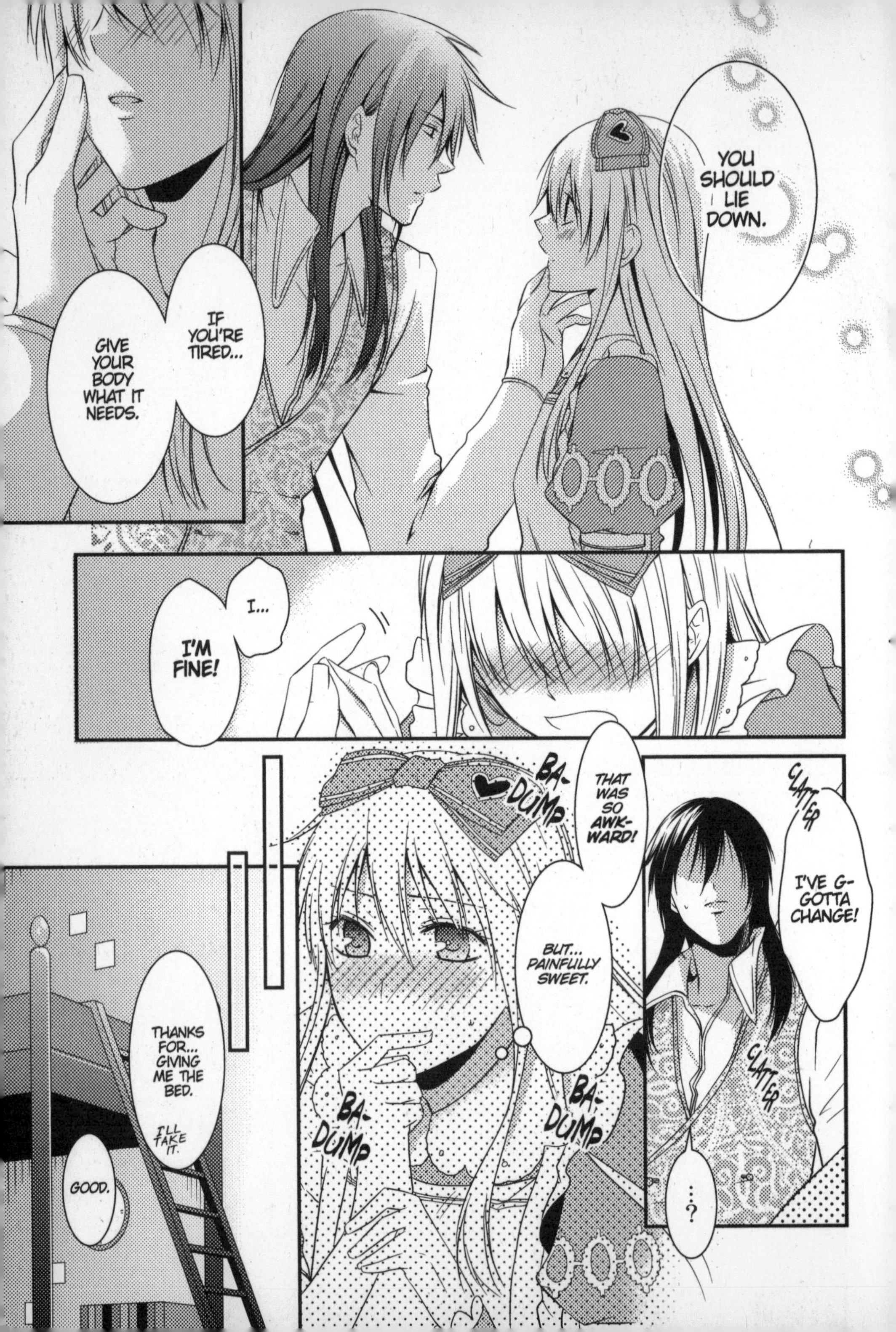
YOU SHOULD LIE DOWN.
IF YOU'RE TIRED...
GIVE YOUR BODY WHAT IT NEEDS.
I...
I'M FINE!
CLATTER
I'VE G-GOTTA CHANGE!
CLATTER
...?
BA-DUMP
THAT WAS SO AWK-WARD!
BUT... PAINFULLY SWEET.
BA-DUMP
BA-DUMP
THANKS FOR... GIVING ME THE BED.
I'LL TAKE IT.
GOOD.

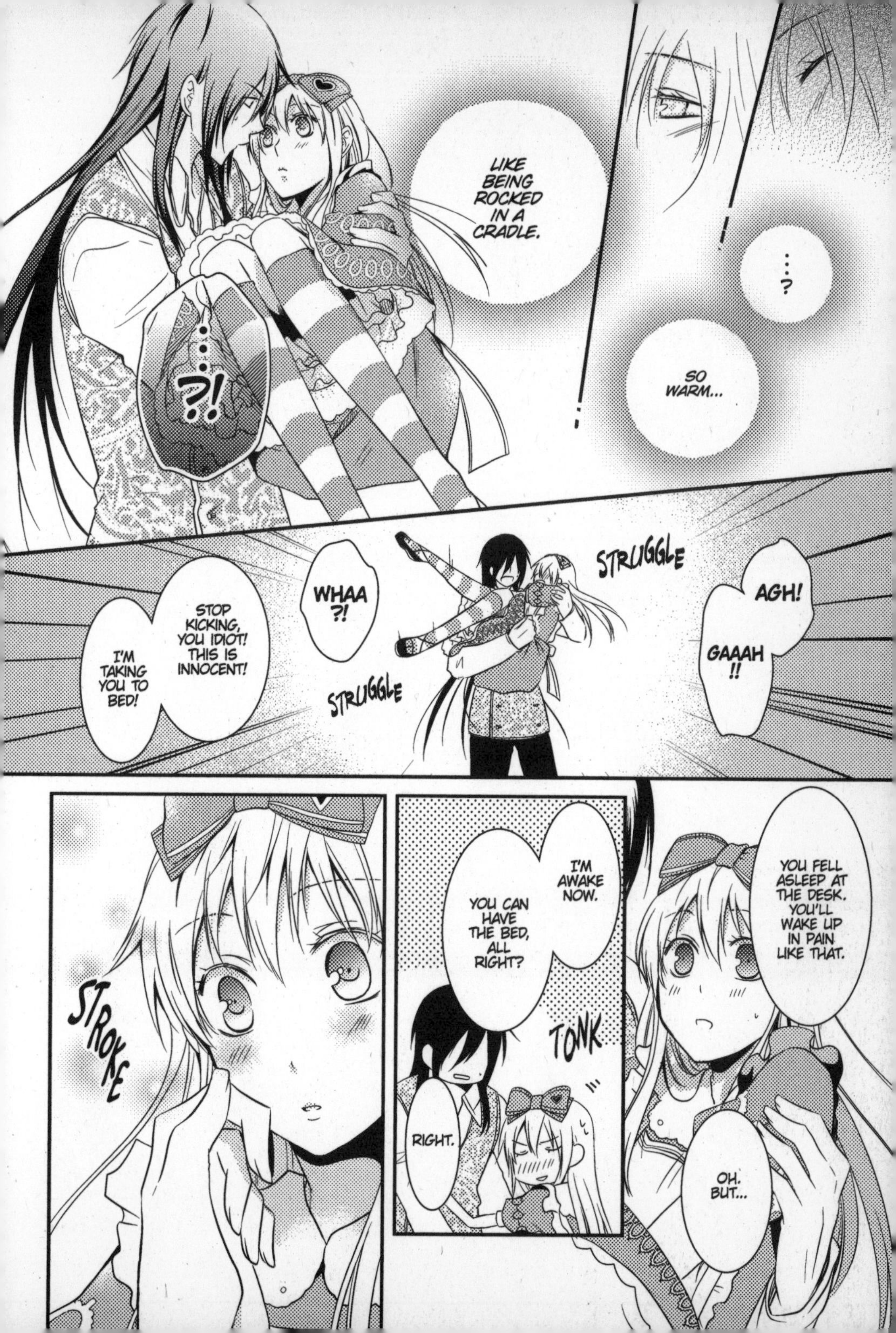
...?
SO WARM...
LIKE BEING ROCKED IN A CRADLE.
...?!
AGH!
GAAAH!!
STRUGGLE
WHAA?!
STRUGGLE
STOP KICKING, YOU IDIOT! THIS IS INNOCENT!
I'M TAKING YOU TO BED!
YOU FELL ASLEEP AT THE DESK. YOU'LL WAKE UP IN PAIN LIKE THAT.
OH. BUT...
I'M AWAKE NOW.
YOU CAN HAVE THE BED, ALL RIGHT?
TONK
RIGHT.
STROKE

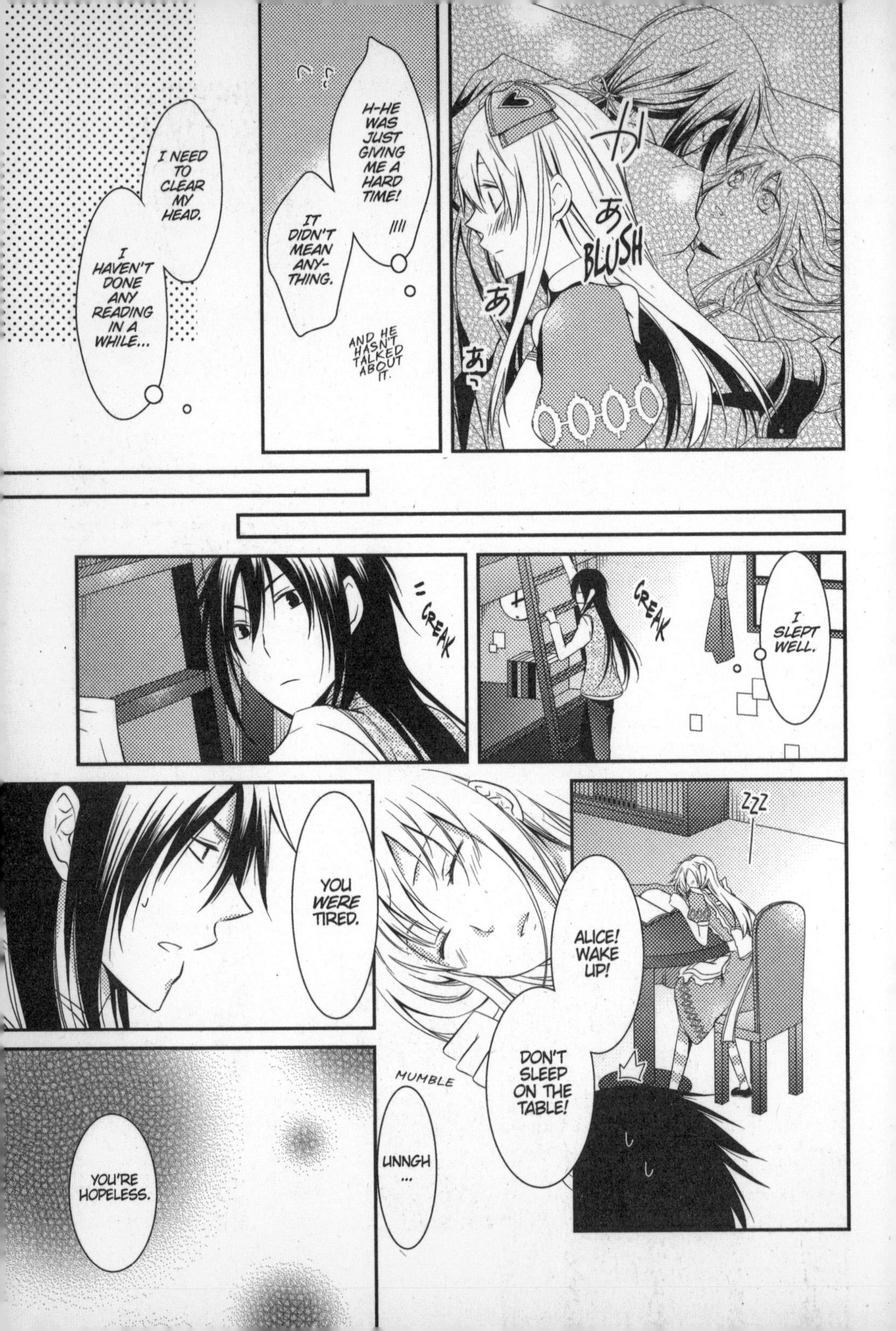
BLUSH
H-HE WAS JUST GIVING ME A HARD TIME!
IT DIDN'T MEAN ANYTHING.
AND HE HASN'T TALKED ABOUT IT.
I NEED TO CLEAR MY HEAD.
I HAVEN'T DONE ANY READING IN A WHILE...
CREAK
I SLEPT WELL.
CREAK
ZZZ
ALICE! WAKE UP!
DON'T SLEEP ON THE TABLE!
YOU WERE TIRED.
MUMBLE
UNNGH...
YOU'RE HOPELESS.

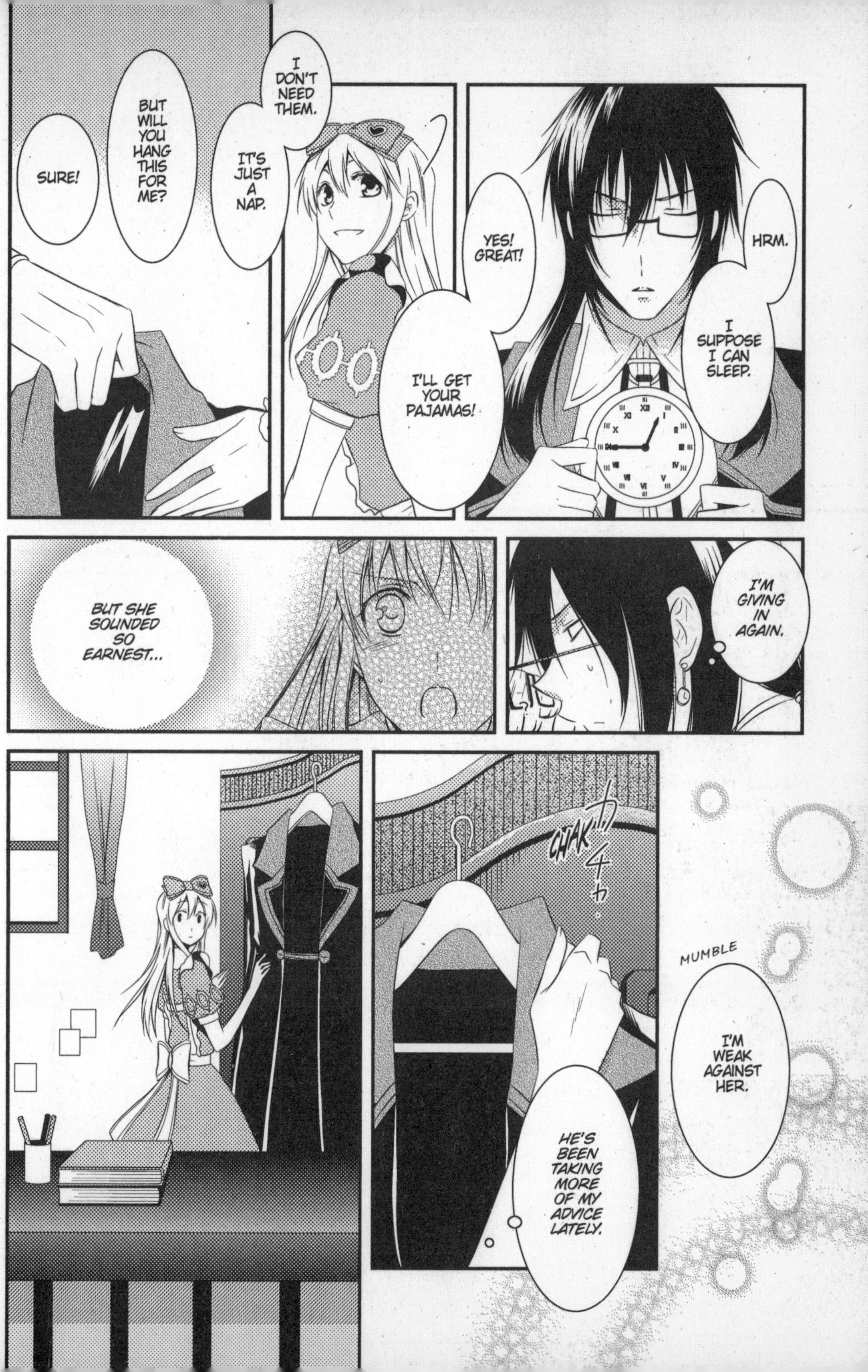
HRM.
I SUPPOSE I CAN SLEEP.
YES! GREAT!
I'LL GET YOUR PAJAMAS!
I DON'T NEED THEM.
IT'S JUST A NAP.
BUT WILL YOU HANG THIS FOR ME?
SURE!
I'M GIVING IN AGAIN.
BUT SHE SOUNDED SO EARNEST...
MUMBLE
I'M WEAK AGAINST HER.
CHAK
HE'S BEEN TAKING MORE OF MY ADVICE LATELY.

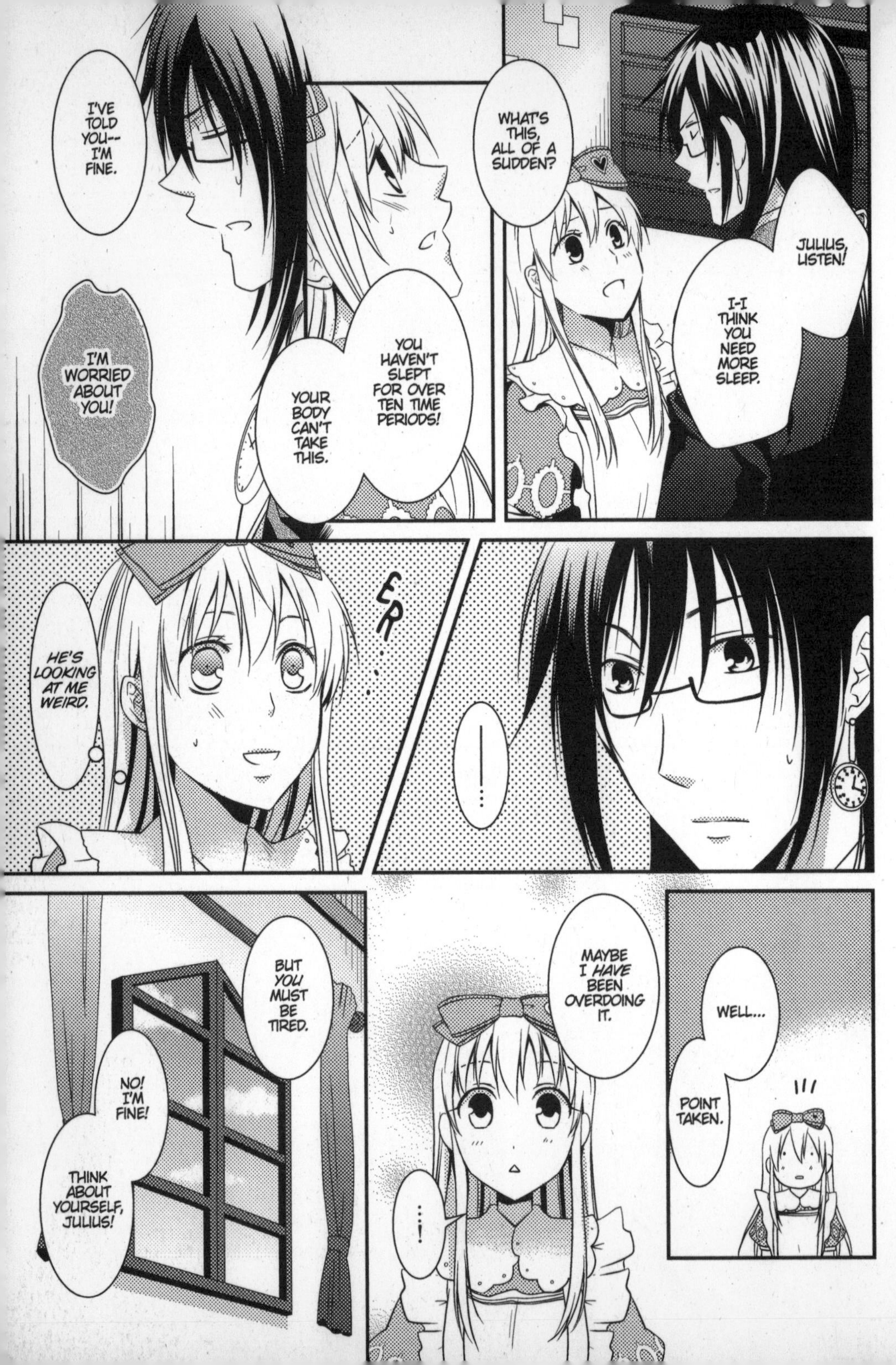
JULIUS, LISTEN!
I-I THINK YOU NEED MORE SLEEP.
WHAT'S THIS, ALL OF A SUDDEN?
YOU HAVEN'T SLEPT FOR OVER TEN TIME PERIODS!
YOUR BODY CAN'T TAKE THIS.
I'VE TOLD YOU-- I'M FINE.
I'M WORRIED ABOUT YOU!
!...
ER...
HE'S LOOKING AT ME WEIRD.
WELL...
POINT TAKEN.
MAYBE I *HAVE* BEEN OVERDOING IT.
...!
BUT *YOU* MUST BE TIRED.
NO! I'M FINE!
THINK ABOUT YOURSELF, JULIUS!

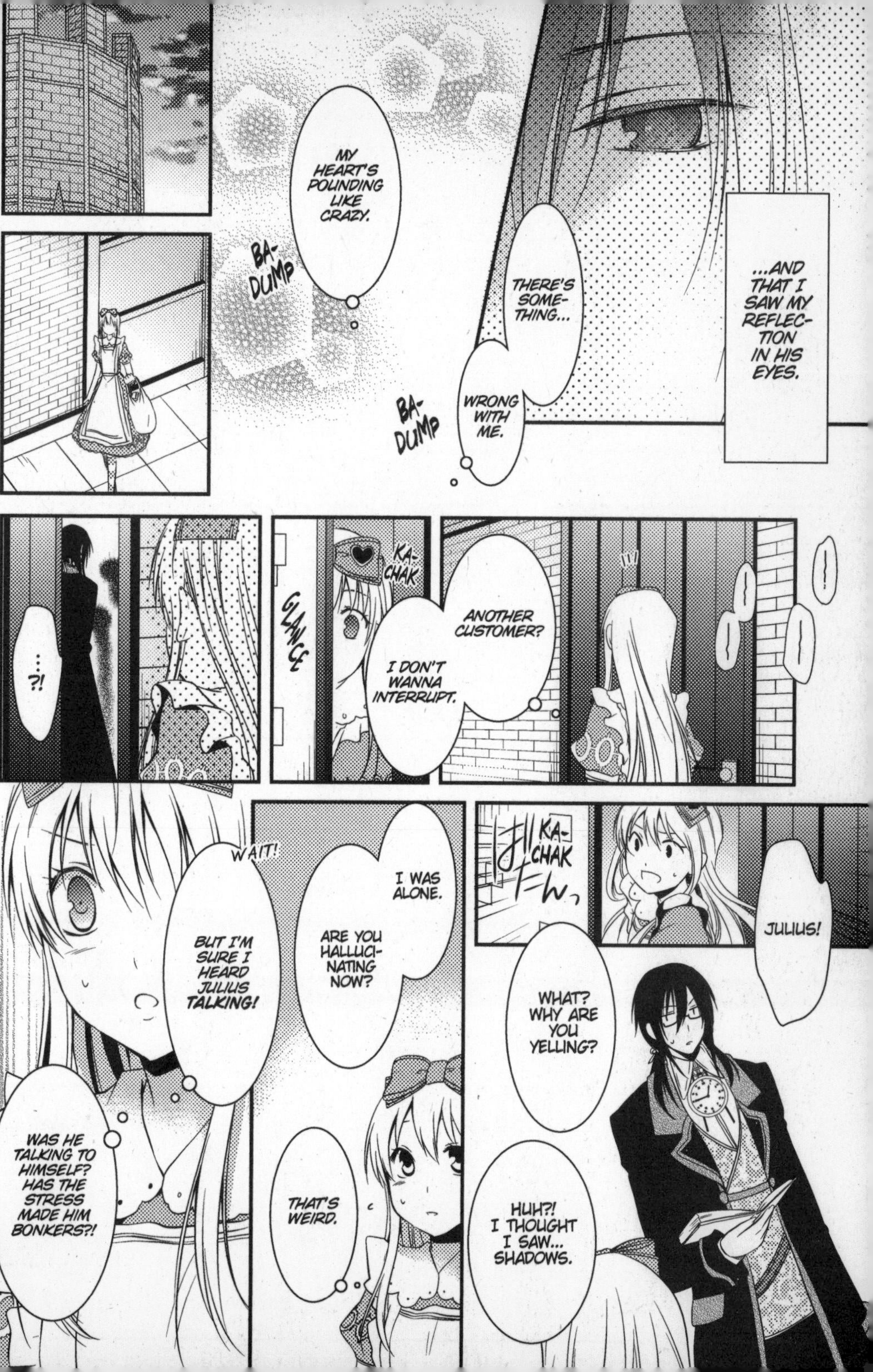
...AND THAT I SAW MY REFLECTION IN HIS EYES.
THERE'S SOMETHING...
WRONG WITH ME.
BA-DUMP
MY HEART'S POUNDING LIKE CRAZY.
BA-DUMP
!
KA-CHAK
ANOTHER CUSTOMER?
I DON'T WANNA INTERRUPT.
GLANCE
...?!
KA-CHAK
JULIUS!
WHAT? WHY ARE YOU YELLING?
HUH?! I THOUGHT I SAW... SHADOWS.
WAIT!
I WAS ALONE.
ARE YOU HALLUCINATING NOW?
THAT'S WEIRD.
BUT I'M SURE I HEARD JULIUS TALKING!
WAS HE TALKING TO HIMSELF? HAS THE STRESS MADE HIM BONKERS?!

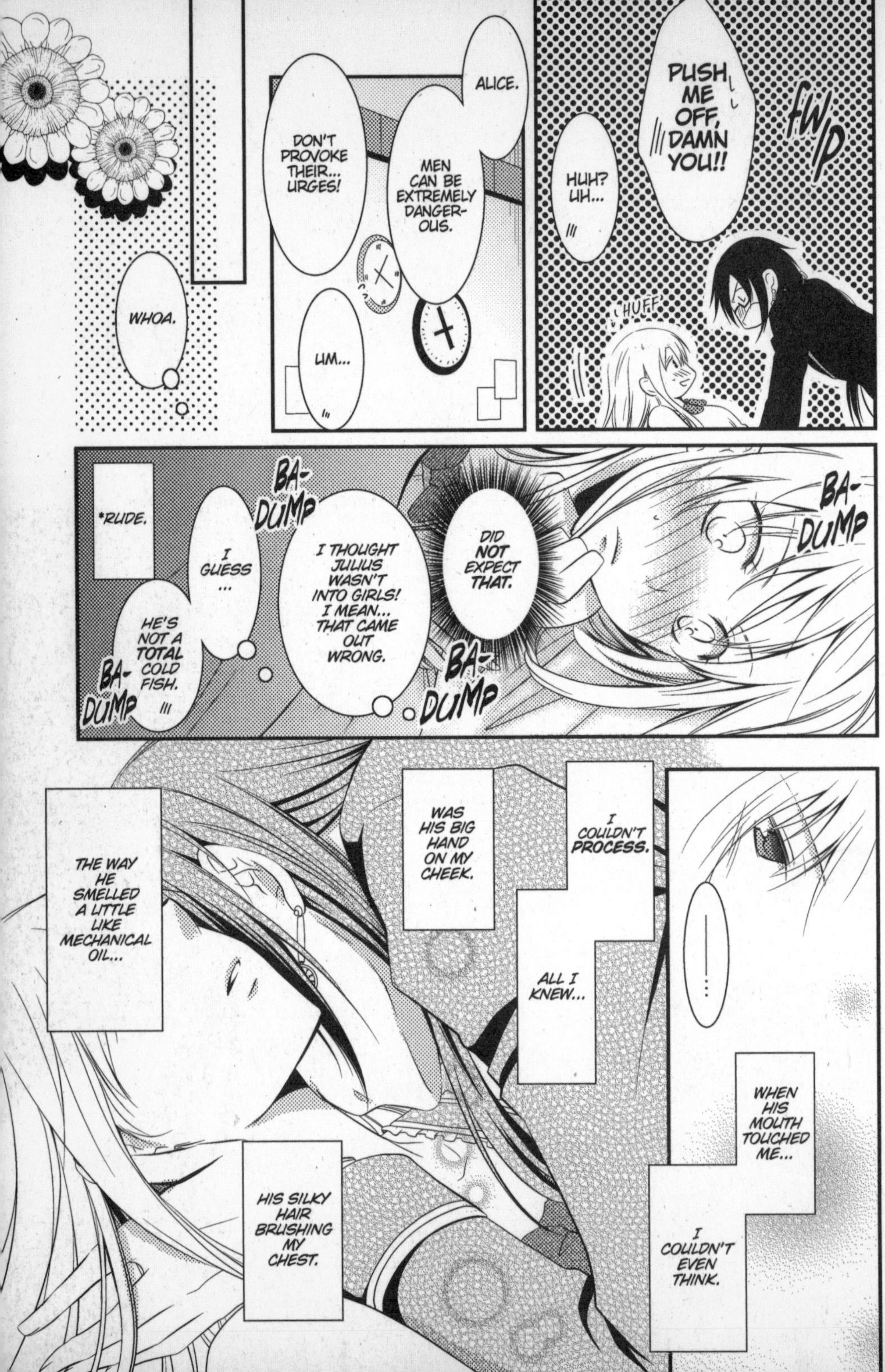
PUSH ME OFF, DAMN YOU!!
FWIP
HUH? UH...
HUFF
ALICE.
MEN CAN BE EXTREMELY DANGER-OUS.
DON'T PROVOKE THEIR... URGES!
UM...
WHOA.
BA-DUMP
DID NOT EXPECT THAT.
BA-DUMP
I THOUGHT JULIUS WASN'T INTO GIRLS! I MEAN... THAT CAME OUT WRONG.
BA-DUMP
I GUESS...
HE'S NOT A TOTAL COLD FISH.
BA-DUMP
*RUDE.
......
I COULDN'T PROCESS.
ALL I KNEW...
WAS HIS BIG HAND ON MY CHEEK.
WHEN HIS MOUTH TOUCHED ME...
I COULDN'T EVEN THINK.
THE WAY HE SMELLED A LITTLE LIKE MECHANICAL OIL...
HIS SILKY HAIR BRUSHING MY CHEST.

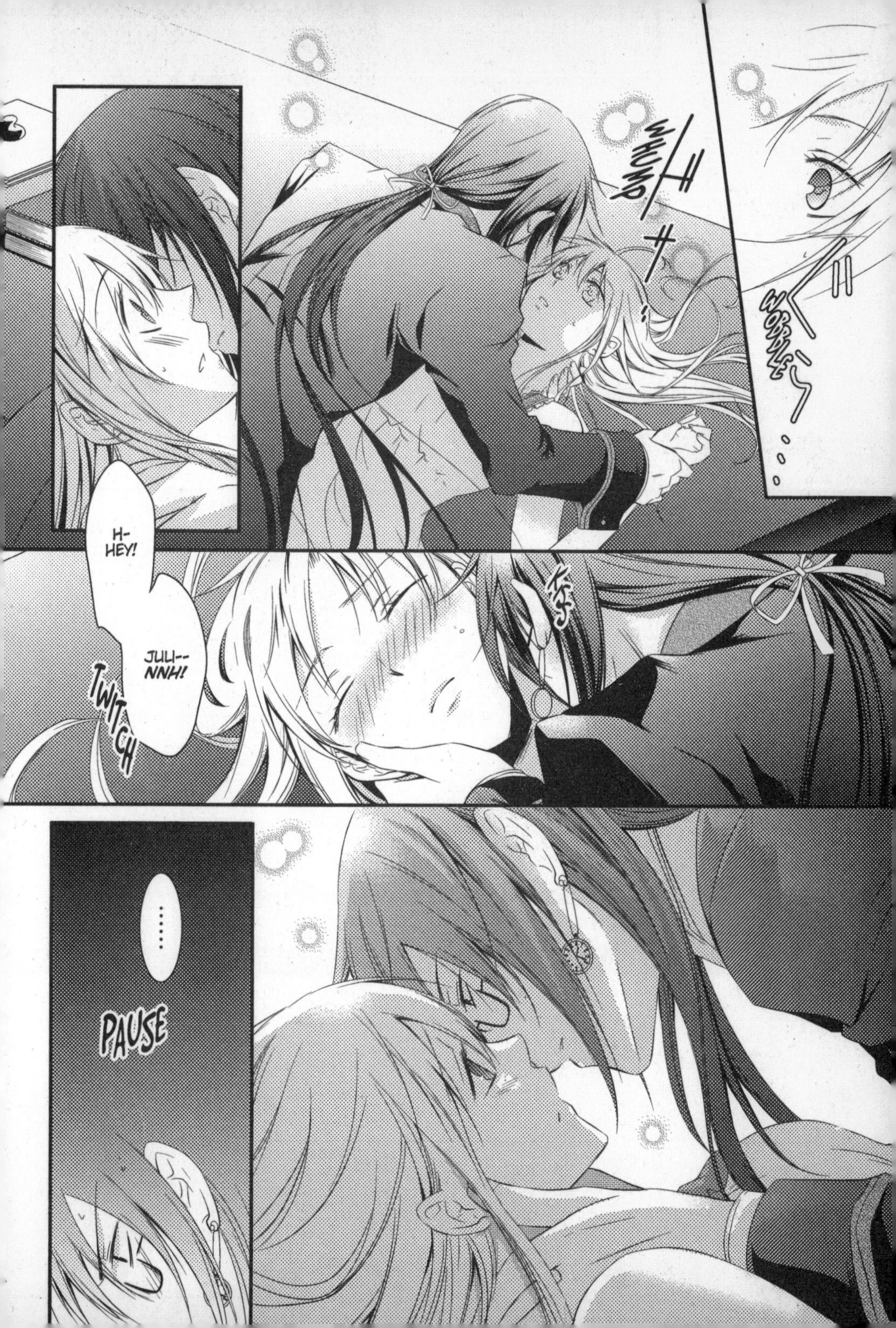
WOBBLE...
WHUMP
KISS
H-HEY!
JULI--NNH!
TWITCH
......
PAUSE

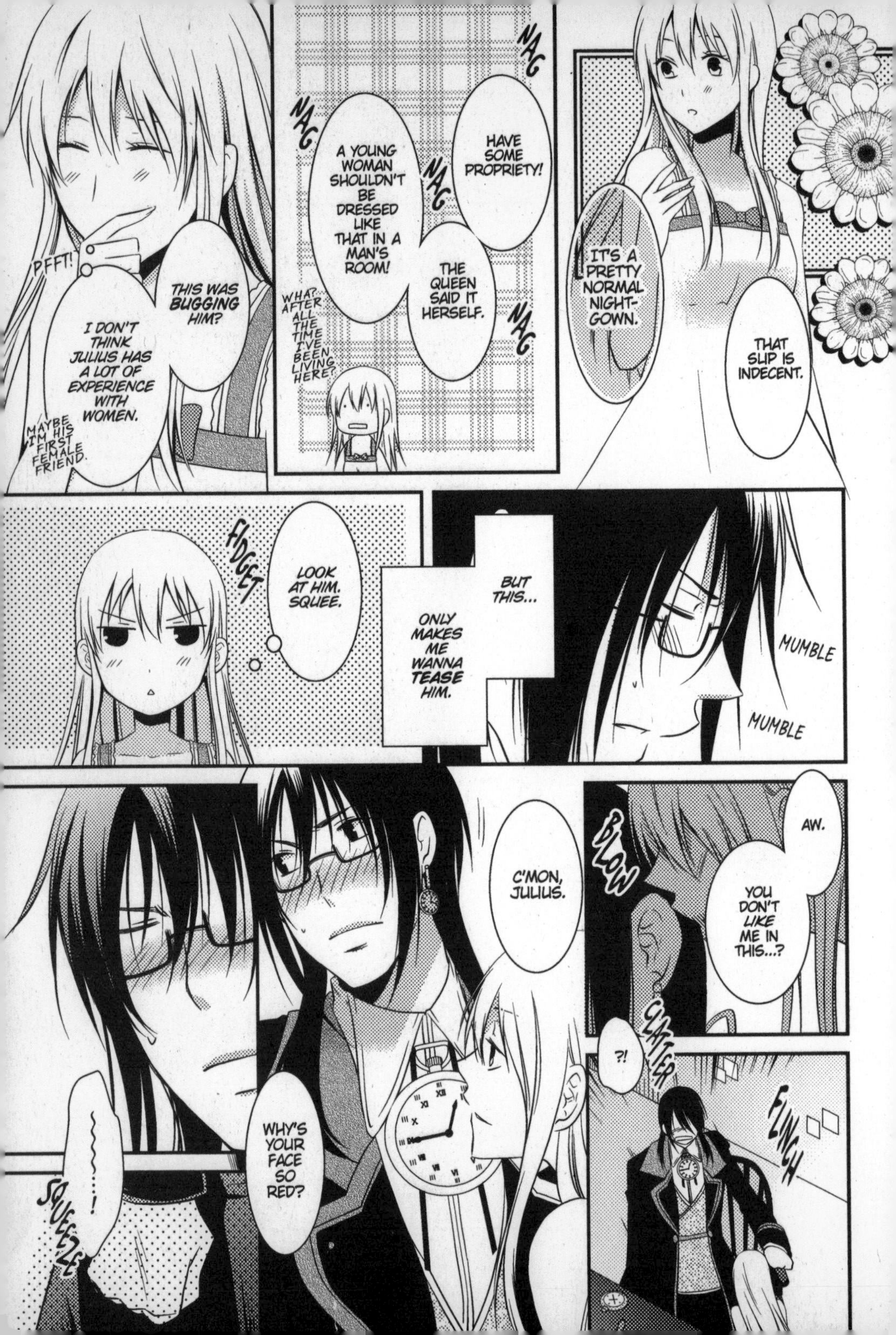
THAT SLIP IS INDECENT.
IT'S A PRETTY NORMAL NIGHT-GOWN.
NAG
HAVE SOME PROPRIETY!
NAG
A YOUNG WOMAN SHOULDN'T BE DRESSED LIKE THAT IN A MAN'S ROOM!
NAG
THE QUEEN SAID IT HERSELF.
NAG
WHAT? AFTER ALL THE TIME I'VE BEEN LIVING HERE?
PFFT!
THIS WAS BUGGING HIM?
I DON'T THINK JULIUS HAS A LOT OF EXPERIENCE WITH WOMEN.
MAYBE I'M HIS FIRST FEMALE FRIEND.
MUMBLE
MUMBLE
BUT THIS...
ONLY MAKES ME WANNA TEASE HIM.
FIDGET
LOOK AT HIM. SQUEE.
AW.
YOU DON'T LIKE ME IN THIS...?
BLOW
FLINCH
CLATTER
?!
C'MON, JULIUS.
WHY'S YOUR FACE SO RED?
......!
SQUEEZE

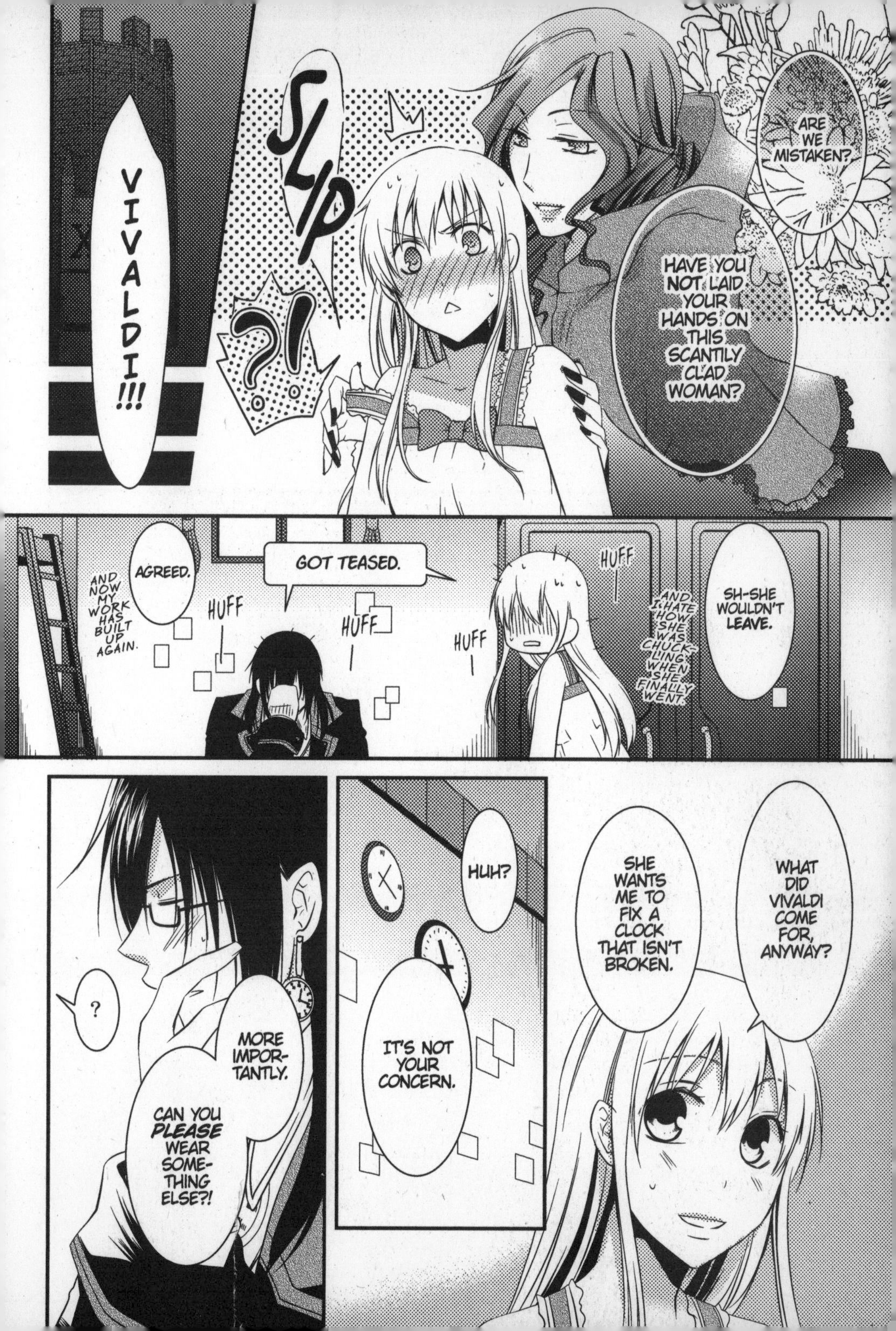
ARE WE MISTAKEN?
HAVE YOU NOT LAID YOUR HANDS ON THIS SCANTILY CLAD WOMAN?
SLIP
?!
VIVALDI!!!
SH-SHE WOULDN'T LEAVE.
AND I HATE HOW SHE WAS CHUCKLING WHEN SHE FINALLY WENT.
HUFF
HUFF
HUFF
HUFF
GOT TEASED.
AGREED.
AND NOW MY WORK HAS BUILT UP AGAIN.
WHAT DID VIVALDI COME FOR, ANYWAY?
SHE WANTS ME TO FIX A CLOCK THAT ISN'T BROKEN.
HUH?
IT'S NOT YOUR CONCERN.
?
MORE IMPORTANTLY.
CAN YOU PLEASE WEAR SOMETHING ELSE?!

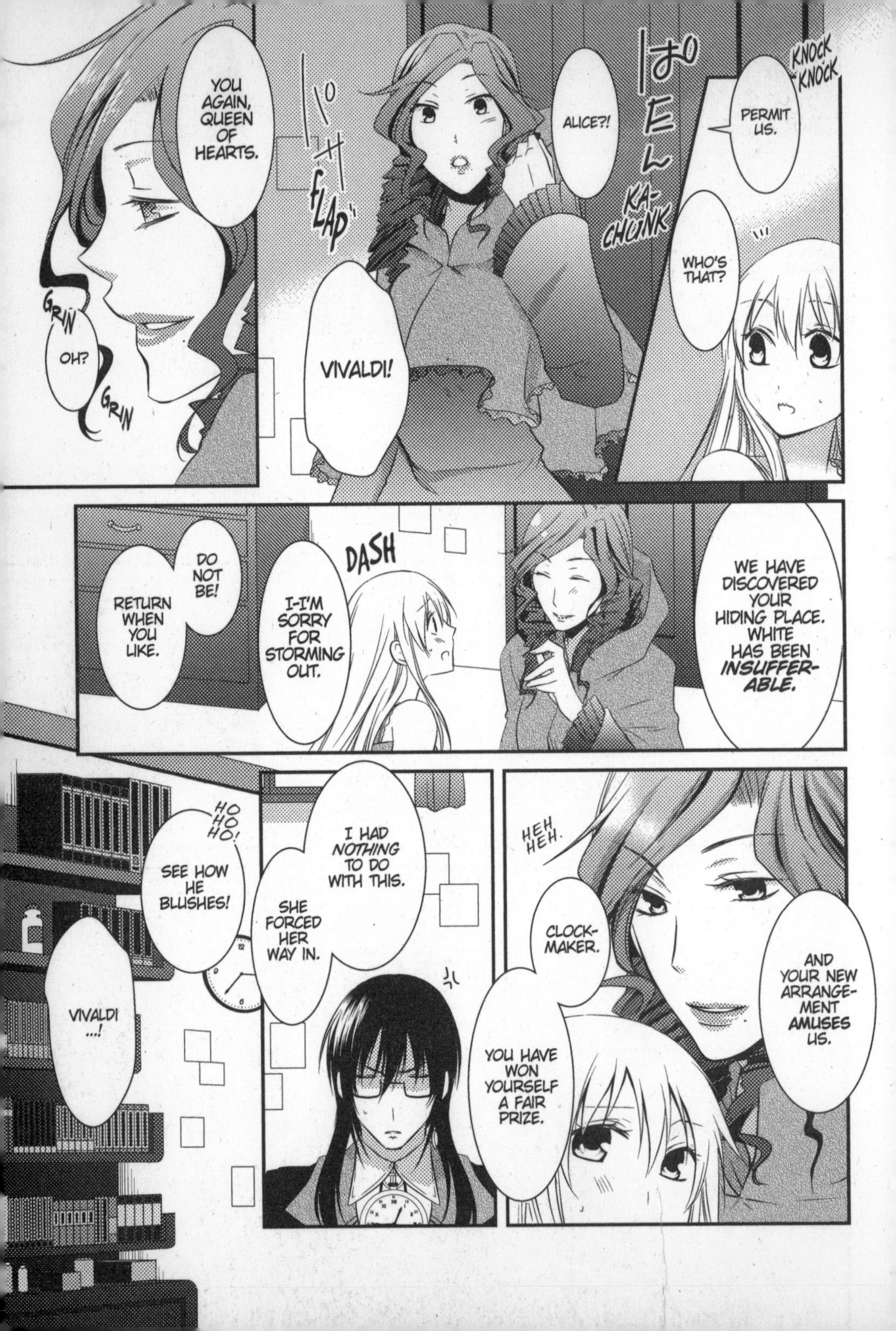
KNOCK KNOCK
PERMIT US.
...
WHO'S THAT?
KA-CHUNK
ALICE?!
FLAP
VIVALDI!
YOU AGAIN, QUEEN OF HEARTS.
GRIN
OH?
GRIN
WE HAVE DISCOVERED YOUR HIDING PLACE. WHITE HAS BEEN *INSUFFERABLE.*
DASH
I-I'M SORRY FOR STORMING OUT.
DO NOT BE!
RETURN WHEN YOU LIKE.
HEH HEH.
AND YOUR NEW ARRANGEMENT AMUSES US.
CLOCK-MAKER.
YOU HAVE WON YOURSELF A FAIR PRIZE.
I HAD *NOTHING* TO DO WITH THIS.
SHE FORCED HER WAY IN.
HO HO HO!
SEE HOW HE BLUSHES!
VIVALDI ...!

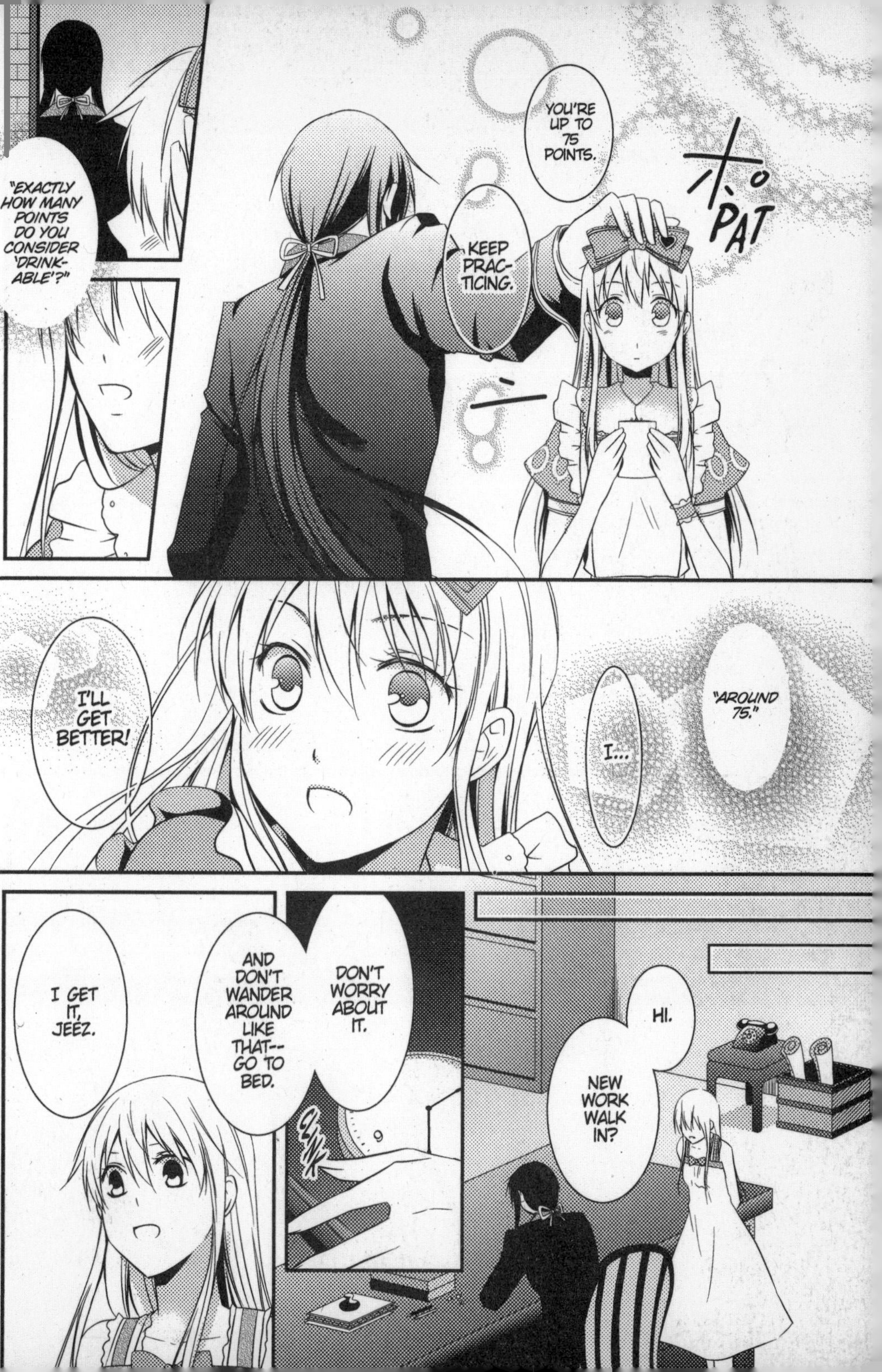
YOU'RE UP TO 75 POINTS.
PAT
KEEP PRACTICING.
"EXACTLY HOW MANY POINTS DO YOU CONSIDER 'DRINKABLE'?"
"AROUND 75."
I...
I'LL GET BETTER!
HI.
NEW WORK WALK IN?
DON'T WORRY ABOUT IT.
AND DON'T WANDER AROUND LIKE THAT--GO TO BED.
CLINK
I GET IT, JEEZ.

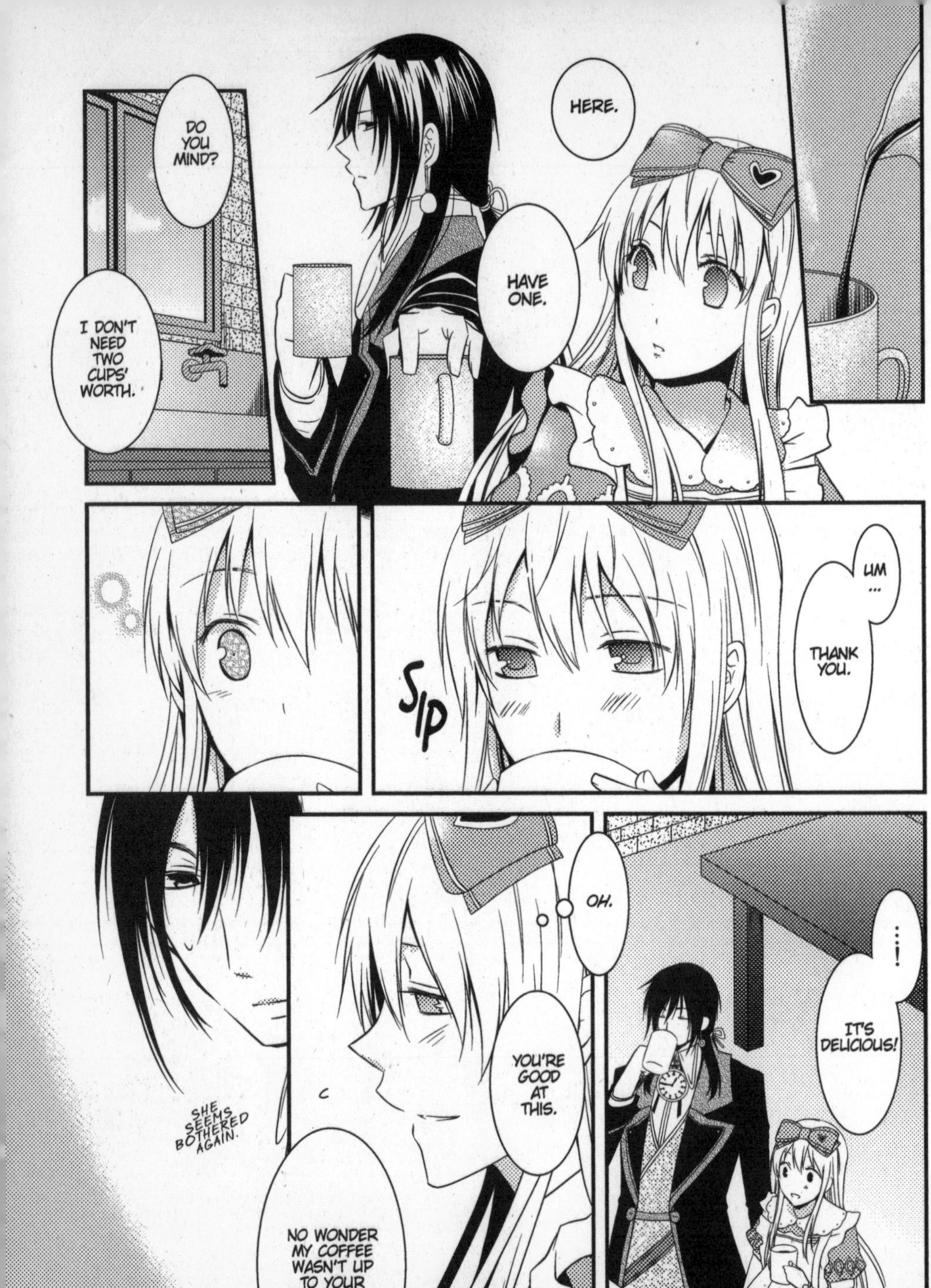
HERE.
HAVE ONE.
DO YOU MIND?
I DON'T NEED TWO CUPS' WORTH.
UM ... THANK YOU.
SIP
...!
IT'S DELICIOUS!
OH.
YOU'RE GOOD AT THIS.
NO WONDER MY COFFEE WASN'T UP TO YOUR STANDARDS.
SHE SEEMS BOTHERED AGAIN.

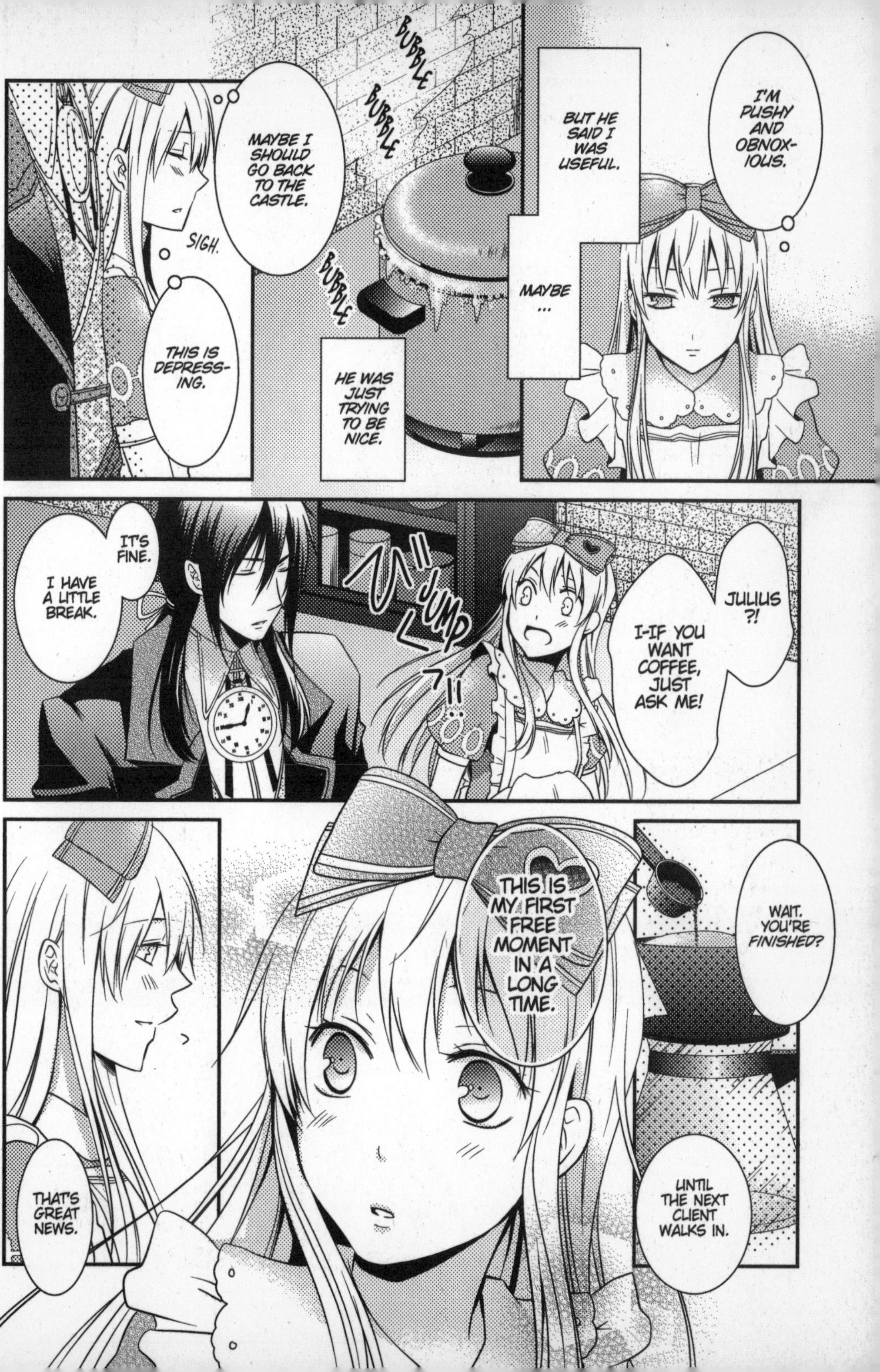
I'M PUSHY AND OBNOX-IOUS.
BUT HE SAID I WAS USEFUL.
MAYBE ...
BUBBLE
BUBBLE
HE WAS JUST TRYING TO BE NICE.
BUBBLE
MAYBE I SHOULD GO BACK TO THE CASTLE.
SIGH.
THIS IS DEPRESS-ING.
JULIUS?!
I-IF YOU WANT COFFEE, JUST ASK ME!
JUMP
IT'S FINE.
I HAVE A LITTLE BREAK.
WAIT. YOU'RE FINISHED?
UNTIL THE NEXT CLIENT WALKS IN.
THIS IS MY FIRST FREE MOMENT IN A LONG TIME.
THAT'S GREAT NEWS.

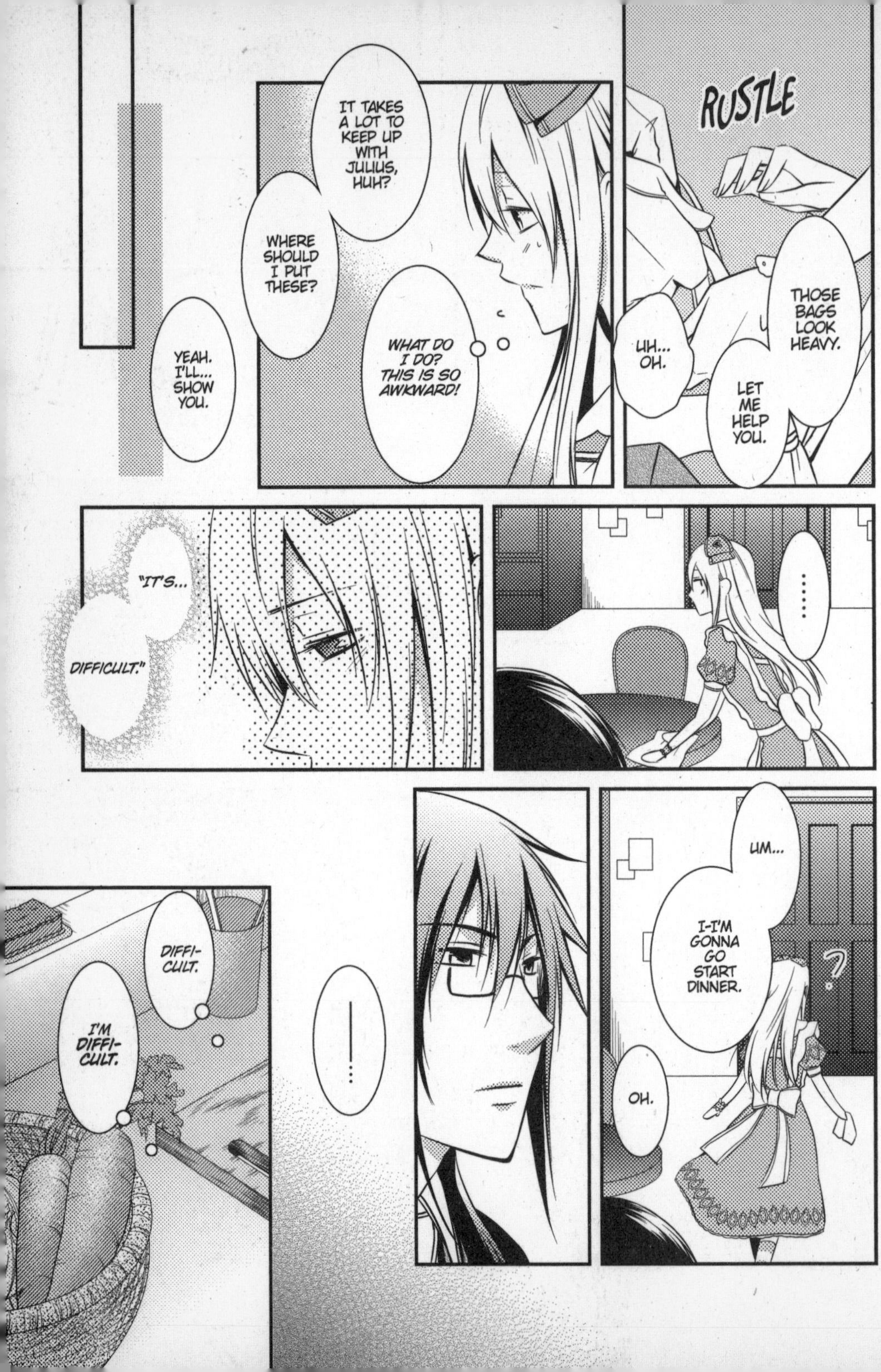
RUSTLE
THOSE BAGS LOOK HEAVY.
LET ME HELP YOU.
UH... OH.
IT TAKES A LOT TO KEEP UP WITH JULIUS, HUH?
WHERE SHOULD I PUT THESE?
WHAT DO I DO? THIS IS SO AWKWARD!
YEAH. I'LL... SHOW YOU.
......
"IT'S...
DIFFICULT."
UM...
I-I'M GONNA GO START DINNER.
?
OH.
—......
DIFFI-CULT.
I'M DIFFI-CULT.

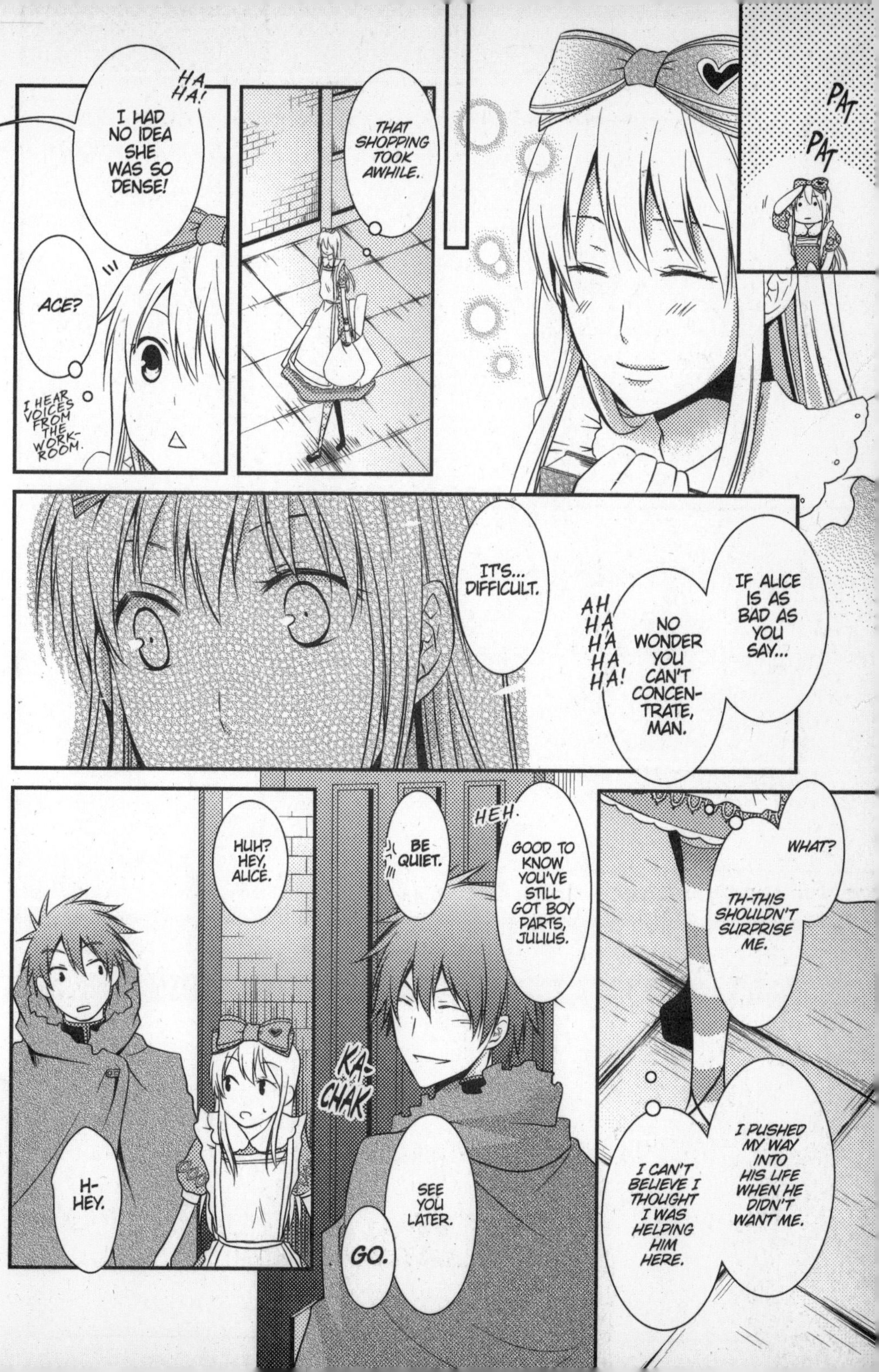
PAT PAT
THAT SHOPPING TOOK AWHILE.
I HEAR VOICES FROM THE WORK-ROOM.
ACE?
HA HA!
I HAD NO IDEA SHE WAS SO DENSE!
IF ALICE IS AS BAD AS YOU SAY...
NO WONDER YOU CAN'T CONCEN-TRATE, MAN.
AH HA HA HA HA HA!
IT'S... DIFFICULT.
WHAT?
TH-THIS SHOULDN'T SURPRISE ME.
I PUSHED MY WAY INTO HIS LIFE WHEN HE DIDN'T WANT ME.
I CAN'T BELIEVE I THOUGHT I WAS HELPING HIM HERE.
HEH.
GOOD TO KNOW YOU'VE STILL GOT BOY PARTS, JULIUS.
BE QUIET.
KA-CHAK
SEE YOU LATER.
GO.
HUH? HEY, ALICE.
H-HEY.

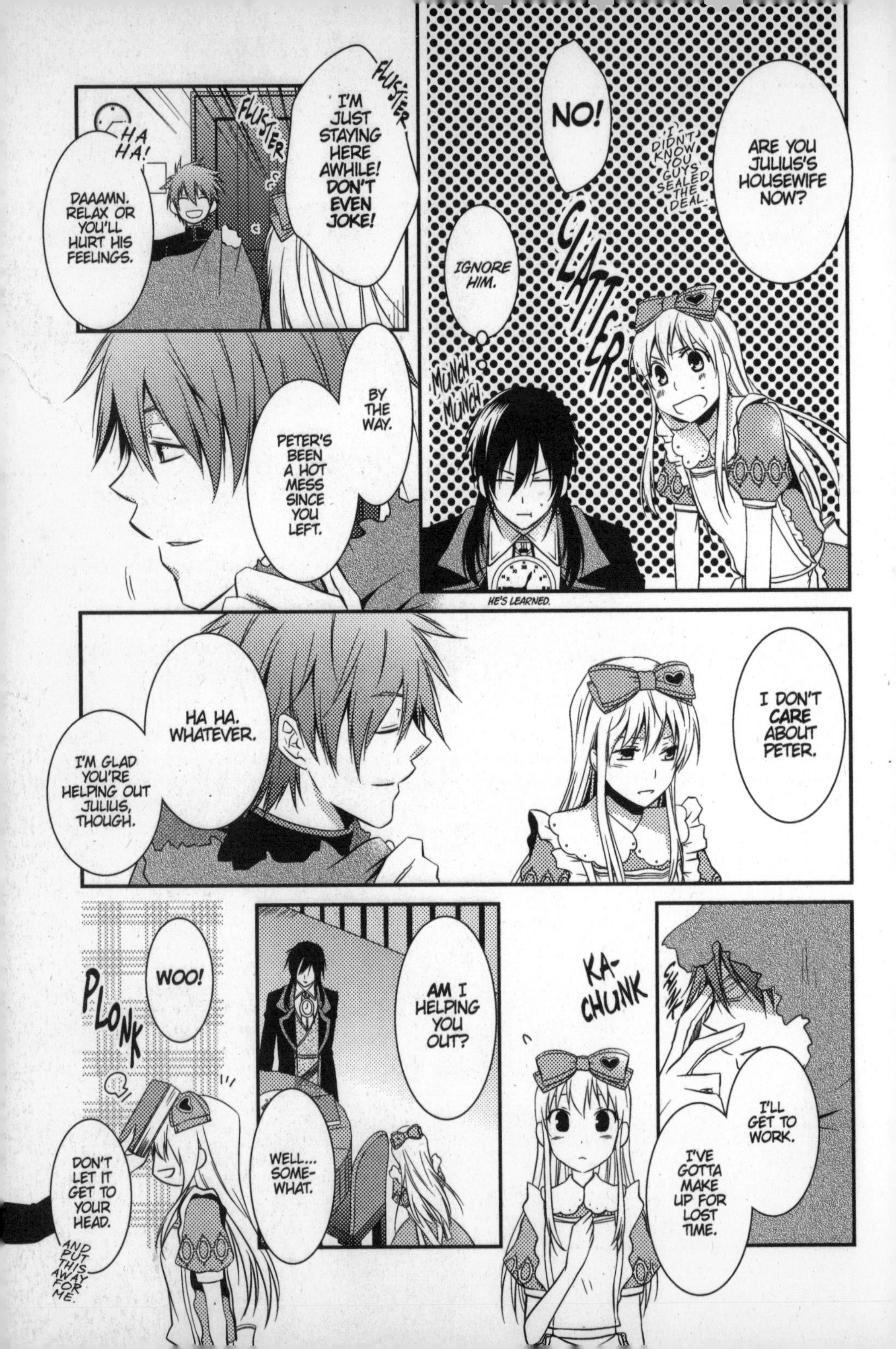
ARE YOU JULIUS'S HOUSEWIFE NOW?
I DIDN'T KNOW YOU GUYS SEALED THE DEAL.
NO!
CLATTER
IGNORE HIM.
MUNCH MUNCH
HE'S LEARNED.
FLUSTER
I'M JUST STAYING HERE AWHILE! DON'T EVEN JOKE!
FLUSTER
HA HA!
DAAAMN. RELAX OR YOU'LL HURT HIS FEELINGS.
BY THE WAY.
PETER'S BEEN A HOT MESS SINCE YOU LEFT.
I DON'T CARE ABOUT PETER.
HA HA. WHATEVER.
I'M GLAD YOU'RE HELPING OUT JULIUS, THOUGH.
CHUNK
I'LL GET TO WORK.
I'VE GOTTA MAKE UP FOR LOST TIME.
KA-CHUNK
AM I HELPING YOU OUT?
WELL... SOME-WHAT.
WOO!
PLONK
DON'T LET IT GET TO YOUR HEAD.
AND PUT THIS AWAY FOR ME.

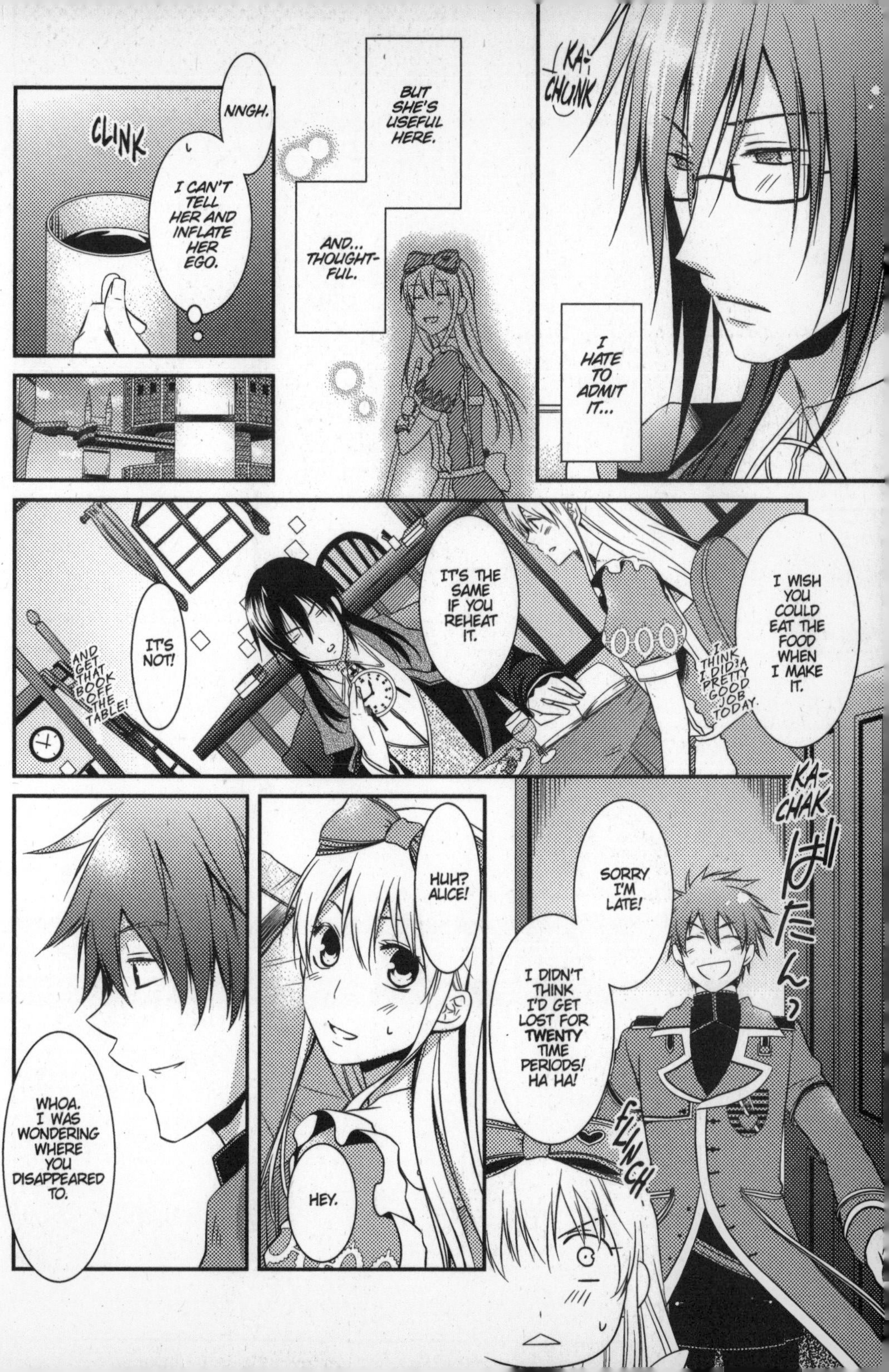
KA-CHUNK
I HATE TO ADMIT IT...
BUT SHE'S USEFUL HERE.
AND... THOUGHTFUL.
NNGH.
CLINK
I CAN'T TELL HER AND INFLATE HER EGO.
I WISH YOU COULD EAT THE FOOD WHEN I MAKE IT.
I THINK I DID A PRETTY GOOD JOB TODAY.
IT'S THE SAME IF YOU REHEAT IT.
IT'S NOT!
AND GET THAT BOOK OFF THE TABLE!
KA-CHAK
ばたんっ
SORRY I'M LATE!
I DIDN'T THINK I'D GET LOST FOR TWENTY TIME PERIODS! HA HA!
FLINCH
HUH? ALICE!
HEY.
WHOA. I WAS WONDERING WHERE YOU DISAPPEARED TO.

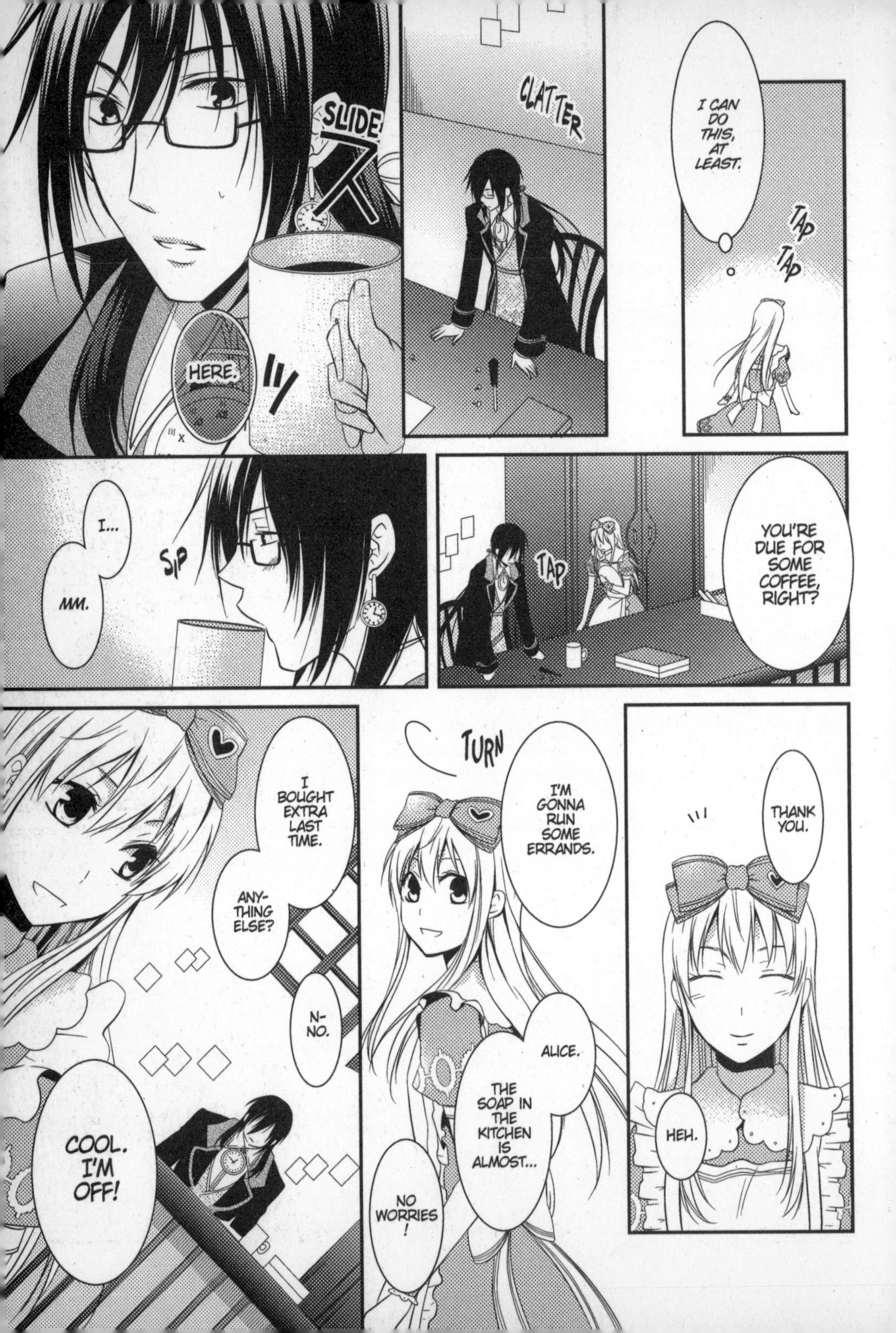
I CAN DO THIS, AT LEAST.
TAP TAP
CLATTER
SLIDE
HERE.
YOU'RE DUE FOR SOME COFFEE, RIGHT?
TAP
I...
SIP
MM.
THANK YOU.
HEH.
TURN
I'M GONNA RUN SOME ERRANDS.
ALICE.
THE SOAP IN THE KITCHEN IS ALMOST...
NO WORRIES!
I BOUGHT EXTRA LAST TIME.
ANYTHING ELSE?
N-NO.
COOL. I'M OFF!

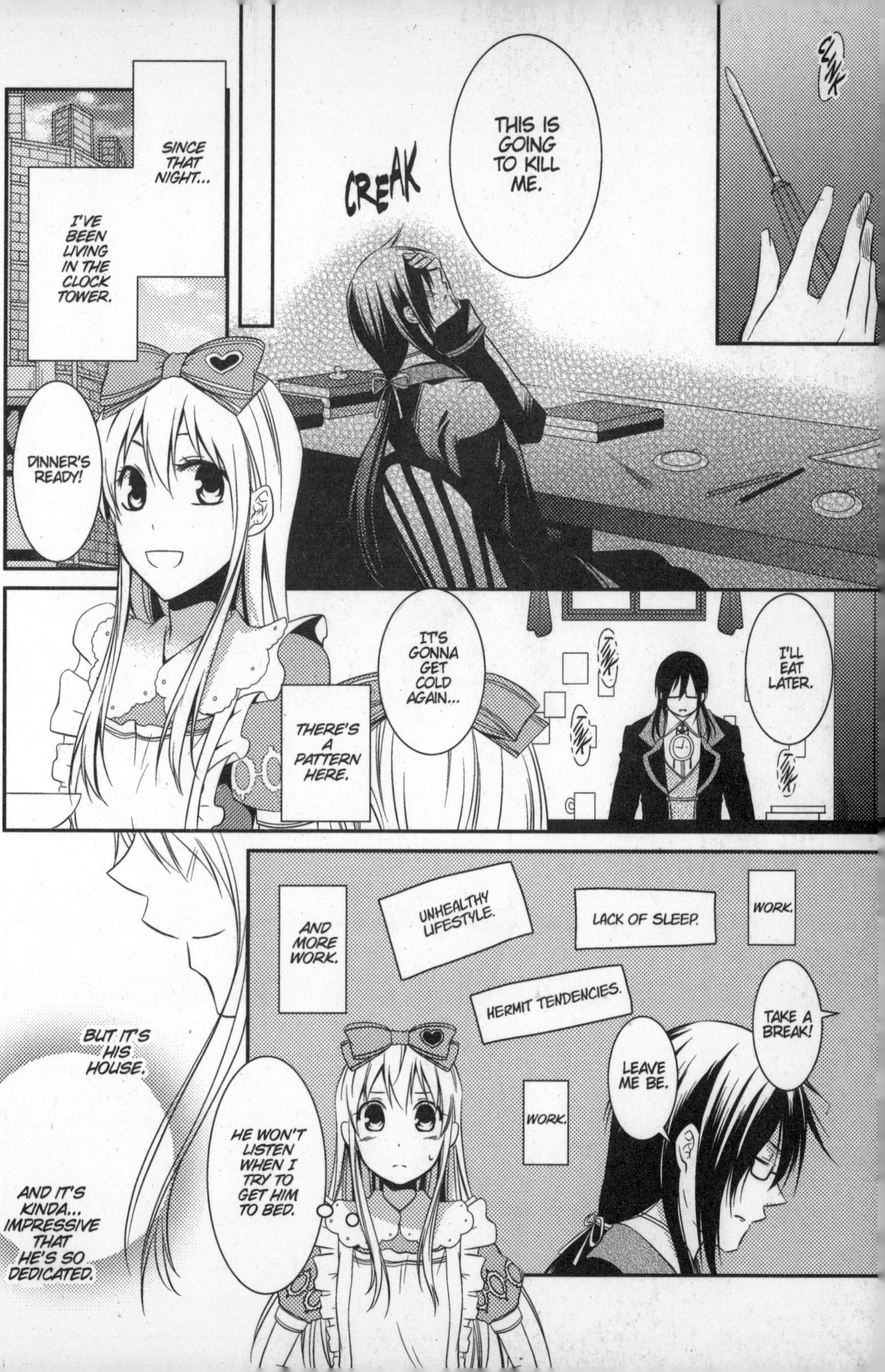
CLINK
THIS IS GOING TO KILL ME.
CREAK
SINCE THAT NIGHT...
I'VE BEEN LIVING IN THE CLOCK TOWER.
DINNER'S READY!
I'LL EAT LATER.
TINK
TINK
TINK
IT'S GONNA GET COLD AGAIN...
THERE'S A PATTERN HERE.
WORK.
LACK OF SLEEP.
UNHEALTHY LIFESTYLE.
AND MORE WORK.
HERMIT TENDENCIES.
TAKE A BREAK!
LEAVE ME BE.
WORK.
HE WON'T LISTEN WHEN I TRY TO GET HIM TO BED.
BUT IT'S HIS HOUSE.
AND IT'S KINDA... IMPRESSIVE THAT HE'S SO DEDICATED.

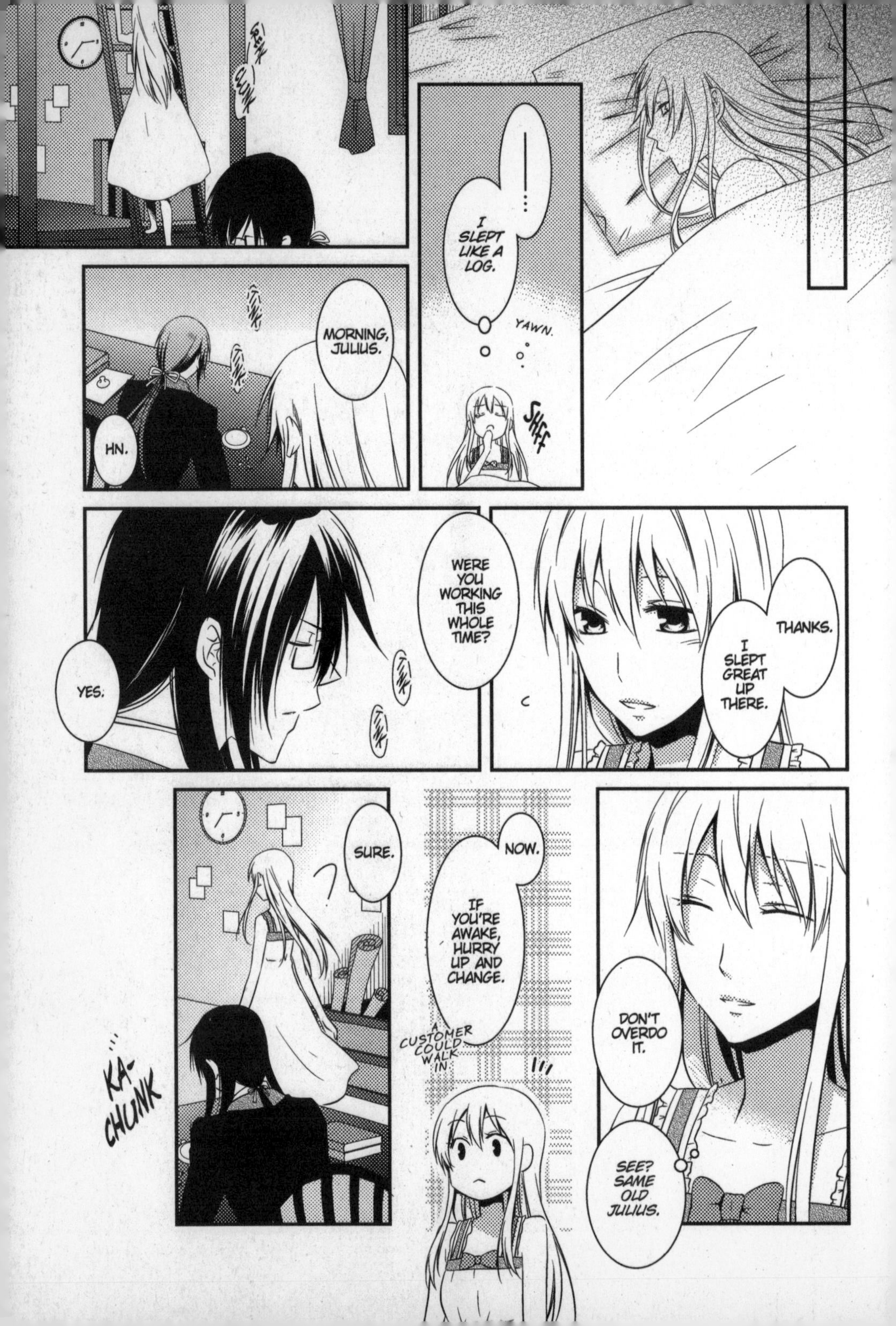
!
...
I SLEPT LIKE A LOG.
YAWN.
SHFF
CREAK CLUNK
MORNING, JULIUS.
TINK
TINK
HN.
THANKS.
I SLEPT GREAT UP THERE.
WERE YOU WORKING THIS WHOLE TIME?
TINK
TINK
YES.
DON'T OVERDO IT.
SEE? SAME OLD JULIUS.
NOW.
IF YOU'RE AWAKE, HURRY UP AND CHANGE.
A CUSTOMER COULD WALK IN
SURE.
KA-CHUNK

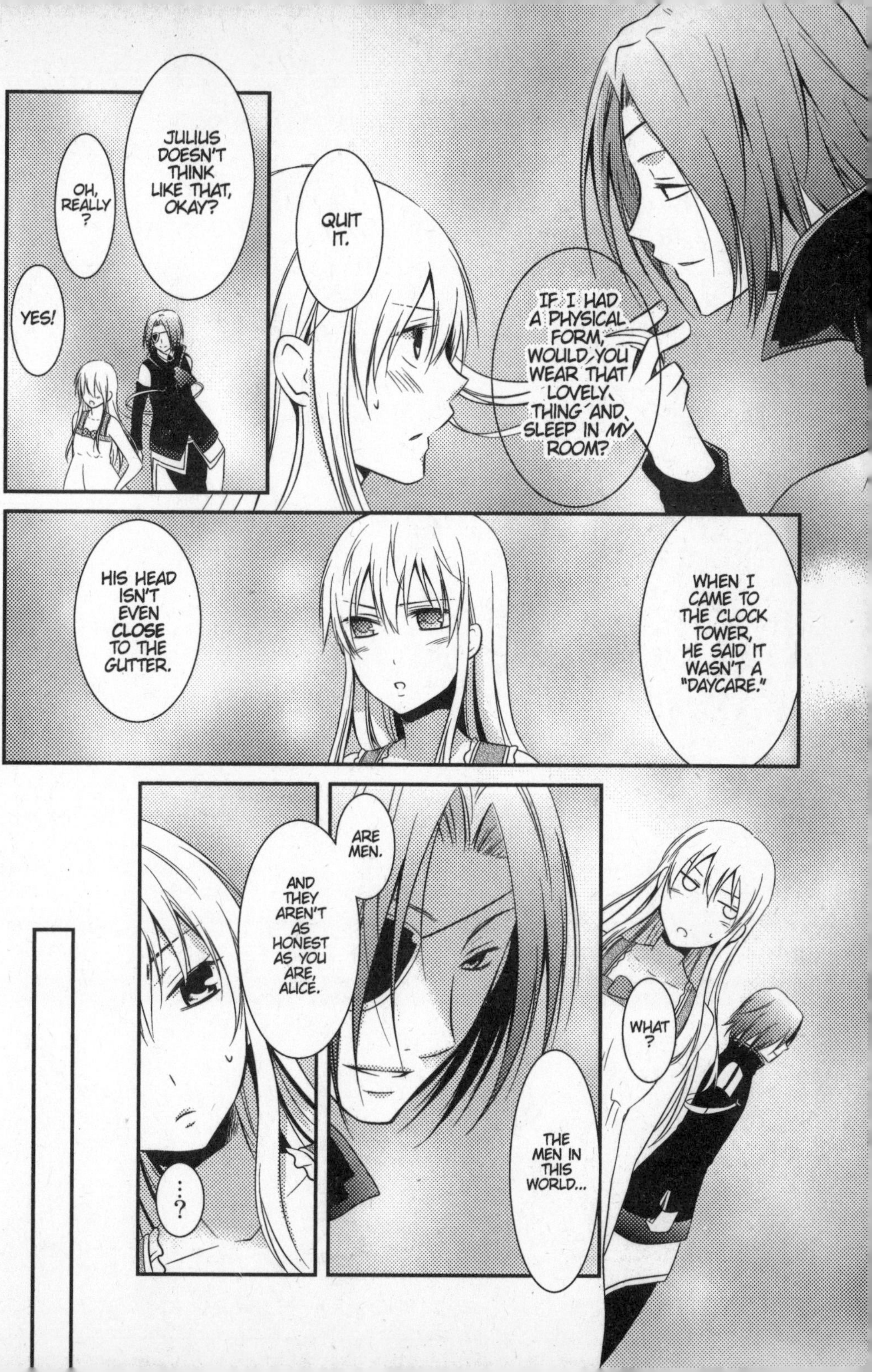

IF I HAD A PHYSICAL FORM, WOULD YOU WEAR THAT LOVELY THING AND SLEEP IN MY ROOM?
QUIT IT.
JULIUS DOESN'T THINK LIKE THAT, OKAY?
OH, REALLY?
YES!
WHEN I CAME TO THE CLOCK TOWER, HE SAID IT WASN'T A "DAYCARE."
HIS HEAD ISN'T EVEN CLOSE TO THE GUTTER.
WHAT?
THE MEN IN THIS WORLD...
ARE MEN.
AND THEY AREN'T AS HONEST AS YOU ARE, ALICE.
...?

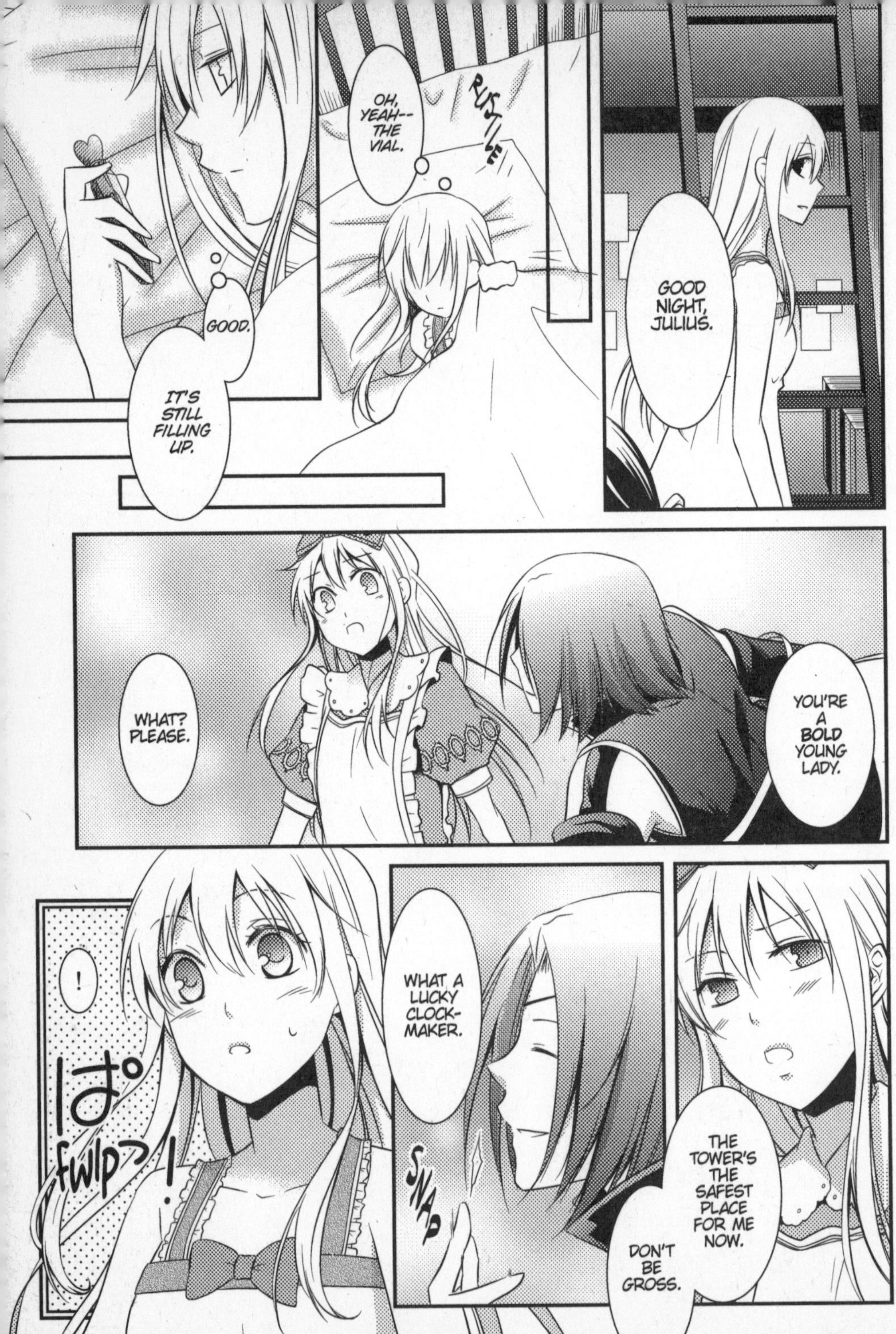
GOOD NIGHT, JULIUS.
OH, YEAH-- THE VIAL.
RUSTLE
GOOD.
IT'S STILL FILLING UP.
YOU'RE A BOLD YOUNG LADY.
WHAT? PLEASE.
THE TOWER'S THE SAFEST PLACE FOR ME NOW.
DON'T BE GROSS.
WHAT A LUCKY CLOCK-MAKER.
SNAP
!
ぱっ!
fwip

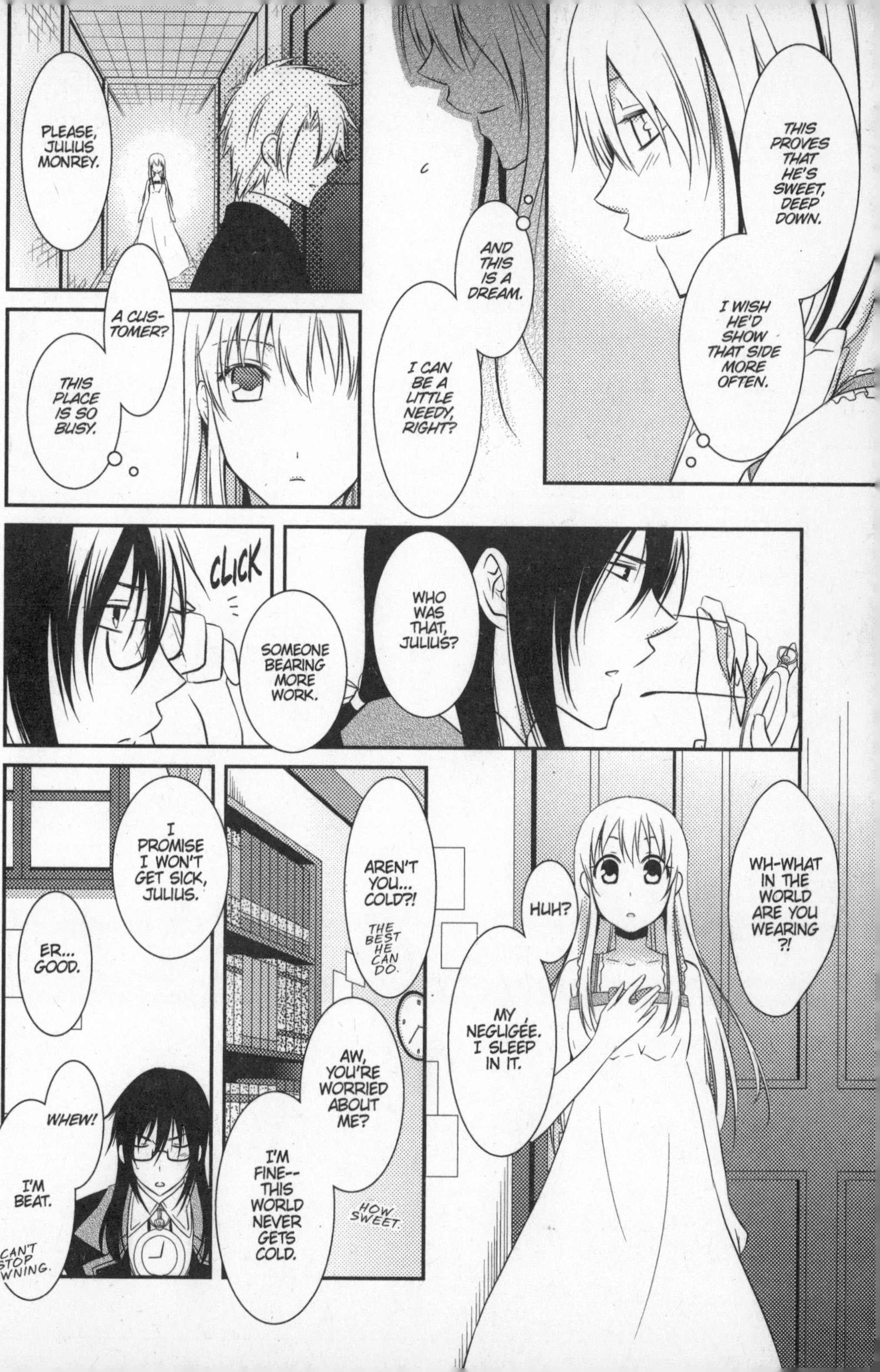
THIS PROVES THAT HE'S SWEET, DEEP DOWN.
I WISH HE'D SHOW THAT SIDE MORE OFTEN.
AND THIS IS A DREAM.
I CAN BE A LITTLE NEEDY, RIGHT?
PLEASE, JULIUS MONREY.
A CUS-TOMER?
THIS PLACE IS SO BUSY.
WHO WAS THAT, JULIUS?
CLICK
SOMEONE BEARING MORE WORK.
WH-WHAT IN THE WORLD ARE YOU WEARING?!
HUH?
MY NEGLIGÉE. I SLEEP IN IT.
AREN'T YOU... COLD?!
THE BEST HE CAN DO.
AW, YOU'RE WORRIED ABOUT ME?
I'M FINE-- THIS WORLD NEVER GETS COLD.
HOW SWEET.
I PROMISE I WON'T GET SICK, JULIUS.
ER... GOOD.
WHEW!
I'M BEAT.
I CAN'T STOP YAWNING.

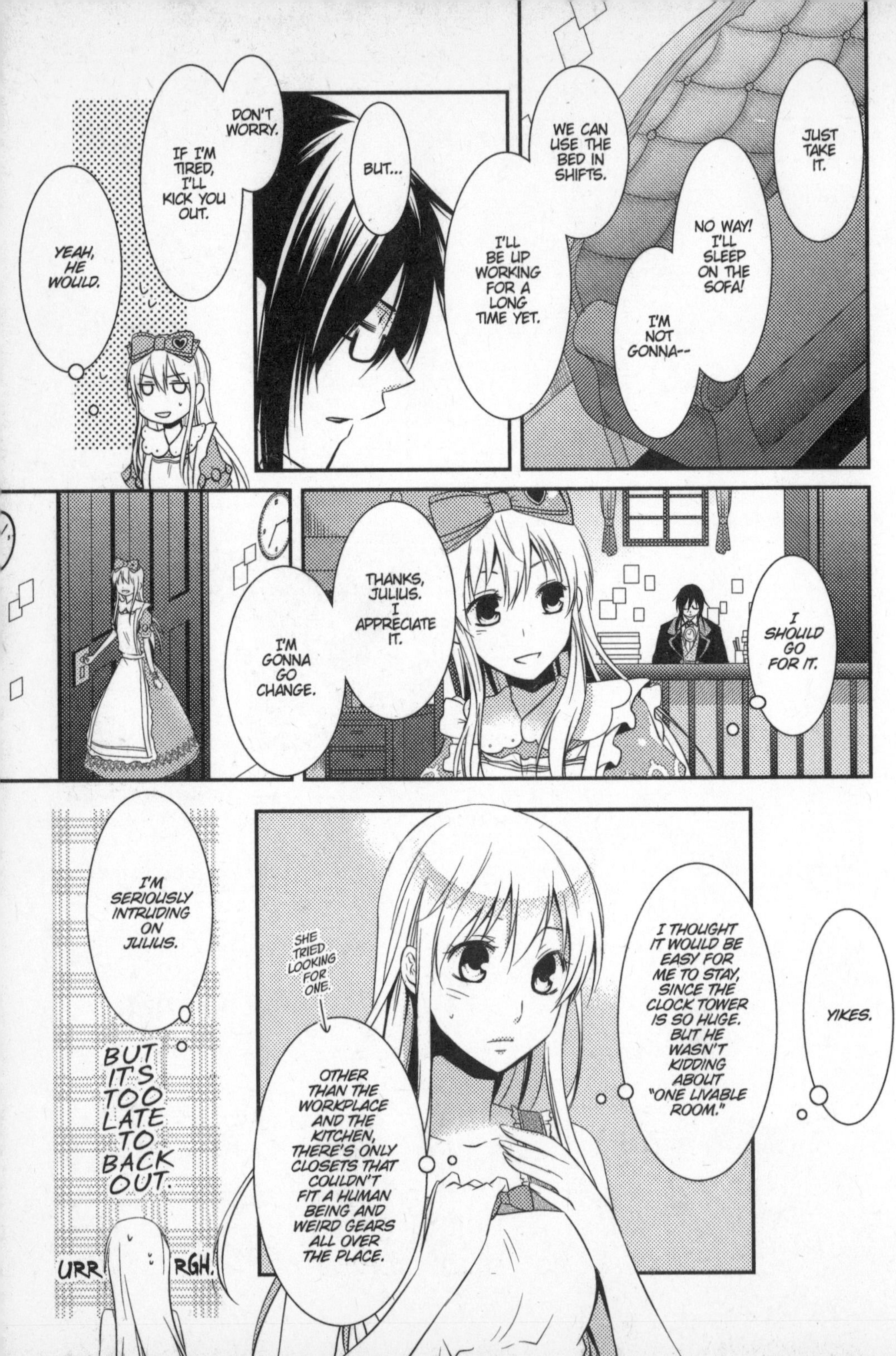
JUST TAKE IT.
NO WAY! I'LL SLEEP ON THE SOFA!
I'M NOT GONNA--
WE CAN USE THE BED IN SHIFTS.
I'LL BE UP WORKING FOR A LONG TIME YET.
BUT...
DON'T WORRY.
IF I'M TIRED, I'LL KICK YOU OUT.
YEAH, HE WOULD.
I SHOULD GO FOR IT.
THANKS, JULIUS. I APPRECIATE IT.
I'M GONNA GO CHANGE.
YIKES.
I THOUGHT IT WOULD BE EASY FOR ME TO STAY, SINCE THE CLOCK TOWER IS SO HUGE. BUT HE WASN'T KIDDING ABOUT "ONE LIVABLE ROOM."
SHE TRIED LOOKING FOR ONE.
OTHER THAN THE WORKPLACE AND THE KITCHEN, THERE'S ONLY CLOSETS THAT COULDN'T FIT A HUMAN BEING AND WEIRD GEARS ALL OVER THE PLACE.
I'M SERIOUSLY INTRUDING ON JULIUS.
BUT IT'S TOO LATE TO BACK OUT.
URRRGH.

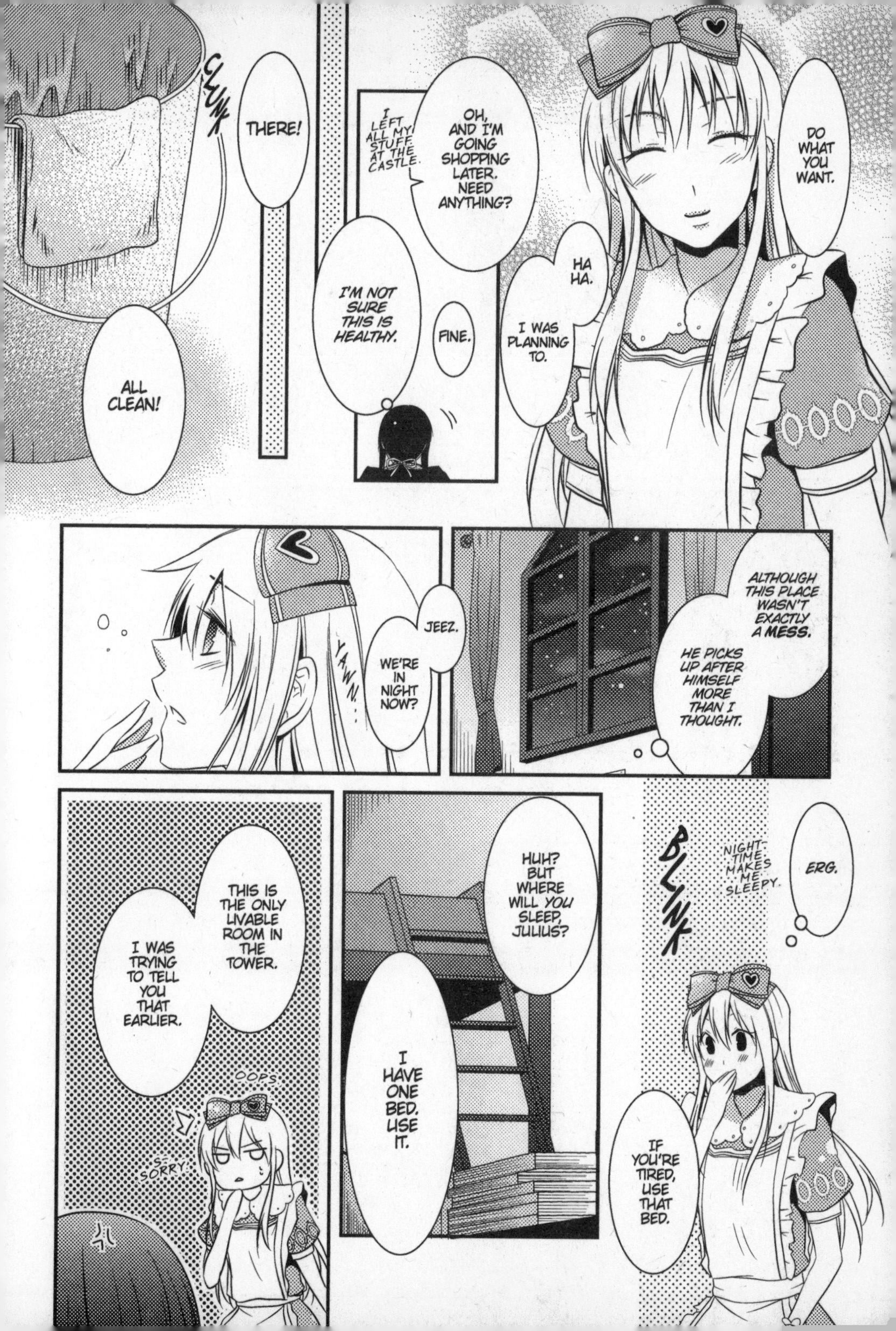
DO WHAT YOU WANT.
HA HA.
I WAS PLANNING TO.
OH, AND I'M GOING SHOPPING LATER. NEED ANYTHING?
I LEFT ALL MY STUFF AT THE CASTLE.
FINE.
I'M NOT SURE THIS IS HEALTHY.
CLUNK
THERE!
ALL CLEAN!
ALTHOUGH THIS PLACE WASN'T EXACTLY A MESS.
HE PICKS UP AFTER HIMSELF MORE THAN I THOUGHT.
JEEZ.
WE'RE IN NIGHT NOW?
YAWN...
ERG.
NIGHT-TIME MAKES ME SLEEPY.
BLINK
IF YOU'RE TIRED, USE THAT BED.
HUH? BUT WHERE WILL YOU SLEEP, JULIUS?
I HAVE ONE BED. USE IT.
THIS IS THE ONLY LIVABLE ROOM IN THE TOWER.
I WAS TRYING TO TELL YOU THAT EARLIER.
OOPS
S-SORRY.

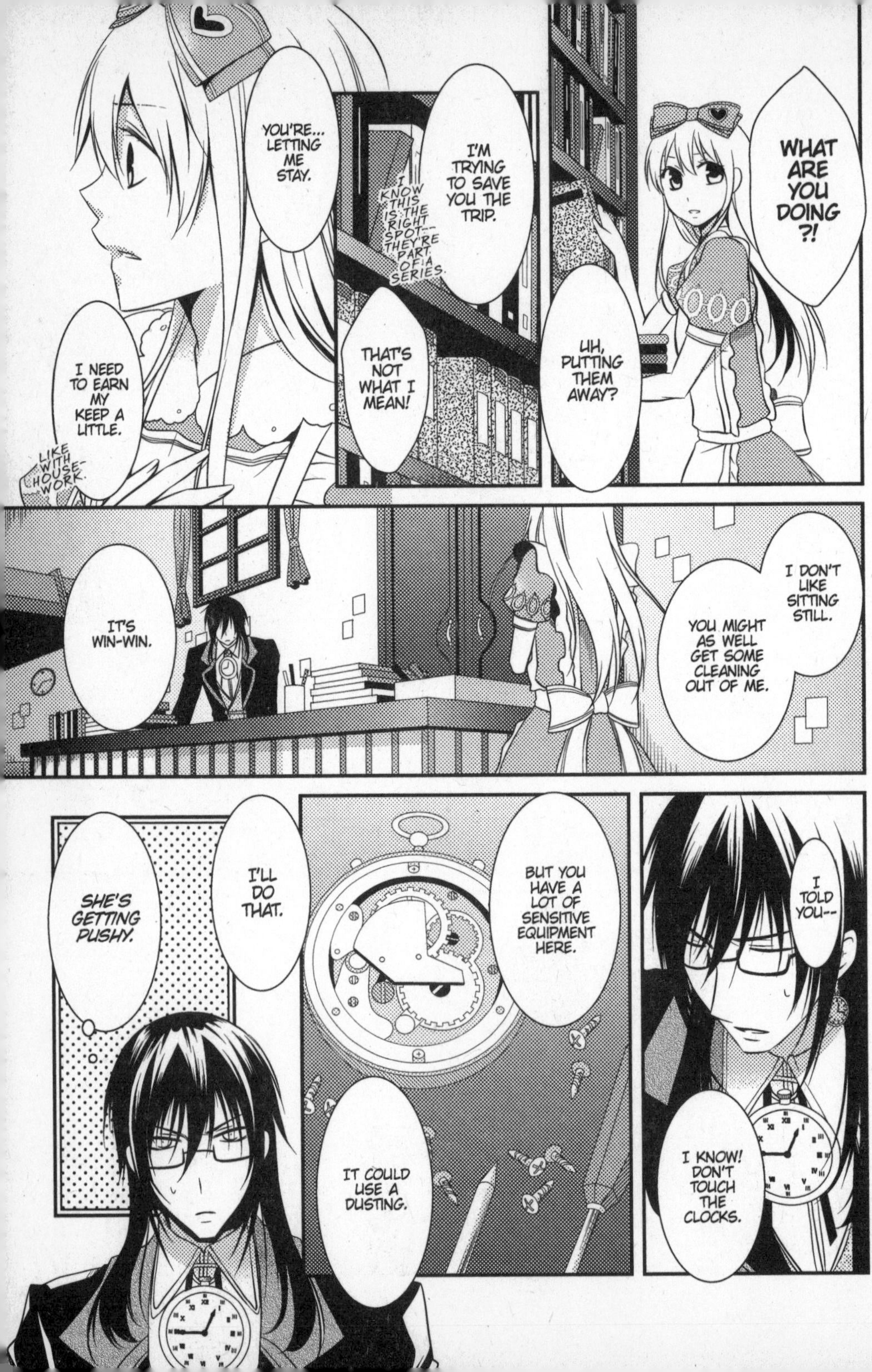
WHAT ARE YOU DOING?!
UH, PUTTING THEM AWAY?
I'M TRYING TO SAVE YOU THE TRIP.
I KNOW THIS IS THE RIGHT SPOT-- THEY'RE PART OF A SERIES.
THAT'S NOT WHAT I MEAN!
YOU'RE... LETTING ME STAY.
I NEED TO EARN MY KEEP A LITTLE.
LIKE WITH HOUSE-WORK.
I DON'T LIKE SITTING STILL.
YOU MIGHT AS WELL GET SOME CLEANING OUT OF ME.
IT'S WIN-WIN.
I TOLD YOU--
I KNOW! DON'T TOUCH THE CLOCKS.
BUT YOU HAVE A LOT OF SENSITIVE EQUIPMENT HERE.
IT COULD USE A DUSTING.
I'LL DO THAT.
SHE'S GETTING PUSHY.

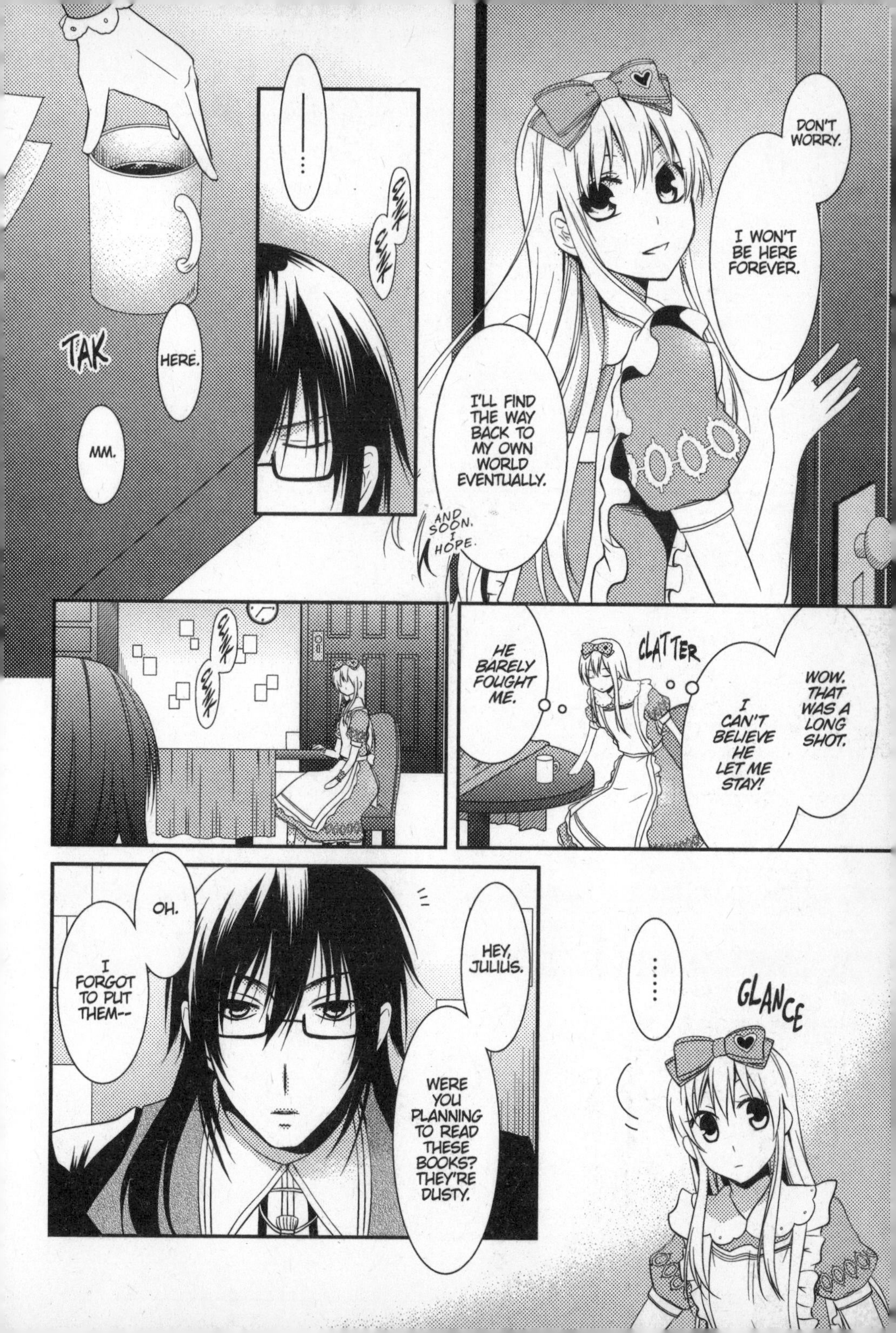
DON'T WORRY.
I WON'T BE HERE FOREVER.
I'LL FIND THE WAY BACK TO MY OWN WORLD EVENTUALLY.
AND SOON, I HOPE.
......
CLINK CLINK
TAK
HERE.
MM.
WOW. THAT WAS A LONG SHOT.
I CAN'T BELIEVE HE LET ME STAY!
CLATTER
HE BARELY FOUGHT ME.
CLINK CLINK
......
GLANCE
HEY, JULIUS.
WERE YOU PLANNING TO READ THESE BOOKS? THEY'RE DUSTY.
OH.
I FORGOT TO PUT THEM--

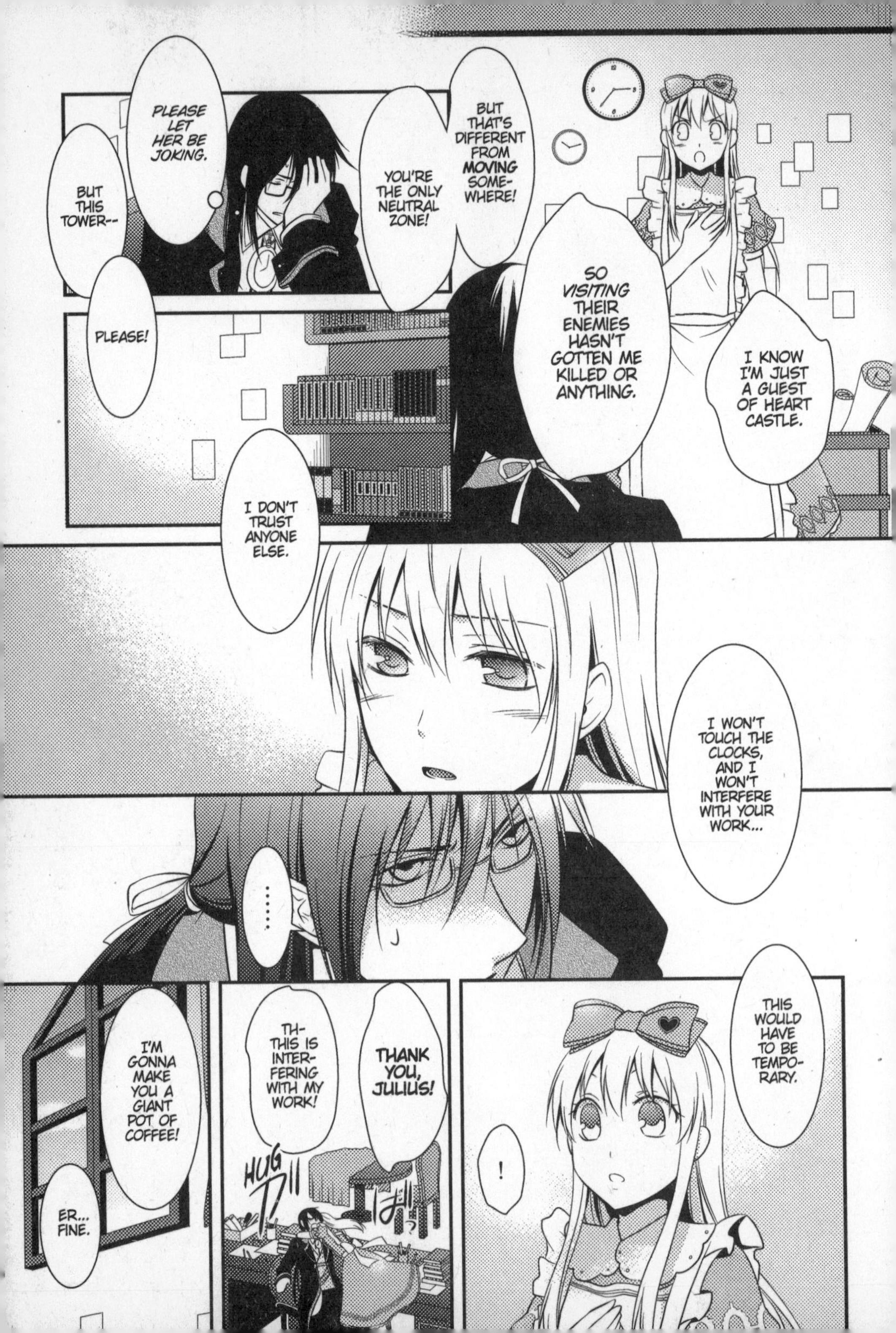

I KNOW I'M JUST A GUEST OF HEART CASTLE.
SO VISITING THEIR ENEMIES HASN'T GOTTEN ME KILLED OR ANYTHING.
BUT THAT'S DIFFERENT FROM MOVING SOMEWHERE!
YOU'RE THE ONLY NEUTRAL ZONE!
PLEASE LET HER BE JOKING.
BUT THIS TOWER--
PLEASE!
I DON'T TRUST ANYONE ELSE.
I WON'T TOUCH THE CLOCKS, AND I WON'T INTERFERE WITH YOUR WORK...
......
THIS WOULD HAVE TO BE TEMPORARY.
!
THANK YOU, JULIUS!
TH-THIS IS INTERFERING WITH MY WORK!
HUG
I'M GONNA MAKE YOU A GIANT POT OF COFFEE!
ER... FINE.

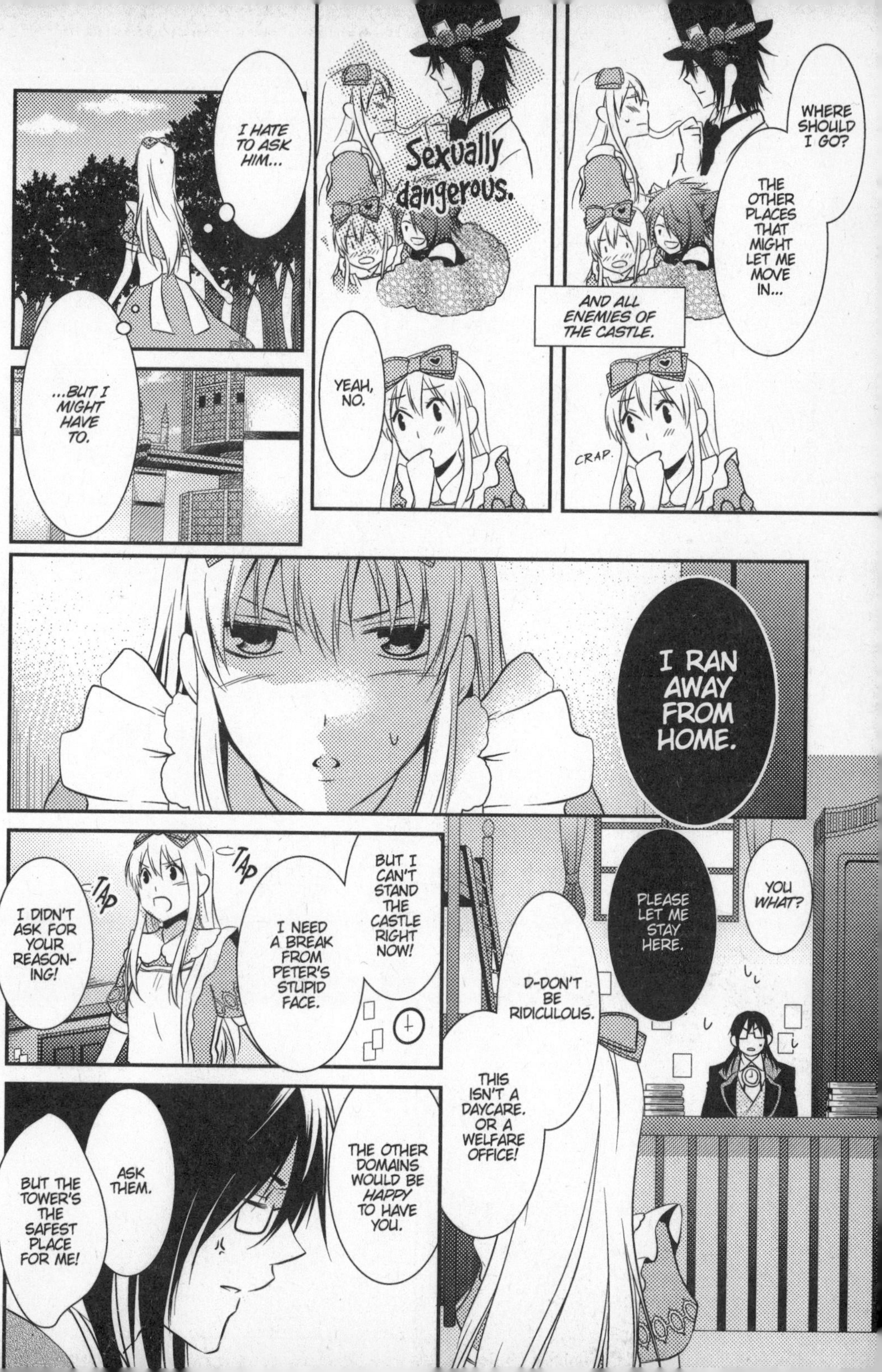

WHERE SHOULD I GO?
THE OTHER PLACES THAT MIGHT LET ME MOVE IN...
AND ALL ENEMIES OF THE CASTLE.
CRAP.
Sexually dangerous.
YEAH, NO.
I HATE TO ASK HIM...
...BUT I MIGHT HAVE TO.
I RAN AWAY FROM HOME.
YOU WHAT?
PLEASE LET ME STAY HERE.
D-DON'T BE RIDICULOUS.
THIS ISN'T A DAYCARE. OR A WELFARE OFFICE!
BUT I CAN'T STAND THE CASTLE RIGHT NOW!
I NEED A BREAK FROM PETER'S STUPID FACE.
TAP
TAP
I DIDN'T ASK FOR YOUR REASONING!
THE OTHER DOMAINS WOULD BE HAPPY TO HAVE YOU.
ASK THEM.
BUT THE TOWER'S THE SAFEST PLACE FOR ME!

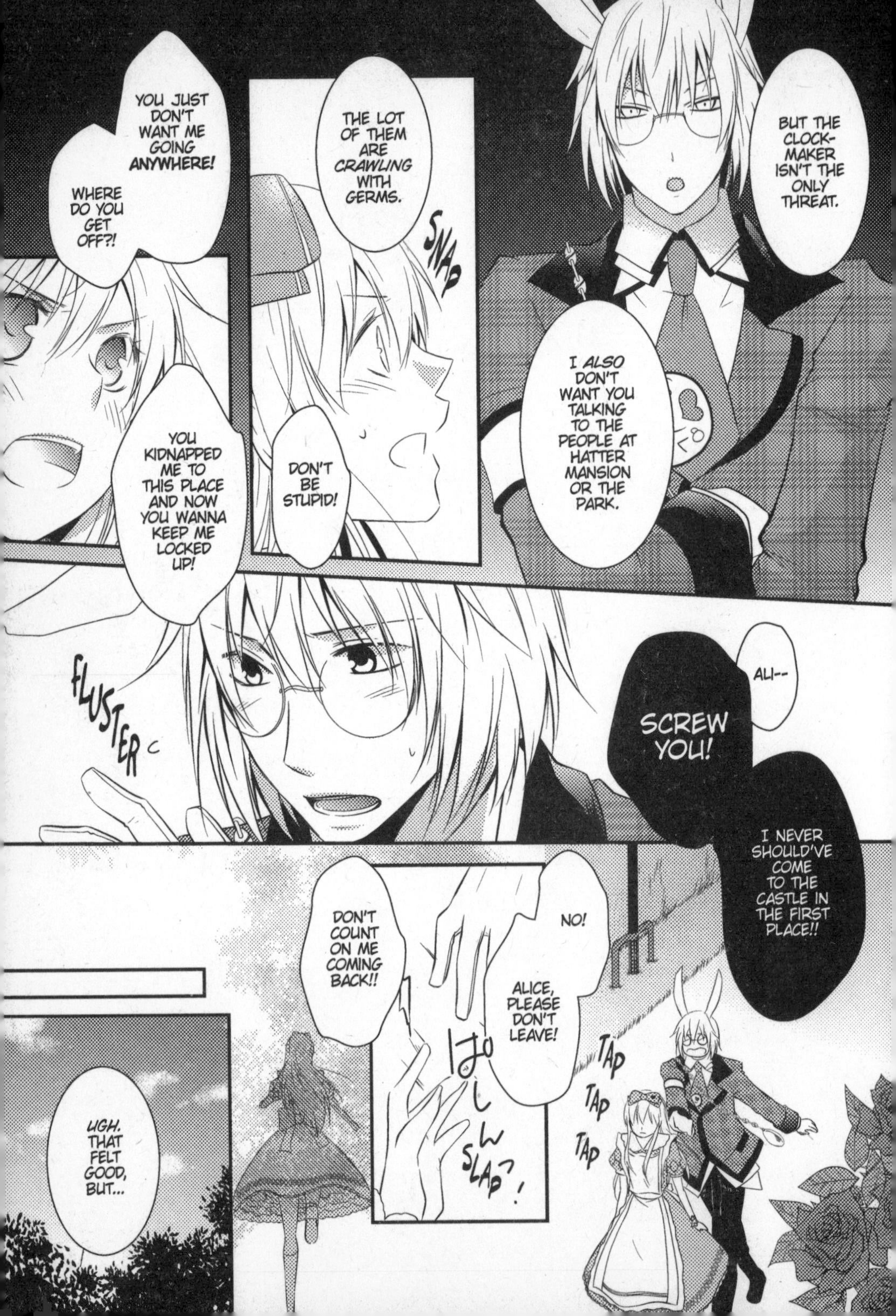
BUT THE CLOCK-MAKER ISN'T THE ONLY THREAT.
I ALSO DON'T WANT YOU TALKING TO THE PEOPLE AT HATTER MANSION OR THE PARK.
THE LOT OF THEM ARE CRAWLING WITH GERMS.
SNAP
DON'T BE STUPID!
YOU JUST DON'T WANT ME GOING ANYWHERE!
WHERE DO YOU GET OFF?!
YOU KIDNAPPED ME TO THIS PLACE AND NOW YOU WANNA KEEP ME LOCKED UP!
ALI--
SCREW YOU!
FLUSTER
I NEVER SHOULD'VE COME TO THE CASTLE IN THE FIRST PLACE!!
NO!
ALICE, PLEASE DON'T LEAVE!
TAP
TAP
TAP
DON'T COUNT ON ME COMING BACK!!
SLAP
UGH. THAT FELT GOOD, BUT...

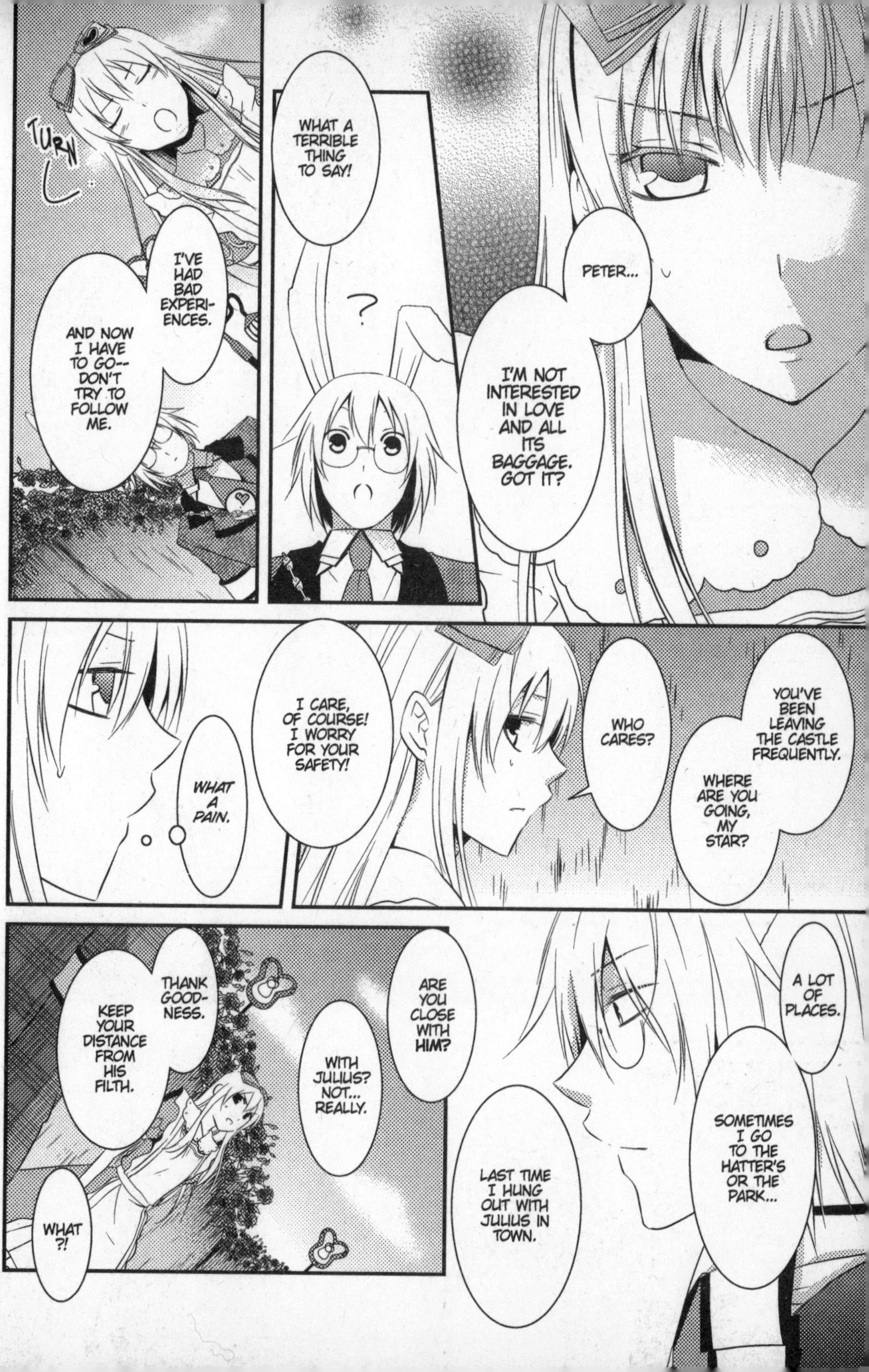
PETER...
I'M NOT INTERESTED IN LOVE AND ALL ITS BAGGAGE. GOT IT?
WHAT A TERRIBLE THING TO SAY!
?
TURN
I'VE HAD BAD EXPERIENCES.
AND NOW I HAVE TO GO-- DON'T TRY TO FOLLOW ME.
YOU'VE BEEN LEAVING THE CASTLE FREQUENTLY.
WHERE ARE YOU GOING, MY STAR?
WHO CARES?
I CARE, OF COURSE! I WORRY FOR YOUR SAFETY!
WHAT A PAIN.
A LOT OF PLACES.
SOMETIMES I GO TO THE HATTER'S OR THE PARK...
LAST TIME I HUNG OUT WITH JULIUS IN TOWN.
ARE YOU CLOSE WITH HIM?
WITH JULIUS? NOT... REALLY.
THANK GOODNESS.
KEEP YOUR DISTANCE FROM HIS FILTH.
WHAT ?!

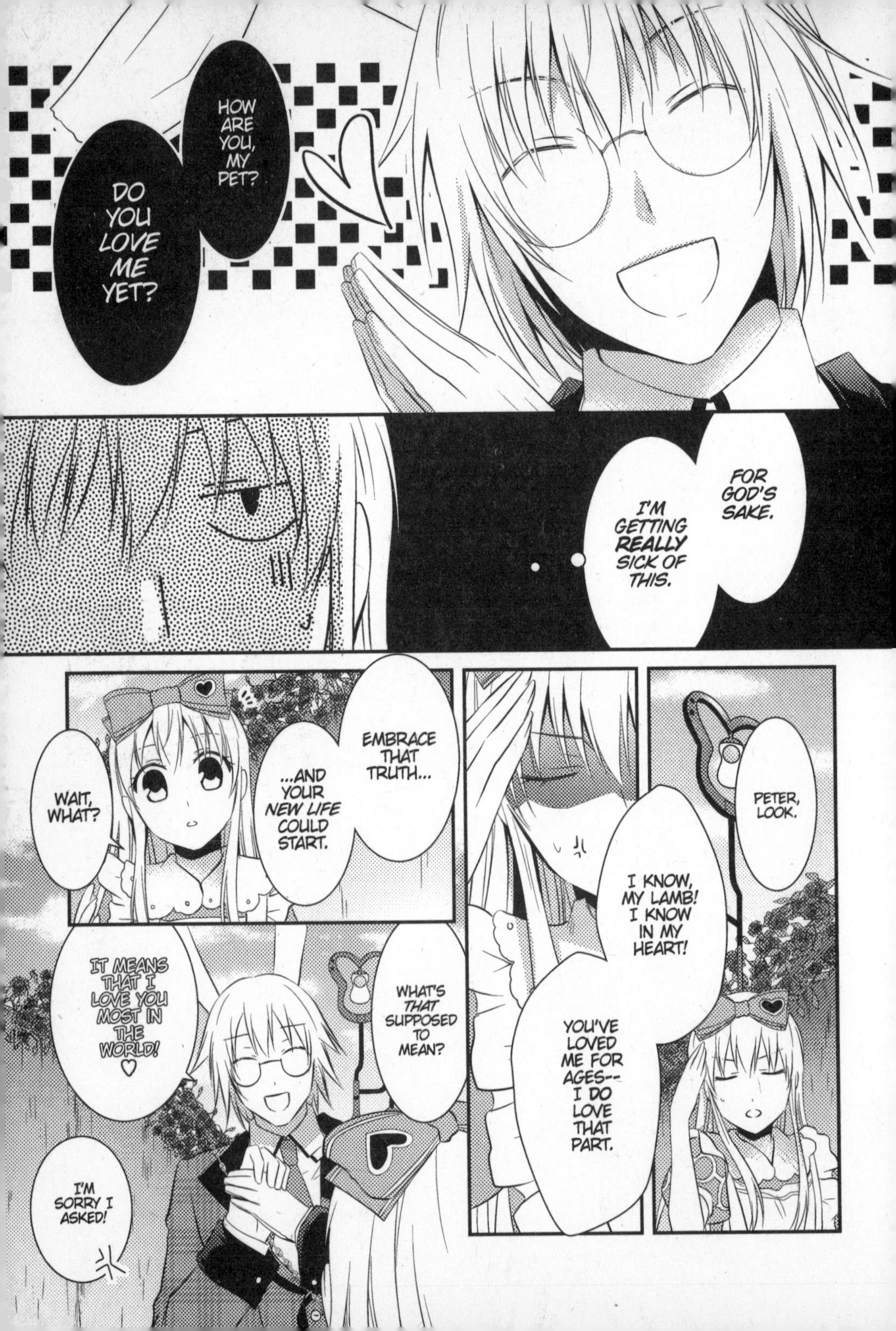
HOW ARE YOU, MY PET?
DO YOU LOVE ME YET?
FOR GOD'S SAKE.
I'M GETTING **REALLY** SICK OF THIS.
PETER, LOOK.
I KNOW, MY LAMB! I KNOW IN MY HEART!
YOU'VE LOVED ME FOR AGES-- I DO LOVE THAT PART.
EMBRACE THAT TRUTH...
...AND YOUR *NEW LIFE* COULD START.
WAIT, WHAT?
WHAT'S *THAT* SUPPOSED TO MEAN?
IT MEANS THAT I LOVE YOU MOST IN THE WORLD! ♡
I'M SORRY I ASKED!

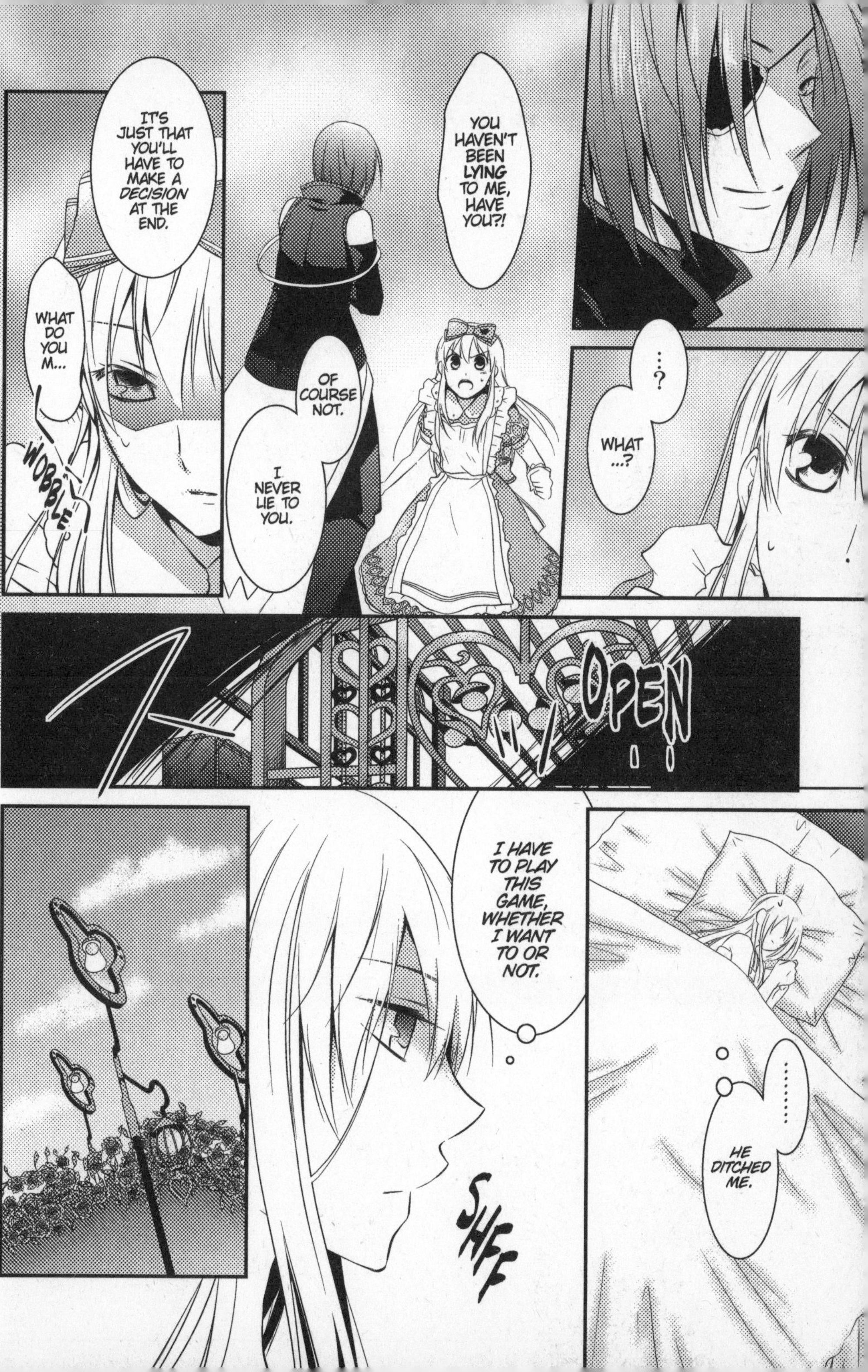
...?
WHAT ...?
YOU HAVEN'T BEEN LYING TO ME, HAVE YOU?!
OF COURSE NOT.
I NEVER LIE TO YOU.
IT'S JUST THAT YOU'LL HAVE TO MAKE A *DECISION* AT THE END.
WHAT DO YOU M...
WOBBLE
OPEN
....
HE DITCHED ME.
I HAVE TO PLAY THIS GAME, WHETHER I WANT TO OR NOT.
SHFF

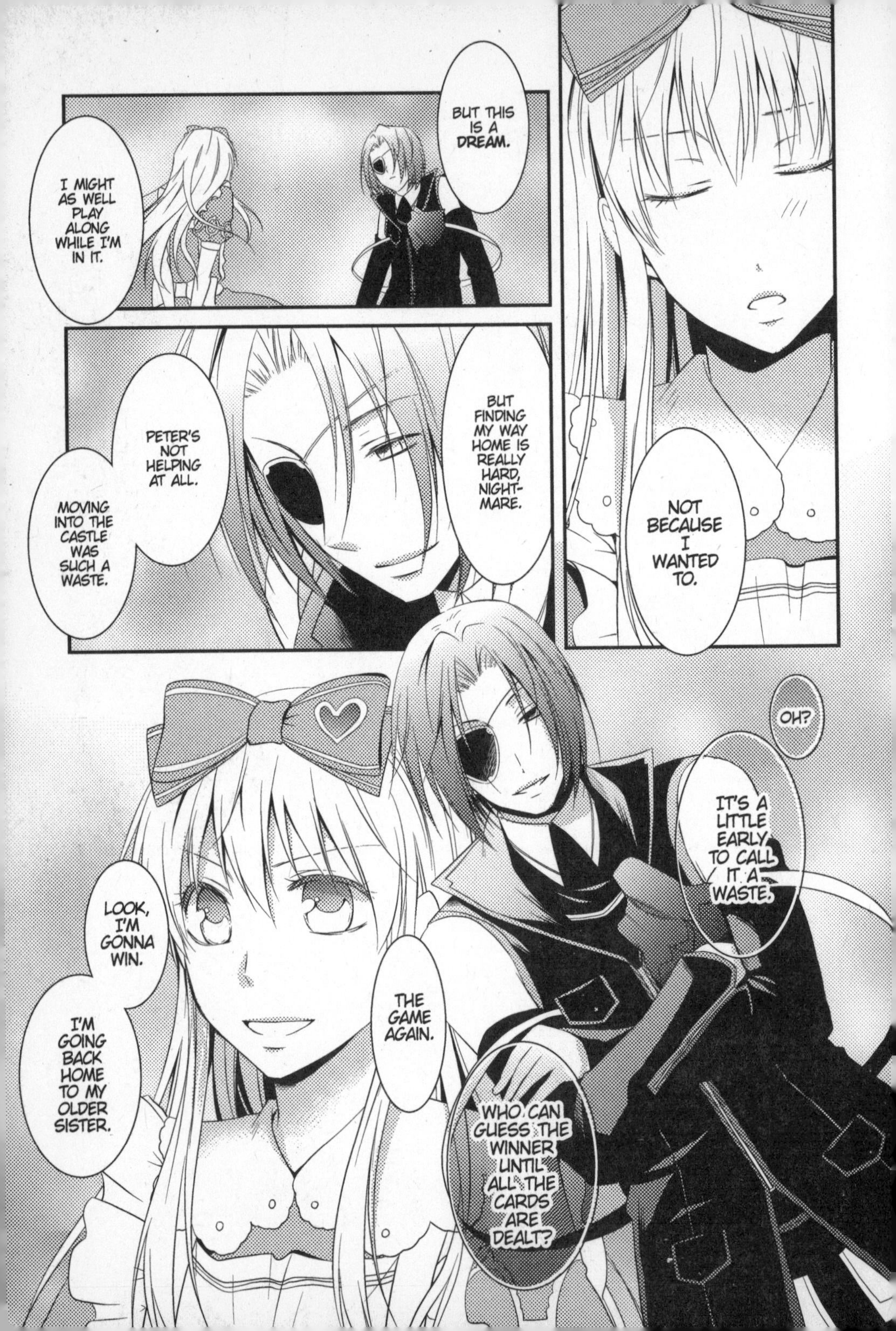
NOT BECAUSE I WANTED TO.
BUT THIS IS A DREAM.
I MIGHT AS WELL PLAY ALONG WHILE I'M IN IT.
BUT FINDING MY WAY HOME IS REALLY HARD, NIGHT-MARE.
PETER'S NOT HELPING AT ALL.
MOVING INTO THE CASTLE WAS SUCH A WASTE.
OH?
IT'S A LITTLE EARLY TO CALL IT A WASTE.
WHO CAN GUESS THE WINNER UNTIL ALL THE CARDS ARE DEALT?
THE GAME AGAIN.
LOOK, I'M GONNA WIN.
I'M GOING BACK HOME TO MY OLDER SISTER.

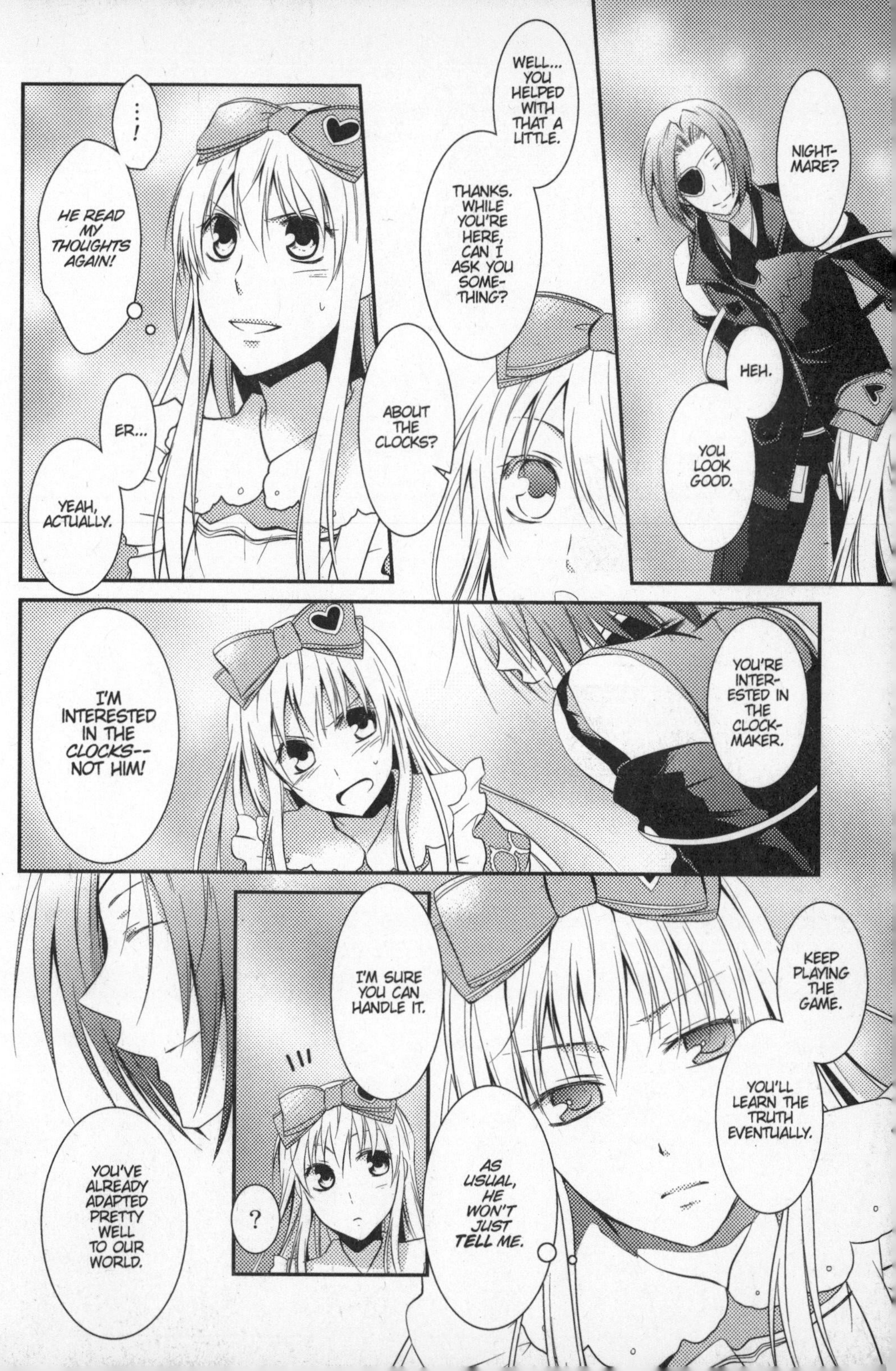
NIGHT-MARE?
HEH.
YOU LOOK GOOD.
WELL... YOU HELPED WITH THAT A LITTLE.
THANKS. WHILE YOU'RE HERE, CAN I ASK YOU SOME-THING?
ABOUT THE CLOCKS?
...!
HE READ MY THOUGHTS AGAIN!
ER...
YEAH, ACTUALLY.
YOU'RE INTER-ESTED IN THE CLOCK-MAKER.
I'M INTERESTED IN THE CLOCKS-- NOT HIM!
KEEP PLAYING THE GAME.
YOU'LL LEARN THE TRUTH EVENTUALLY.
AS USUAL, HE WON'T JUST TELL ME.
I'M SURE YOU CAN HANDLE IT.
?
YOU'VE ALREADY ADAPTED PRETTY WELL TO OUR WORLD.

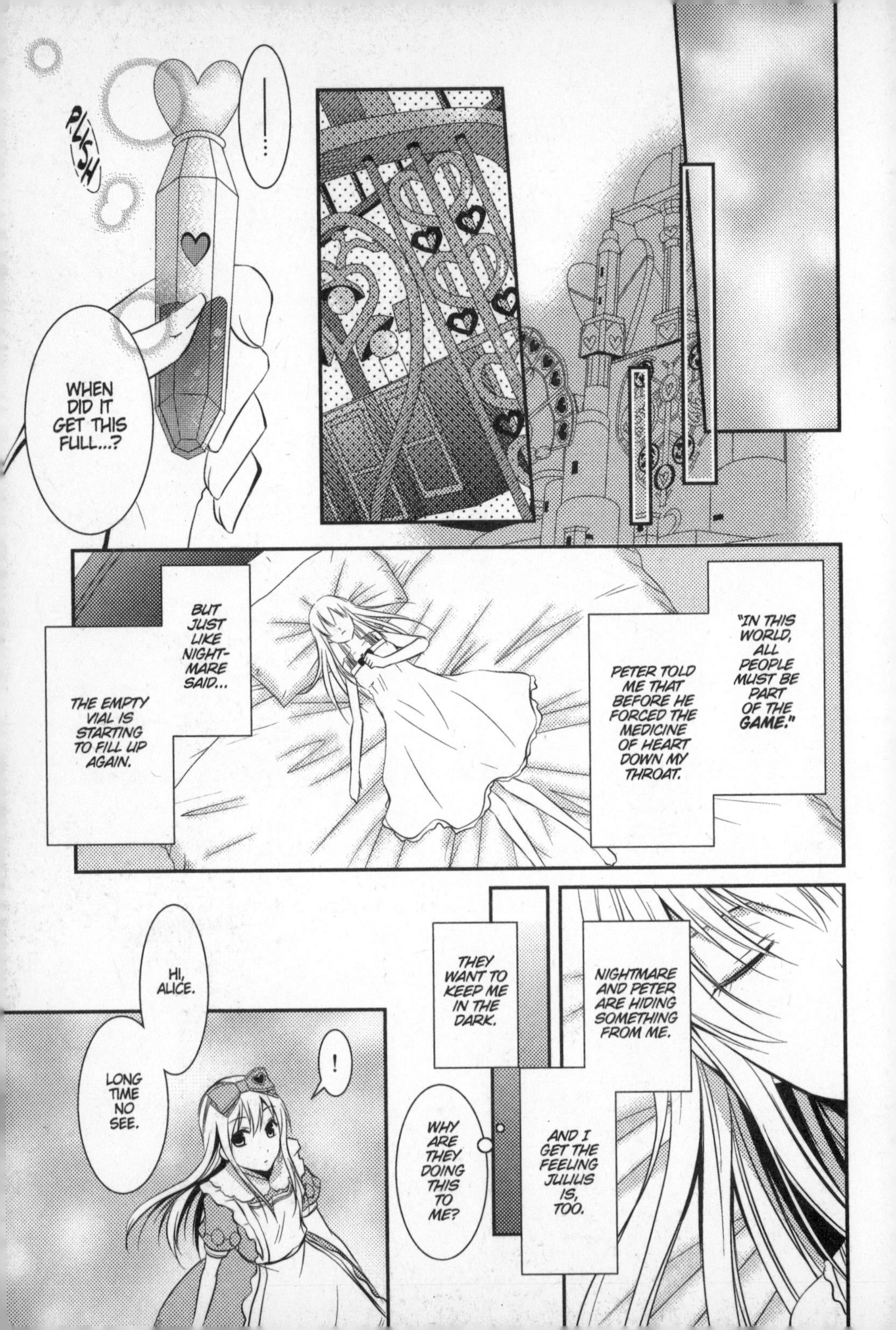
—......
PLISH
WHEN DID IT GET THIS FULL...?
"IN THIS WORLD, ALL PEOPLE MUST BE PART OF THE **GAME.**"
PETER TOLD ME THAT BEFORE HE FORCED THE MEDICINE OF HEART DOWN MY THROAT.
BUT JUST LIKE NIGHTMARE SAID...
THE EMPTY VIAL IS STARTING TO FILL UP AGAIN.
NIGHTMARE AND PETER ARE HIDING SOMETHING FROM ME.
THEY WANT TO KEEP ME IN THE DARK.
AND I GET THE FEELING JULIUS IS, TOO.
WHY ARE THEY DOING THIS TO ME?
HI, ALICE.
!
LONG TIME NO SEE.

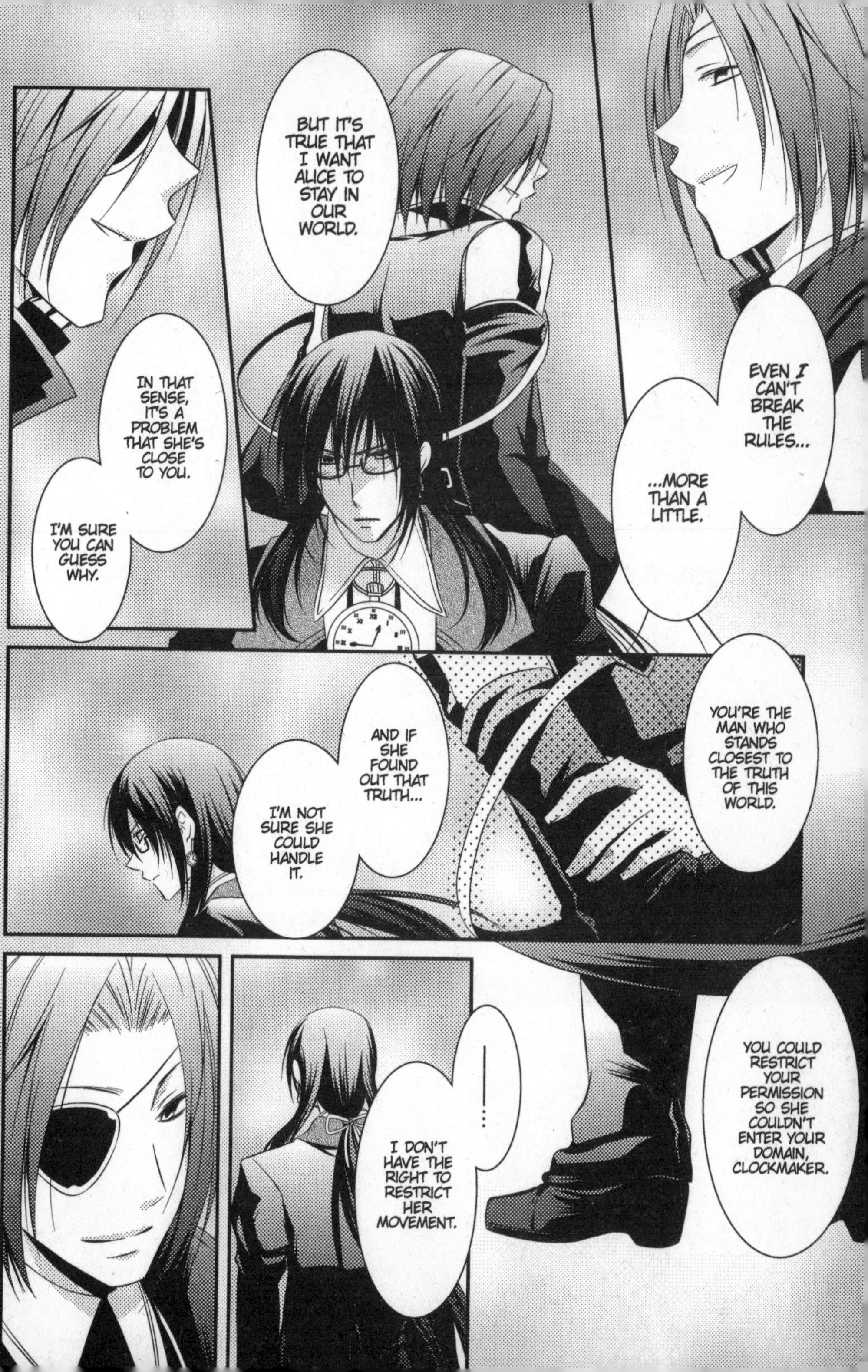
EVEN I CAN'T BREAK THE RULES...
...MORE THAN A LITTLE.
BUT IT'S TRUE THAT I WANT ALICE TO STAY IN OUR WORLD.
IN THAT SENSE, IT'S A PROBLEM THAT SHE'S CLOSE TO YOU.
I'M SURE YOU CAN GUESS WHY.
YOU'RE THE MAN WHO STANDS CLOSEST TO THE TRUTH OF THIS WORLD.
AND IF SHE FOUND OUT THAT TRUTH...
I'M NOT SURE SHE COULD HANDLE IT.
YOU COULD RESTRICT YOUR PERMISSION SO SHE COULDN'T ENTER YOUR DOMAIN, CLOCKMAKER.
......
I DON'T HAVE THE RIGHT TO RESTRICT HER MOVEMENT.

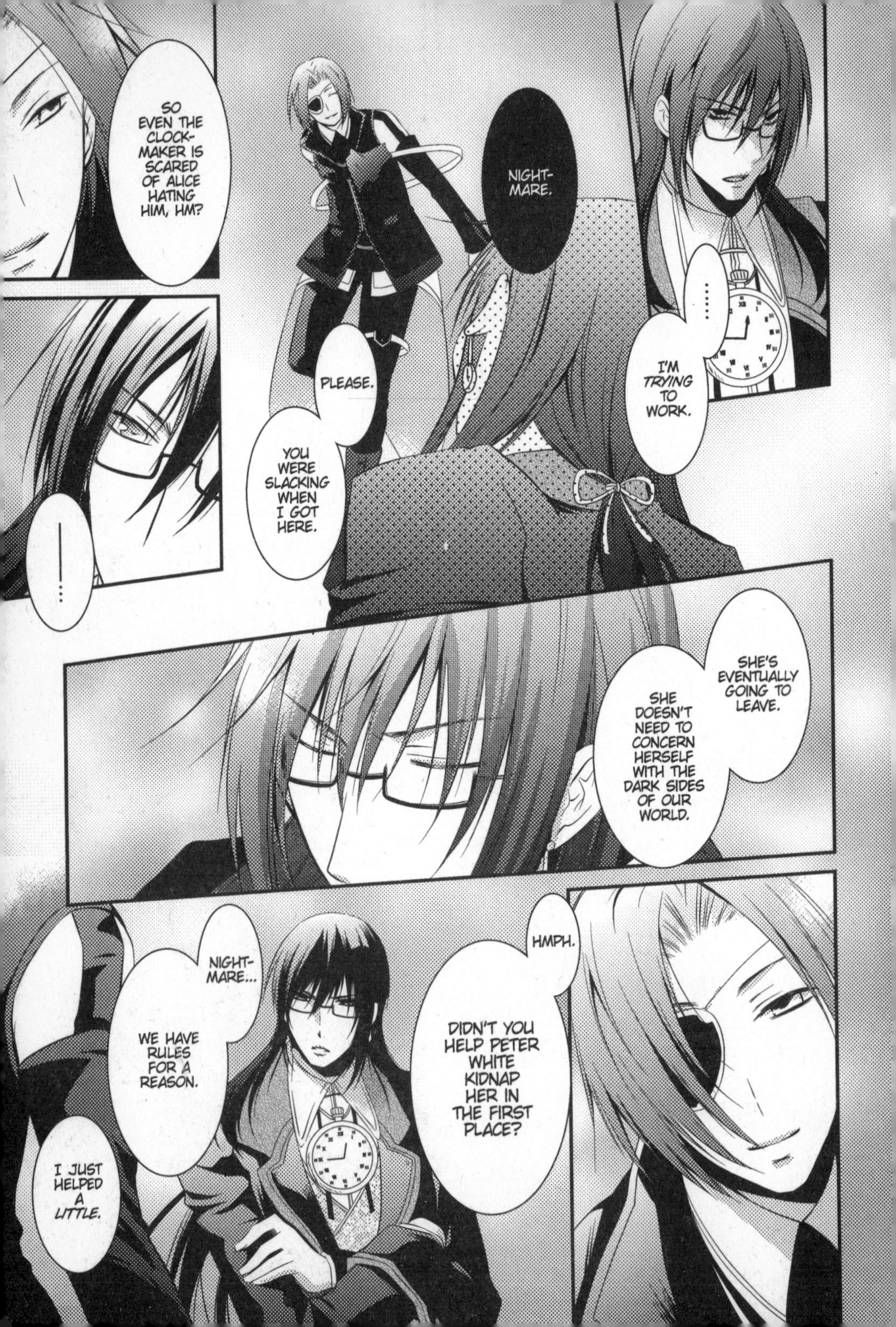
NIGHT-MARE.
......
I'M *TRYING* TO WORK.
PLEASE.
YOU WERE SLACKING WHEN I GOT HERE.
SO EVEN THE CLOCK-MAKER IS SCARED OF ALICE HATING HIM, HM?
......
SHE'S EVENTUALLY GOING TO LEAVE.
SHE DOESN'T NEED TO CONCERN HERSELF WITH THE DARK SIDES OF OUR WORLD.
HMPH.
DIDN'T YOU HELP PETER WHITE KIDNAP HER IN THE FIRST PLACE?
NIGHT-MARE...
WE HAVE RULES FOR A REASON.
I JUST HELPED A *LITTLE*.

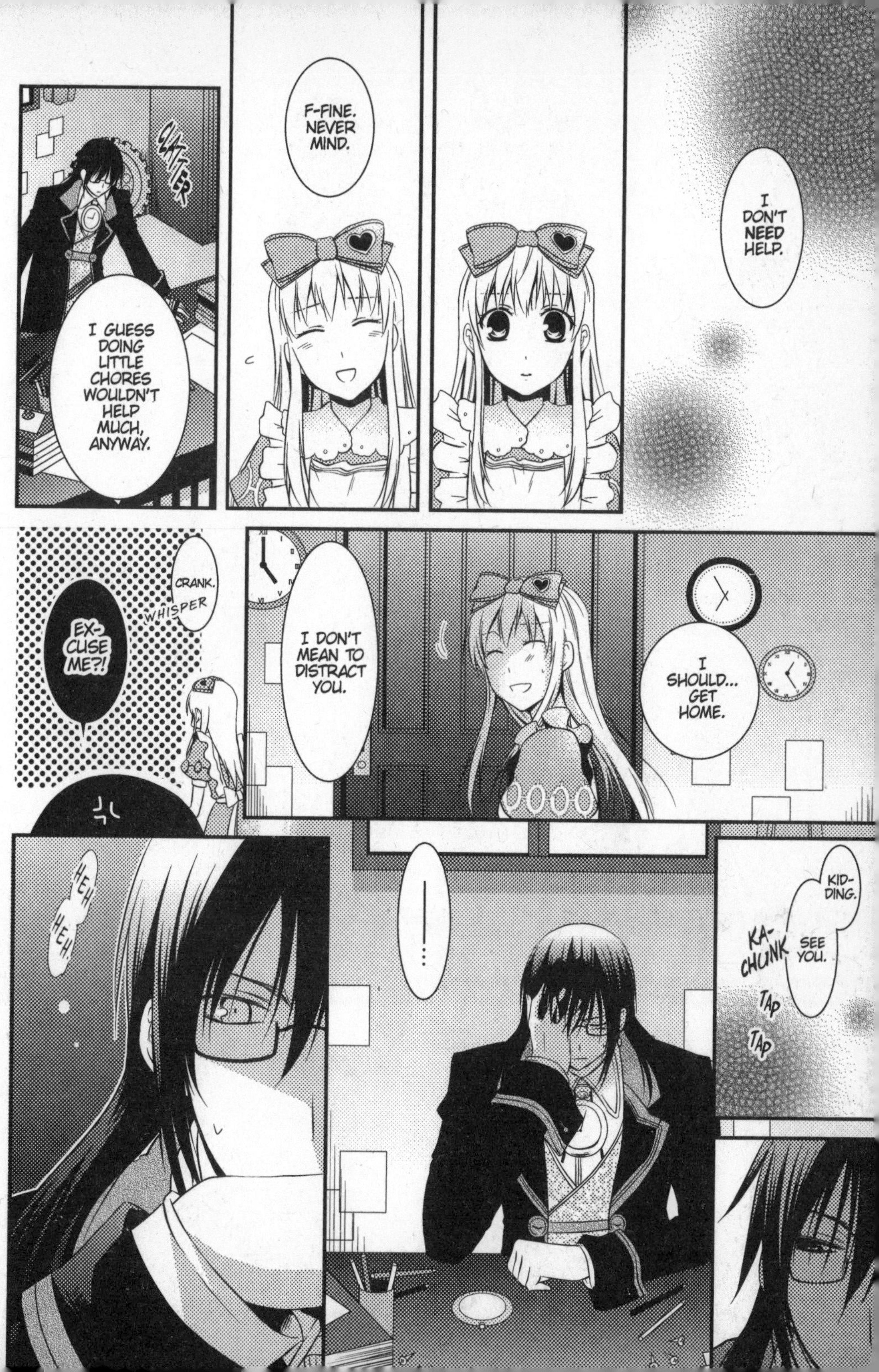
I DON'T NEED HELP.
F-FINE. NEVER MIND.
CLATTER
I GUESS DOING LITTLE CHORES WOULDN'T HELP MUCH, ANYWAY.
I SHOULD... GET HOME.
I DON'T MEAN TO DISTRACT YOU.
CRANK.
WHISPER
EX-CUSE ME?!
KID-DING.
KA-CHUNK
SEE YOU.
TAP
TAP
!...
HEH HEH.

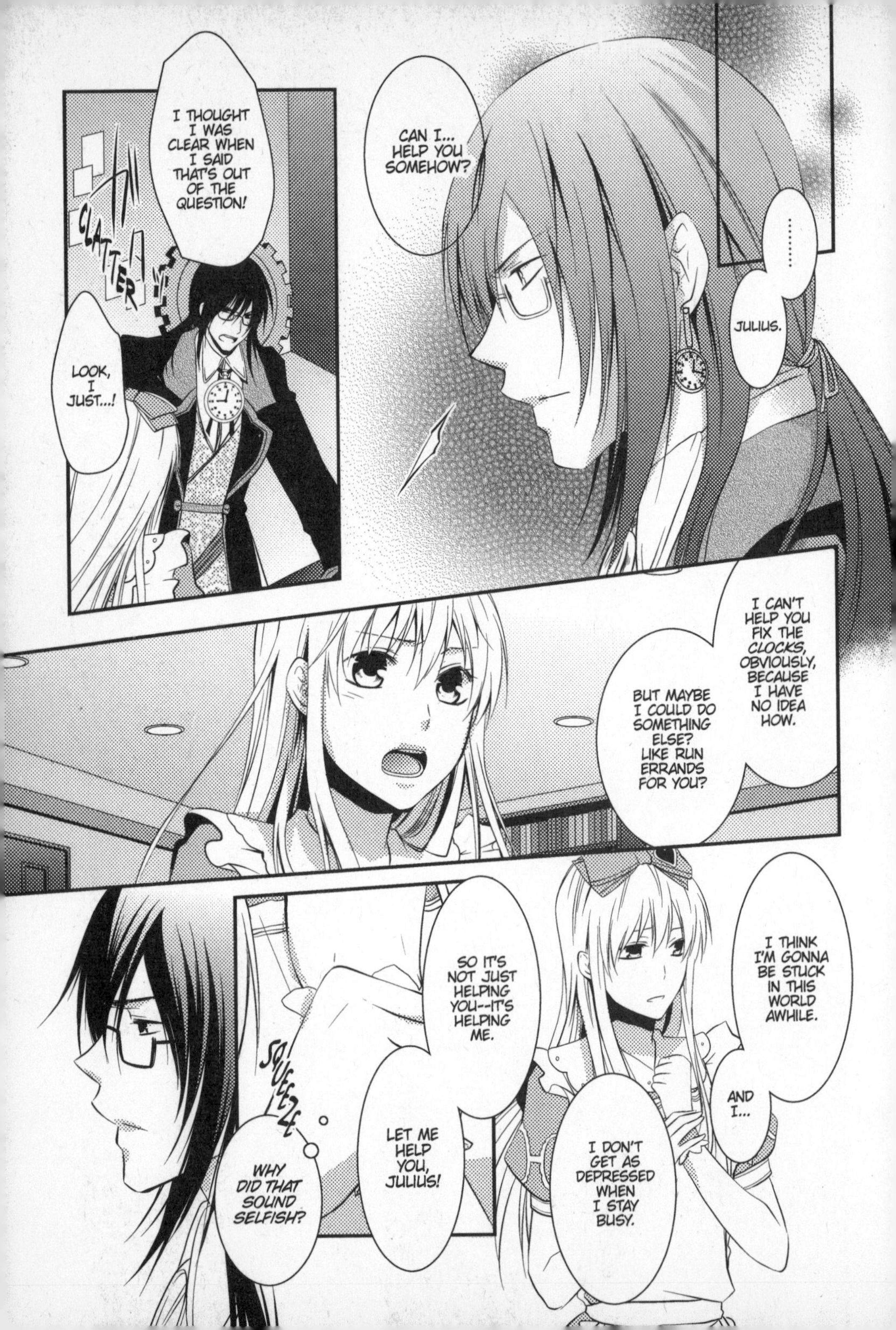
……
JULIUS.
CAN I... HELP YOU SOMEHOW?
I THOUGHT I WAS CLEAR WHEN I SAID THAT'S OUT OF THE QUESTION!
CLATTER
LOOK, I JUST...!
I CAN'T HELP YOU FIX THE *CLOCKS*, OBVIOUSLY, BECAUSE I HAVE NO IDEA HOW.
BUT MAYBE I COULD DO SOMETHING ELSE? LIKE RUN ERRANDS FOR YOU?
I THINK I'M GONNA BE STUCK IN THIS WORLD AWHILE.
AND I...
I DON'T GET AS DEPRESSED WHEN I STAY BUSY.
SO IT'S NOT JUST HELPING YOU--IT'S HELPING ME.
LET ME HELP YOU, JULIUS!
SQUEEZE
WHY DID THAT SOUND SELFISH?

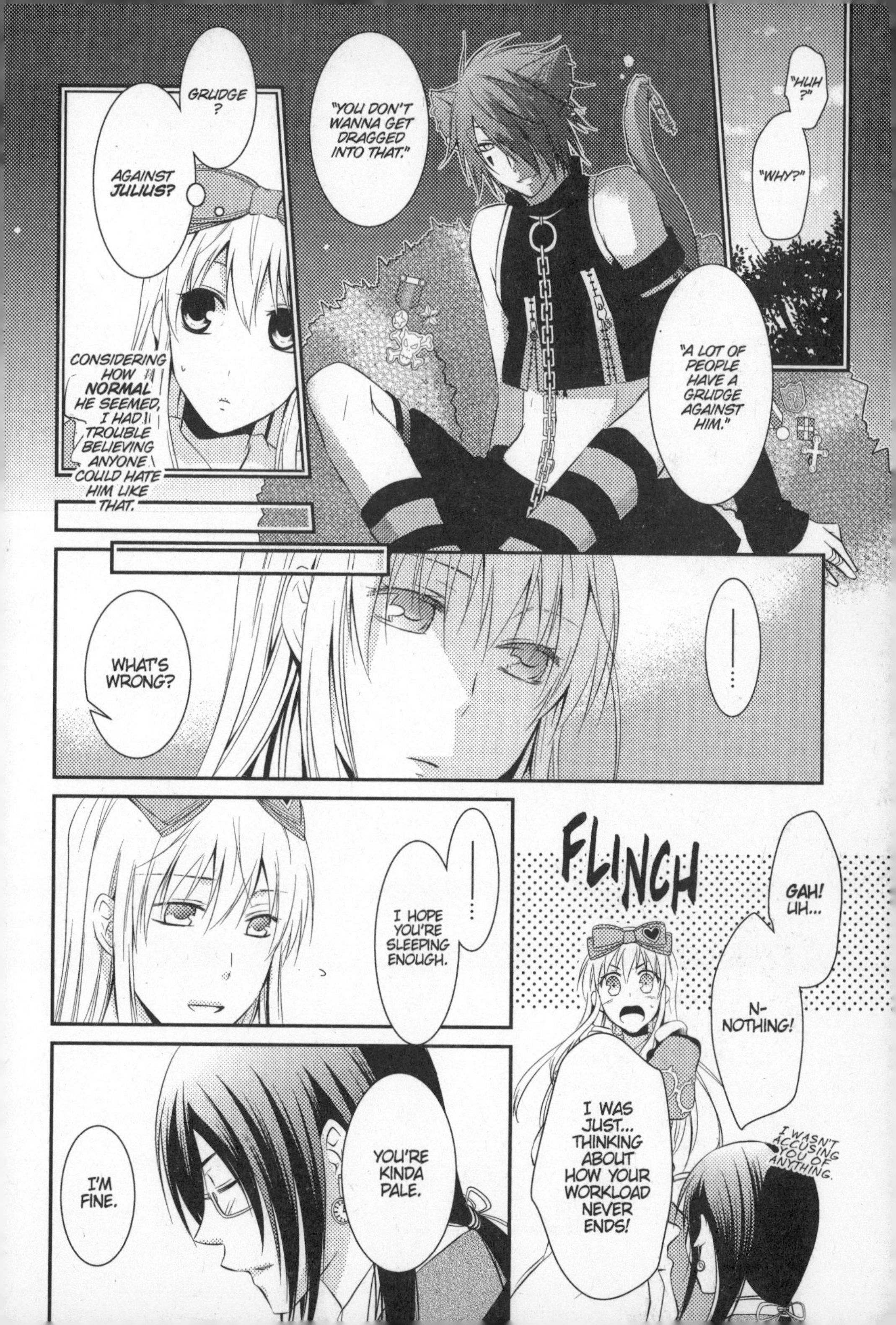
"HUH?"
"WHY?"
"A LOT OF PEOPLE HAVE A GRUDGE AGAINST HIM."
"YOU DON'T WANNA GET DRAGGED INTO THAT."
GRUDGE?
AGAINST JULIUS?
CONSIDERING HOW NORMAL HE SEEMED, I HAD TROUBLE BELIEVING ANYONE COULD HATE HIM LIKE THAT.
!...
WHAT'S WRONG?
FLINCH
GAH! UH...
N-NOTHING!
I WAS JUST... THINKING ABOUT HOW YOUR WORKLOAD NEVER ENDS!
I WASN'T ACCUSING YOU OF ANYTHING.
!...
I HOPE YOU'RE SLEEPING ENOUGH.
YOU'RE KINDA PALE.
I'M FINE.

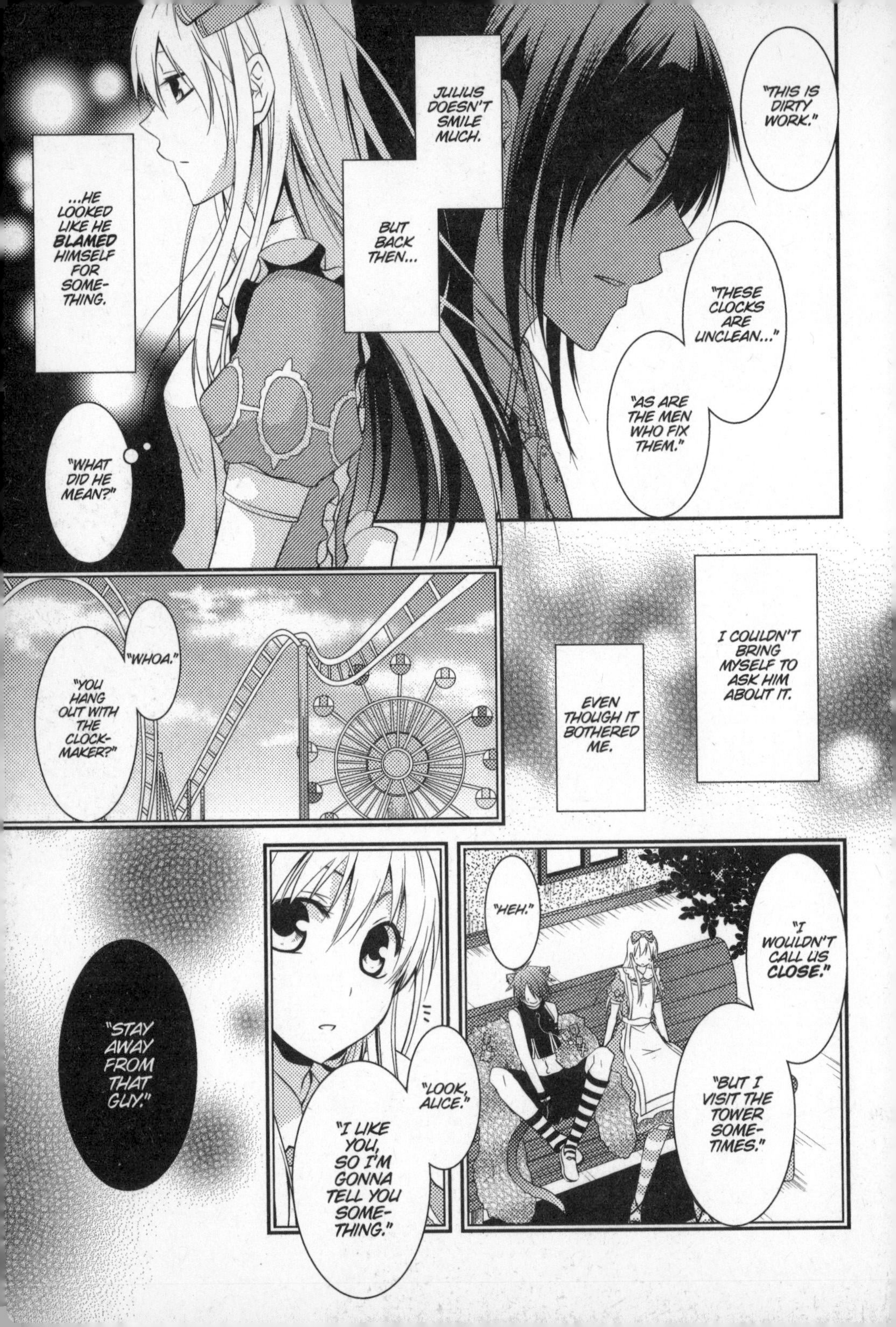
"THIS IS DIRTY WORK."
"THESE CLOCKS ARE UNCLEAN..."
"AS ARE THE MEN WHO FIX THEM."
JULIUS DOESN'T SMILE MUCH.
BUT BACK THEN...
...HE LOOKED LIKE HE BLAMED HIMSELF FOR SOME-THING.
"WHAT DID HE MEAN?"
I COULDN'T BRING MYSELF TO ASK HIM ABOUT IT.
EVEN THOUGH IT BOTHERED ME.
"WHOA."
"YOU HANG OUT WITH THE CLOCK-MAKER?"
"I WOULDN'T CALL US CLOSE."
"HEH."
"BUT I VISIT THE TOWER SOME-TIMES."
"LOOK, ALICE."
"I LIKE YOU, SO I'M GONNA TELL YOU SOME-THING."
"STAY AWAY FROM THAT GUY."

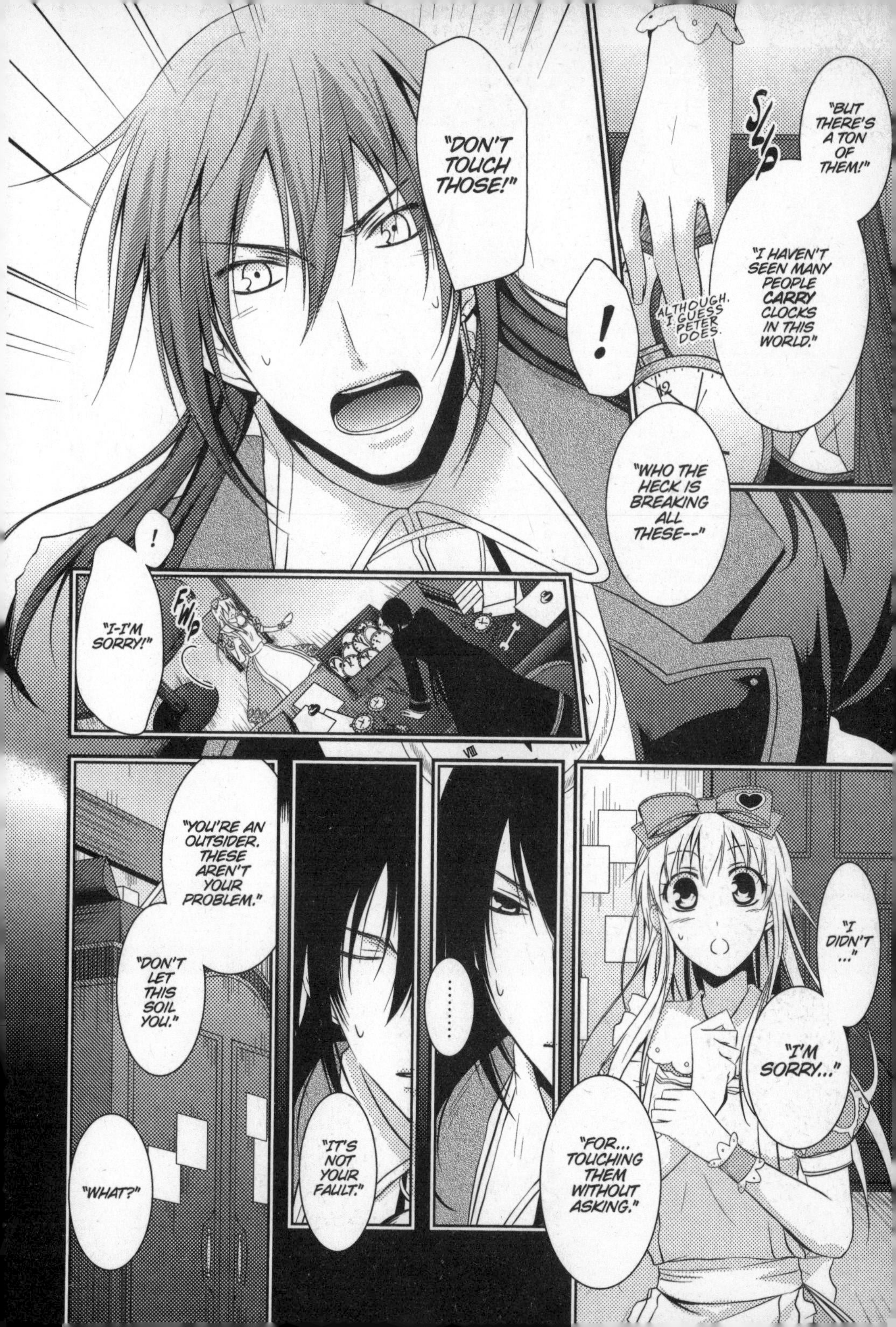
SLIP
"BUT THERE'S A TON OF THEM!"
"I HAVEN'T SEEN MANY PEOPLE CARRY CLOCKS IN THIS WORLD."
ALTHOUGH, I GUESS PETER DOES.
!
"WHO THE HECK IS BREAKING ALL THESE--"
"DON'T TOUCH THOSE!"
!
FWIP
"I-I'M SORRY!"
"I DIDN'T ..."
"I'M SORRY..."
"FOR... TOUCHING THEM WITHOUT ASKING."
......
"IT'S NOT YOUR FAULT."
"YOU'RE AN OUTSIDER. THESE AREN'T YOUR PROBLEM."
"DON'T LET THIS SOIL YOU."
"WHAT?"

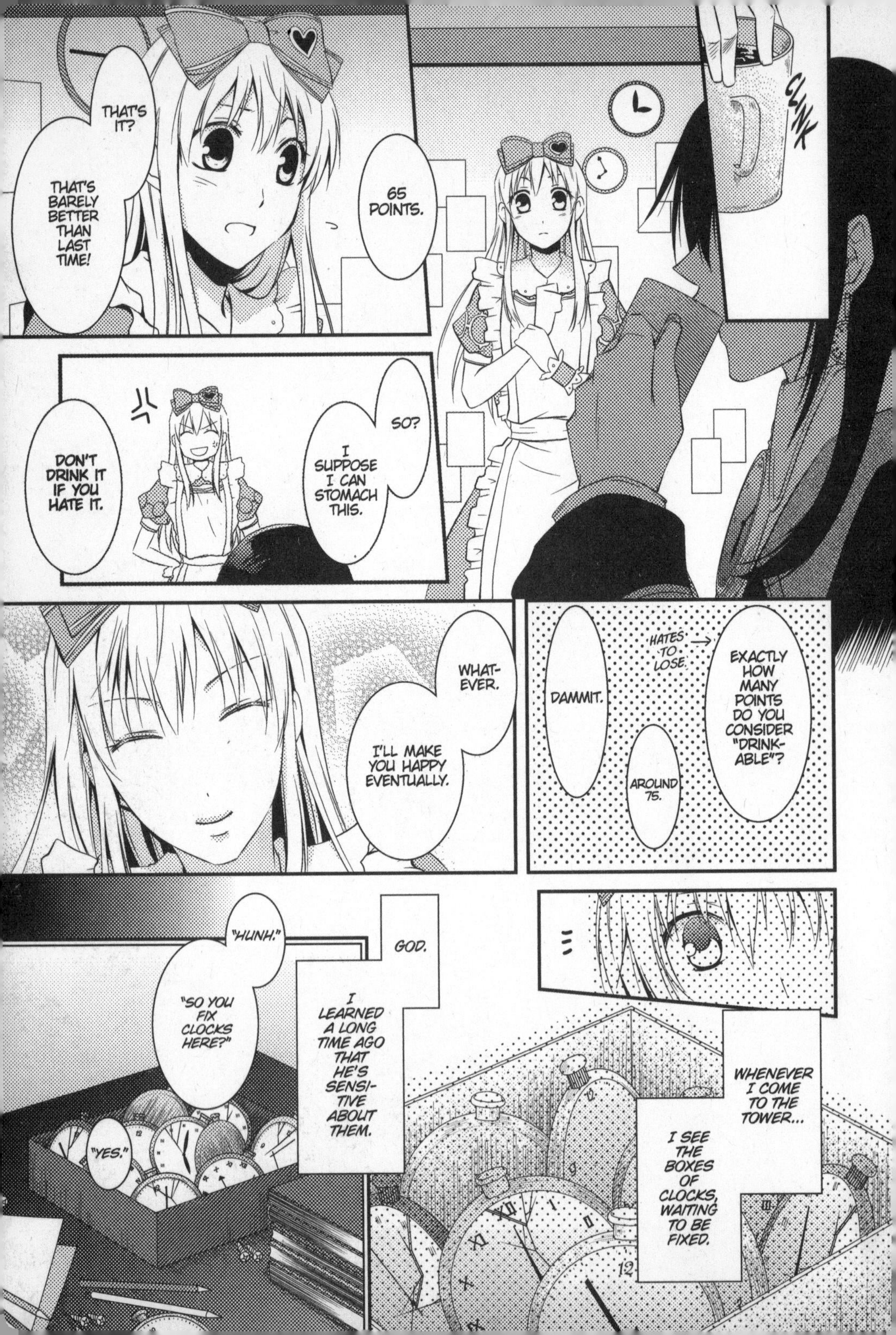
CLINK
65 POINTS.
THAT'S IT?
THAT'S BARELY BETTER THAN LAST TIME!
SO?
I SUPPOSE I CAN STOMACH THIS.
DON'T DRINK IT IF YOU HATE IT.
EXACTLY HOW MANY POINTS DO YOU CONSIDER "DRINK-ABLE"?
HATES TO LOSE →
AROUND 75.
DAMMIT.
WHAT-EVER.
I'LL MAKE YOU HAPPY EVENTUALLY.
WHENEVER I COME TO THE TOWER...
I SEE THE BOXES OF CLOCKS, WAITING TO BE FIXED.
GOD.
I LEARNED A LONG TIME AGO THAT HE'S SENSI-TIVE ABOUT THEM.
"HUNH."
"SO YOU FIX CLOCKS HERE?"
"YES."

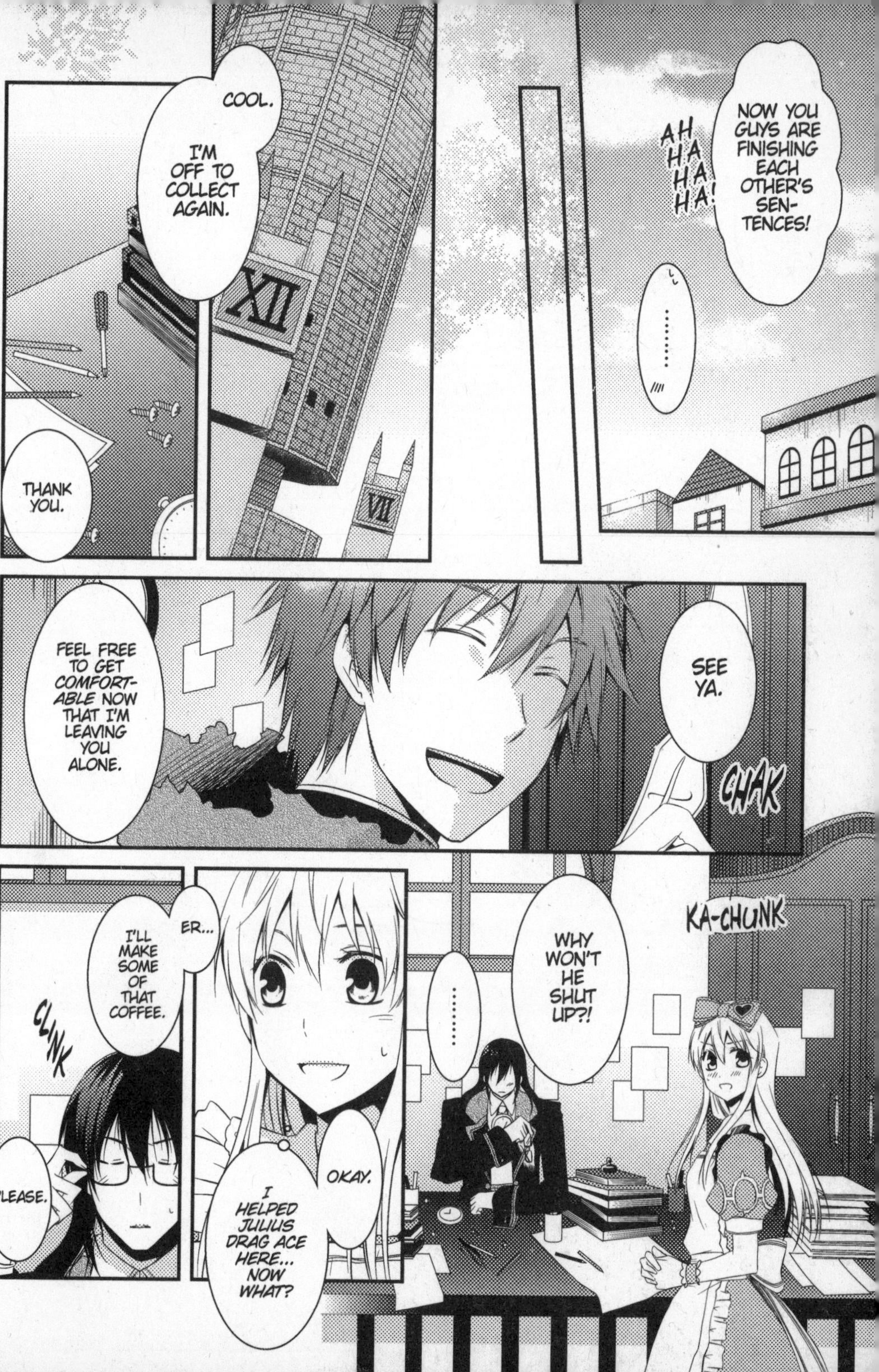
NOW YOU GUYS ARE FINISHING EACH OTHER'S SEN-TENCES!
AH HA HA HA!
......
COOL.
I'M OFF TO COLLECT AGAIN.
THANK YOU.
SEE YA.
CHAK
FEEL FREE TO GET COMFORT-ABLE NOW THAT I'M LEAVING YOU ALONE.
KA-CHUNK
WHY WON'T HE SHUT UP?!
......
OKAY.
I HELPED JULIUS DRAG ACE HERE... NOW WHAT?
ER...
I'LL MAKE SOME OF THAT COFFEE.
CLINK
PLEASE.

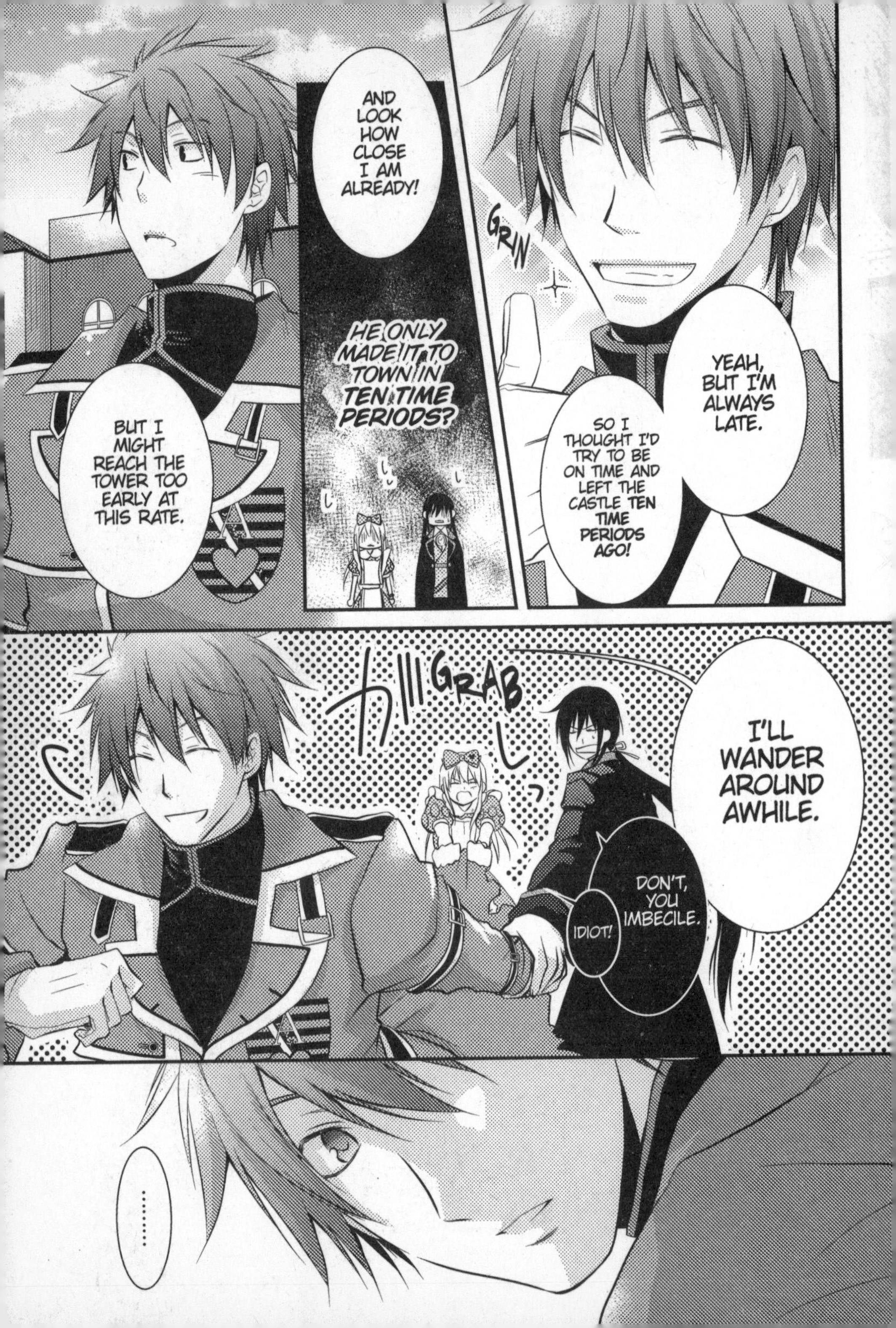

YEAH, BUT I'M ALWAYS LATE.
SO I THOUGHT I'D TRY TO BE ON TIME AND LEFT THE CASTLE TEN TIME PERIODS AGO!
GRIN
AND LOOK HOW CLOSE I AM ALREADY!
HE ONLY MADE IT TO TOWN IN TEN TIME PERIODS?
BUT I MIGHT REACH THE TOWER TOO EARLY AT THIS RATE.
I'LL WANDER AROUND AWHILE.
GRAB
DON'T, YOU IMBECILE.
IDIOT!
……

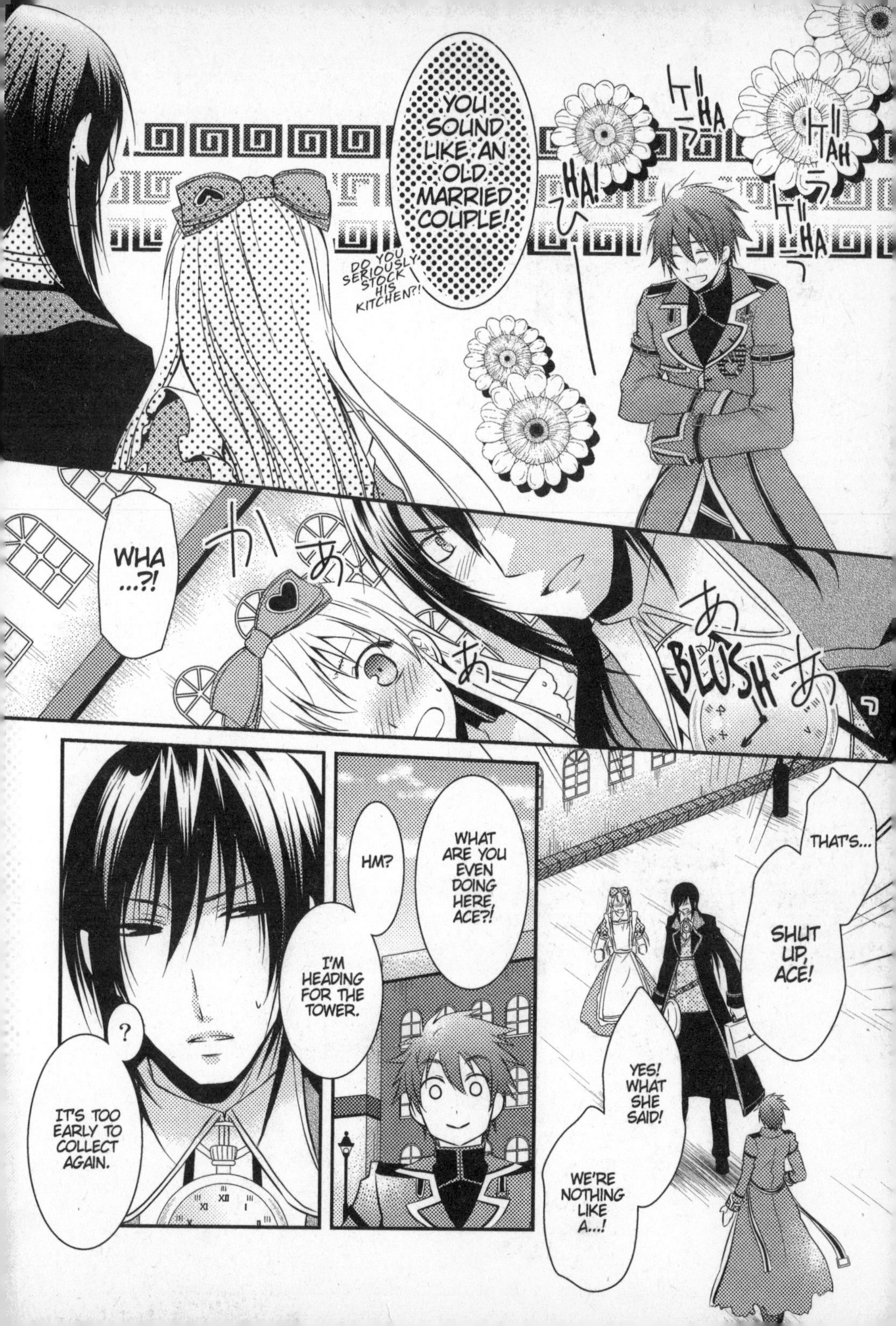
HAH
HA
HA
HA!
YOU SOUND LIKE AN OLD MARRIED COUPLE!
DO YOU SERIOUSLY STOCK HIS KITCHEN?!
BLUSH
WHA...?!
THAT'S...
SHUT UP, ACE!
YES! WHAT SHE SAID!
WE'RE NOTHING LIKE A...!
WHAT ARE YOU EVEN DOING HERE, ACE?!
HM?
I'M HEADING FOR THE TOWER.
?
IT'S TOO EARLY TO COLLECT AGAIN.

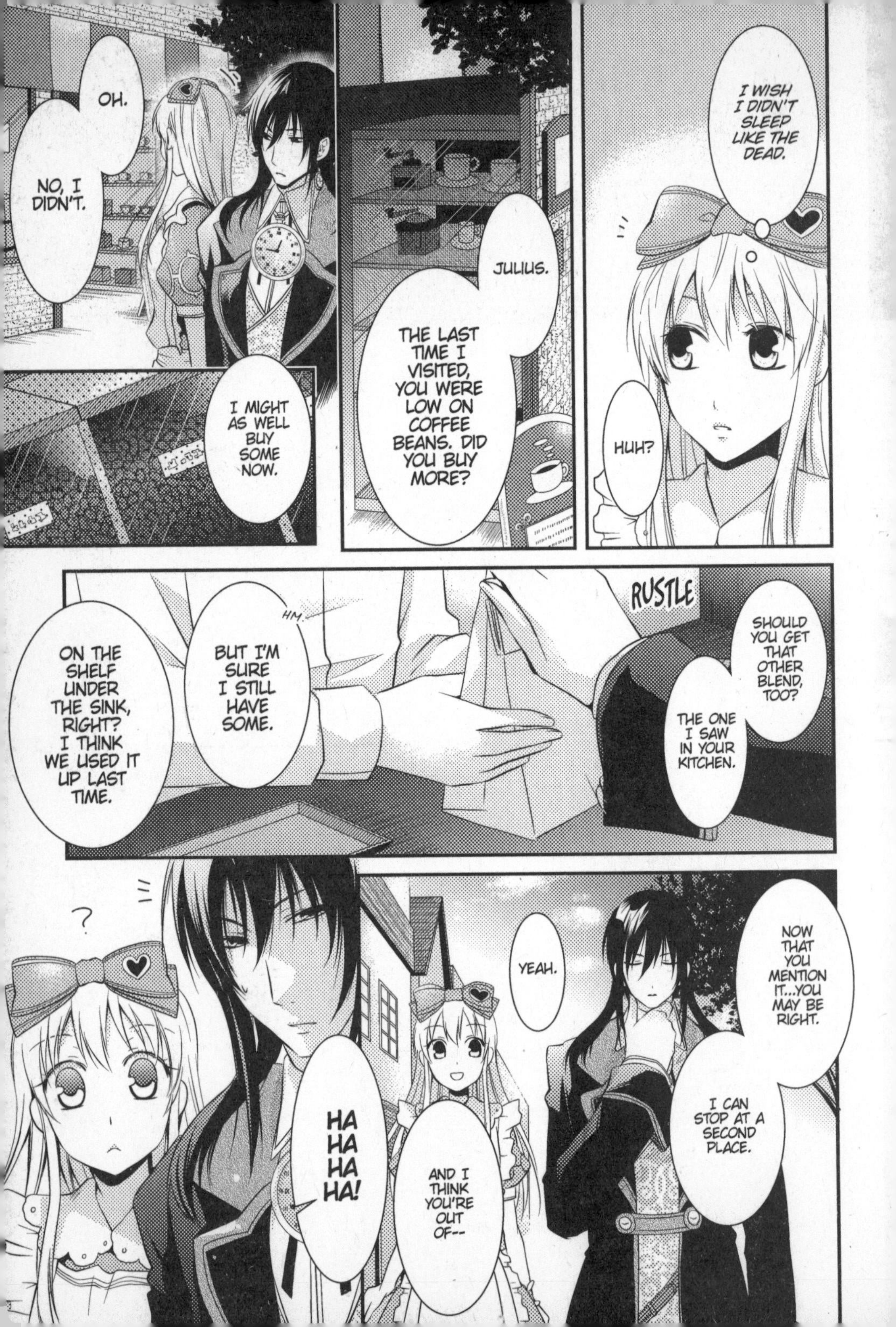
I WISH I DIDN'T SLEEP LIKE THE DEAD.
HUH?
JULIUS.
THE LAST TIME I VISITED, YOU WERE LOW ON COFFEE BEANS. DID YOU BUY MORE?
OH.
NO, I DIDN'T.
I MIGHT AS WELL BUY SOME NOW.
RUSTLE
SHOULD YOU GET THAT OTHER BLEND, TOO?
THE ONE I SAW IN YOUR KITCHEN.
HM.
BUT I'M SURE I STILL HAVE SOME.
ON THE SHELF UNDER THE SINK, RIGHT? I THINK WE USED IT UP LAST TIME.
NOW THAT YOU MENTION IT...YOU MAY BE RIGHT.
YEAH.
I CAN STOP AT A SECOND PLACE.
AND I THINK YOU'RE OUT OF--
HA HA HA HA HA!
?

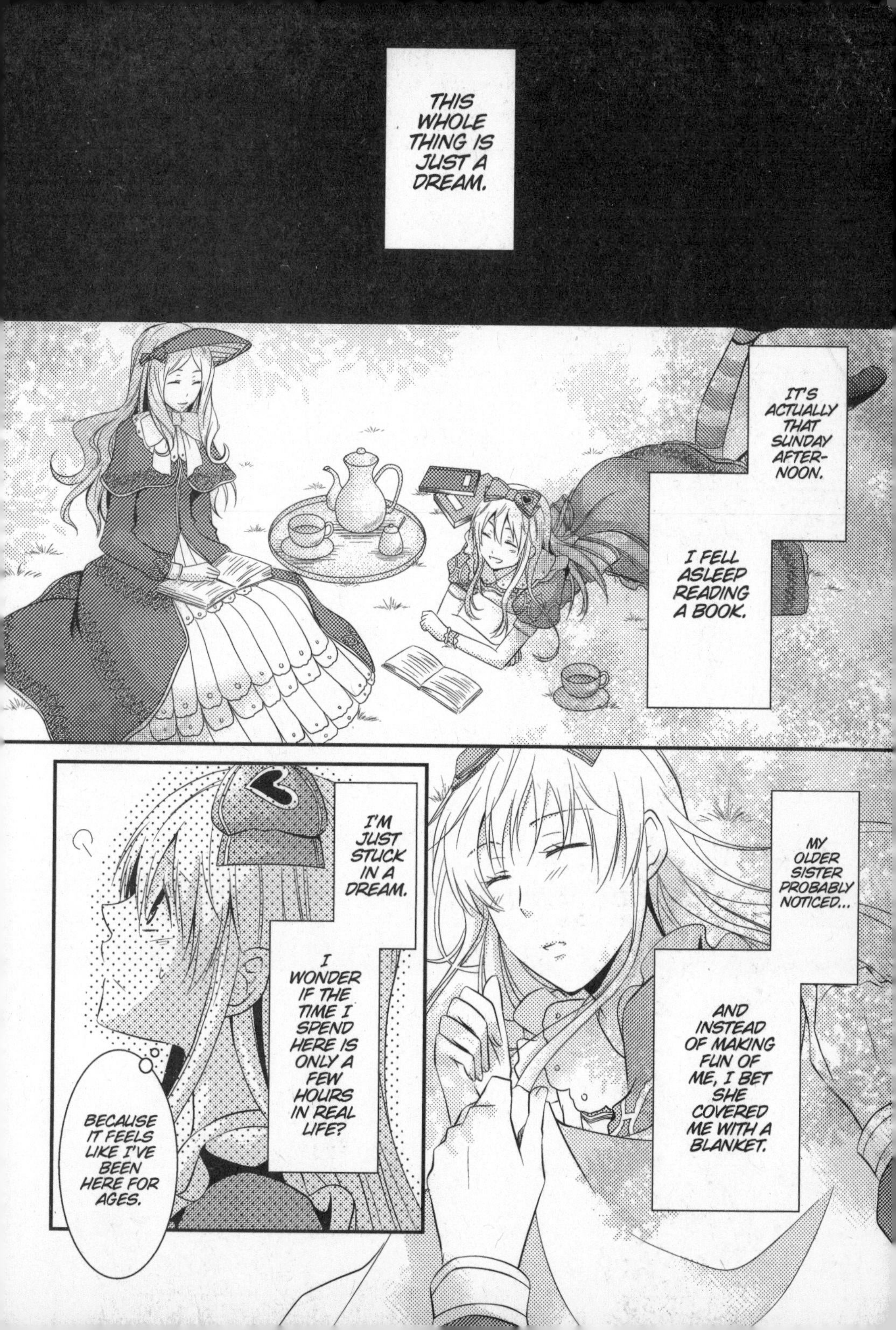
THIS WHOLE THING IS JUST A DREAM.
IT'S ACTUALLY THAT SUNDAY AFTER-NOON.
I FELL ASLEEP READING A BOOK.
MY OLDER SISTER PROBABLY NOTICED...
AND INSTEAD OF MAKING FUN OF ME, I BET SHE COVERED ME WITH A BLANKET.
I'M JUST STUCK IN A DREAM.
I WONDER IF THE TIME I SPEND HERE IS ONLY A FEW HOURS IN REAL LIFE?
BECAUSE IT FEELS LIKE I'VE BEEN HERE FOR AGES.

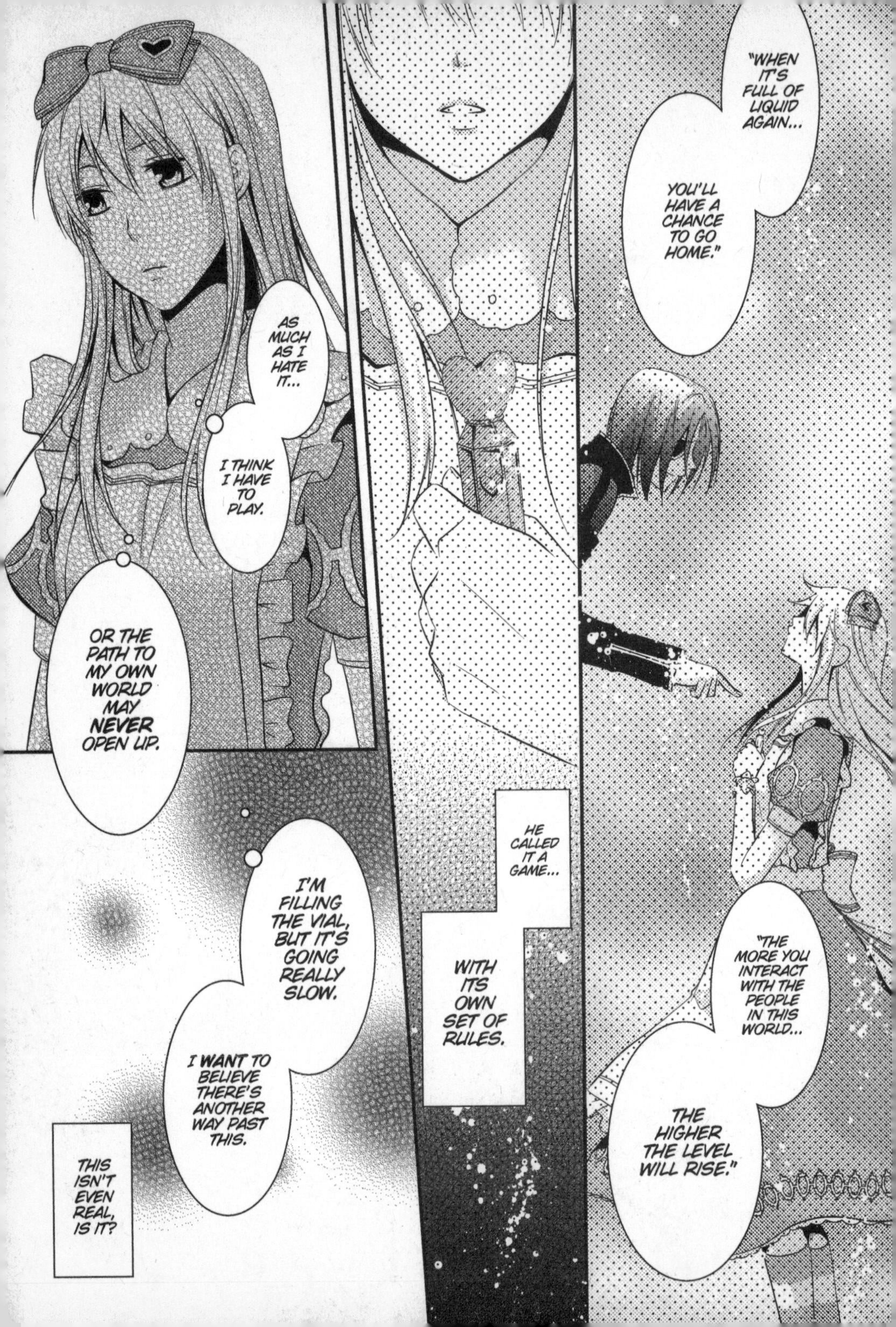
"WHEN IT'S FULL OF LIQUID AGAIN...
YOU'LL HAVE A CHANCE TO GO HOME."
"THE MORE YOU INTERACT WITH THE PEOPLE IN THIS WORLD...
THE HIGHER THE LEVEL WILL RISE."
HE CALLED IT A GAME...
WITH ITS OWN SET OF RULES.
AS MUCH AS I HATE IT...
I THINK I HAVE TO PLAY.
OR THE PATH TO MY OWN WORLD MAY NEVER OPEN UP.
I'M FILLING THE VIAL, BUT IT'S GOING REALLY SLOW.
I WANT TO BELIEVE THERE'S ANOTHER WAY PAST THIS.
THIS ISN'T EVEN REAL, IS IT?

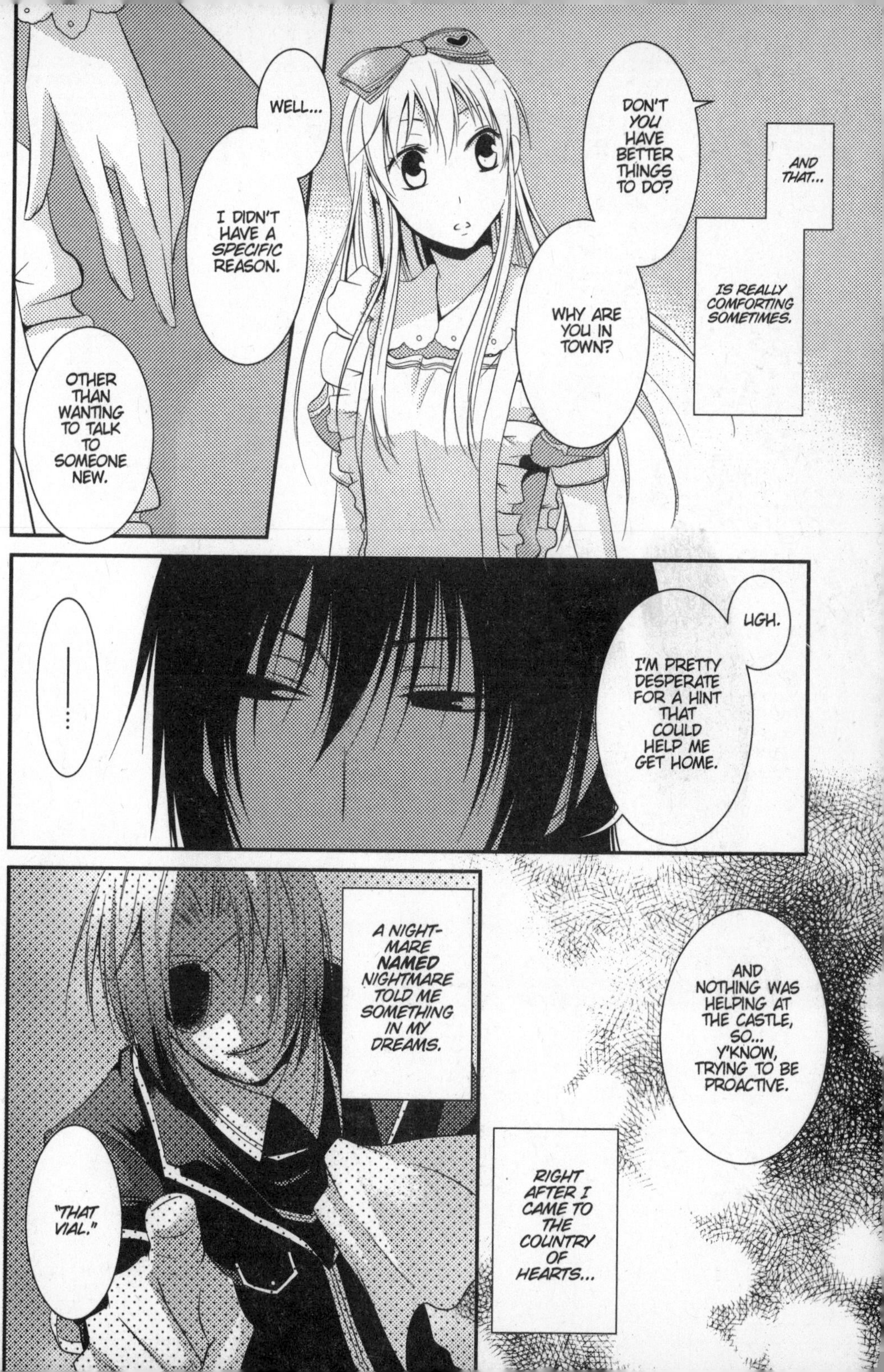
AND THAT... IS REALLY COMFORTING SOMETIMES.
DON'T YOU HAVE BETTER THINGS TO DO?
WHY ARE YOU IN TOWN?
WELL...
I DIDN'T HAVE A SPECIFIC REASON.
OTHER THAN WANTING TO TALK TO SOMEONE NEW.
UGH.
I'M PRETTY DESPERATE FOR A HINT THAT COULD HELP ME GET HOME.
—...
AND NOTHING WAS HELPING AT THE CASTLE, SO... Y'KNOW, TRYING TO BE PROACTIVE.
RIGHT AFTER I CAME TO THE COUNTRY OF HEARTS...
A NIGHTMARE **NAMED** NIGHTMARE TOLD ME SOMETHING IN MY DREAMS.
"THAT VIAL."

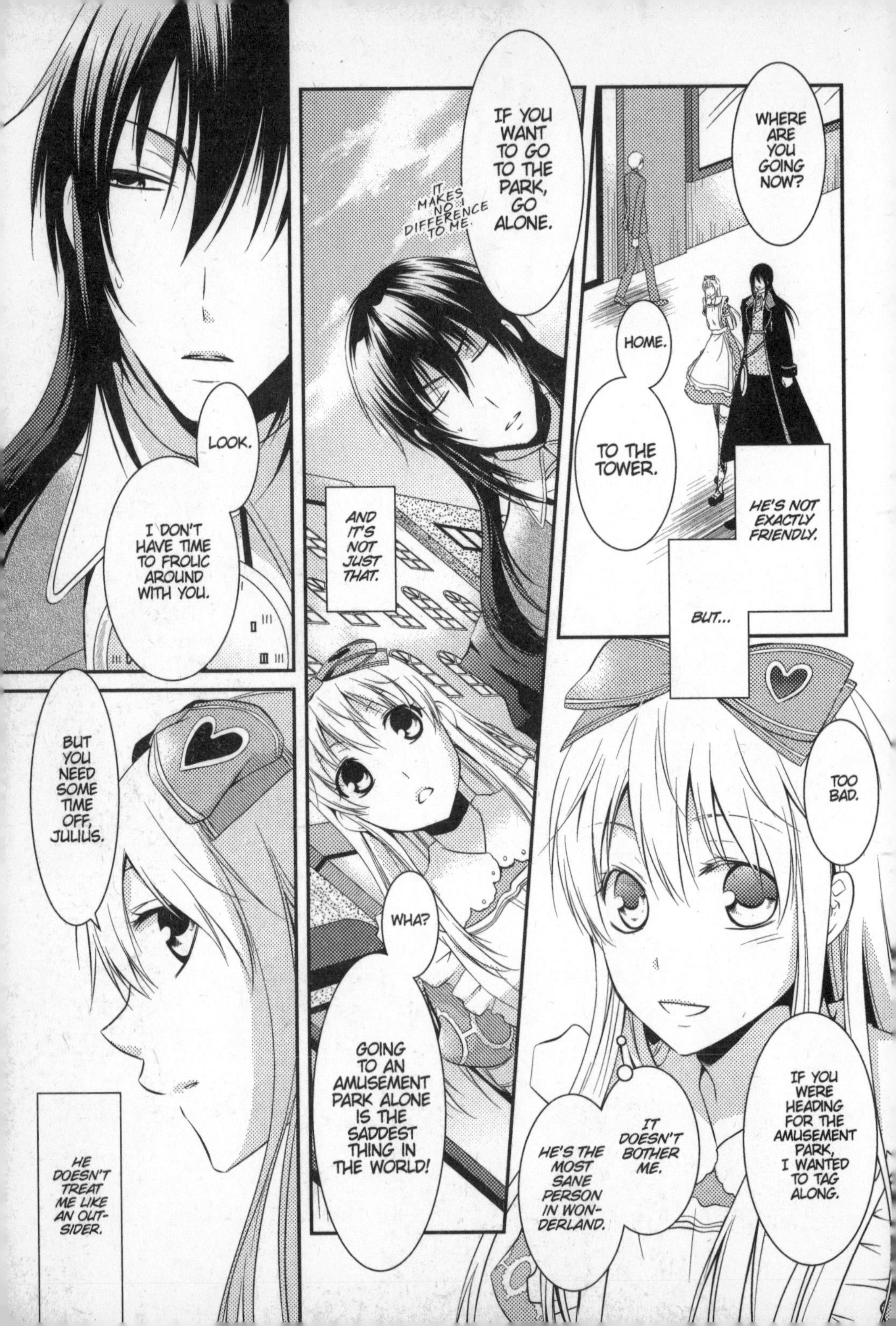
WHERE ARE YOU GOING NOW?
HOME.
TO THE TOWER.
HE'S NOT EXACTLY FRIENDLY.
BUT...
TOO BAD.
IF YOU WERE HEADING FOR THE AMUSEMENT PARK, I WANTED TO TAG ALONG.
IT DOESN'T BOTHER ME.
HE'S THE MOST SANE PERSON IN WONDERLAND.
IF YOU WANT TO GO TO THE PARK, GO ALONE.
IT MAKES NO DIFFERENCE TO ME.
AND IT'S NOT JUST THAT.
WHA?
GOING TO AN AMUSEMENT PARK ALONE IS THE SADDEST THING IN THE WORLD!
LOOK.
I DON'T HAVE TIME TO FROLIC AROUND WITH YOU.
BUT YOU NEED SOME TIME OFF, JULIUS.
HE DOESN'T TREAT ME LIKE AN OUT-SIDER.

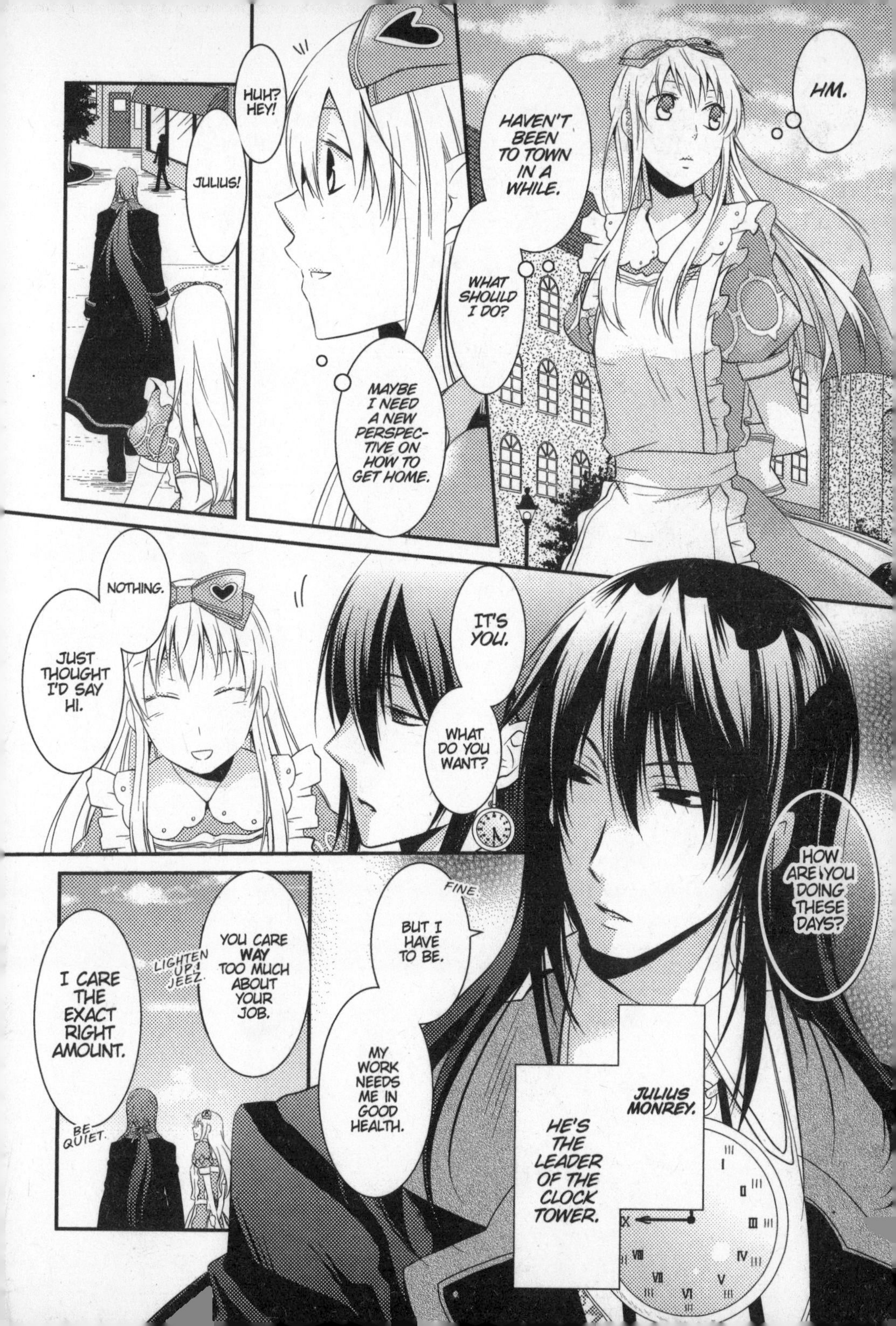
HM.
HAVEN'T BEEN TO TOWN IN A WHILE.
WHAT SHOULD I DO?
MAYBE I NEED A NEW PERSPECTIVE ON HOW TO GET HOME.
HUH? HEY!
JULIUS!
IT'S YOU.
WHAT DO YOU WANT?
NOTHING.
JUST THOUGHT I'D SAY HI.
HOW ARE YOU DOING THESE DAYS?
FINE.
BUT I HAVE TO BE.
MY WORK NEEDS ME IN GOOD HEALTH.
JULIUS MONREY.
HE'S THE LEADER OF THE CLOCK TOWER.
YOU CARE WAY TOO MUCH ABOUT YOUR JOB.
LIGHTEN UP! JEEZ.
I CARE THE EXACT RIGHT AMOUNT.
BE QUIET.

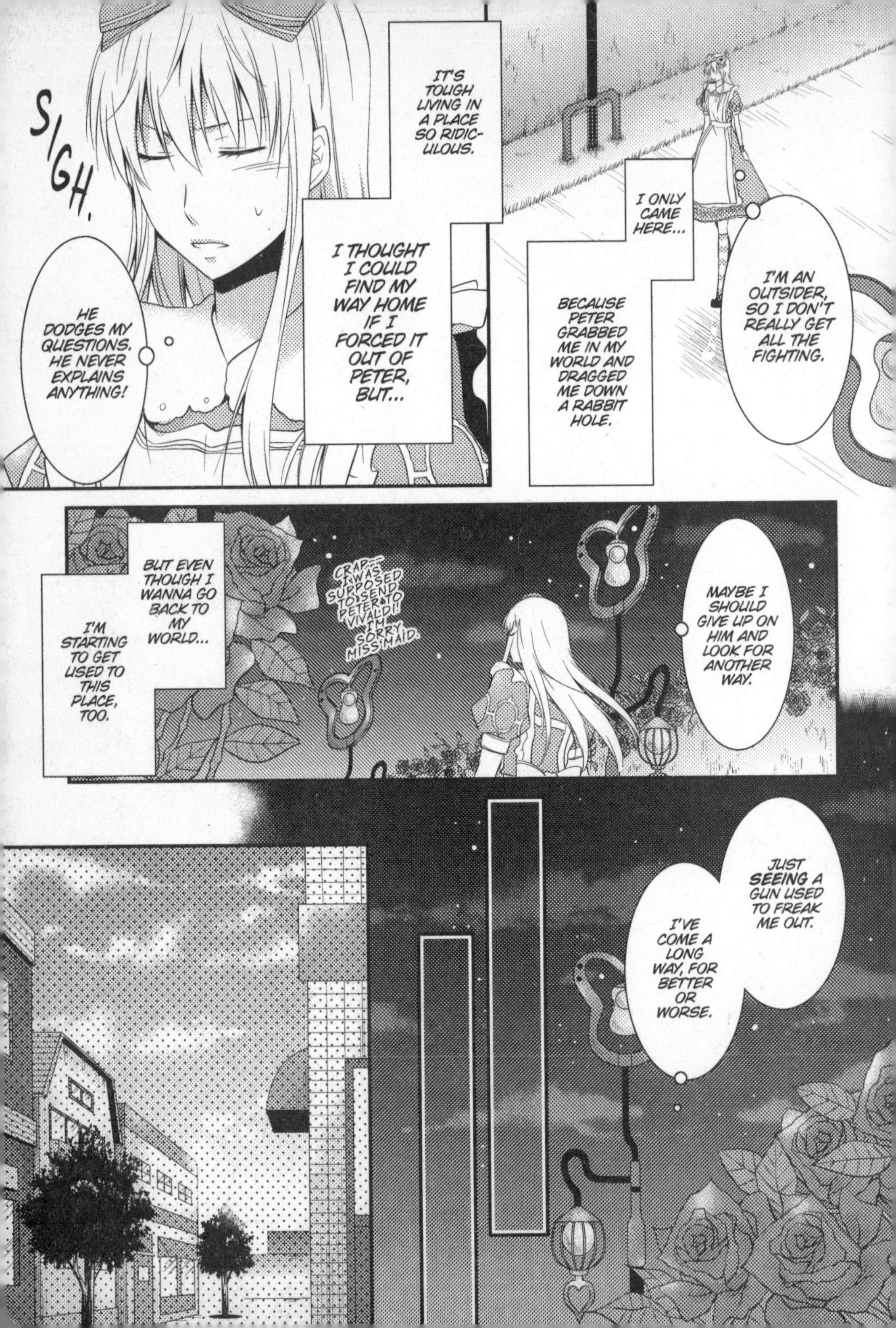
I'M AN OUTSIDER, SO I DON'T REALLY GET ALL THE FIGHTING.
I ONLY CAME HERE...
BECAUSE PETER GRABBED ME IN MY WORLD AND DRAGGED ME DOWN A RABBIT HOLE.
IT'S TOUGH LIVING IN A PLACE SO RIDICULOUS.
I THOUGHT I COULD FIND MY WAY HOME IF I FORCED IT OUT OF PETER, BUT...
SIGH.
HE DODGES MY QUESTIONS. HE NEVER EXPLAINS ANYTHING!
MAYBE I SHOULD GIVE UP ON HIM AND LOOK FOR ANOTHER WAY.
CRAP— I WAS SUPPOSED TO SEND PETER TO VIVALDI! I'M SORRY, MISS MAID.
BUT EVEN THOUGH I WANNA GO BACK TO MY WORLD...
I'M STARTING TO GET USED TO THIS PLACE, TOO.
JUST SEEING A GUN USED TO FREAK ME OUT.
I'VE COME A LONG WAY, FOR BETTER OR WORSE.

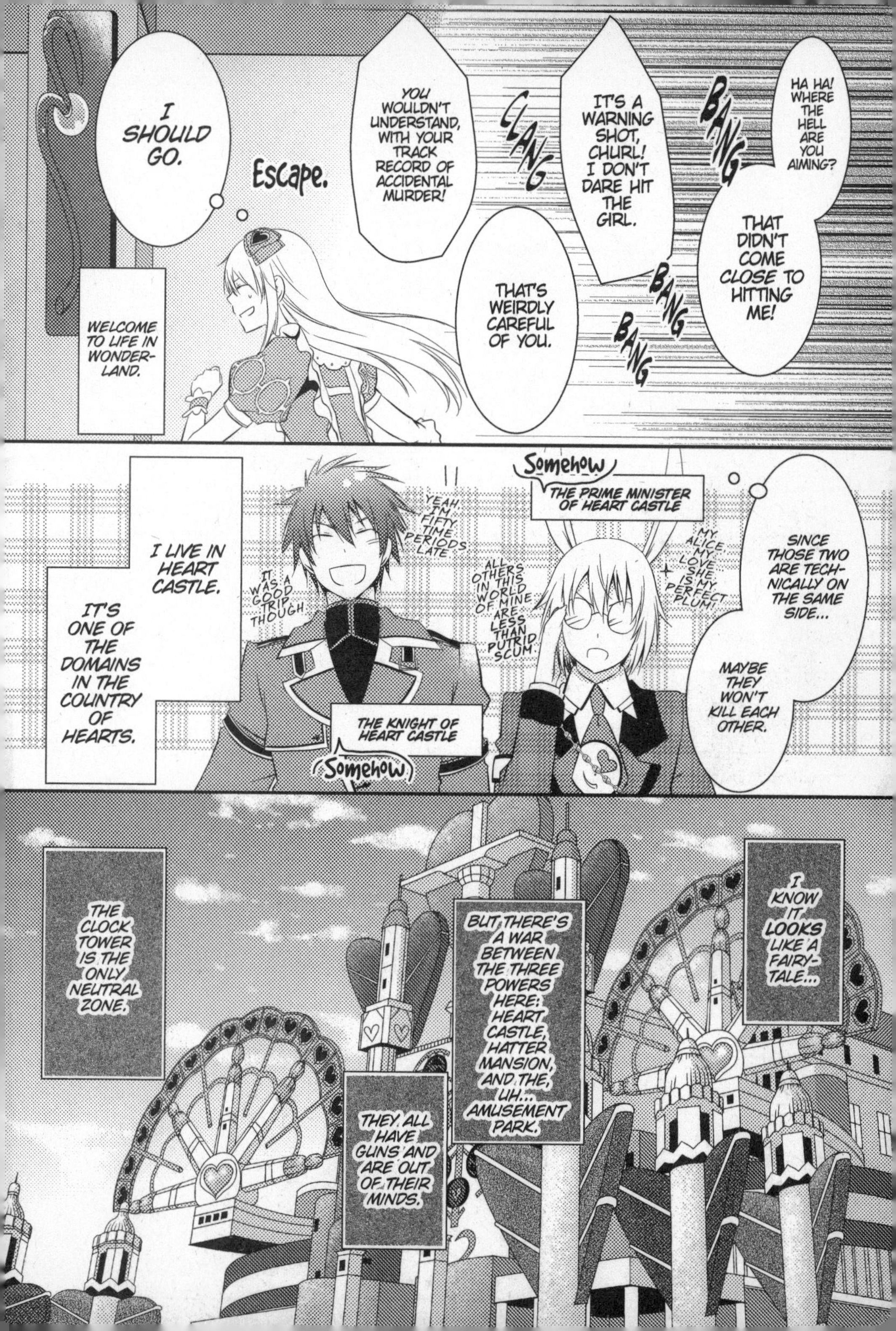
HA HA! WHERE THE HELL ARE YOU AIMING?
THAT DIDN'T COME CLOSE TO HITTING ME!
BANG
BANG
BANG
BANG
IT'S A WARNING SHOT, CHURL! I DON'T DARE HIT THE GIRL.
CLANG
THAT'S WEIRDLY CAREFUL OF YOU.
YOU WOULDN'T UNDERSTAND, WITH YOUR TRACK RECORD OF ACCIDENTAL MURDER!
I SHOULD GO.
Escape.
WELCOME TO LIFE IN WONDER-LAND.
SINCE THOSE TWO ARE TECHNICALLY ON THE SAME SIDE...
MAYBE THEY WON'T KILL EACH OTHER.
Somehow
THE PRIME MINISTER OF HEART CASTLE
MY ALICE, MY LOVE. SHE IS MY PERFECT PLUM!
ALL OTHERS IN THIS WORLD OF MINE ARE LESS THAN PUTRID SCUM.
YEAH, I'M FIFTY TIME PERIODS LATE.
IT WAS A GOOD TRIP THOUGH
THE KNIGHT OF HEART CASTLE
Somehow
I LIVE IN HEART CASTLE.
IT'S ONE OF THE DOMAINS IN THE COUNTRY OF HEARTS.
I KNOW IT LOOKS LIKE A FAIRY-TALE...
BUT THERE'S A WAR BETWEEN THE THREE POWERS HERE: HEART CASTLE, HATTER MANSION, AND THE, UH... AMUSEMENT PARK.
THEY ALL HAVE GUNS AND ARE OUT OF THEIR MINDS.
THE CLOCK TOWER IS THE ONLY NEUTRAL ZONE.

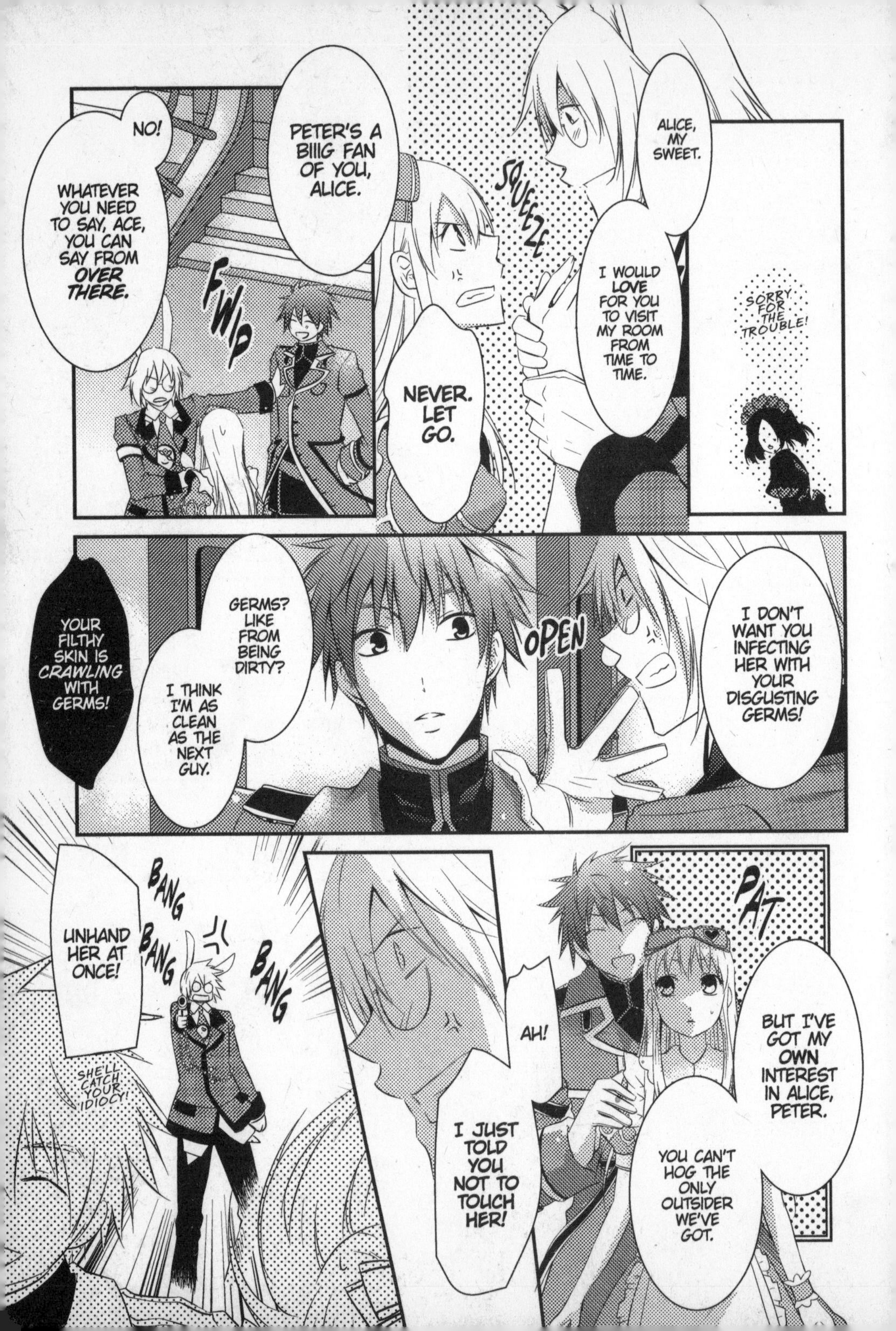
ALICE, MY SWEET.
SQUEEZE
I WOULD LOVE FOR YOU TO VISIT MY ROOM FROM TIME TO TIME.
SORRY FOR THE TROUBLE!
NEVER. LET GO.
PETER'S A BIIIG FAN OF YOU, ALICE.
NO!
WHATEVER YOU NEED TO SAY, ACE, YOU CAN SAY FROM OVER THERE.
FWIP
I DON'T WANT YOU INFECTING HER WITH YOUR DISGUSTING GERMS!
OPEN
GERMS? LIKE FROM BEING DIRTY?
I THINK I'M AS CLEAN AS THE NEXT GUY.
YOUR FILTHY SKIN IS CRAWLING WITH GERMS!
PAT
BUT I'VE GOT MY OWN INTEREST IN ALICE, PETER.
YOU CAN'T HOG THE ONLY OUTSIDER WE'VE GOT.
AH!
I JUST TOLD YOU NOT TO TOUCH HER!
BANG
BANG
BANG
BANG
UNHAND HER AT ONCE!
SHE'LL CATCH YOUR IDIOCY!

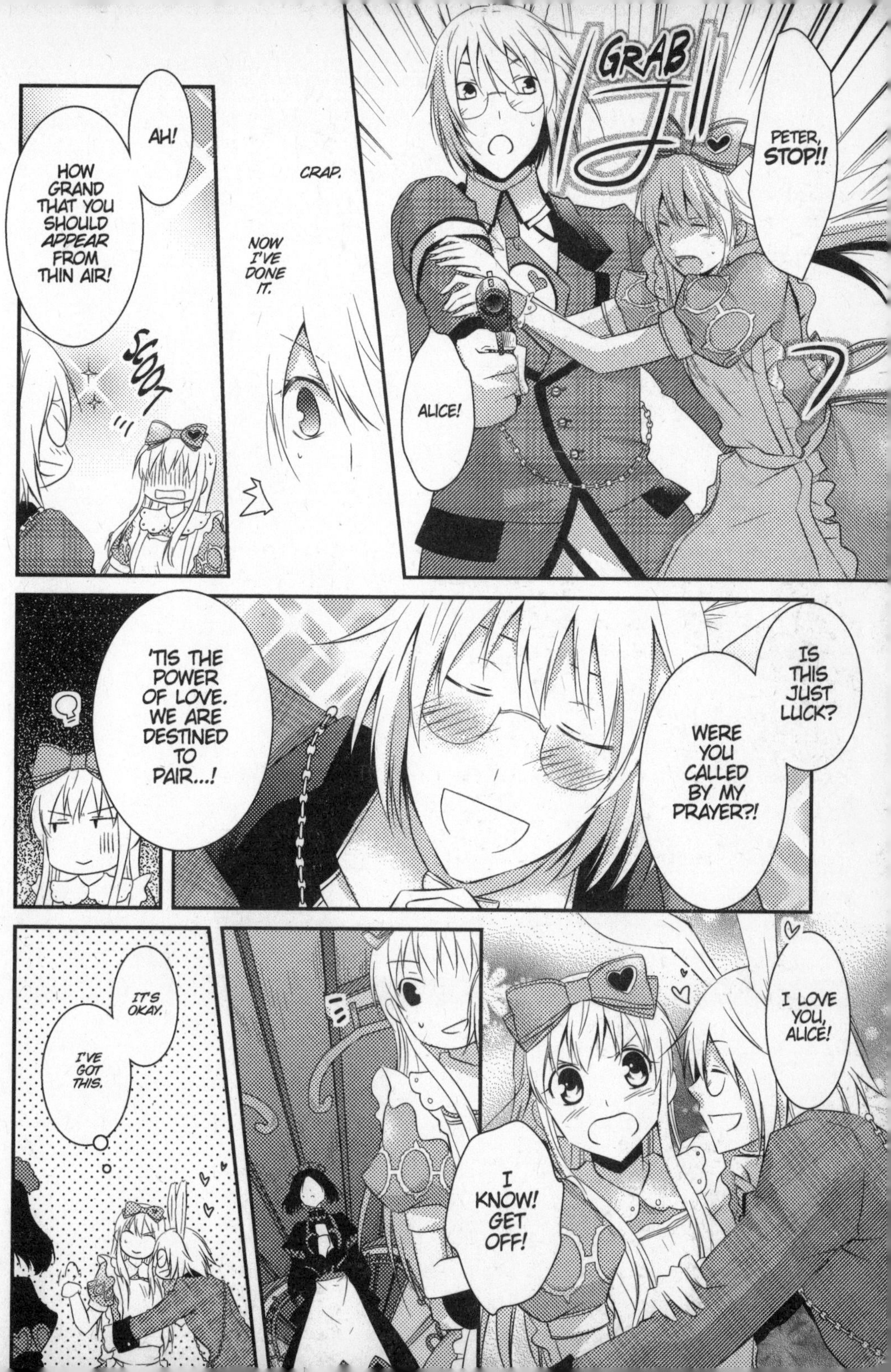
GRAB
PETER, STOP!!
ALICE!
CRAP.
NOW I'VE DONE IT.
AH!
HOW GRAND THAT YOU SHOULD APPEAR FROM THIN AIR!
SHOOM
IS THIS JUST LUCK?
WERE YOU CALLED BY MY PRAYER?!
'TIS THE POWER OF LOVE. WE ARE DESTINED TO PAIR...!
I LOVE YOU, ALICE!
I KNOW! GET OFF!
IT'S OKAY.
I'VE GOT THIS.

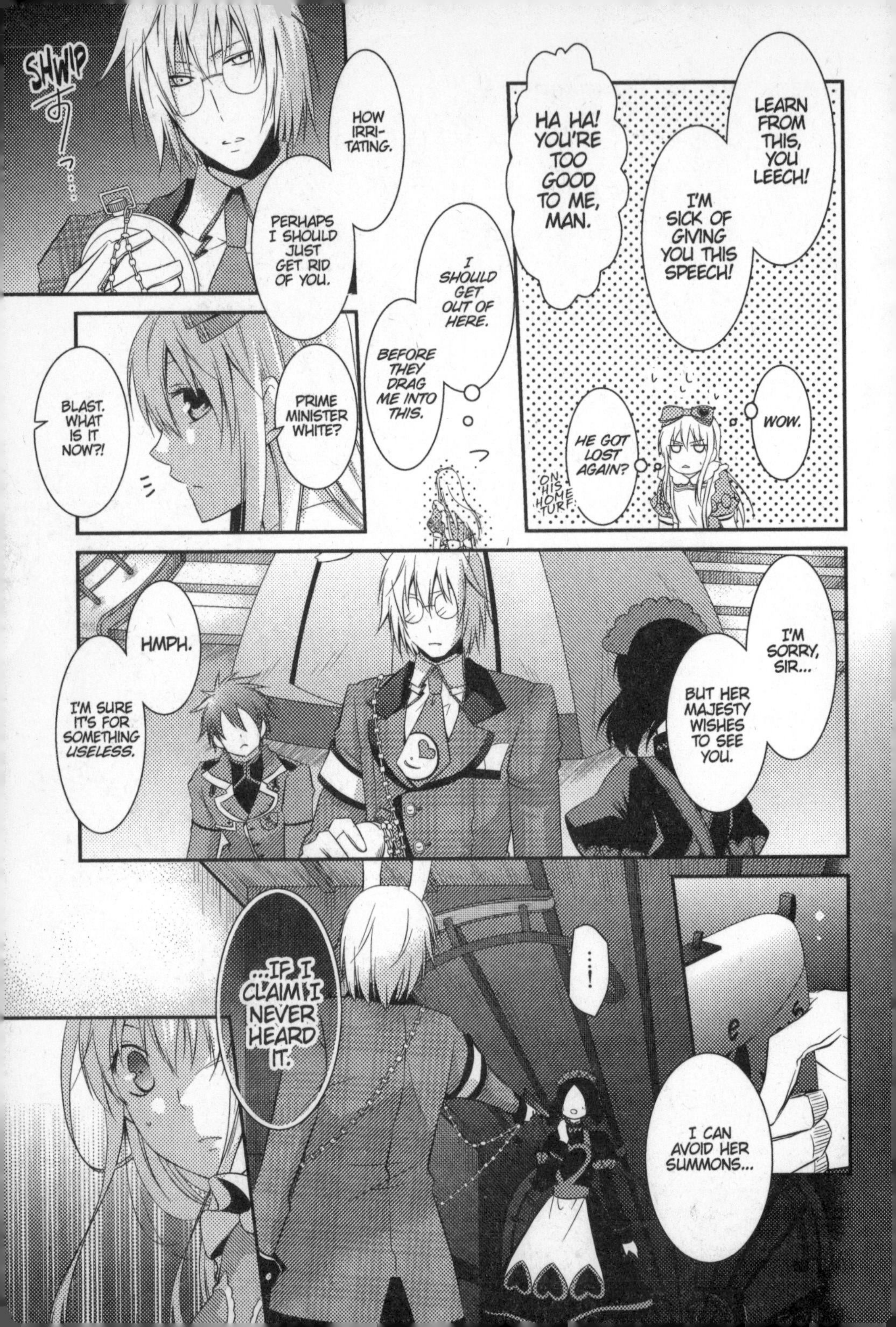
LEARN FROM THIS, YOU LEECH!
I'M SICK OF GIVING YOU THIS SPEECH!
HA HA! YOU'RE TOO GOOD TO ME, MAN.
WOW.
HE GOT LOST AGAIN?
ON HIS HOME TURF.
SHWIP
HOW IRRI-TATING.
PERHAPS I SHOULD JUST GET RID OF YOU.
I SHOULD GET OUT OF HERE.
BEFORE THEY DRAG ME INTO THIS.
PRIME MINISTER WHITE?
BLAST. WHAT IS IT NOW?!
I'M SORRY, SIR...
BUT HER MAJESTY WISHES TO SEE YOU.
HMPH.
I'M SURE IT'S FOR SOMETHING *USELESS*.
...!
I CAN AVOID HER SUMMONS...
...IF I CLAIM I NEVER HEARD IT.

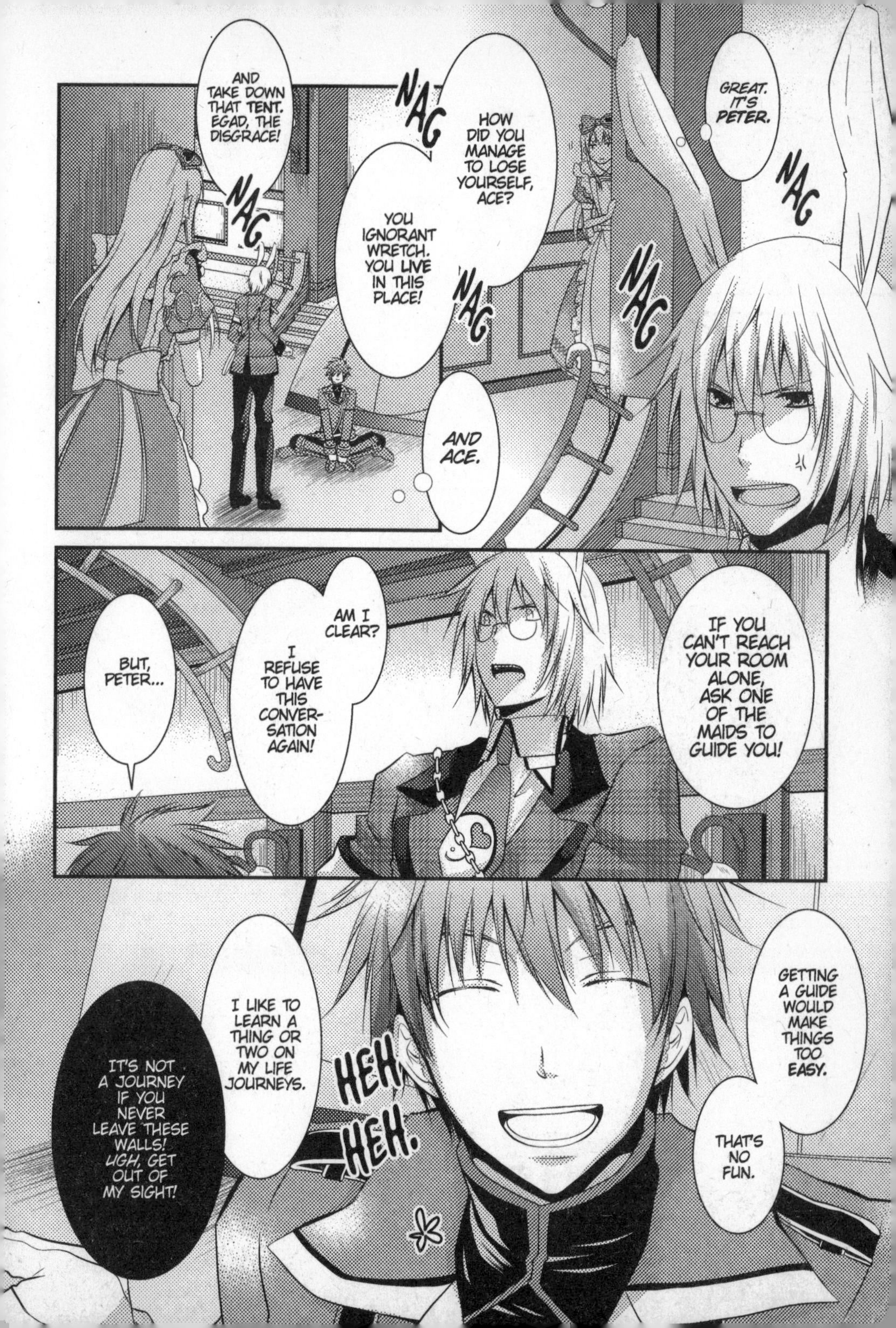
GREAT. IT'S PETER.
AND ACE.
NAG NAG
HOW DID YOU MANAGE TO LOSE YOURSELF, ACE?
NAG NAG
AND TAKE DOWN THAT TENT. EGAD, THE DISGRACE!
NAG NAG
YOU IGNORANT WRETCH. YOU LIVE IN THIS PLACE!
NAG NAG
IF YOU CAN'T REACH YOUR ROOM ALONE, ASK ONE OF THE MAIDS TO GUIDE YOU!
AM I CLEAR?
I REFUSE TO HAVE THIS CONVERSATION AGAIN!
BUT, PETER...
GETTING A GUIDE WOULD MAKE THINGS TOO EASY.
THAT'S NO FUN.
HEH HEH.
I LIKE TO LEARN A THING OR TWO ON MY LIFE JOURNEYS.
IT'S NOT A JOURNEY IF YOU NEVER LEAVE THESE WALLS! UGH, GET OUT OF MY SIGHT!

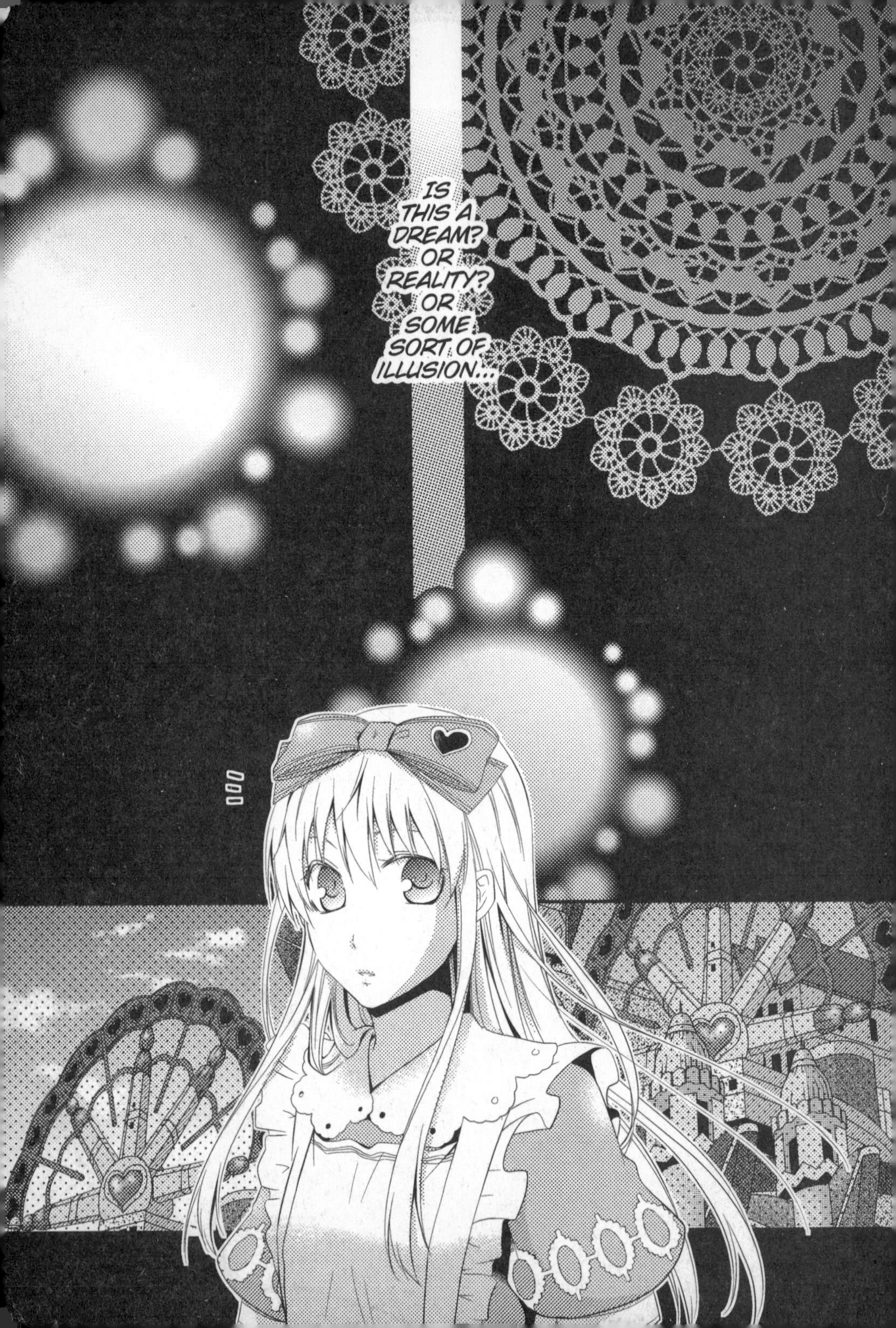
IS THIS A DREAM? OR REALITY? OR SOME SORT OF ILLUSION...

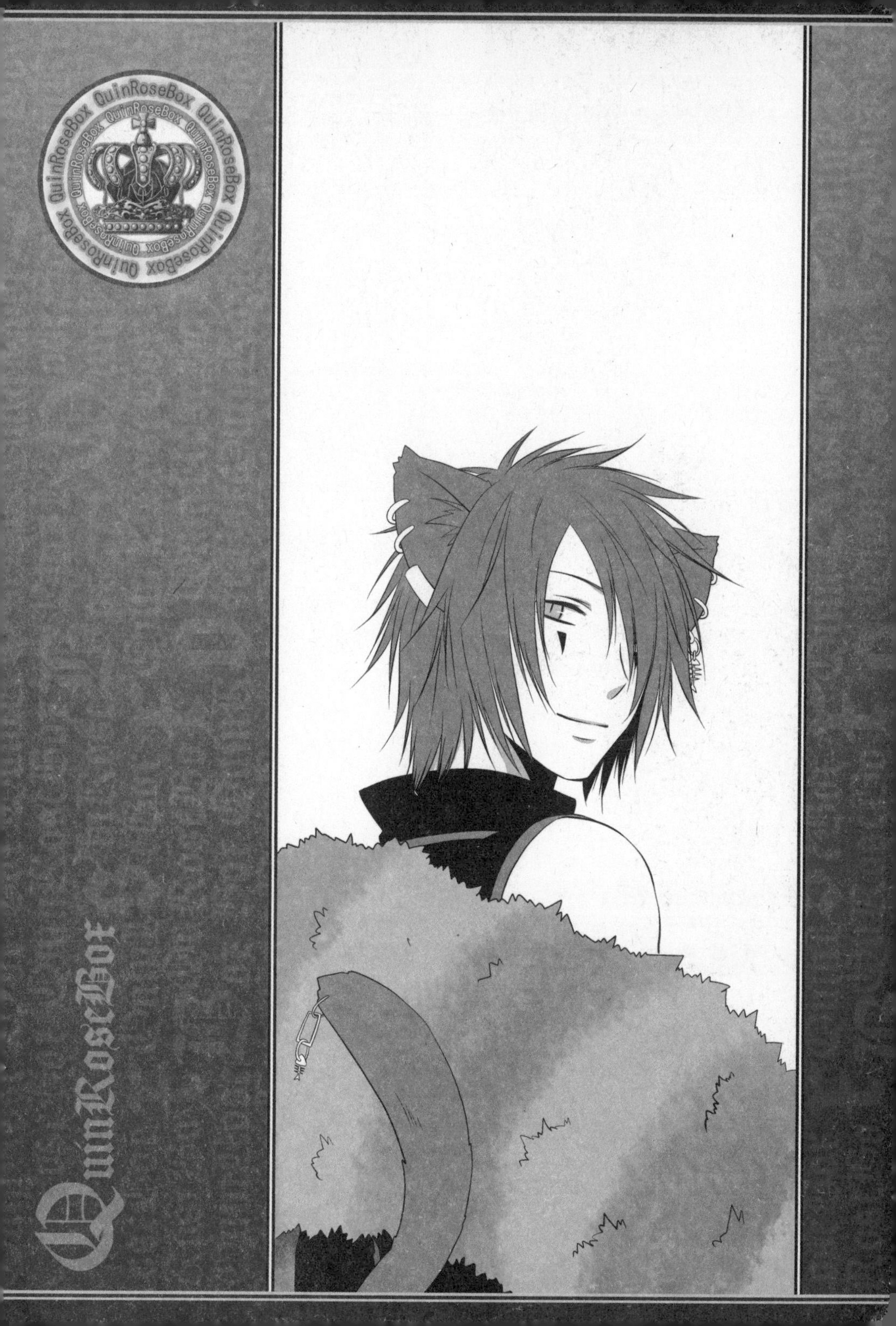

QuinRoseBox

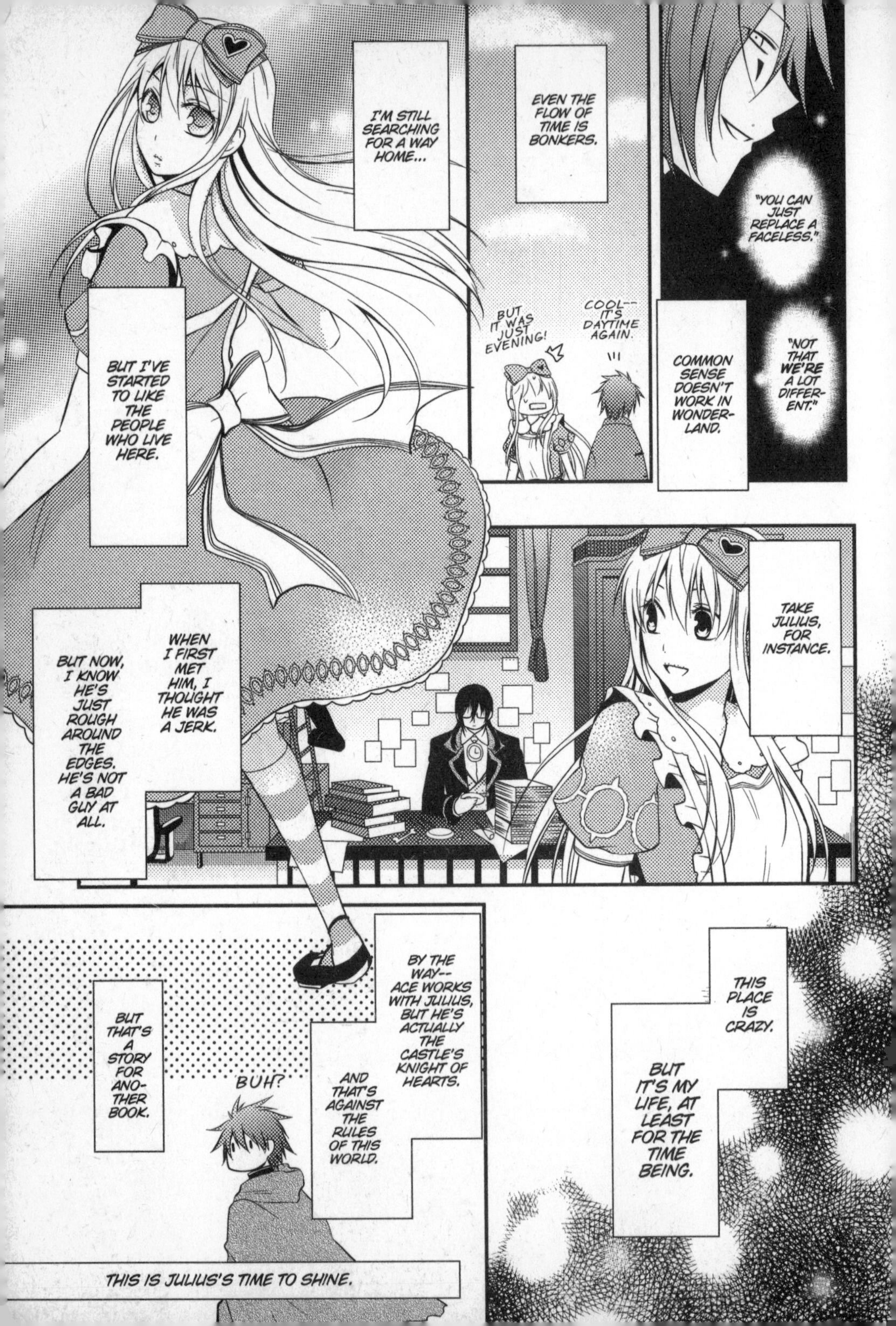
"YOU CAN JUST REPLACE A FACELESS."
"NOT THAT WE'RE A LOT DIFFERENT."
COMMON SENSE DOESN'T WORK IN WONDERLAND.
EVEN THE FLOW OF TIME IS BONKERS.
COOL--IT'S DAYTIME AGAIN.
BUT IT WAS JUST EVENING!
I'M STILL SEARCHING FOR A WAY HOME...
BUT I'VE STARTED TO LIKE THE PEOPLE WHO LIVE HERE.
TAKE JULIUS, FOR INSTANCE.
WHEN I FIRST MET HIM, I THOUGHT HE WAS A JERK.
BUT NOW, I KNOW HE'S JUST ROUGH AROUND THE EDGES. HE'S NOT A BAD GUY AT ALL.
THIS PLACE IS CRAZY.
BUT IT'S MY LIFE, AT LEAST FOR THE TIME BEING.
BY THE WAY--ACE WORKS WITH JULIUS, BUT HE'S ACTUALLY THE CASTLE'S KNIGHT OF HEARTS.
AND THAT'S AGAINST THE RULES OF THIS WORLD.
BUH?
BUT THAT'S A STORY FOR ANOTHER BOOK.
THIS IS JULIUS'S TIME TO SHINE.

An introduction to the world of Alice

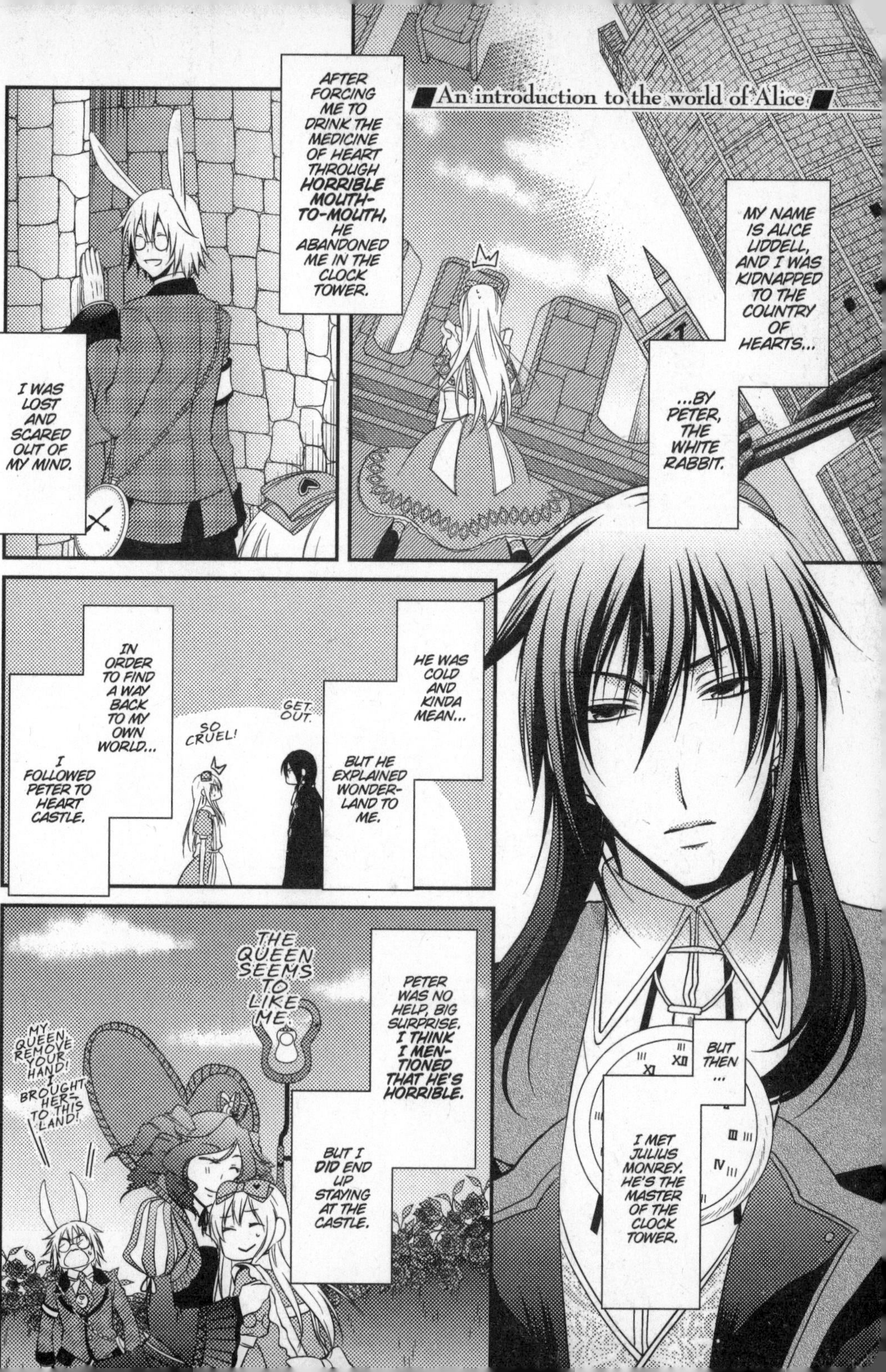
MY NAME IS ALICE LIDDELL, AND I WAS KIDNAPPED TO THE COUNTRY OF HEARTS...
...BY PETER, THE WHITE RABBIT.
AFTER FORCING ME TO DRINK THE MEDICINE OF HEART THROUGH HORRIBLE MOUTH-TO-MOUTH, HE ABANDONED ME IN THE CLOCK TOWER.
I WAS LOST AND SCARED OUT OF MY MIND.
BUT THEN...
I MET JULIUS MONREY. HE'S THE MASTER OF THE CLOCK TOWER.
HE WAS COLD AND KINDA MEAN...
BUT HE EXPLAINED WONDERLAND TO ME.
GET OUT.
SO CRUEL!
IN ORDER TO FIND A WAY BACK TO MY OWN WORLD...
I FOLLOWED PETER TO HEART CASTLE.
PETER WAS NO HELP, BIG SURPRISE. I THINK I MENTIONED THAT HE'S HORRIBLE.
BUT I DID END UP STAYING AT THE CASTLE.
THE QUEEN SEEMS TO LIKE ME.
MY QUEEN, REMOVE YOUR HAND! I BROUGHT HER TO THIS LAND!

Alice in Country of Hearts
Character Information

Elliot March
VA: Tsuguo Mogami

The No. 2 of the Hatter Family and Blood's right-hand man, Elliot is an ex-criminal and an escaped convict. Very short-tempered, he used to be a "very bad guy" who shot before asking questions. After partnering up with Blood, he rounded out and changed to a "slightly bad guy" who thinks for about three seconds before shooting. In his mind, this is a vast improvement.

Blood Dupre
VA: Katsuyuki Konishi

The dangerous leader of the crime syndicate known as the Hatter Family. Since he enjoys plotting more than working directly, he controls everything from the shadows. He's incredibly smart, but due to his temperamental moods and his desire to keep things "interesting," he often digs his own grave in his secret plans.

Alice Liddell
VA: Rie Kugimiya

She grew up to be a responsible young woman after losing her mother early, but Alice still carries a complex toward her older sister. She respects her older sister very much, but is frustrated about always being compared to her. Since her first love fell for her older sister, she has no confidence in herself when it comes to romance.

Vivaldi
VA: Yuuko Kaida

Ruthless and cruel, the Queen of Hearts is an arrogant beauty with a wild temper. She's enemies with the Hatter and Gowland. Impatient at heart, Vivaldi takes her fury out on everyone around her, including her subordinates, whom she considers pawns. Anyone **not** working for her doesn't even register as existing.

Tweedle Dum
VA: Jun Fukuyama

The second "Bloody Twin" and a dead ringer for his brother—in both appearance and personality. As they often change places, it's uncertain which one is the older twin.

Tweedle Dee
VA: Jun Fukuyama

Gatekeeper of the Hatter territory, and one of the dark, sneaky twins. They sometimes show an innocent side, but they usually have a malicious agenda. Also known as the "Bloody Twins" due to their unsavory activities.

Ace
VA: Daisuke Hirakawa

The knight of Hearts and the ex-subordinate of Vivaldi. He's left the castle and is currently wandering. He's a very unlucky and unfortunate man, yet he remains strangely positive, thus he tends to plow forward and make mistakes that only worsen his situation. He's one of the few friends of the clockmaker, Julius.

Julius Monrey
VA: Takehito Koyasu

The clockmaker, a gloomy machine expert who easily falls into depression. He lives in the Clock Tower and doesn't get out much. He always thinks of everything in the most negative way and tends to distrust people, but he gets along with Ace. He had some part in the imprisonment of the March Hare, Elliot, and is thus the target of Elliot's hatred.

Peter White
VA: Kouki Miyata

Don't be fooled by the cute ears—Peter is the dangerous guide who dragged Alice to Wonderland in the first place. He claims to always be worried about the time, despite having a strange grasp on it. Rumors say his heart is as black as his hair is white.

Nightmare
VA: Tomokazu Sugita

A sickly nightmare. He appears in Alice's dream, sometimes to guide her—and other times, to **misguide** her.

Mary Gowland
VA: Kenyuu Horiuchi

The owner of the Amusement Park. He hides his hated first name, Mary, but pretty much everyone already knows it. His full name is a play on words that sounds like "Merry Go Round" when said quickly. If his musical talent was given a numerical value, it would be closer to negatives than zero.

Boris Airay
VA: Noriaki Sugiyama

A riddle-loving cat with a signature smirk. He sometimes gives hints to his riddles, but the hints usually just cause more confusion. He also has a tendency to pose questions and never answer them.

Alice in the Country of Hearts

ハートの国の
アリス

~Wonderful Wonder World ~

- STORY -

This is a love adventure game. It is based on *Alice in Wonderland*, but evolves into a completely different story.

The main character is far from a romantic. In fact, she's especially sick of love relationships.

She's pulled (against her will) into the dangerous Country of Hearts, which is not as peaceful as the name makes it sound. The Hatters are a mafia family, and even the employees of the Amusement Park carry weapons.

The leaders of the three domains are constantly trying to kill each other. Many of the skirmishes are the result of territory grabs by three major powers trying to control more land: the Hatter, the Queen of Hearts, and Gowland.

After drinking some strange medicine (again, against her will), the main character is unable to return to her world. She quickly decides that she's trapped in a dream and allows herself to enjoy(?) the extraordinary experience she's been thrown into.

What territory will she stay with and who will she interact with to get herself home? And will this girl, so jaded about love, fall into a relationship she doesn't expect?

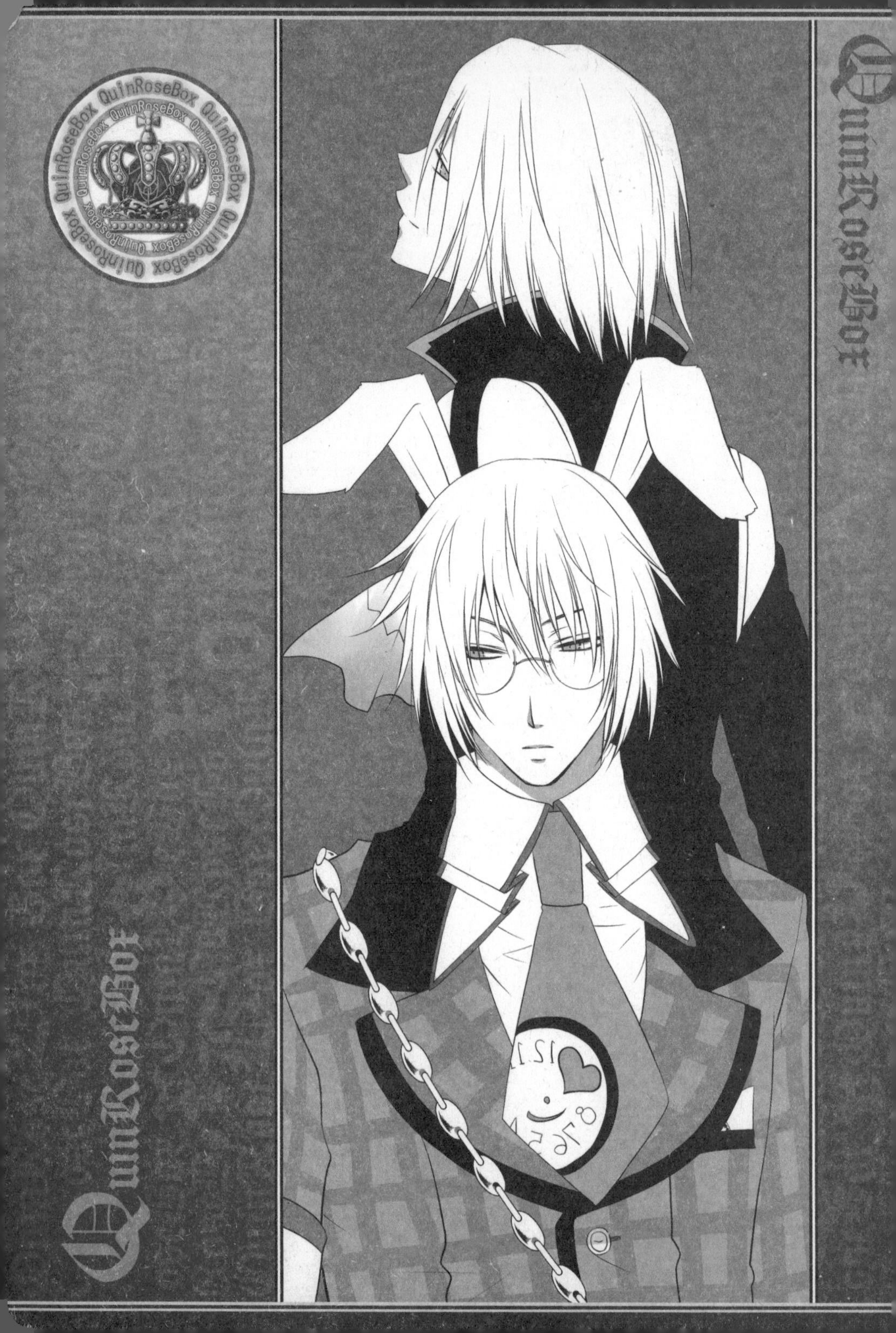
QuinRoseBox
QuinRoseBox

Alice IN THE COUNTRY OF Hearts
THE CLOCKMAKER'S STORY

story by **QuinRose**

art by **Mamenosuke Fujimaru**

STAFF CREDITS

translation	**Angela Liu**
adaptation	**Lianne Sentar**
lettering	**Roland Amago**
layout	**Bambi Eloriaga-Amago**
cover design	**Nicky Lim**
proofreader	**Shanti Whitesides, Katherine Bell**
editor	**Adam Arnold**
publisher	**Jason DeAngelis** **Seven Seas Entertainment**

ISBN: 978-1-937867-64-5

Printed in Canada

First Printing: August 2013

10 9 8 7 6 5 4 3 2 1

FOLLOW US ONLINE: **www.gomanga.com**

READING DIRECTIONS

This book reads from *right to left*, Japanese style. If this is your first time reading manga, you start reading from the top right panel on each page and take it from there. If you get lost, just follow the numbered diagram here. It may seem backwards at first, but you'll get the hang of it! Have fun!!

Alice in the Country of Hearts
~The Clockmaker's Story~

Mamenosuke Fujimaru

藤丸 豆ノ介